Chess Stars Openings

Squeezing the Gambits:

the Benko, Budapest, Albin and Blumenfeld

Kiril Georgiev

Chess Stars

www.chess-stars.com

Current Theory and Practice Series

Squeezing the Gambits: the Benko, Budapest, Albin and Blumenfeld

Translation and editing by Semko Semkov
Cover design by Kalojan Nachev

Printed in Bulgaria
ISBN: 978-954 8782 75-3

Contents

Bibliography

Books

My One Hundred Best Games, A.Dreev, Chess Stars 2007
The Benko Gambit, J.Pinski, Quality Chess 2005
Grandmaster Repertoire: 1.d4 Volume One, B.Avrukh, Quality Chess 2009
The Fabulous Budapest Gambit, V. Moskalenko, New In Chess 2007

Electronic/Periodicals

Mega Database, Chess Base
Albin's Counter-Gambit for Experts, R.Kasimdzhanov, Chess Base 2008
Chess Base Magazine 114, Chess base 2006
Chess Informant, Sahovsky Informator
New in Chess Yearbook, Interchess
Chess Today

Internet resources

The Week In Chess (chesscenter.com)
10 Days (Chessmix.com)
Internet Chess Club (chessclub.com)
ChessPublishing.com forum
Chesspro.ru

Introduction

In this book I will try to teach you how to put Black into a positional squeeze in the most popular gambits against 1.d4.

Remember the old aphorism that the best way of meeting a gambit is accepting it? This may be true, but only for absolutely incorrect systems, such as 1.d4 e5 2.dxe5 d6? Of course, here we take everything and sail forth to converting our material advantage. But look at another example:

1.d4 ♘f6 2.c4 c5 3.d5 b5 4.cxb5 a6 5.bxa6 g6 6.♘c3 ♗xa6 7.♘f3 d6 8.g3 ♗g7 9.♗g2 ♘bd7 10.♖b1 ♕a5 11.0-0 0-0 12.♕c2 ♘b6 13.♖d1 ♘fd7 14.♗d2 ♘c4 15.♗e1 ♖fb8, Banikas-Tregubov, Kallithea 2009:

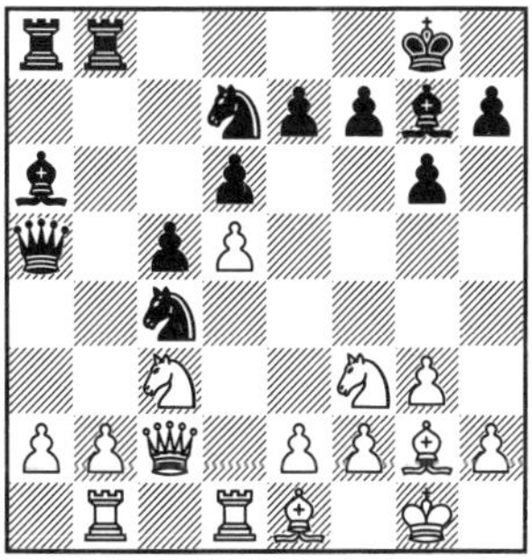

Would you really go for this position as White if you did not know that it was assessed as one of the newest and most sophisticated set-ups against the Benko?

White is a pawn up, but all his pieces are huddled on the first two ranks. Both rooks are humble defenders of the weak pawns. One imprecise move, and White's position will crumble down. Common sense suggests that unless White plays like a machine, he should better seek another approach in that opening.

I do not want to get involved into theoretical disputes over the Benko Accepted. I only claim that White's choice is dubious from practical point of view. The more mistakes you usually commit in your games, the more dangerous it is.

I think that instead of trying to refute those gambits by clutching to an extra pawn, it is better to play good positional chess, occupy the centre, and deny any counterplay to the opponent.

Now comes my strongest argument in favour of the Positional approach: it allows to greatly decrease the role of computer assisted home analysis. Such considerations will soon become a leading factor in the process of constructing a repertoire.

The game of chess has reached a major crossroads in its existence.

Due to the rising of the invincible computer monsters, it will either disappear, as it has happened with checkers, or it will branch to different formats: computer chess and human chess. Of course, nothing would stop human players to use a bunch of engines for home preparation. Thus, a lot of more or less forced variations and even whole sharp systems will simply vanish from practice since they will be deeply analysed to finite evaluations. It would be at least impractical to choose sharp concrete variations against weaker players because of the risk of stumbling into a home made theoretical mine.

Therefore, in order to survive the opening, the better players would have to adopt a solid positional approach based on understanding. In such circumstances, computers are not too helpful because of the great numbers of branches of similar worth.

Avoiding home preparation is only one part of the problem. The more important task is how to outplay the opponent.

Unlike computers, humans cannot always seek for the best move, executing tons of calculations. They must be saving time and energy so they rely on typical plans, general principles and also involve some degree of prophylaxis in their decisions. When we play over the board, we should always be aware that we are prone to mistakes. By accepting the gambits, we put ourselves in a precarious situation where the price of every move is higher than normal. When we are on the defensive, such mistakes would be often decisive. It would be of little consolation that in the postmortem we could claim an advantage in the form of an extra pawn, for example.

My task in this book will be to help you build a viable, stable and durable repertoire against the major gambits. Note that the systems I propose are safer and much easier to play, but they are in no way inferior to any other. For instance, after 1.d4 ♘f6 2.c4 c5 3.d5 b5 4.♘f3 g6 5.cxb5 a6, the move 6.b6 fares the decent 58% while 6.bxa6 yields only 48%. Two moves earlier, 4.♘f3 achieves 60% to only 52% for 4.cxb5.

My repertoire does not require a lot of memorising since the main lines do not feature an all-in clash. Both sides can choose plenty of different move orders so I focus on plans and ideas. I also explain what to do after the opening, which pieces to exchange and which ones to cherish. And, of course, I provide a full, step by step, branch by branch theoretical coverage in the “Step by Step” chapters.

You will be surprised how easily it could be to play against those gambits if one knows what to do.

Read first the “Main Ideas” chapters! They give explanations which you will not find in the “Step by Step” coverage.

Kiril Georgiev
2010

The Benko Gambit Declined

Part 1

Main Ideas

1.d4 ♘f6 2.c4 c5 3.d5 b5 4.♘f3 g6 5.cxb5 a6 6.b6

Objectives and Move Order

The Benko is a demanding opening. It is highly unbalanced strategically, and one cannot treat it by general considerations. The piercing dark-squared bishop on the h8-a1 diagonal and the open b-file create tons of tactics. The missing c4-pawn turns White's centre unstable and vulnerable to undermining by ...f7-f5 or ...e6. That's why our first tasks will be quick development and consolidation. Next, we should restrict Black's counterplay by imposing blockade on the squares c4 and b5 (or b6). Only when we get a firm grip on the position, could we think about launching a kingside attack.

Here are two model games of the most devoted fan of the Benko Declined lately, V.Milov, which best illustrate White's strategy:

V.Milov–Rincon Bascon
Dos Hermanas 2006

1.d4 ♘f6 2.c4 c5 3.d5 b5 4.♘f3 g6 5.cxb5 a6 6.b6 d6 7.♘c3 ♗g7 8.e4 0-0 9.a4 ♕xb6 10.♘d2 ♘bd7 11.♗e2 a5 12.♘c4 ♕d8 13.0-0 ♘b6 14.♘a3

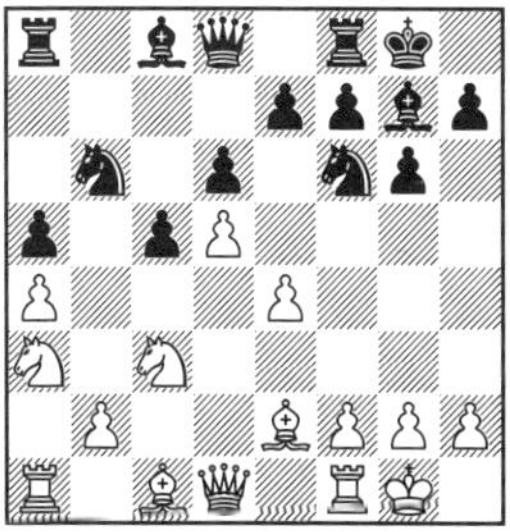

Stage 1 is completed. White has castled, c4 is under control.

14...♘e8 15.♗f4 ♘c7 16.♖c1 ♗a6 17.♗xa6 ♘xa6 18.b3 ♘d7 19.♘c4 ♘b4 20.♕d2 ♘b6 21.♘b5

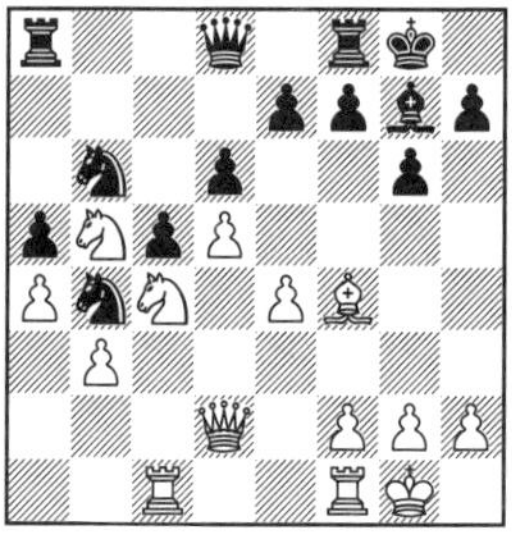

Stage 2 is over as well. Black is deprived of any counterplay. The c4-square is blockaded, the b-file is plugged. We'll be often observing Black in such a predicament. His knight on b4 is a pathetic sight. It spent 5 moves to arrive there, where it is totally useless. White is finally ready for the kingside assault.

21...♘xc4 22.bxc4 ♕d7 23.♖fe1 f6 24.♗g3 g5 25.f4 gxf4 26.♗xf4 ♖ac8 27.♖c3 ♔h8 28.♖h3 ♕g4 29.♖g3 ♕h4 30.♖f1 ♖g8 31.♖ff3

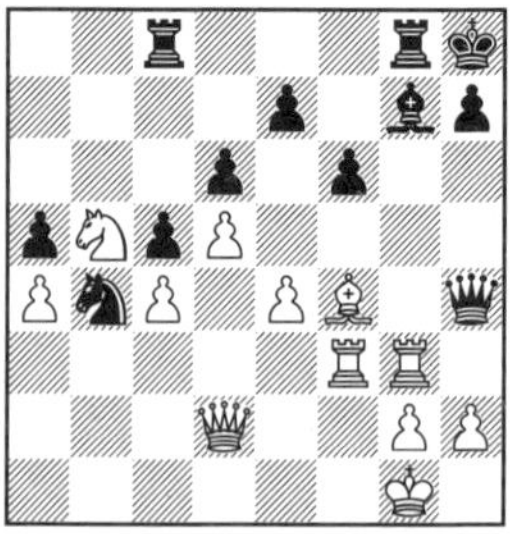

White is already winning, seemingly without having calculated a single variation. His play has been purposeful, with a clear plan.

31...f5 32.exf5 ♕f6 33.♗g5 ♕f8 34.♖h3 ♗f6 35.♖xh7+! ♔xh7 36.♖h3+ ♔g7 37.♗h6+ ♔f7 38.♗xf8 ♖cxf8 39.♘c7 ♖h8 40.♖xh8 ♖xh8 41.♕e2 ♗d4+ 42.♔h1 ♗e5 43.g3 ♖h6 44.♔g2 ♔f6 45.h3 ♔xf5 46.♕g4+ ♔f6 47.♕e6+ ♔g7 48.♕xe7+ ♔g8 49.♘e6 ♖g6 50.g4 ♘d3 51.♕f8+ ♔h7 52.♕f5 ♘e1+ 1-0

In the next game, Black lets White's a-pawn to a5. Thus he obtains the b5-square for his minor pieces, but the overall picture is similar. White bars the b-file with a knight at b6, instead of b5:

V.Milov–Abrahamyan
Minneapolis 2005

1.d4 ♘f6 2.c4 c5 3.d5 b5 4.♘f3 g6 5.cxb5 a6 6.b6 d6 7.♘c3 ♘bd7 8.e4 ♗g7 9.a4 ♕xb6 10.a5 ♕b4 11.♘d2 0-0 12.♗e2 ♘e8 13.0-0 ♘c7 14.♘c4 ♕b7 15.♘a4 ♘b5

Compared to the first diagram from the previous page, White's pieces on the queenside are shifted forward. This spatial advantage enables another good plan for White. Besides attacking the black king, he can also open up the left wing by b2-b4. This is even the main plan in the structures with a white pawn on a5.

16.♘ab6 ♘xb6 17.♘xb6 ♖a7 18.♖b1 ♗d7 19.♗g5 ♖e8 20.♕d2 ♘d4 21.♗c4 ♗b5 22.♕d3 ♗xc4 23.♕xc4 ♘b5 24.♕d3 ♕b8

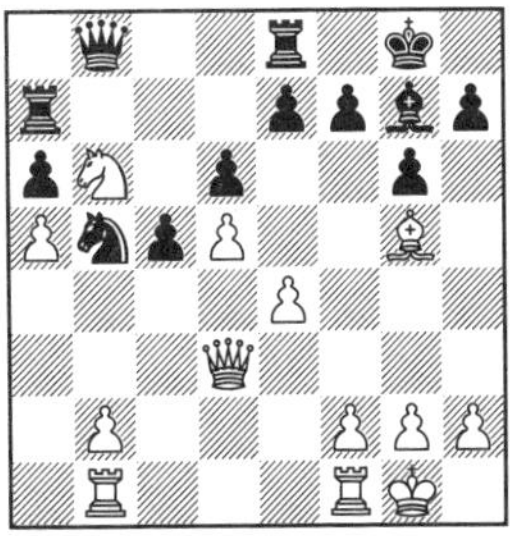

Here b2-b4 gives a stable edge, but Milov prefers the kingside attack:

25.f4 ♖c7 26.f5! ♘d4 27.♖bc1 ♗e5 28.♗f4 ♗xf4 29.♖xf4 ♖f8 30.fxg6 fxg6 31.♖xf8+ ♕xf8 32.♖f1 ♕b8 33.h4 ♘b5 34.h5 ♕e8 35.e5!

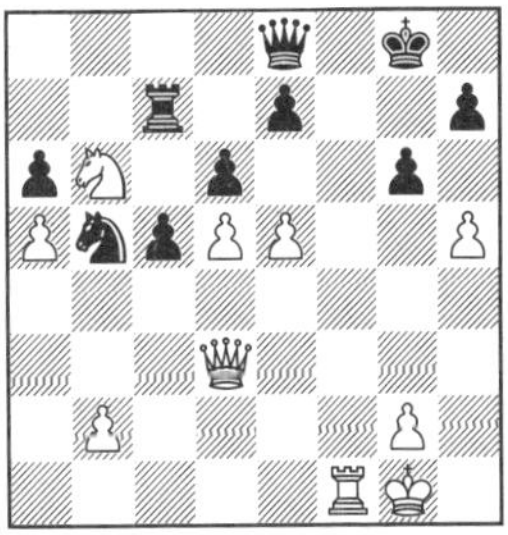

During the last 10 moves Milov demonstrated a nearly full set of White's most important techniques in the kingside attack: he began with f4-f5, then came the turn of the h-pawn, while finally e4-e5 serves as the *coup de grâce*.

35...dxe5 36.♕g3 ♘d6 37.♕xe5 gxh5 38.♖f3 h4 39.♕g5+ ♔h8 40.♕h6 ♘f7 41.♕h5 ♔g8 42.♕xh4 ♖b7 43.♕g4+ ♔h8 44.♕h5 e5 45.d6 e4 46.♖f1 1-0

White deals the decisive blow nearly always on the right wing, but that happens in deep middlegame. In the opening, we have other concerns. Let us consider them in turn.

Our primary task in the opening after 1.d4 ♘f6 2.c4 c5 3.d5 b5 will be quick development.

For that, we need to achieve e2-e4.

Recently 4.♕c2 has come into fashion, but this move removes the support for our main trump, the d5-pawn. That offers Black the possibility of open up the centre by ...e6 which results in very sharp play and many forced variations. Another common sense argument against this move is that the queen might turn misplaced on c2. Still, in Part 2 I examine shortly the 4.♕c2 system which could be a solid alternative to our main repertoire.

In many cases the main ideas of the Positional Benko with b6 are applicable to that system, too.

The most natural way to prepare e2-e4 is 4.♘c3, but it does not work due to 4...b4. Obviously, we must define the situation on the queenside first. Our aim is to obtain this pawn structure:

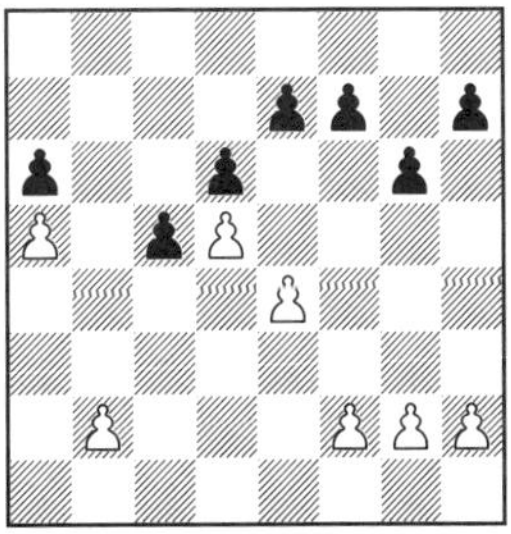

Note that we want it WITH the

a6-pawn, in order to keep the black heavy pieces shut behind it. Before the b6-system became popular, White often tried to achieve that by immediately attacking the b5-pawn with 4.a4 bxc4 5.♘c3 d6 6.e4 g6 7.♗xc4

Diagram 1

Let us compare this position with the next one (which arises after 1.d4 ♘f6 2.c4 c5 3.d5 b5 4.♘f3 g6 5.cxb5 a6 6.b6 ♕xb6 7.♘c3 d6 8.e4):

Diagram 2

On Diagram 2, the knight is on f3. This is compensated in the first case by the move a4 which is indispensable anyway. In Diagram 1, White has an extra move – ♗c4, but this is hardly the best square for the bishop since it deprives the f3-knight of its ideal stand. Moreover, on ...♗a6 White has nothing better, but spend a tempo on ♗b5 which suggests that we can hardly claim a clear extra tempo up in comparison to Diagram 2.

In Diagram 2 Black has 2 extra moves – ...♕b6 and ...a6. And here is the big catch. **The pawn on a6 is a horrible "asset".** It deprives Black's minor pieces of the a6-square. It is also a target in many variations where White fixes it by a2-a4-a5. Finally, the b6-square is weakened and, as we saw in game 2 V.Milov-Abrahamyan, White often plants there a knight.

Summarising: Diagram 2 shows a better version of the same pawn structure.

So we reject 4.a4 and confine our choice to:

1. 4.cxb5 a6 5.b6, or
2. 4.♘f3 g6 (4...d6) 5.cxb5 a6 6.b6.

Both move orders are possible and you can vary them, but I recommend the latter one.

Let us consider the pros and cons.

1. 4.cxb5 a6 5.b6

Pros: This is the most straightforward path to the desired structure. Black cannot evade it by 4...b4.

Cons: Black can attack the centre by 5...e6. That brings about independent pawn structures so I devoted a separate part of the book to them. The learning overhead of this variation is relatively small, but White's choice is very limited. Black can drag us more or less forcedly into a pretty dry heavy pieces middlegame with meager winning chances for White. If you face a strong opponent or prefer to minimise risk, that is a perfect choice.

The critical line goes 1.d4 ♘f6 2.c4 c5 3.d5 b5 4.cxb5 a6 5.b6 e6 6.♘c3 ♘xd5 7.♘xd5 exd5 8.♕xd5 ♘c6 9.♘f3 ♖b8 10.e4 ♗e7 11.♗d2 0-0 12.♗c4 ♖xb6 13.♗c3 d6 14.0-0 ♗e6 15.♕d3 ♗xc4 16.♕xc4 ♗f6 when a lot of variations lead to a complete extermination of the minor pieces, e.g. 17.♖ad1 ♗xc3 18.bxc3 ♕f6 19.♖d3 ♖e8 20.♕a4 ♔f8 21.♖fd1 ♘e5 22.♘xe5 ♕xe5 23.♖e3

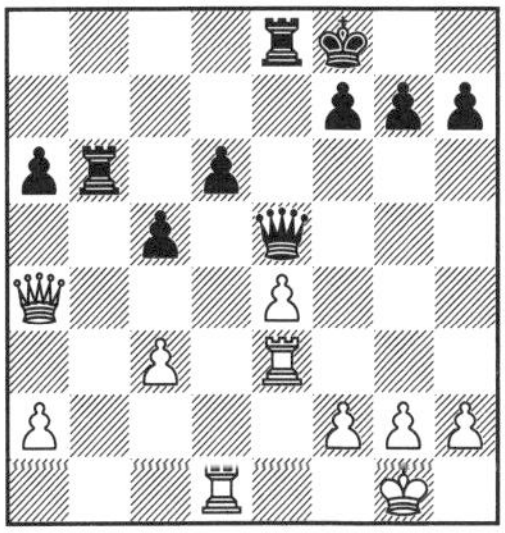

See **game 14 Kuljasevic-Andrews**, USA tt ICC, 2007 (p.120). White has the draw in the pocket and he exerts lasting pressure, but I think that the other move order leads to more fresh positions:

2. 4.♘f3

Pros: This is a flexible move which keeps all options open. The majority of games feature 4...g6 or 4...d6 when we reach the b6 system by 5.cxb5 a6 6.b6. That way we sidestep the variations with 4...e6.

Cons: The only drawback I can see is the necessity of learning two more systems as Black can lead the game into closed strategic positions by 4...b4 or initiate sharp complications by 4...♗b7. I consider them in Part 2. However, these options should not be of particular concern to us since play is rich and promising for White. I often meet in chess literature the old myth that 4...♗b7 allegedly gives Black sufficient counterplay. Modern practice and my analyses do not confirm that at all. In fact, at higher level, very few players opt lately for 4...♗b7 and they are usually crushed in the opening.

A Little Background

I have always played the Benko with both colours. In my junior years, I followed the fashion and used to take on b5 following up with 5.e3. Here is one memorable game which practically earned me my Junior World title:

Kiril Georgiev–Bareev
Wch U20 Belfort, 1983

1.d4 ♘f6 2.c4 c5 3.d5 b5 4.cxb5 a6 5.e3 e6 6.♘c3 exd5 7.♘xd5 ♗b7 8.♘xf6+ ♕xf6 9.♘f3 ♗e7 10.bxa6 ♗xa6 11.♗d3 ♕e6 12.a4 0-0 13.0-0 ♗f6 14.♖a3 d5 15.♖e1 ♘c6 16.e4 ♗xd3 17.exd5 ♕xd5 18.♖xd3 ♕a2 19.♖d6 ♖fd8 20.♖xd8+ 1-0

About that time, the popularity of 5.e3 began to fade and White players gradually turned their attention to the Benko Accepted. However, the chess world noticed the efforts of the 20-years old future champion Kasparov to develop new ways of fighting the Benko. It is true, he employed 5.b6 only in simultan and exhibition games, but every opening experiment of the young superstar had a strong impact, especially on the younger players. At that time Kasparov treated the b6-system very aggressively, with an early f4. (That was not new, as we can find the game Ogaard-Mortensen, Kiel 1978 in database, for example.)

Kasparov–Illescas Cordoba
Barcelona sim 1984

1.d4 ♘f6 2.c4 c5 3.d5 b5 4.cxb5 a6 5.b6 d6 6.♘c3 ♘bd7 7.a4 ♘xb6 8.a5 ♘bd7 9.e4 g6 10.f4 ♗g7 11.♗c4 0-0 12.♘f3 ♘e8 13.0-0 ♘c7

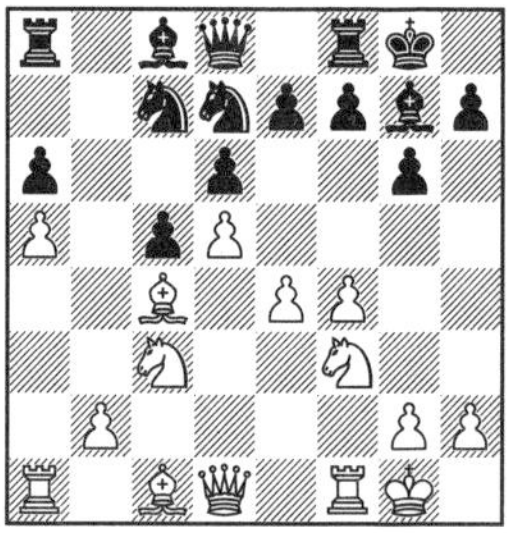

Although this approach is tempting, it offers Black considerable counterattacking chances. My style was more solid and I wanted a sounder solution of the opening problems. So I turned my attention to 4.a4:

Kiril Georgiev–Vaisser
San Bernardino 1989

1.d4 ♘f6 2.c4 c5 3.d5 b5 4.a4 bxc4 5.♘c3 d6 6.e4 g6 7.♗xc4 ♗g7 8.h3 ♗a6 9.♗b5+ ♗xb5 10.axb5 0-0 11.♘f3 ♘bd7 12.0-0 ♘e8 13.♖e1 ♘c7 14.♗f4

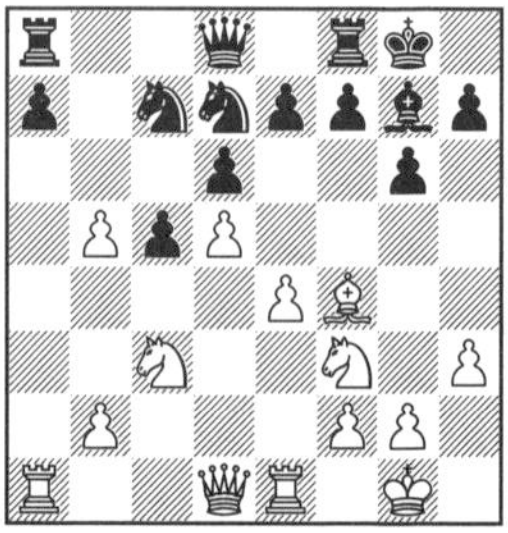

We see here many ideas I advocate in the book, but the fact that Black's pawn is still on a7 (instead of a5, like in the examples in the book) allows the equalising:

14...a6! 15.bxa6 ♖xa6 16.♖xa6 ♘xa6 17.e5 dxe5 18.♘xe5 ♘xe5 19.♗xe5 ♘b4 20.♗xg7 ♔xg7 Draw.

Then I was already ripe for 4.♘f3, but my first serious tournament test was a little later, in the game:

Kiril Georgiev–Topalov
Elenite 1992

1.d4 ♘f6 2.c4 c5 3.d5 b5 4.♘f3 g6 5.cxb5 a6 6.b6 ♕xb6 7.♘c3 ♗g7 8.e4 0-0 9.♗e2 d6 10.♘d2 ♘bd7 11.0-0 ♖b8 12.♘c4 ♕c7 13.♗f4 ♘b6 14.e5 ♘e8 15.exd6 exd6 16.♕d2 ♘xc4 17.♗xc4 ♘f6 18.♖fe1 ♘g4 19.♖ad1 ♗d4 20.♗g3 f5 21.♖e2 ♖b4 22.b3 ♕g7

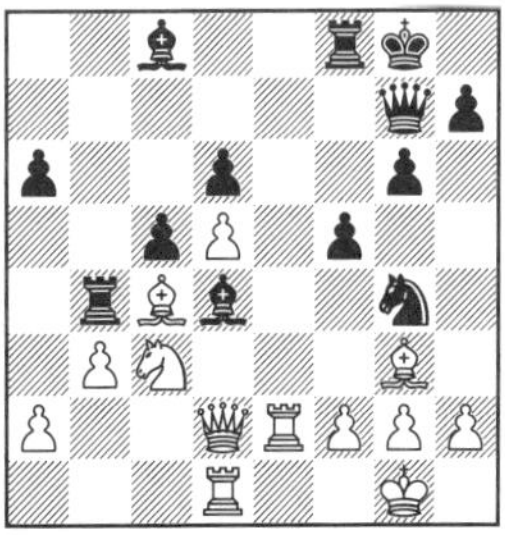

23.♗xd6!! ♗xc3 24.♕f4 ♖d8 25.♖e7 ♕f6 26.♗xc5 ♖b7 27.♖xb7 ♗e5 28.d6+ ♔h8 29.♕f3 ♗xh2+ 30.♔f1 ♗e5 31.♕d5 ♗xb7 32.♕xb7 ♕h4 33.d7 ♗f6 34.a4 ♕h5 35.♖d6 ♘e5 36.♕d5 ♘xc4 37.bxc4 ♗g7 38.♖e6 g5 39.♗b6 1-0

It was a nice win indeed, but the opening did not bring me a real advantage. Something was missing and perhaps it was the positional plan connected with a2-a4-a5. Shirov employed it in several games, but he still linked it with an early f4. No wonder he was getting into crazy complications.

Another favourite plan from those years was to develop the bishop to c4 and the king's knight went to e2 in order to leave a free lane to the f-pawn.

Meanwhile, Shirov's numerous victories brought a burst of popularity of the b6-system and it was gradually becoming the main alternative to the Benko Accepted. Even Karpov, who is fairly conservative in his opening tastes, tried it. The following game was a true strategic revelation. We can find in it most of the principles I try to explain in this book:

Karpov–Belotti
FRA France, 1993

1.d4 ♘f6 2.c4 c5 3.d5 b5 4.cxb5 a6 5.b6 d6 6.♘c3 ♕xb6 7.e4 g6 8.♘f3 ♗g7 9.♘d2 0-0 10.♘c4 ♕c7 11.♗e2 ♘bd7 12.♗f4 ♘b6 13.♘e3 ♘fd7 14.♖c1 a5 15.a4 ♘b8 16.♘b5 ♕d8 17.b3 ♘a6 18.0-0 ♘b4 19.♕d2 ♗a6 20.♖fd1 ♘d7

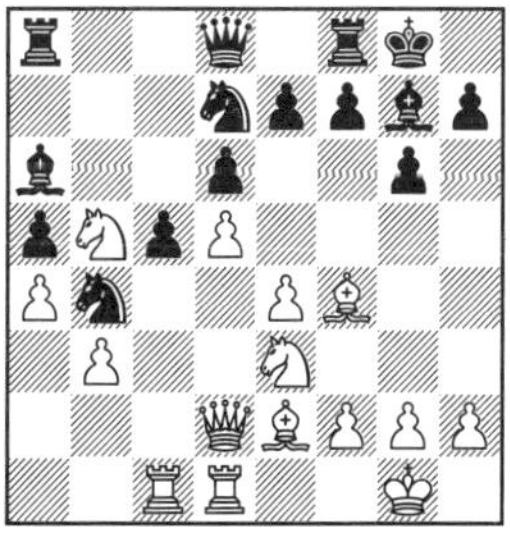

White has accomplished his opening aims. He completed development and took control of c4 and b5. The next objectives of Karpov are to kill in advance any attempt for counterplay.

21.f3 ♘f6 22.♗c4 ♘e8 23.♖e1 ♘c7 24.♘a3 ♕d7 25.♔h1 ♗d4 26.♗h6 ♖fb8 27.♘g4 ♗xc4 28.♘xc4 ♘e8 29.♗e3 ♗xe3 30.♖xe3 ♘f6 31.♘f2 ♕d8 32.♖ce1 ♕f8

Only now Karpov embarks upon White's main plan – a kingside attack with f4. He is conducting the offensive with extreme precautions though:

33.f4 ♕g7 34.♖d1 ♘h5 35.♘h3 ♘f6 36.♕e2 ♕h6 37.♖f3 ♕h5 38.♘f2 ♕h6 39.g3 ♕g7 40.♔g2 h5 41.♘h3 ♖d8 42.♘g5 ♘h7 43.♘xh7 ♔xh7

Here finally follows the thematic thrust:

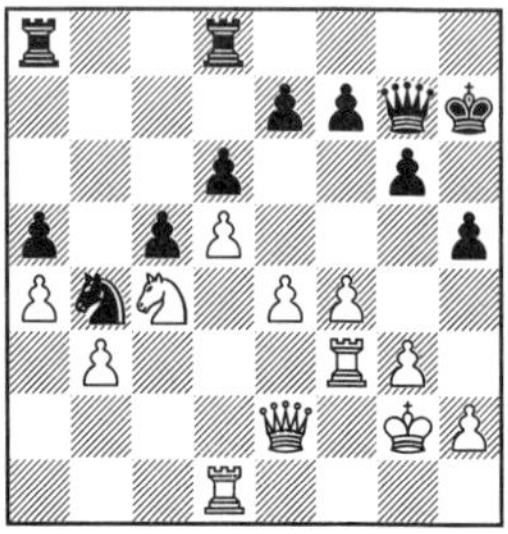

44.f5! f6 45.fxg6+ ♔xg6 46.♖f5 ♖h8 47.♖df1 ♖h6 48.e5 dxe5 49.♖xe5 ♖a7 50.d6 1-0

I should also mention the great contribution of Dreev who created several positional masterpieces. In the 90ies he used the straightforward move order with 4.cxb5 a6 5.b6, but in 2007 I saw him moving to 4.♘f3.

I also will be assuming 4.♘f3 as our weapon of choice.

Basic Plans and Pawn Structures

The Benko Declined is a calm system which allows a great number of different move orders and transpositions. It assumes a battle of plans rather than of moves. You would easier find your way between interweaving branches if you grasped first the basic ideas of that opening. Then you could check the "Step by Step" chapter for more concrete guidance.

The main position of the b6-system arises after **1.d4 ♘f6 2.c4 c5 3.d5 b5 4.♘f3 g6 5.cxb5 a6 6.b6 d6 7. ♘c3 ♗g7 8.e4 0-0**

This is the most flexible move order for Black because he keeps open all his options for regaining the pawn. He can capture on b6 by queen, by his queen's knight, or even by his king's knight after ...♘f6-d7xb6.

9.a4

The thrust of the a-pawn forces Black to define the pawn structure on the queenside. If he wants to take by knight, he must answer 9...a5. The alternative is 9...♕xb6, yielding space on the queenside. The ensuing different structures imply different middlegame scenarios. In the first case, White plays in the centre and on the kingside, while in the second one his main goal is to open the queenside by b2-b4 and hit the a6-pawn. So I'll examine them separately.

Black plays 9...a5

9...a5 10.♗b5

The possibility for this move is the main reason for playing 9.a4 instead of developing the bishop to e2.

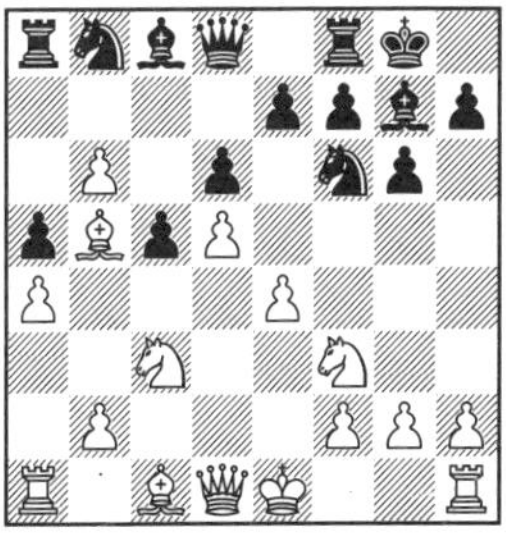

The b5-bishop has several tasks:

1. It restricts Black's counterplay by plugging the b-file. Naturally, it has no right to retreat, no matter how Black will attack it – by bishop or by knight. Should Black exchange it, we'll take by the a-pawn, keeping the b-file closed and hitting the a5-pawn, for instance:

10...♗a6 11.0-0 ♗xb5 12.axb5 ♘bd7

13.b7 ♖b8 14.♘d2! ♖xb7 15.♘c4 ♖a7 16.h3± with a positional domination.

2. On b5 the bishop is more useful than on e2, since the e-file remains free for our rook, which is able to support the breakthrough e4-e5. Note that Black cannot effectively contest the e-file due to the X-ray of our bishop toward e8.

3. The bishop is able to inflict serious damage by going even further – to c6 as we'll see a little later.

So we lead the bishop to b5. What is next? It depends mostly on Black's move 10. If he chooses the rare 10...♘fd7!?, I suggest to use the absence of Black's knight from the kingside and provoke a weakening of Black's castling position by 11.h4! h5. Then we'll trade the only defender of the black king: 12.♗g5 ♘xb6 13.♕d2 ♘a6 14.♗h6 ♗g4 (14...♘c7 15.♗xg7 ♔xg7 16.♘d4!) 15.♗xg7 ♔xg7

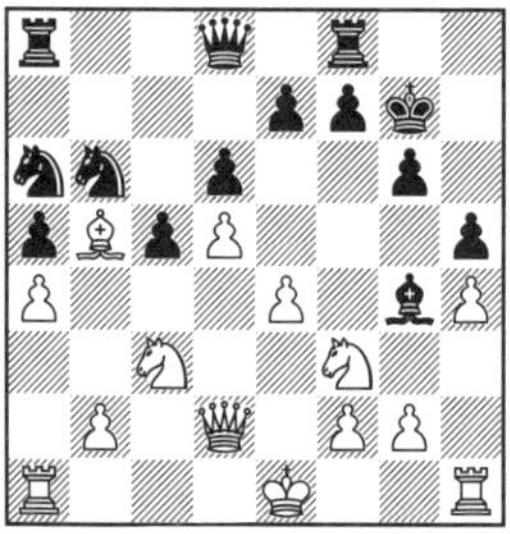

16.♘h2! ♗d7 17.0-0. This position is similar to the other lines, but the insertion of h4 h5 should enhance the effect of the imminent f4-f5. I examine this variation in "Step by Step" chapter, line A3.

If Black directs the queen's knight to b6, we follow up with:

10...♘bd7 11.0-0 ♘xb6

The evaluation of this position depends on whether White will be able to break in the centre before Black removed the blockade on the b-file. My conclusion is that White is ahead with his play.

You should remember not to waste time on prophylaxis with h3.

In that case Black will manage to hit first: 12.h3 ♘e8 13.♖e1 ♘c7 14.♗f4 ♗a6 15.♕c2 ♗xb5 16.axb5 ♕d7, winning the b5-pawn.

Instead, White could develop by 12.♗f4, followed by 13.♕d2, but I prefer to prepare e4-e5 with:

12.♖e1

The fine point is that now 12...♘e8 13.♗f4! (waiting for the e8-knight to go to c7) 13...♘c7 will let in 14.♗c6 ♖b8 15.e5! ♗f5 16.exd6 exd6 17.♗g5 f6 18.♗d2 ♘c4 19.♘b5 ♘xb2 20.♕e2 ♗d3 21.♕e3. White's pieces are much more active, for example: 21...♗xb5 22.axb5 ♘xb5 23.♕e6+! ♔h8 24.♕e2±.

12...f6 14.♗c6 ♖b8 15.♘b5

A typical position for this line. The a5-pawn is weak and we are going to attack it by ♗d2. Our b5-knight could go even deeper inside Black's camp – to a7.

Black's only counterplay is connected with ...f6-f5 so we should leave our knight on f3. I examine that in detail in line A4.

Notice that Black can trade his bishop for our knight: 12...♗g4 13.h3 ♗xf3 14.♕xf3 ♘e8

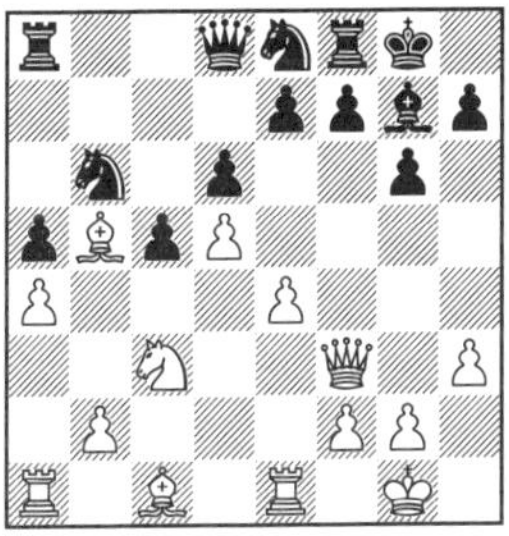

This position is rather unpleasant for Black as he is deprived of any counterplay. Without his light-square bishop, he will be unable to break the blockade on b5. That means, we will be remaining the active side for many moves. We could exchange the defender of Black's king – the g7-bishop – by ♗d2-c3 and prepare e4-e5, or advance the h-pawn.

I'll only mention Black's option of capturing on b6 by queen, since it does not fit in the schema with ...a5. Black will anyway have to retreat the queen, thus losing a tempo. We continue as in the other line with ♖e1, only instead of developing the bishop to f4 we put it on g5 to underline the weakness of the e7-pawn.

Points to remember:

- Do not play h3. With the black pawn on a5, any exchange of the enemy light-squared bishop (either for our f3-knight or for our bishop) is in White's favour;
- Prepare e4-e5, but wait for ♘e8-c7 first;
- Paralise the queenside by ♗c6 and ♘b5;
- Aim to exchange the g7-bishop – by ♗f4, ♕d2, ♗h6 or ♗f4-d2-c3;
- Watch out for ...f5;
- We commonly meet ...e6 by taking dxe6.

Middlegame Plans

I devote the next pages on concrete examples which should prepare you for practical battles. The more such positions you know, the better decisions you will make over the board.

The Benko Declined does not require much calculation if you treat it correctly. In fact, it is not even too important that you make always the best moves. The stable pawn structure allows long manoeuvring which does not affect the evaluation of the position.

However, the fact that you'll not be able to choose the best move by calculation, requires strategic thinking and knowledge of typical . When you look at the board, you would often be able to associate the position with some diagram from this book and follow the model.

Here are examples of White's light-squared strategy where Black parted with his bishop:

Game 2 Shaked–Shirov
Tilburg 1997

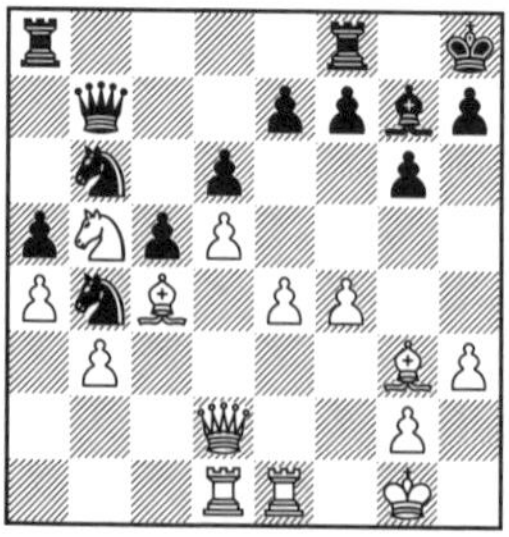

Position after 25.b3

White has total bind on the queenside and the centre, which is a premise for a successful attack on the black king. The typical plan is linked with f4-f5 and exchange of Black's bishop. See the commentaries in the "Complete Games" chapter.

Khmelniker–Georgescu
Plovdiv 2008

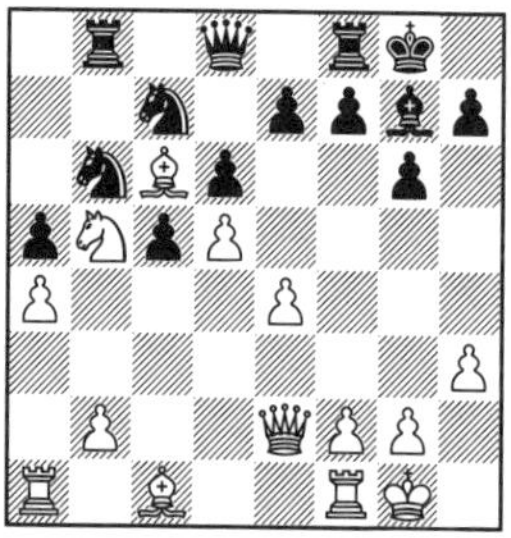

Position after 17.♘b5

Black could not stand the b5-knight and took it: 17...♘xb5. As we know, White should have recaptured by 18.axb5! with a solid edge, for example, 18...a4 19.♗f4, intending h4-h5 and discouraging 19...f5 in view of 20.e5. Instead, he chose 18.♗xb5 ♘d7 19.♕c2 (19.♗g5! h6 20.♗f4) 19...f5 and Black organised some counterplay.

Early in the opening, we keep our bishop on b5. Later on, however, when we are fully developed and our queenside rook is no longer eyeing the black pawn at a5 (in case Black exchanges on b5), we should gladly trade it in order to make room for our knight:

Game 1 Gleizerov–Draganic
Biel 2008

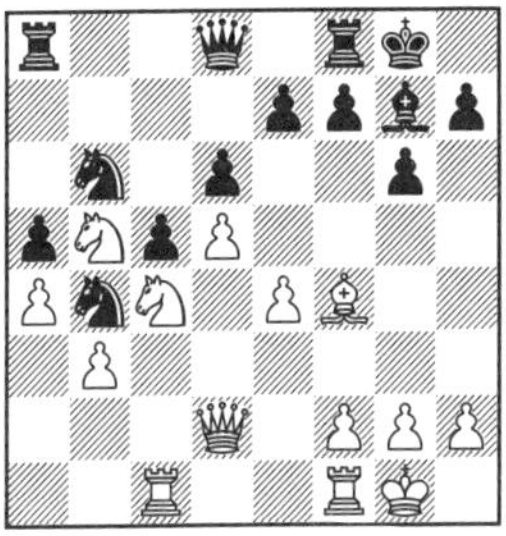

Position after 21.♘b5

White will put his rooks in the centre and push f4. Then he will choose between e4-e5 or f4-f5, depending on Black's concrete setup.

Shaked–Bosboom
Wijk aan Zee 1998

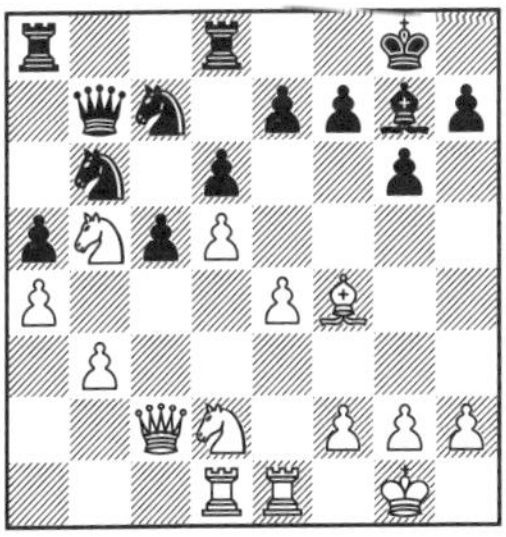

Position after 21...♘c7

Black is seeking counterplay in the centre, but White is perfectly coordinated: 22.♘a3 e6?! 23.♘dc4 exd5. Here best would have been 24.♘xd6 ♕c6 25.♘ab5±.

I noted many times the role of Black's light-squared bishop for the contest of the b5 and c4-squares. The other important piece in that battle is the f6-knight, which goes to c7. Without that knight, Black cannot hope for counterplay.

Grabarczyk–Kachur
Barlinek 2006

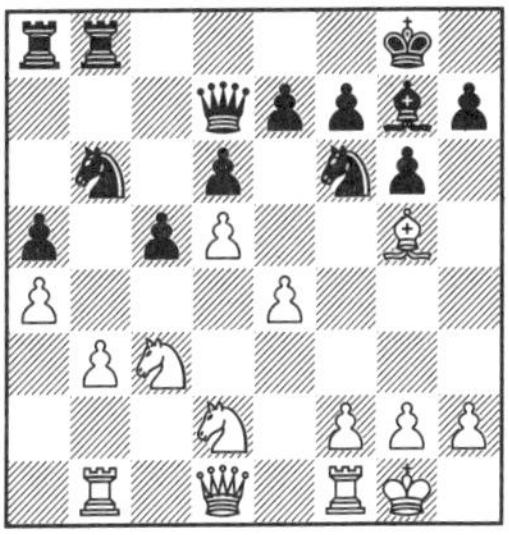

Position after 16...♖fb8

Although I do not advice to give our bishop for the enemy knight (since it will be more difficult to mate the opponent later), Grabarczyk's decision: 17.♗xf6, has a solid positional reason. After 17...♗xf6 18.♘b5 ♘c8 19.♘c4 ♘a7 20.♘ba3 ♘c8 21.♕d2 ♕d8 22.f4 ♖b4 23.e5± White dominated the centre.

Typical Tactical Motives

Semkov–Knaak
Yerevan 1988

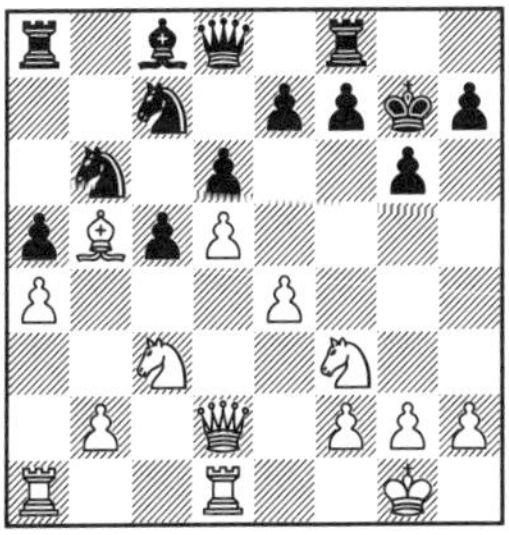

Position after 16...♗b7-c8?

Black leaves his knight on b6 undefended. In combination with a king on g7 (which often happens after ♗c1-f4-h6xg7), that triggers the tactical mine 17.♘d4! with a big edge. It is far from trivial and in the game both opponents missed it! Notice that instead of 16...♗c8?, 16...f5 would have also stumbled into 17.exf5 ♖xf5 18.♘d4!.

Remember this hit as it is an important part of White's arsenal in the pawn structure with ...a5.

Matveeva–E.Atalik
Elista 2002

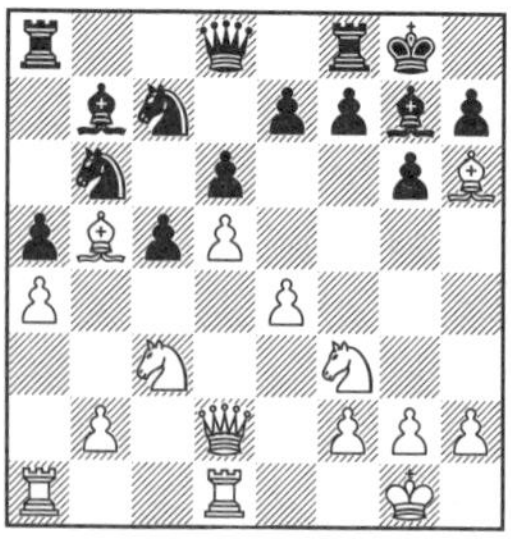

Position after 15.♗h6

We see the same pattern from the previous example. Now 15...f5 looks tempting, but then 16.exf5 ♖xf5 17.♗xg7 ♔xg7 18.♘d4!± would have been very awkward.

Counterplay

Let me repeat once again: our primary task in the Benko Declined is to deprive Black of counterplay. We already saw how to tame his queenside attempts. The following examples show what White should be trying to avoid.

Alwais whatch out for the breakthrough ...f7-f5. Topalov is one of the few players who always sought kingside play with ...f5. Modern engines also seem to love this break.

Gleizerov–Fayyazi
Teheran 2006

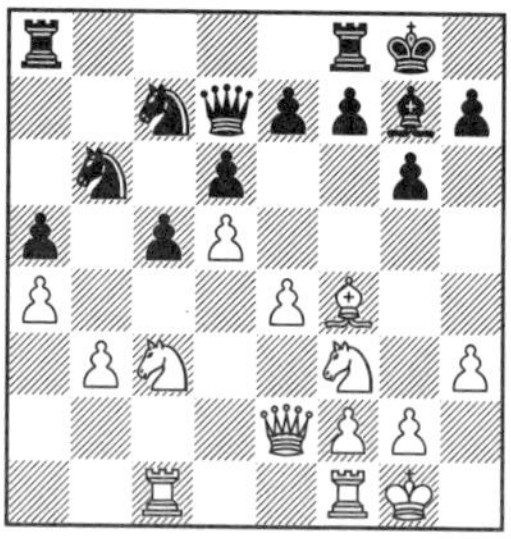

Position after 18.b3

White has not manoeuvred well and the d5-pawn is shaky. Black could have underlined it by 18...f5! intercepting the initiative. Instead, he chose the mundane 18...♖fb8 and gradually lost.

Shipov–Zubov
blitz, bereg.ru Int, 2003

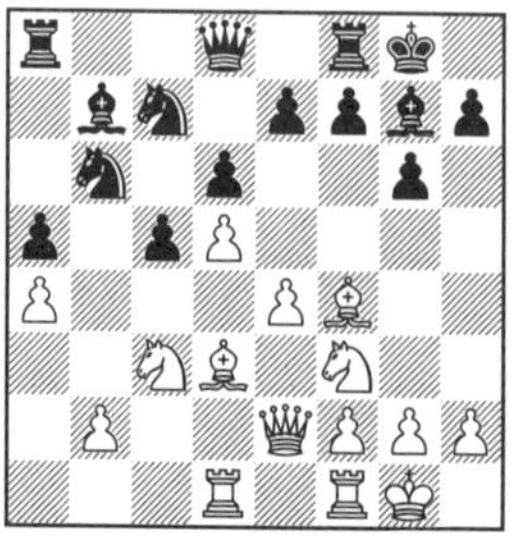

Position after 15.♗d3

White's d5-pawn is hanging. In such positions ...f5 is always dangerous. Black could have shaped best this idea by 15...♕d7 16.♕c2 f5!, e.g. 17.e5 c4 18.♗e2 ♘cxd5 19.♘xd5 ♗xd5 20.exd6 e6∓.

The other break in the centre, ...e6, is another active option of Black.

C.Ionescu–Jianu
Bucharest 2005

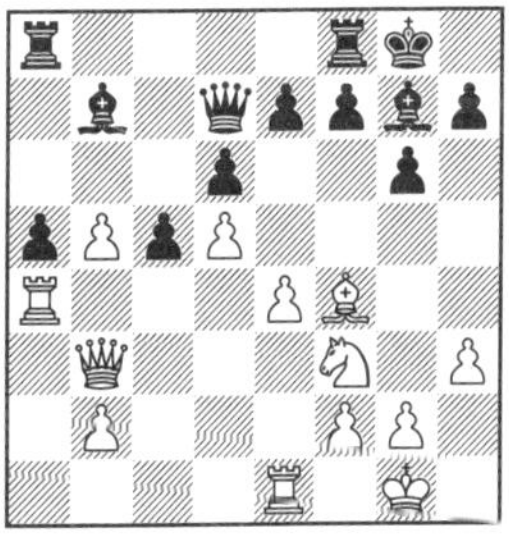

Position after 18.♖xa4

18...f5 here does not work due to 19.e5!, but the other breakthrough in the centre, 18...e6!, equalised.

Inarkiev–Vuckovic
Pardubice 2004

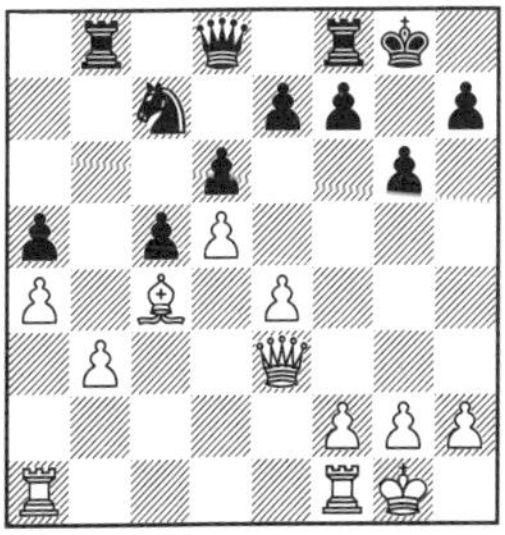

Position after 23.♗c4

White has lost tempi in the opening and could not find time for putting his rooks to d1 and e1. That offers Black the opportunity for undermining the centre by 23...e6! with some counterplay.

Instead, he made the typical mistake of doing pseudo-active moves on the queenside and was quickly overrun after 23...♖b4? 24.f4.

In most cases, however, the ...e6 break is less efficient than ...f5 and only opens the centre in White's favour:

Macieja–Berg
Warsaw 2008

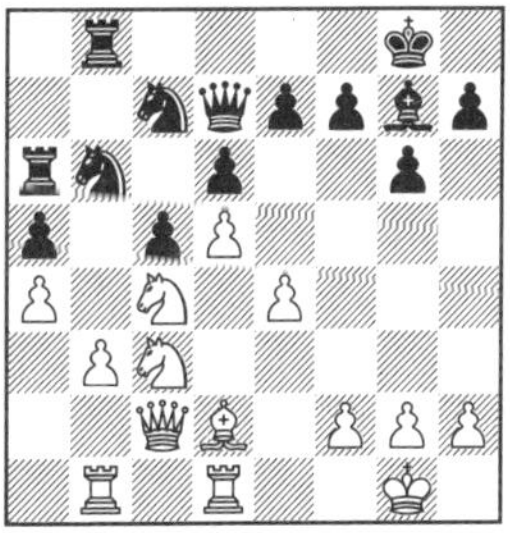

Position after 19.♗d2

White's setup in this example is not perfect (the rooks would have stayed better on d1 and e1), but he has achieved the main task of the positional Benko – c4 is under firm control and Black's counterplay is non-existent.

Berg tried to break the unfavourable for him pattern by 19...e6?!, and eventually made a draw, but White was much better after 20.dxe6 ♕xe6 21.♕d3 ♘c8 22.♘d5±.

Panchenko–Petr
Pardubice 1993

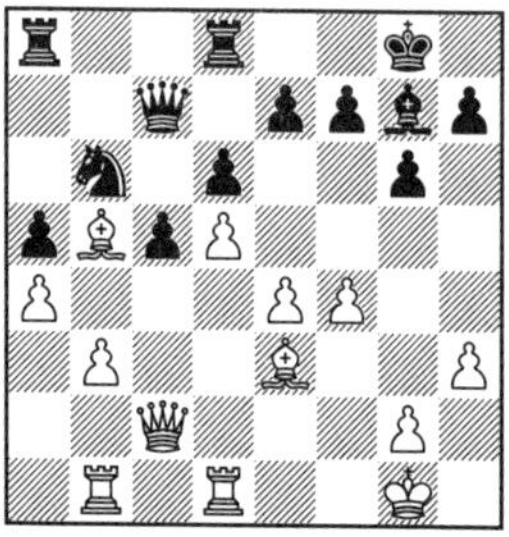

Position after 28.♗b5

28...e6?! 29.dxe6 fxe6 30.f5 ♗e5 31.♗g5 ♖f8 32.fxe6 ♘c8 33.♗d7 ♗f6 34.♗xf6 ♖xf6 35.♕c3 ♖f8 1-0

Attack on the kingside

Once we have deprived the opponent of counterplay and bolstered our pawn centre, we can pass to the stage of converting our advantage. That is usually achieved by a kingside attack.

Delchev–Granero Roca
Benidorm 2007

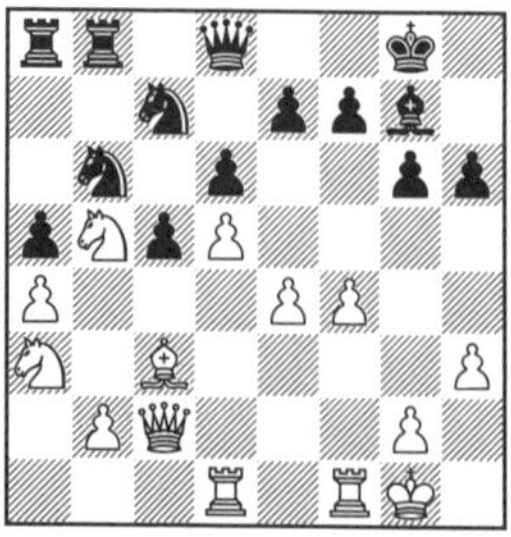

Position after 24...♘c7

We begin with f4-f5 in order to gain space on the flank and eliminate freeing attempts as ...f7-f5 or ...e7-e6. Then we can lift a rook to the h-file:

25.f5! ♘xb5 26.♘xb5 ♘d7 27.fxg6 fxg6 28.e5 dxe5 29.♕xg6 ♖b6 30.d6 exd6 31.♖f7 ♕f8 32.♖xf8+ ♘xf8 33.♕e4 1-0

Inarkiev–Vuckovic
Pardubice 2004

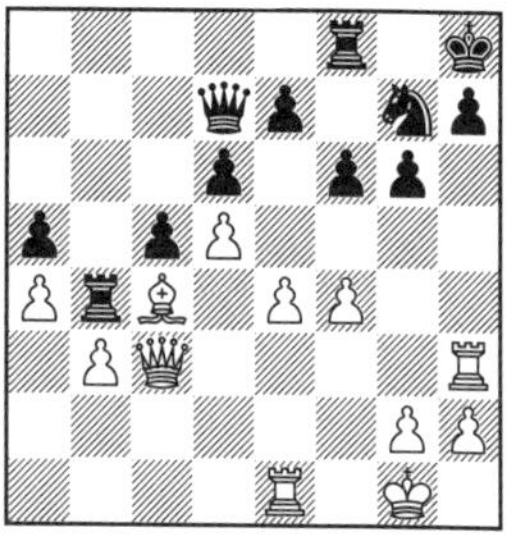

Position after 28...♕d7

Now simplest would have been 29.f5! g5 (29...gxf5 30.♕e3 ♖f7 31.♕h6 ♘e8 32.♗b5 ♖xb5 33.axb5 ♕xb5 34.exf5) 30.♖h6 ♖f7 31.♕h3 ♘e8 32.♗b5 ♕d8 33.♕h5+–.

The game went 29.♕g3 when Black blundered by 29...♖f7 and resigned. However, even the more stubborn defence 29...♖g8 should be hopeless after 30.f5! g5 31.♖h6. Here is a possible continuation of the attack: 31...♘e8 32.♕g4 ♘c7 33.♖e3 ♖g7 34.h4 ♕e8 35.hxg5 ♖xg5 36.♕h3 ♖g7 37.♖g3 ♕f8 38.♖hg6 ♖f7 39.♕h4 ♖b8 (39...♘a8 40.♗b5) 40.♗e2 ♖b4 41.♗h5+–.

Black refrains from ...a5

The most popular approach of the second players is to recapture on b6 by queen and let us play a4-a5. We'll certainly oblige, but not before having inserted ♘f3-d2!

6...♕xb6 7.♘c3 d6

8.♘d2

Let me elaborate on the diagram position. In the previous lines we considered lines where White invariably played e4 followed up by a4. The knight remained on f3 in order to support e4-e5. With a black queen on b6 and the pawn still on a6, we need to modify our plans. The reasons are:

1. We do not want to face the pin ...♗g4. Had Black played ...a6-a5, we would have gladly allowed the exchange of our knight since we would get full control of b5. Thus Black would not have any counterplay down the b-file. Without ...a6-a5 though, it makes sense to keep our knight since it is destined to reach c4 and even b6.

2. The straightforward plan with 8.a4 ♗g7 9.a5 ♕b4 10.♖a4 ♕b7 11.e4 0-0 12.♗e2 ♗d7 13.♖a3 ♗b5 offers Black considerable counterchances. Therefore we should wait for ...♘bd7. Then a4-a5 would be fine.

8...♗g7 9.e4 0-0

You should remember the tricky move order with 9...♘bd7 10.a4 ♕b4, when best is 11.a5! – see "Step by Step", page 32.

10.a4 ♘bd7 11.a5

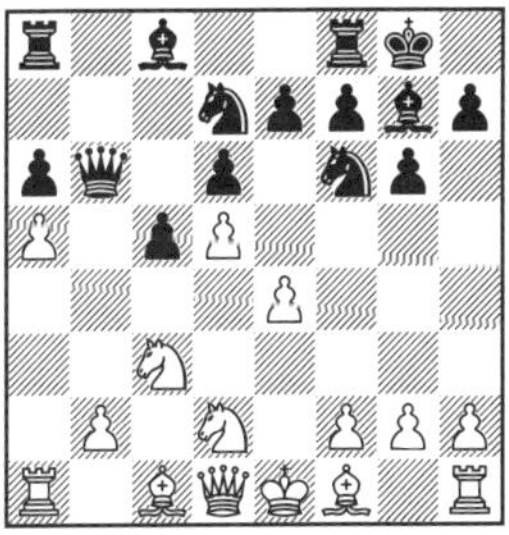

This pawn structure is considered in "Step by Step", line B. Black has tried here all possible retreats. I will focus now on the typical plans.

Basically, we want to play on the queenside where the a6-pawn is a tempting target both in the middlegame or endgame.

Firstly, we must neutralise Black's pressure down the b-file by sticking a knight on b6 (by ♘d2-

c4, ♘c3-a4). Then we set our other pieces with b2-b4 in mind. Opening up the queenside would unleash the power of White's rooks and underline Black's lack of space.

White's setup slightly varies depending on the retreat of Black's queen – to c7, d8, b7, b4, or a7.

I will break down White's play in the opening to three important steps:

1. Occupying the b6-square

White's first task is to complete development and direct both knights toward b6 by ♘d2-c4, ♘c3-a4.

This setup is universal and it does not depend on where Black retreats the queen after a4-a5.

Bareev–Bartel
Warsaw, 1999

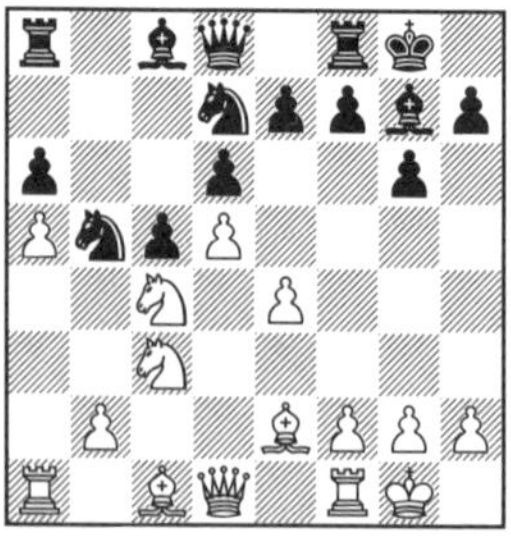

Position after 14...♘b5

Black concluded the long knight manoeuvre, but on d4 his knight would be more of a scarecrow. It would be efficient there only in conjunction with pressure along the b-file so we must answer: 15.♘a4! ♘d4 16.♗d3 ♘e5 17.♘xe5 ♗xe5 18.♘b6, with a clear advantage. White can then udermine d4 by b2-b4 or go for a direct attack with f4-f5.

C.Flear–Lumsdon
Brocco 1991

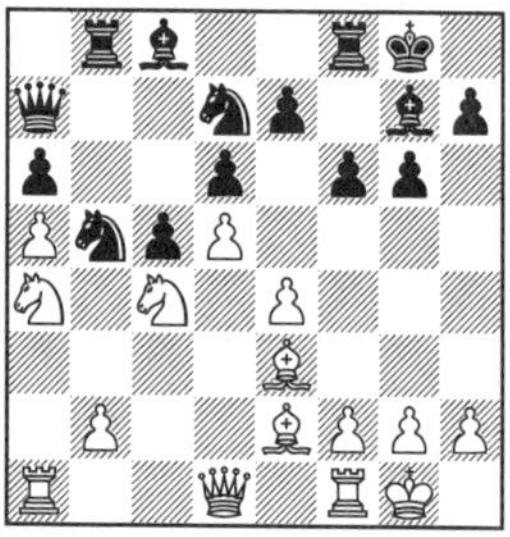

Position after 17.♘a4

Black's strategy is a failure. He was struggling after 17...f5 18.exf5 gxf5 19.♗g5 ♘e5 20.♘ab6.

Kacheishvili–D.Gurevich
Philadelphia 2009

Position after 14...♘e5

Here Black anticipated White's play (since 15.♘b6 would drop the e4-pawn), but at the high price of splitting its pawn chain and plugging the g7-bishop. These structural defects define White's edge. We can even ignore the exchange after 15.♘xe5 dxe5 16.♕c2 e6 17.♖d1 (17...♕b7 18.♗e3!) 17...♖d4 18.♗e3 ♖d8 19.♘a4!

2. The light-squared bishop goes to e2

The only exception is when Black's queen went to b7: 11...♕b7 12.♘c4 ♘e8 13.♗d3 ♘c7 14.0-0 ♘b5 15.♘a4 ♖b8

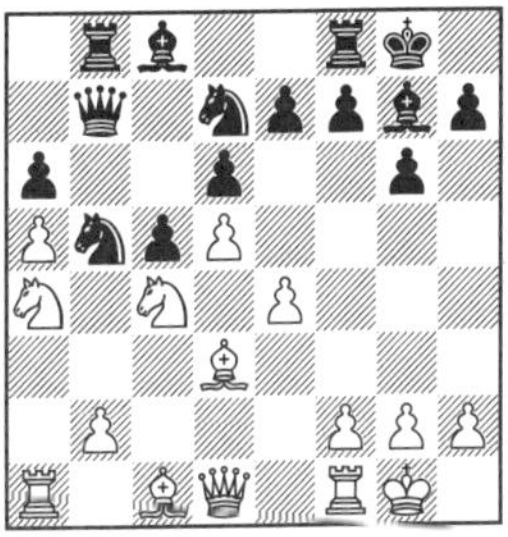

Now we prepare b4 by 16.♖b1!

3. The dark-squared bishop remains on c1

Commonly we develop our bishop only when the opening stage is over and the plans of both sides are clearly defined. Then it can go to d2 to support b4, or to e3 if Black had brought a knight to d4. Note that f4 is probably the worst place for this piece, in contrast with the structures when Black played a6-a5 himself. The reason is mostly that ...f7-f5 becomes more efficient since the bishop would be hanging on f4.

There is one specific line where the early ♗g5! is essential: when Black's queen retreats to a7. From here the queen does not defend e7 (as it does from d8), nor does it hit b2. That makes ♗g5! very awkward after ...♘f6-e8:

11...♕a7 12.♘c4 ♖b8 (12...♘e8 13.♗g5! f6 14.♗e3) 13.♗e2 ♘e8 14.♗g5! f6 15.♗e3.

Middlegame Plans

When development is completed and White has installed a knight on b6, he should focus on organising b2-b4.

This breakthrough is very important for White for many reasons. It undermines the only black outpost on d4 and denies the enemy any possible counterplay down the b-file. At the same time it fixes White's spatial advantage on the queenside by trading the weak b2-pawn for the strong one on c5. If we shape well this break and execute it at the right moment, Black will be doomed to a difficult defence without counterchances.

Mertanen–Vetemaa
Tampere 2000

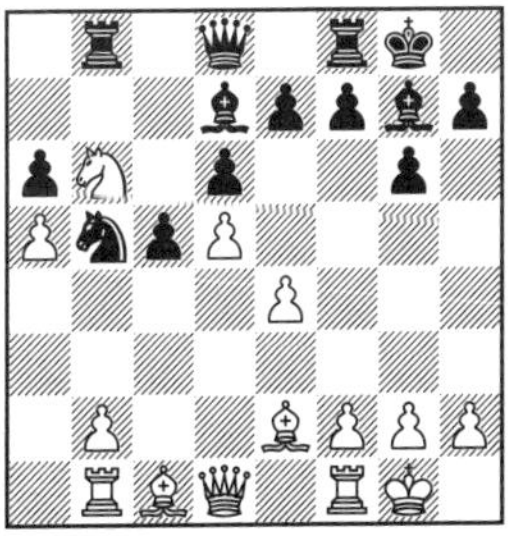

Position after 18.♖b1

18...♘c7

Preparing ...♗b5 while defending the a6-pawn.

19.♗d2! ♗b5 20.b4±.

Curiously enough, when the situation is ripe for b2-b4, the other typical plan in the Benko Declined – with f4-f5, is usually also good:

Game 4 V.Milov–Abrahamyan Minneapolis 2005

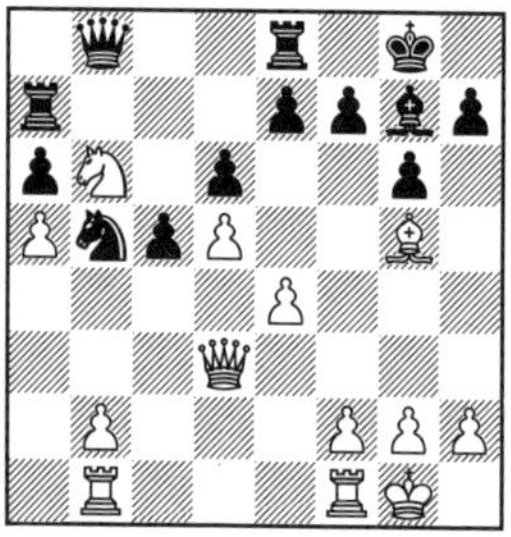

Position after 24...♕b8

All previous play until that moment "screams" for 25.b4 with a lasting advantage. However, Black is so passive, that the kingside attack is also rather unpleasant and possibly more effective: 25.f4!? ♖c7 26.f5 – see page 10.

Finally, an example where White combined both plans.

In the position on the next diagram Black is so cramped, that White could probably win only on the kingside. Instead, Portisch finds an elegant and safe solution. He breaks through the left wing: 50.b4!, with a decisive advantage.

Game 6 Portisch–Malakhatko Istanbul 2000

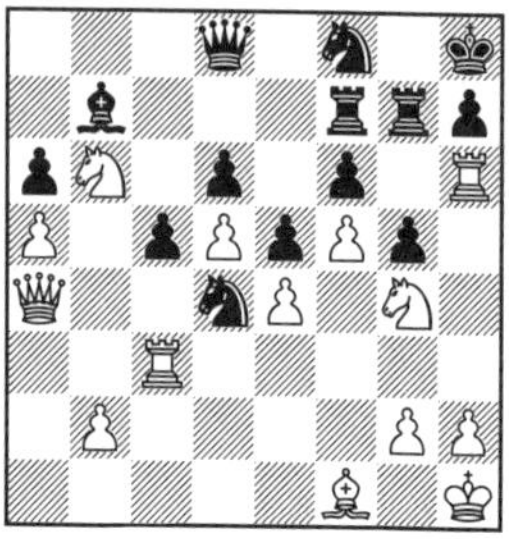

Position after 49...♔h8

Typical Tactical Motives

The opposition of a rook at b1 vs. a black queen on the same file often enables tactical tricks:

Lomineishvili–Pham Bich Ngoc Ningbo 02.09.2009

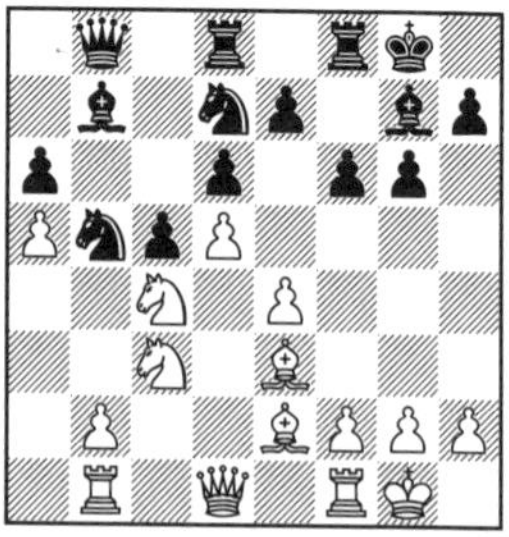

Position after 18...♘b5

19.♘xb5 axb5 20.b4!! bxc4 21.bxc5 ♘xc5 22.♗xc5 dxc5 23.a6 and White won.

Counterplay

We should always keep in mind Black's main ideas for counterplay: ...f5 or pressure down the b-file.

Rogozenco–Heinemann
Hamburg 1998

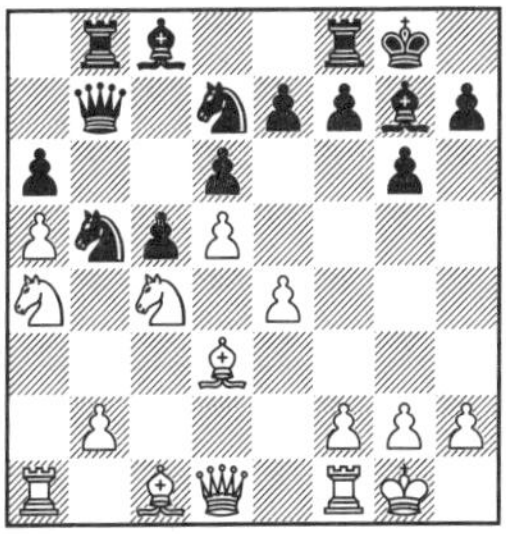

Position after 15...♖b8

White followed "by the book" 16.♘ab6?! ♘xb6 17.♘xb6, when 17...f5! would have given Black counterchances in view of 18.♘xc8 ♖bxc8 19.exf5 c4! 20.♗e2 c3. Instead, 16.♖b1 would have anticipated any tactics while keeping ♘ab6 in store.

V.Milov–Rincon Bascon
Dos Hermanas 2006

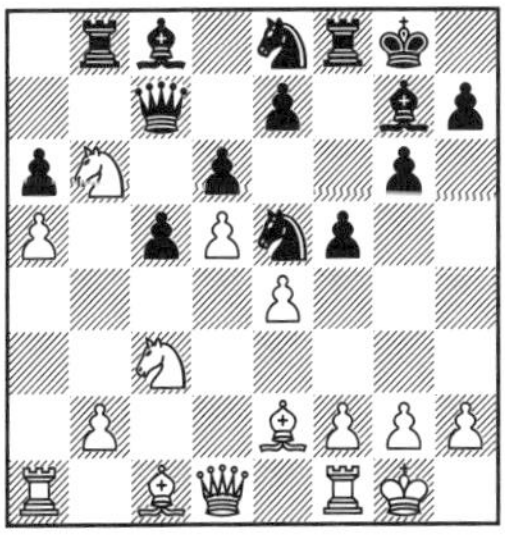

Position after 15...f5

The break ...f5 is inefficient here since Black's pieces are passive and the d5-pawn is well protected: 16.exf5 ♗xf5 17.♗e3± left Black with numerous weaknesses. The attempt to occupy d3 cost a pawn following 17...c4? 18.♖a4 ♘f6 19.♗xc4.

In the next example White manoeuvred without a clue and put his rook to the passive square a2.

Ricardi–Kiril Georgiev
Moscow, ol., 1994

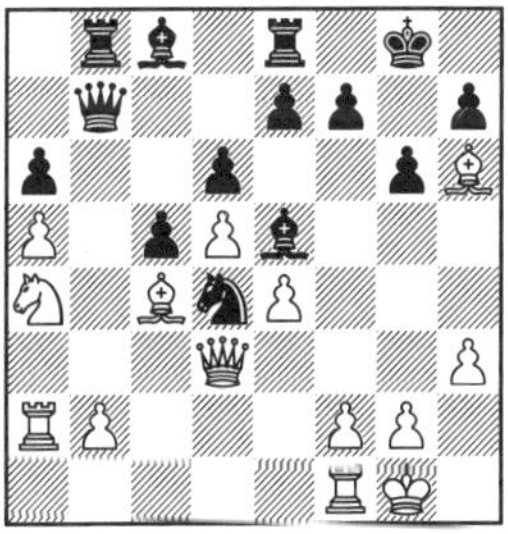

Position after 21.♘a4

That gave me the initiative after 21...♘b3! 22.♗e3 ♕b4. The exchange of the a-pawns lead to a typical symmetrical position with slightly better chances for Black: 23.♘b6 ♘xa5 24.♗d2 ♕xb6 25.♗xa5 ♕b7 26.♗c3 ♗xc3 27.bxc3 ♗d7 28.♗xa6 ♗b5 29.♗xb5 ♕xb5.

Such a position may look drawish, but in practise White finds it difficult to defend.

Pressure along the b-file is the main motive in Black's play. Sometimes he is even willing to sacrifice material to remove White's barricade on b6:

Game 5 Porfiriadis–Ermenkov
Athens 1993

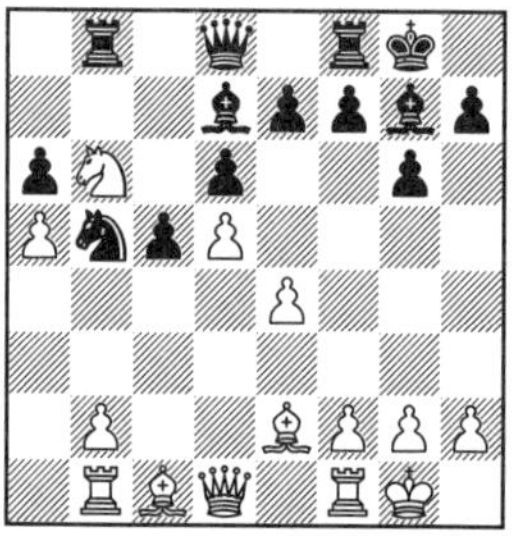

Position after 18.♖b1

White's knight on b6 is so awkward that Black chooses to kill it even at the cost of the exchange: 18...♖xb6!? 19.axb6 ♕xb6.

Do not underestimate the enemy counterplay in such positions! White needs to play very concretely. He must urgently provoke weaknesses on the kingside or he risks to get overrun on the queenside. See this interesting game in the "Complete Games" chapter.

Points to remember:

- Do not play a4-a5 until Black's knight occupied d7;
- Paralise the queenside by ♘d2-c4, ♘c3-a4;
- Aim for b2-b4;
- Watch out for ...f5.

Part 1

Step by Step

1.d4 ♘f6 2.c4 c5 3.d5 b5 4.♘f3 g6 5.cxb5 a6 6.b6

6...d6

Black often recaptures early on b6: 6...♕xb6. Then 7.♘c3 d6 8.♘d2! ♗g7 9.e4 commonly transposes to line B. There are a few variations of independent significance which I examine on the next page – see 8...♕xb6.

7. ♘c3 ♗g7 8.e4

8...0-0

8...♘bd7 9.a4 should transpose to the main line, for instance:

a) 9...a5 10.♗b5, line A,

b) 9...♘xb6 10.a5 ♘bd7 11.♗e2 0-0 12.0-0 ♘e8 13.♘d2, line B5.

c) 9...♕xb6 10.a5 ♕b4 (The other retreats transpose to line B.) 10.♘d2, see line a) on the next page.

8...♗g4 appears only in three games in my database. Perhaps the main reason is that the b6-pawn is still alive and the second players do not like the concrete variation 9.♕a4+ (9.e5 ♘fd7! is unclear) 9...♘fd7 10.♘d2 0-0 11.b7 ♖a7 12.♕c2 Black's setup is rather clumsy. His bishop has no retreat square, the b8-knight is also problematic, for instance, 12...♘b6 13.♗d3 ♖xb7

14.0-0 ♕c7 15.b3 with a strong grip on the queenside, which is a precondition for a successful attack on the other wing with f2-f4.

8...♕xb6 is the most popular answer. While many games transpose to variations from the current chapter, the early capture by the queen makes Black's strategy less flexible. That gives White more options, namely he can try plans without early a4.

In the next lines I will show you how to transpose safely to the main lines of the current part.

9.♘d2!

We can also start with 9.a4, but Black could then pin our knight by 9...♗g4. While this is not a terrible threat, it is better to sidestep this possibility.

a) 9...♘bd7 10.a4 ♕b4 11.a5! (11.♗e2 ♘e5 was unclear in V.Milov-Carlsen, Kemer 2007. The fine point is that Black's knight has freed the d7-square so 12.a5 would be already inefficient due to 12...♗d7) 11...♘e5 (everybody plays here 11...0-0, but after 12.♗e2 White is better, see line B2) 12.♖a4 ♕b7 13.f4 ♘ed7 14.♗c4 0-0 15.0-0±;

b) 9...0-0 10.a4 and:

b1) 10...♘bd7 transposes to the main line.

b2) 10...♕b4 11.♗e2! is line B2.

b3) 10...♕c7 11.a5 is line B1.

b4) 10...a5 11.♗b5 – see line A2.

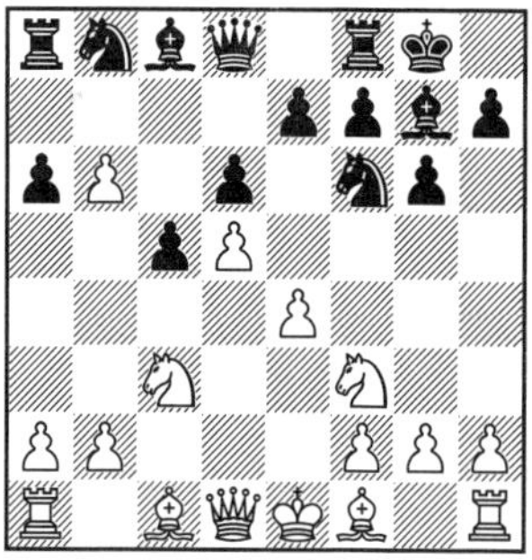

9.a4

This aims to define the pawn structure on the queenside. White is planning to fix at the right moment the a6-pawn by a4-a5. Should Black oppose this by playing ...a6-a5 himself, then White's bishop will land on b5.

9.♗e2 is also possible, but it is linked with another plan which I do not consider in this book. White's idea in this case is to play in the centre and prepare e4-e5. He often refrains from a4 at all. I would not say that this plan is worse than our main line, but it is not so straightforward and requires deeper understanding of the strategic nuances.

Note that the tempting 9.♕b3 is pointless as Black will capture the b6-pawn anyway: 9...♗b7 10.♘d2 ♘bd7 11.♘c4 a5 12.a4 (12.♘a4 kept temporarily the extra pawn, but Black had a strong initiative after 12...♖e8 13.0-0 e6 14.dxe6 ♖xe6 15.♗c4 ♖e7∞ Van Welly-Ivanchuk, 2002) 12...♖a6 13.♗d2 ♘xb6 14.♘e3 ♖a8 15.♗b5 ♗a6 16.0-0 ♗xb5 17.axb5 a4 with a good game, Seirawan-Van Wely, Merrillville 1997.

Now main continuations are:
A. 9...a5
B. 9...♕xb6

A. 9...a5

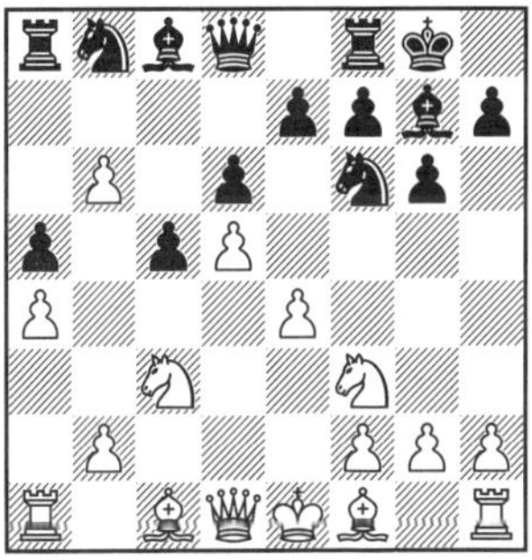

10.♗b5

10.♗e2!? is a worthy alternative. White's strategy is the same as in the main line, but there are notable specifics which I will try to explain below.

First of all, 10...♘fd7, which is a challenging reply to 10.♗b5, no longer works here, because White's attack after 11.h4 h5 (11...♕xb6 looks reckless: 12.h5 ♘e5 13.♘xe5 ♗xe5 14.♘b5 ♘a6 when every developing move should be good for White, for instance, 15.♗d2!? ♗xb2 16.♖b1 ♗g7 17.♕c1↑) 12.g4 hxg4 13.♘g5 ♘f6 14.b7 ♗xb7 15.♗xg4 is quite promising, e.g. 15...♘bd7 16.h5 ♘xg4 17.♕xg4 ♘f6 18.♕d1 gxh5 19.♖xh5 ♕d7 20.♖h4↑.

Perhaps Black should try the flexible 10...♘a6!?. It leads to unexplored positions, for instance, 11.0-0 ♘d7!? 12.♗f4.

The most common reply, however, is 10...♘bd7?! 11.0-0

11...♘xb6

11...♕xb6 12.♘d2 is another topical line, see **game 1 Gleizerov-Draganic**, Biel 2008.

12.♗g5 ♘e8 13.♕d2 ♘c7 14.♗h6 ♗a6 15.♗xg7 ♔xg7 16.♗xa6 ♖xa6 17.♖fe1 f6 18.b3 ♕d7 19.♕c2 ♖aa8 20.♘d2 ♖ab8 21.h3 ♖b7 22.♕d3 ♖bb8, V.Milov-Aveskulov, Oak Brook 2007 when 23.♘d1 e6 24.♘e3± would have fixed White's advantage.

After 10.♗b5, Black should decide how to recapture the pawn:

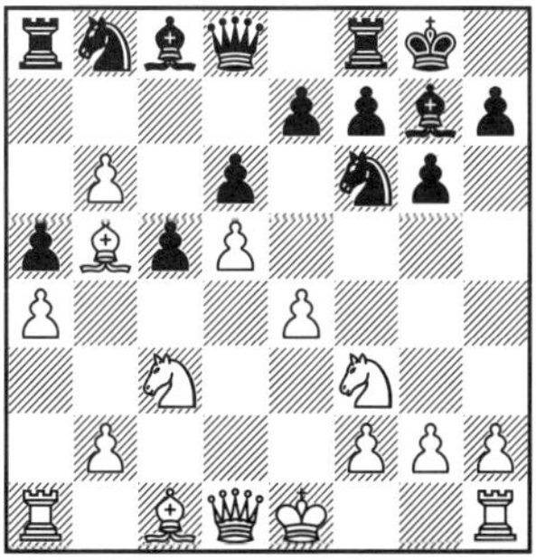

A1. 10...♗a6
A2. 10...♕xb6
A3. 10...♘fd7
A4. 10...♘bd7

Note that White should meet 10...♘a6 by 11.♘d2! (11.0-0 ♘fd7!? would throw us out of the repertoire) when 11...♕xb6 will transpose to line A3.

A1. 10...♗a6 11.0–0 ♗xb5 12.axb5 ♘bd7

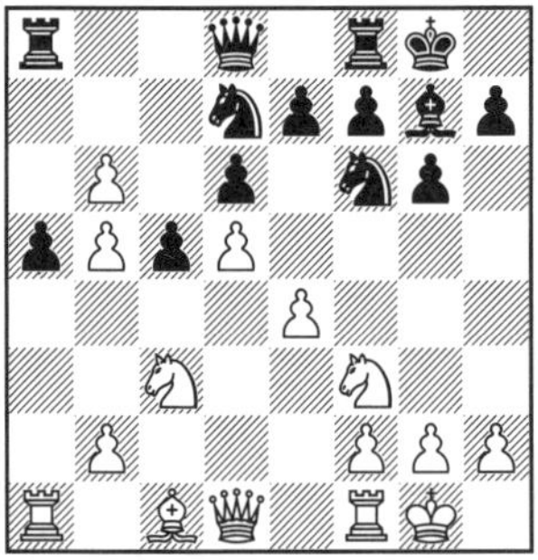

This is a rare variation which is interesting mostly with the fact that Milanovic chose it twice in blitz against Navrotescu in 2005, and won both games. However, in the second game White apparently found the best reply:

13.b7 ♖b8

White should meet 13...♖a7, intending to capture the awkward pawn by queen after ...♕b8, with 14.♗g5 ♕b8 15.♕d2 ♘b6 16.♗h6, when 16...♘c4 17.♕c1 ♗xh6 18.♕xh6 ♘xb2 loses to 19.♘g5 ♘c4 20.e5+–.

14.♘d2!

In the game White won a pawn by 14.♕a4 ♖xb7 15.♕xa5, but Black has good counterplay in that case. In the Benko Declined, White is commonly better off with equal pawns.

14...♖xb7 15.♘c4 ♖a7 16.h3±

White clearly dominates the board.

A2. 10...♕xb6 11.0–0

I chose the text as main line for consistency, since in line A4 we meet 10...♘bd7 by 11.0-0, when 11...♕xb6 would transpose to A2. However, now that Black has captured already by queen, we can confidently play 11.♘d2 instead of castling. This option is important for the move order with early ...♕xb6. In most cases play should transpose to the main line: 11...♘a6 (11...♗a6 12.♘c4 ♕d8 turned bad for Black in V.Alekseev-Mandelbaum, Pelaro 2002 after 13.0-0 ♘e8 14.♗f4 ♘c7 15.e5±) 12.♘c4 ♕c7 (12...♕d8 13.0-0 ♘b4 14.♗g5 ♘g4 15.♕d2 f5 16.exf5 ♗xf5 17.♖ae1 ♖f7 18.h3 ♘f6 19.♘e3 ♗d7 20.♖e2⩲) 13.0-0 or 13.♗g5 ♘b4 14.0-0.

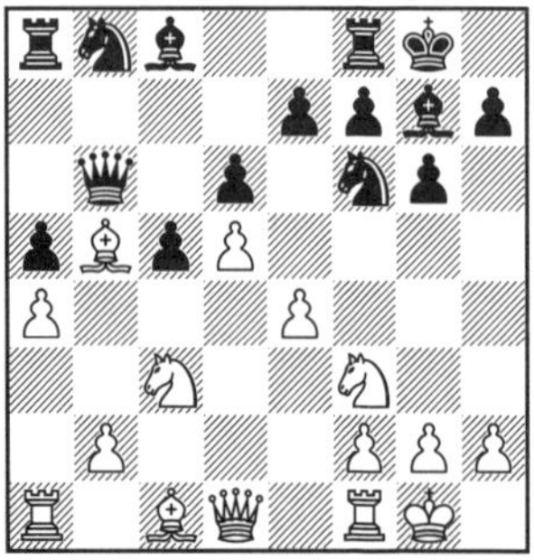

11...♘bd7

11...♘a6 has similar ideas with line A3, but here Black is practically a tempo behind since he plays ...♕d8xb6-c7. That leaves him without clear counterplay after:

12.♗g5!

Note that 12.e5 dxe5 13.♘xe5 ♘b4 14.♘c6 e6 is fine for Black as he obtains good piece play.

The other important thing you should remember is to develop the bishop to g5. From there it attacks e7 and does not provide Black with a tempo to strike back with ...f5 as it happened in the game Maksimenko-M.Markovic, Novi Sad 2000 which went 12.♘d2 ♘b4 13.♘c4 ♕c7 14.♗f4?! ♘h5 15.♗e3 f5⇄.

12...♘b4 13.h3

This is aimed not against ...♗g4, but against ...♘g4-e5.

13...♗b7 (13...♗a6 14.♘d2) 14.♘d2 ♕c7 15.♘c4

White took firm control of the light squares and needs only a couple of tempi to bring his heavy pieces into the centre. Then he will continue with the usual kingside attack. Obviously Black should oppose some breakthrough in the centre, but that also suites White: 15...♖ad8 16.♕d2 e6 17.♖ad1 (or 17.dxe6 fxe6 18.♖ad1 d5 19.exd5 exd5 20.♗f4 ♕c8 21.♘d6!±) 17...exd5 18.exd5± .

12.♖e1

On the previous move I considered positions where Black's queen's knight was going to b4. In that case the thematic break e4-e5 is not efficient as the d5-pawn is too vulnerable. With a knight on d7, however, e4-e5 is on the agenda again so White should not waste time on prophylaxis:

12.h3 ♗a6 13.♗g5 ♗xb5 14.axb5 ♕b7

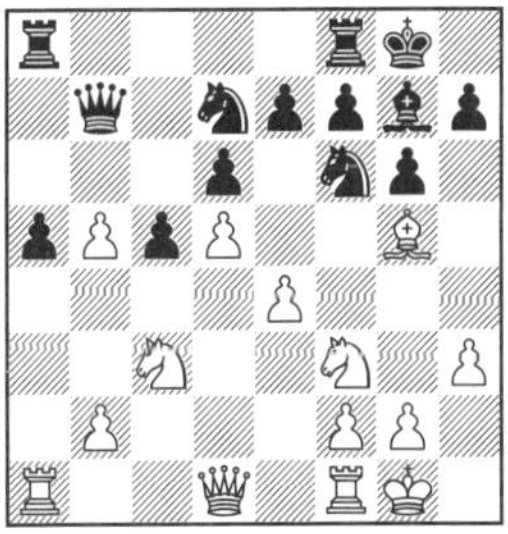

The b5-pawn is weak here so Black should get sufficient counterplay with the manoeuvre ...♘f6-e8-c7. In the diagram position White can drag Black's knight to b6 in order to remove the hit on b5 by:

15.♘d2 (Or 15.♕e2 ♖fb8 16.♖a2 h6 17.♗e3 ♘e8 18.♖fa1 ♘c7) 15...♘b6 16.♕e2 ♖fb8 17.♖a2 ♘e8 18.♖fa1 a4=.

12...♘g4

V.Milov-Zaikov, Reno 2005, saw 12...♘e8 13.♗g5 ♕d8 14.♕d2 ♘c7 15.♗c6 ♖a6 16.♗h6 (16.h4 was also interesting) 16...♘b6 17.♗xg7 ♔xg7 18.e5 (18.♘b5 f6 19.b3 ♘d7 20.♘a3±) 18...♗g4 19.exd6 exd6 20.♘e4 (20.♘d4) 20...♗xf3 21.♕c3+ f6 22.♕xf3± and White went on to win.

13.♗g5 ♕d8 14.♘d2 ♘b6 15.h3 ♘e5 16.f4 ♘ed7 17.♘f3

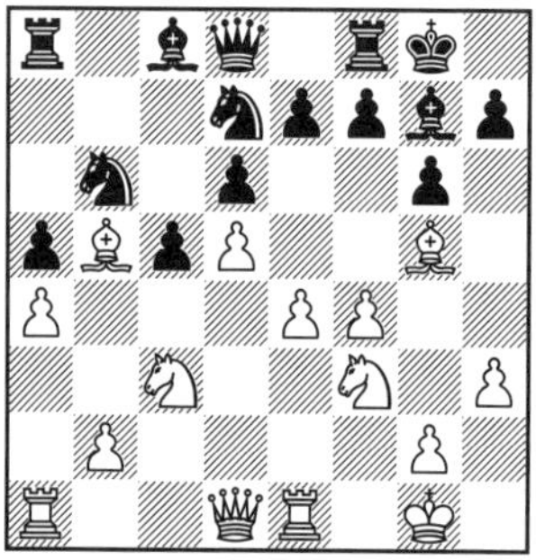

White is clearly ahead with his play in the centre.

A3. 10...♘fd7

This is the most challenging continuation. Black aims to reach a typical aggressive setup with two extra tempi. He'll play ...♘dxb6, ...♘b8-a6-b4 and ...♗c8-a6 (or d7). As we'll see in line A4, after the common ...♘b8-d7xb6 and ...♘f6-e8-c7, Black usually has not time for ...♘a6-b4 since White is first to attack in the centre.

Let us see whether White can hinder the enemy's plan by standard means:

11.0-0 ♘xb6 12.♖e1 ♘a6

12...♗g4 is passive. 13.h3 ♗xf3 14.♕xf3 ♘8d7 15.♕e2 ♖c8 16.♗e3 c4 17.♗a6 ♖b8 occurred in Moskalenko-S.Soloviov, Val Thorens 1990 when White should have played the energetic 18.♘b5!, with an edge: 18...♘c5 19.♗xc5 dxc5 20.♘a7± or 18...♖a8 19.♗b7 ♖b8 20.♗c6 ♘e5 (20...♘c5 21.♗xc5 dxc5 22.e5 ♘xd5 23.♖ad1 e6 24.♕e4±) 21.♘d4 ♘d3 22.♖f1 ♘c5 23.♗b5 ♗xd4 24.♗xd4 ♘b3 25.♖ad1 ♘xd4 26.♖xd4 ♕c7 27.♖c1±.

13.♗g5 ♘b4 14.♖b1 h6 15.♗d2

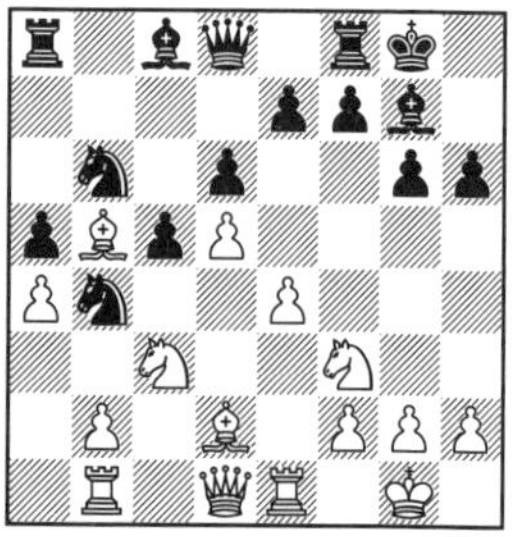

Alterman-Nedobora, Israel 2008 reached this position. White's setup is not too impressive. Black can follow up with 15...♗d7, intending to trade bishops and secure the d3-square for his knight.

It is quite evident that White should try to exploit the drawbacks of 10...♘d7 with more concrete play:

11.h4!?

White's main plan in the Benko Declined is to finish off the game with a kingside attack. Commonly, he needs first to neutralise the enemy counterplay in the centre and on the queenside, and only then think about advancing f4 or h4. Even the slightest delay in development with h3, for instance, can provide Black with time to undermine the centre. On the other hand, 10...♘d7 dramatically reduces his options, linked with ...e6. We should not miss the opportunity to launch immediately the attack. After the text, Black cannot ignore our threats as he risks to be crushed quickly:

11...♘xb6?! 12.h5 ♘a6 (or 12...♗g4 13.hxg6 fxg6 14.♗e2) 13.♘g5 h6 14.♘xf7 ♖xf7 15.hxg6 ♖f6 16.♕h5 ♕f8 17.0-0! intending to launch the f- and g-pawns. So he must answer:

11...h5

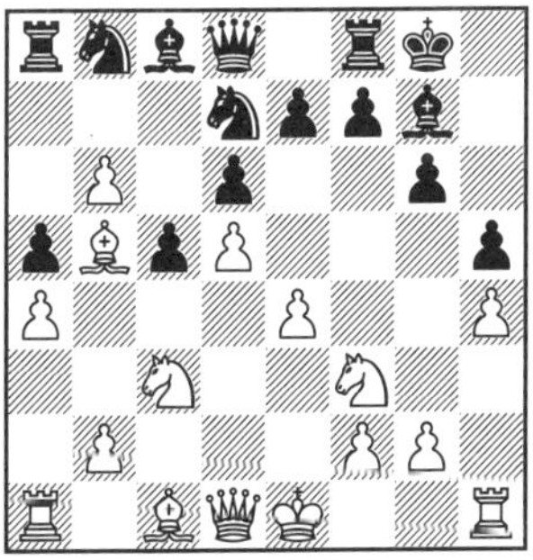

This is a completely different story compared to the variations with 11.0-0. The weakening of the g6-square may be still inconspicuous, but in future it will have a strong impact on the game. To start with, ...f6 does not seem a solid way to prevent e4-e5 anymore. Another problem of Black is that he would not be able to repel a knight from g5 by ...h7-h6.

At the same time, we should not underestimate Black's defensive resources. As tempting as it seems, 12.g4 does not win by force. I spent quite a few time on that position, but could not find anything serious after 12...hxg4 13.♘g5 ♘f6 14.b7 ♗xb7 15.h5 gxh5

White is undeveloped:

16.♘e2 ♘bd7 17.♘g3 ♗a6 18.♗xa6 18...♖xa6 19.♘xh5 ♘xh5 20.♖xh5 ♘f6 21.♖h4 ♕d7 22.♗d2 ♖b8 23.♗c3 ♖ab6 24.♕d2 ♖b3 25.♔f1 ♕b7. Black's counterplay on the b-file gives him the initiative, e.g. 26.♖e1 ♖xb2 27.♗xb2 ♕xb2↑.

12.♗g5 ♘xb6 13.♕d2 ♘a6 14.♗h6 ♗g4

14...♘c7 leaves the b6-knight unprotected. That enables the thematic hit 15.♗xg7 ♔xg7 16.♘d4! based on the double attack on g7 and b6. White is clearly better with a knight on c6: 16...♘xb5 17.♘c6 ♘c4 18.♕g5 ♕c7 19.axb5 ♘xb2 20.0-0 ♘c4 21.♘e2±, heading for the kingside.

The text is consistent as Black would love to remove the knight.

15.♗xg7 ♔xg7

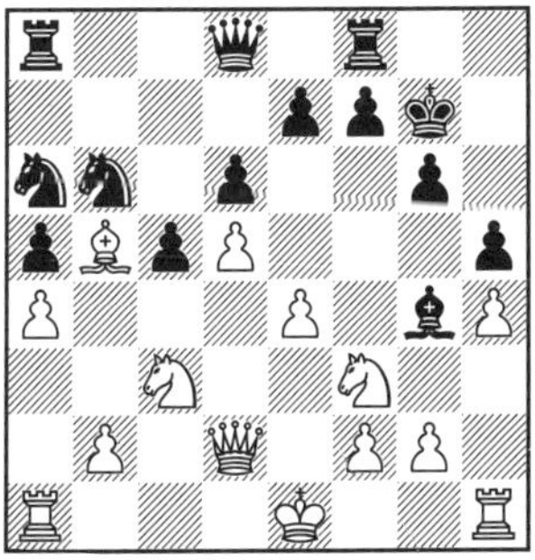

A critical position. I would like very much to bring the f3-knight closer to the enemy king, but 16.♘g5 ♘c7! only helps Black to exchange it. (16...♘b4?! 17.0-0 f6 is worse due to 18.♘e6+ ♗xe6 19.dxe6 ♕c8 20.♘d5 ♘6xd5 21.exd5 with an edge.) Then:

a) 17.f3 ♗d7 and both 18.f4 or 19.g4 stumble into 18...f6;

b) 17.♗e2 f6 18.♘h3 e5 19.dxe6 ♘xe6 20.♗xg4 hxg4 21.♘f4 ♕d7 22.h5 ♘c4 23.♘xe6+ ♕xe6∞;

c) 17.♗c6 ♘c4 18.♕c2 ♖b8 19.♘b5 ♘e5∓.

Apparently, it is better to step back in order to save the knight for better times:

16.♘h2! ♗d7 17.0–0

Again, the position is not fully ripe for an all-in clash: 17.f4 ♘b4 18.f5 ♗xb5 19.axb5 ♘c4 20.♕e2 ♘xb2 21.0-0 ♘2d3 22.g4 hxg4 23.h5 gxh5 24.♘xg4 ♖h8 and White's attack dies away.

17...♗xb5 18.axb5 ♘b4 19.f4 ♖b8

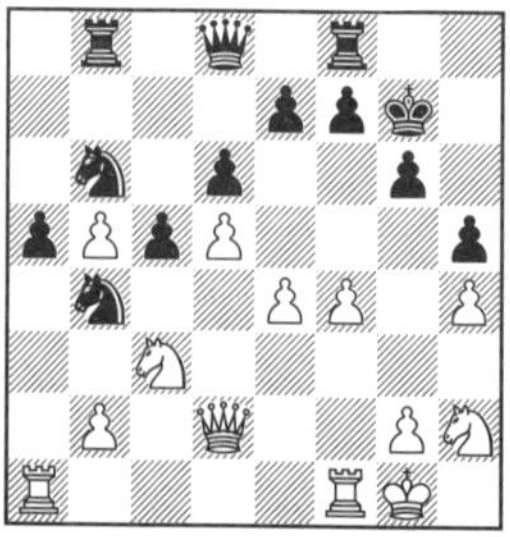

This position requires strategic approach. The black king will not run away. It is only a matter of time for White to start the final attack. But first he should restrain any enemy's activity. For instance, 20.f5 would have offered Black the e5-square after 20...♘c4 21.♕e2 ♘e5 22.♘f3 ♘bd3 23.fxg6 fxg6 24.♘g5 ♖xf1+ 25.♖xf1 ♕b6.

20.♘f3 f6 21.b3±

Black is helpless against the imminent threat of f4-f5.

A4. 10...♘bd7 11.0–0 ♘xb6

11...♕xb6 transposes to line A2.

Black often plays 11...♗b7?!, but this move is at least inaccurate. For instance, after 12.♖fe1 ♘xb6 play would transpose to the main lines so Black gains nothing from this move order. On the other hand, White can exploit the early defining of Black's bishop's development by:

12.♗f4 ♘xb6 13.♕d2

This idea is not so good while the black bishop remains on c8 as it can go to g4 and force White lose a tempo on protection of the f3-knight.

13...♘e8 14.♗h6 ♘c7 15.♗xg7 ♔xg7

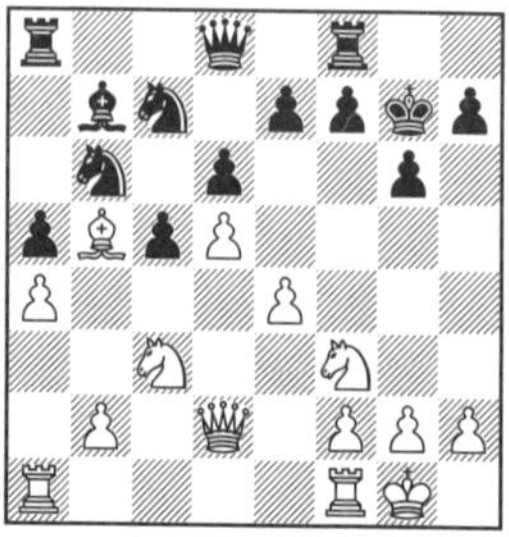

White has achieved his opening goals. He is well developed, the centre and the queenside are under control while Black's castling position is vulnerable. The latter could be underlined by 16.h4, but Black would counterattack by 16...f5 or 16...e6. Therefore, it is better first to bring a rook in the centre. e1 is the best place. The rook supports e5 from there and it is also ready for a lift to h3 via e3. The game Semkov-Knaak, Yerevan 1988 saw instead:

16.♖fd1 ♗c8?

This misses both 17.♘d4! or 17.♗c6 ♖b8 18.♘b5 ♘a6 19.e5±. 16...f5? also fails to 17.exf5 ♖xf5 18.♘d4! so the only move was 16...♘xb5 17.axb5 ♗c8 18.b3! intending to meet 18...♗d7 by 19.e5!

Summarising: Even if Black wants to play ...♗c8-b7, he should better delay it for 1-2 moves.

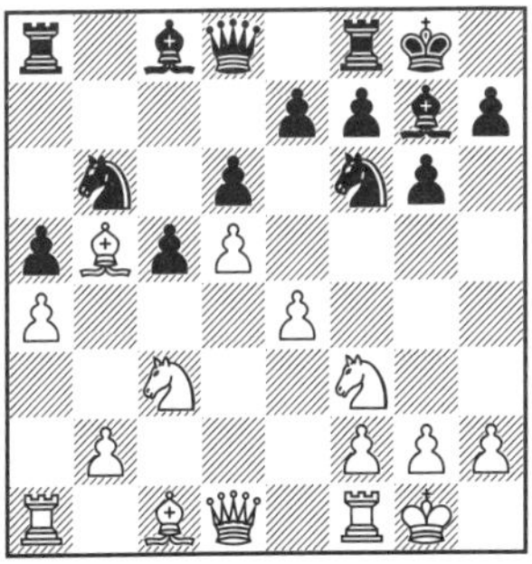

12.♖e1

It is difficult to choose between the text, 12.♗f4 and 12.♕e2. They have similar ideas and only some nuances tip the balance in favour of 12.♖e1.

White has a space advantage so it is normal that his game is more pleasant in general. Still, I think that the prophylactic move:

12.h3, which is as popular as 12.♖e1, reduces his advantage. Black manages to consolidate after:

12...♘e8 (12...e6 13.dxe6 ♗xe6 14.♖e1 should be somewhat better for White) 13.♖e1 ♘c7 14.♗f4 ♗a6

It becomes evident that 12.h3 was superfluous. In the game Moskalenko-Bendersky, Simferopol 1990 White decided to sac a pawn by 15.♕c2 ♗xb5 16.axb5 ♕d7 17.♖ad1 ♘xb5 18.♘xb5 ♕xb5 19.e5, but as attractive as he stands, his opponent has sufficient defensive resources: 19...♕d7 20.♕c1 ♖ad8 21.♗h6 ♕b7 22.♖e4 ♘d7 (22...f6 23.e6 ♔h8 24.♖h4 ♖g8 25.♗e3 ♖ge8 26.♗h6=; 22...dxe5 23.♗xg7 ♔xg7 24.♖h4 ♖h8 25.♕h6+ ♔g8 26.♘xe5 ♖xd5 27.♖e1 ♖d6∞) 22...dxe5 23.♗xg7 ♔xg7 24.♖h4 h5 25.♖xh5 ♖h8=.

12.♕e2 is a decent alternative.

Again, the counterattack in the centre 12...e6 13.dxe6 ♗xe6 leaves Black struggling following 14.♗f4 d5 (or 14...♘h5 15.♗e3) 15.exd5 ♘fxd5 16.♗e5 ♘xc3 17.bxc3 ♗d5 18.♗xg7±, Luch-Zherebukh, Pardubice 2005.

The most consistent reply to

12.♕e2 seems to be 12...♗g4, but even with the tempo lost on ♕e2 White looks better after 13.h3 ♗xf3 14.♕xf3 ♘e8 15.♕e2 ♘c7 16.♗c6 ♖b8 17.♘b5 ♘xb5 18.axb5!. (18.♗xb5 ♘d7 19.♕c2 f5 gave Black counterplay in the game Khmelniker-Georgescu, Plovdiv 2008.)

Black's best plan is:

12...♘e8 13.♖d1 ♘c7 14.♗c6 ♖b8 15.♘b5 ♘a6 and this position is rather unclear despite the good placement of the queen on e2.

12.♗f4 is another good option. It makes sense if White links it with ♕d2 and ♗h6. However, after 12...♘e8, 13.♕d2 seems unconvincing since Black has 13...♗g4.

We see such a development in the game Inarkiev-Vuckovic, Pardubice 2004, where White chose to keep his queen beyond the reach of Black's knight at b6: 13.♕c1 ♗g4 14.♗e2 ♖b8 15.♗h6 ♗xh6 16.♕xh6 ♗xf3 17.♗xf3 ♘c7 18.♗e2 ♘d7 19.♘b5 ♘f6 20.♕e3 ♘xb5 21.♗xb5 ♘e8 22.b3 ♘c7 23.♗c4

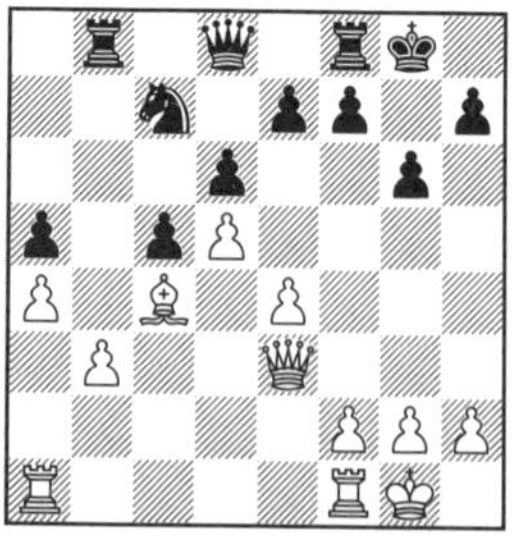

At first sight White has achieved his strategic goal. He retained a spatial advantage and eliminated any counterplay on the left wing. He needs only a couple of moves to bring his rooks in the centre and then he will be ready for ramming the kingside by the h- and f-pawns. One mundane move – 23...♖b4, and Vuckovic was crushed after 24.f4 ♘e8 25.♖f3 ♔h8 26.♕c3+ f6 27.♖e1 ♘g7 28.♖h3 ♕d7 29.♕g3 ♖f7 1-0. Still, in the diagram position Black can probably hold on with 23...e6!, disturbing White's attacking plans.

Therefore, White usually follows up with 13.♖e1 which transposes to the main line.

I would not completely discard 13.♕d2 though, only after 13.♕d2 ♗g4 White should save his knight by retreating it to e1: 14.♘e1 ♘c7 15.♗h6 ♘xb5 16.♗xg7 ♔xg7 17.axb5

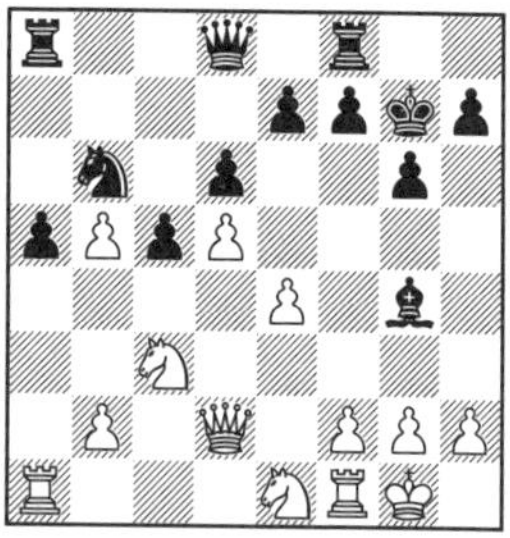

The e1-knight goes to e3 via c2, combining threats to the black king with control over c4.

The usual counterplay with 17...e5 does not work as the bishop would be awkward on e6 after 18.dxe6 ♗xe6 19.f4↑. Remains 17...♖b8 18.♘c2 ♗d7 19.♘e3 ♘a8 20.♖a3 ♘c7 (20...♗xb5 21.♘xb5 ♖xb5 22.♘f5++–) 21.♖xa5 ♘xb5 22.♘xb5 ♗xb5 23.♖fa1. Despite the simplification, White keeps some initiative.

Summarising: 12.♗f4, followed by 13.♕d2, is a natural straightforward plan which offers White good prospects. The only reason I selected 12.♖e1 as the main move is that it restricts Black's choice.

12...♘e8

12...♗g4 commonly leaves Black without much hope for counterplay after 13.h3 ♗xf3 14.♕xf3 ♘e8

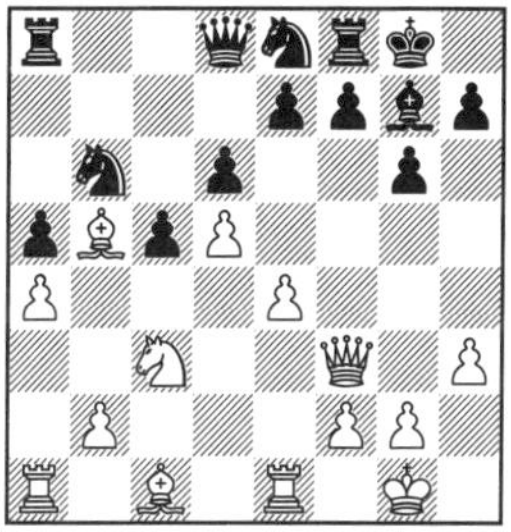

White has a pleasant choice here:

a) 15.♕e2 ♘c7 (15...♖b8 16.♗d2) 16.♗c6 ♖b8 17.♘b5± intending to take on b5 by pawn;

b) 15.♗f4 ♘d7 16.♖ab1 ♘c7 17.♗f1;

c) 15.♗d2!? ♘c7 16.♗c6 ♖b8 17.♕e2 (avoiding 17.♘b5 ♘c4 18.♗c3 ♘e5) 17...♘c8 18.♘b5 ♘a6 19.♗c3 ♘b4 20.♗xg7 ♔xg7 21.e5±.

13.♗f4!?

It might seem that the possibility for breaking through the centre by 13.e5 is the main reason behind 12.♖e1. However, this push is a bit premature as Black's pieces are well prepared to meet it. The point is that the e8-knight will obtain a perfect blockading stand at d6:

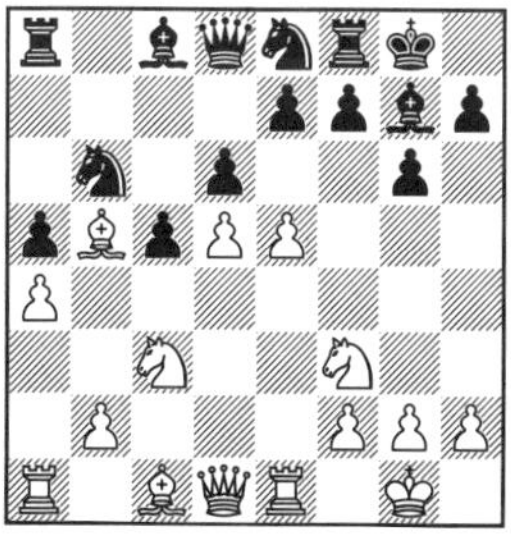

13...♗g4!

13...♗b7 would have ben good if Black could win the d5-pawn. However, tactics work in White's favour:

14.♗f4 ♘c7 15.exd6 exd6 16.♗c6 with some edge:

a) 16...♗xc6 17.dxc6 d5 18.♕b3 ♘e6 19.♗g3±;

b) 16...♗xc3 17.bxc3 ♖b8 18.♗h6 ♗xc6 19.dxc6 ♖e8 20.♕d3 ♘e6 21.♖ed1 d5 22.♘e5 ♘g7 23.♘g4 ♕d6 24.♕f3 ♘h5 25.♗g5 ♔g7 (25...♕xc6 26.c4↑) 26.c7 ♖bc8 27.♗d8±;

c) 16...♖b8 17.♘c4 ♘bxd5 18.♗xd5 ♘xd5 19.♗xd6± ♗xb2 20.♖b1 ♘c3 21.♘xc3 ♗xc3 22.♗xf8 ♕xf8 23.♖e3 ♖d8 24.♕e2.

Therefore, Black should seek exchanges and 13...♗g4! serves best this goal:

14.exd6 ♘xd6 15.♗c6 ♖b8 16.h3 ♗xf3 17.♕xf3 ♘bc4 18.♘b5 ♘e5! (18...♘xb2?! 19.♗g5 f6 20.♗f4 ♘bc4 21.♖e6 ♘e5 22.♕e3 c4 23.♕a7) 19.♕e2 ♖c8 20.♘a7 (20.♗h6 ♘xc6 21.♗xg7 ♔xg7 22.dxc6 ♖xc6 23.♕f3 ♖b6=) 20...♖c7 21.♕a6 ♕b8 eliminating to a draw endgame after 22.♘b5 ♘xb5 23.♕xb5 ♘xc6 24.dxc6 ♕e8 25.♕xc5 ♕xc6 26.♕xa5 ♖fc8 27.♗f4 ♗xb2 28.♗xc7 ♖xc7.

Note that the usual plan with 13.♗c6 ♖b8 14.♘b5 is also possible.

Play might continue with 14...♗g4 15.h3 ♗xf3 16.♕xf3 ♘c4 17.♕e2 ♘e5 18.♗xe8 ♖xe8 19.♖b1 ♕b6 (or 19... c4 20.b3) 20.♗d2 ♘d7 21.♗c3 ♖bc8 22.♕d2 ♕a6 23.f4±.

I prefer to make another developing move which enhances the threat of e4-e5.

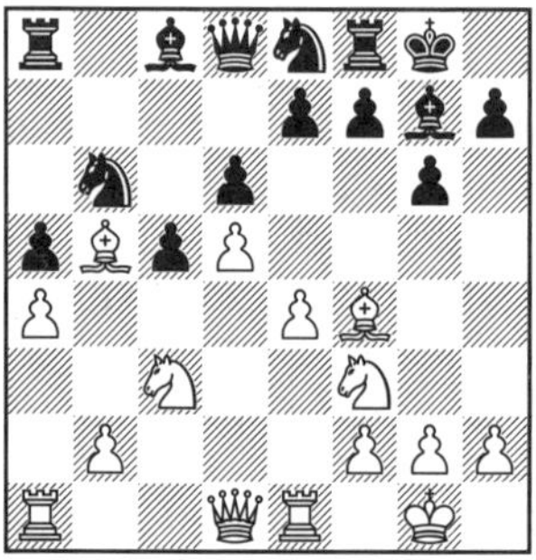

13...f6

The mere fact that Black has to resort to such a move is a point in White's favour.

Instead, 13...♗g4 would be ineffective as White will bolster his control over c4 and deprive the opponent of any counterplay. Compared to the position after 13.e5 ♗g4, here Black has not d6 for his knight and the d5-pawn is not hanging.

13...♘c7 is not good either as it leaves d6 underprotected: 14.♗c6 ♖b8 15.e5 ♗f5 16.exd6!

16.♘b5 allows unnecessary complications after 16...♘cxd5 17.♗xd5 dxe5 18.♗xe5 ♕xd5 19.♗xb8 ♖xb8 20.♕xd5 ♘xd5 21.♖ac1 ♘b4 22.♖xe7 ♘d3 23.♖f1 ♘xb2.

16...exd6 17.♗g5 f6 18.♗d2. Whites pieces are much more active, for example: 18...♘c4 19.♘b5 ♘xb2 20.♕e2 ♗d3 21.♕e3 ♗xb5 22.axb5 ♘c4 23.♕e2 ♘xd2 24.♘xd2 f5 25.♖xa5 ♗c3 26.♖a7 ♖f7 27.♖b1±.

14.♗c6

In the game I.Sokolov-Ponomariov, Hastings 1999, White chose to immediately attack the a5-pawn with 14.♘d2 ♘c7 15.♗c6 (15.♗f1 f5!⇄) 15...♖b8 16.♘b3, but 16...♘c4 17.♘b5 ♘a6!∞ turned out to be unclear. For instance, 18.♕c2 ♘e5 19.♗xe5 fxe5 20.♘a7 ♕b6 21.♘xc8 ♖fxc8 22.♗d7 ♖f8 would be equal so Sokolov played 18.♕e2 ♘e5 19.♗xe5 fxe5 and even won eventually, but it is obvious that Black is not worse. The knight is well placed on f3 and it should remain there in order to restrict counterplay by f6-f5.

14...♖b8 15.♘b5

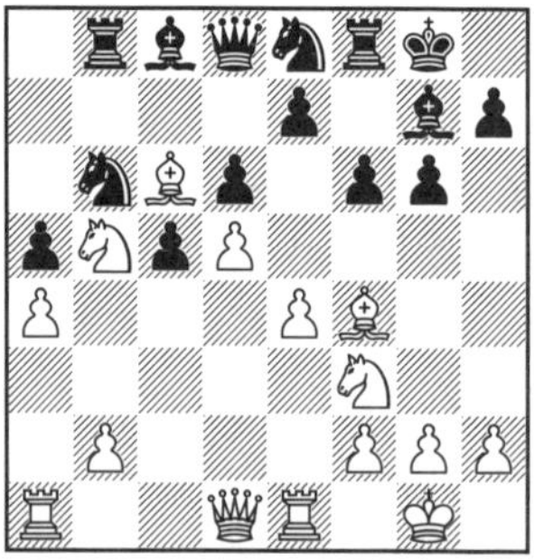

White's position is so good that we can calmly continue improving with 15.♕d3!?, intending to meet 15...♗d7 by 16.♗d2.

Our stem game, Kacheishvili-Felgaer, Ubeda 2001, however, features a more direct approach which is typical when Black refrains from an early ...♗b7. In that case White can incorporate two minor pieces on c6 and b5. They are very awkward for Black since any exchange will produce a dangerous passed pawn at their place. At the same time, the knight at b5 bars the b-file, opens the e1-a5-diagonal, making possible ♗d2, and it is threatening to go even deeper inside Black's camp – to a7.

15...♘c7

Perhaps Black should kill the c6-bishop by 15...♗d7 16.♗d2 (16.♗xd7 ♕xd7 17.b3 ♘c7 18.♘xc7 ♕xc7 19.♖b1 ♕b7 20.♕d3 would face 20... f5, with counterplay.) 16...♗xc6 17.dxc6 ♕c8 18.♗xa5 ♕xc6 although White is on top after 19.b3, e.g. 19... f5 20.e5.

16.♖c1

The source game went 16.♕d2 ♘a6 17.♕xa5 ♘b4 18.♖ed1 ♘c4 19.♕xd8 ♖xd8 when Black has plenty of unpleasant threats: 20.♗d2 ♘xb2 21.♗xb4 cxb4 22.♖db1 f5 23.a5 and here 23...♗a6 would have been better for him.

16...♘a6

16...♘xb5 17.axb5 typically favours White as the a5-pawn could become quite weak.

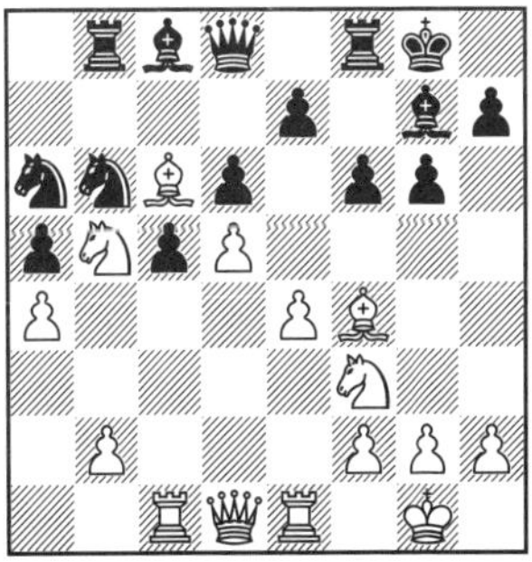

17.♘a7

This move crowns White's strategy. 17...♘b4 loses a pawn to 18.♖xc5 while 17...♗g4 18.♗b5 ♘b4 19.♘c6 ♘xc6 20.dxc6 leaves Black tied up with the defence of the a5-pawn. He also has not any good piece while White can organise a kingside attack.

B. 9...♕xb6

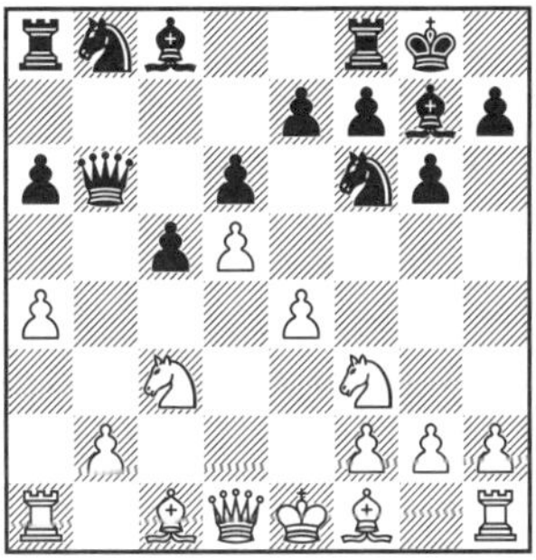

10.♘d2!

About 15 years ago it was established that 10.a5 is premature since it allows Black to activate his bishop from b5 via d7. With this manoeuvre in mind, it is easy to find 10...♕b4! 11.♖a4 ♕b7. Now ...♗d7 will be with tempo and Black will obtain a fine position after the "normal" 12.♗e2 ♗d7 13.♖a3 ♗b5 14.0-0 ♘bd7 as in a game of the still very young then Topalov as Black vs. Campos Moreno, Aviles 1992. Later White tried to discourage ...♗d7-b5 by 12.♘d2. The idea of this move is to grab a pawn after 12...♗d7 13.♖a3 ♗b5 14.♕b3 ♘bd7 15.♘xb5 axb5

16.♕xb5. Although I won a nice game against Van Wely, Groningen 1994, where I played 16...♕c7, objectively the pawn sac is not entirely sound in that particular position. It is much safer to attack the centre by 12...e6! Black has won all the games in my database so far.

Instead, White keeps all options open by choosing the flexible 10.♘d2!

10...♘bd7

10...a5 11.♗b5 is discussed in line A2.

10...♕b4 11.♗e2! ♘bd7 12.a5 transposes to the main line, see B2. Only 11...e6 is of independent significance, but the position after 12.0-0 exd5 13.exd5 ♘bd7 14.♘c4 ♕b8 15.a5 ♖a7, Yevseev-Khropov, St Petersburg 2004, is rather gloom for Black, e.g. 16.♖e1 ♖e8 17.♗f4±.

10...e6 is not a good idea as it only creates a second weakness – on d6. White was clearly better after 11.♘c4 ♕d8 12.♗e2 exd5 13.exd5 ♖a7 14.0-0 ♖e7 15.♗f4 ♘e4 16.♗f3±, Vavrak-Stocek, Tatranske Zruby 2003.

11.a5

Forcing Black to define his plans.

11.♗e2 is not a mistake if we play 12.a5 on the next move, but we will see later that in some lines the bishop could be more useful on d3.

Be sure to fix the centre before castling!

For instance, 11.♗e2 ♕c7 12.0-0?! is already wrong, because Black can bust our setup by 12...♗b7! 13.a5 e6 14.♘c4 ♘xe4! 15.♘xe4 exd5 16.♗f4 ♘e5 17.♗xe5 dxe5 18.♘b6 ♖ad8, Iotov-Giri, Enschede 2008. Who would enjoy such a position as White?!

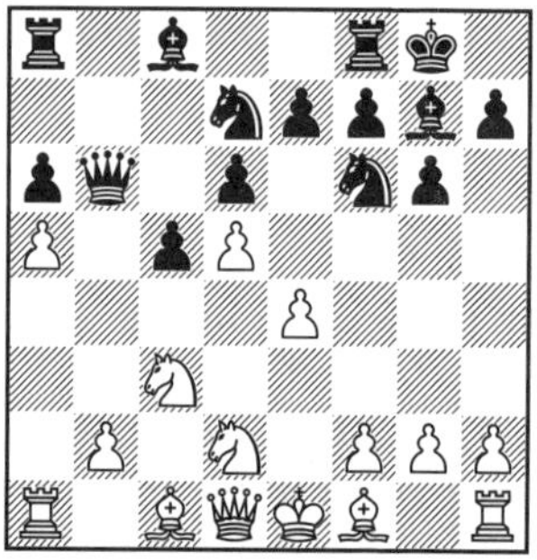

We have reached the typical pawn structure for line B. Black has tried here all possible retreats:

B1. 11...♕c7
B2. 11...♕b4?!
B3. 11...♕b7
B4. 11...♕a7
B5. 11...♕d8

B1. 11...♕c7 12.♗e2

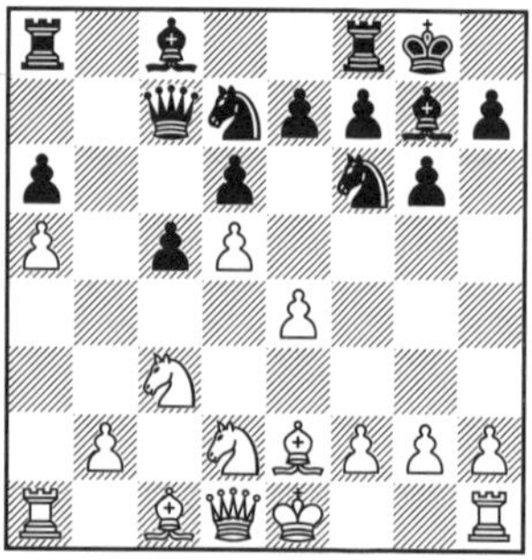

12...♖b8

The plans with counterplay in the centre are less popular because White can immediately attack the d6-pawn:

12...e6 13.♘c4 exd5 14.♘xd5 ♘xd5 15.♕xd5±;

12...♗b7 13.♘c4 ♖fe8 14.♗f4±.

13.0–0 ♘e8

An alternative is 13...♖b4 14.♘c4 ♘e5 (14...♘e8 – see the main line) 15.♘xe5 dxe5 16.♕c2 e6

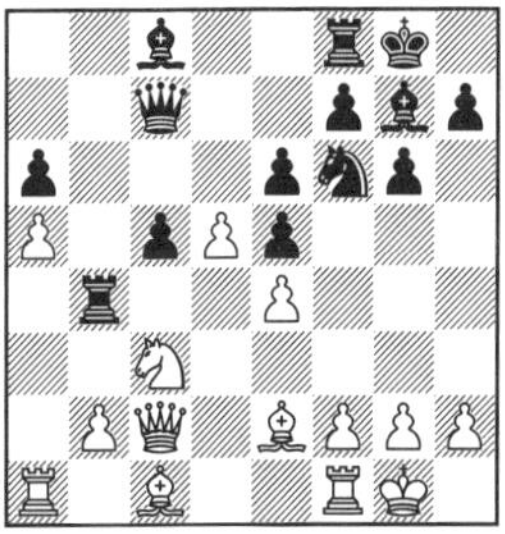

With this move, Black gets rid of his doubled pawns in the centre, but he cannot level entirely the game due to the sensitive a6-pawn.

17.♖d1 (I would not part with my bishop by 17.♗g5 h6 18.♗xf6) 17...♖d4

Kacheishvili-D.Gurevich, Philadelphia 2009 saw 17...♕b7, but it turned out that this move does not really hinder 18.♗e3!. The fine point is that after 18...♖xb2 19.♕c1 White is threatening both 20.♗xa6 and 20.♗xc5. The game went 20...exd5 20.♗xc5 d4 21.♗xf8 ♗xf8 22.♗xa6± to last only a few more moves.

18.♗e3 ♖xd1+

18...♖d8 does not help as White ignores the rook: 19.♘a4! ♖xd1+ 20.♖xd1 exd5 21.♕xc5 ♕xc5 22.♘xc5 d4 23.b4 with a solid advantage in the endgame.

19.♕xd1 ♖d8 20.♕b3±.

White's bishops form a formidable battery against the fragmented pawn chain of the opponent.

14.♘c4 ♘e5

Black scores surprisingly well with the highly inconsistent move:

14...♕d8. Indeed, if he wanted to station the queen on its initial square, he should have done that on move 11. In reply, Dreev developed the dark-squared bishop to g5: 15.♗g5 and to 15...f6 retreated it to h4. Following 16.♗h4 ♘c7 17.f4 ♘b5 18.♗d3 ♖f7 19.♔h1 ♕f8 20.f5 he was slightly better, Dreev-Wang Zili, Beijing 2000. However, 16...f5 would have been more challenging, exploiting that White's minor pieces are somewhat unstable on the fourth rank. While he retains preferable chances after 17.cxf5 ♖xf5 18.♗d3 ♖h5 19.♗g3 ♗d4 20.♗e2 ♖f5 21.♗g4 ♖f8 22.♕e2±, it is probably stronger to keep the pieces more compact in the centre by 16.♗e3! ♘c7 17.♗d3 – discouraging 17...f5 (17...♘e5 18.♘xe5 fxe5 19.♘a4±) which would face 18.exf5 gxf5 19.♖e1 f4 20.♗d2 ♘e5 21.♖xe5!±.

14...♖b4 does not make much sense either, as the rook will be hanging in many variations. In Rogers-West, Sydney 1999, White continued development with 15.♕c2 (preparing to meet 15...♘e5 by 16.♘b6) 15...♕a7 16.♗g5 f6 17.♗d2 ♘c7 and the weakening of the g6-square is a good reason for 18.h4! ♖b8 19.h5±

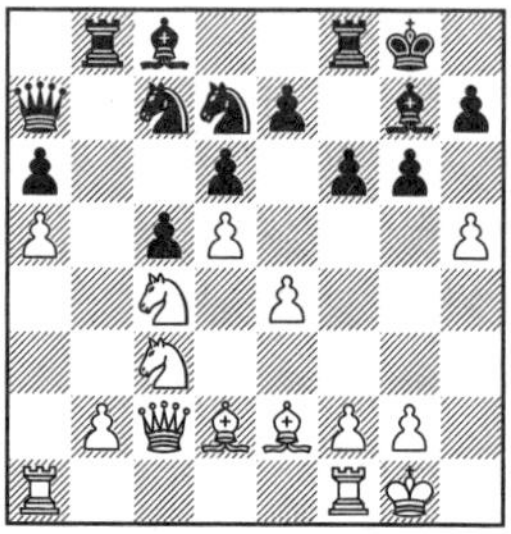

In the game Black desperately pushed 19...f5 which only helped White's attack, but even the more logical 19...♘b5 20.♘xb5 axb5 21.♘e3 c4 would have been difficult for him due to 22.h6 ♗h8 23.♗c3 ♘c5 24.♗d4 and Black is in positional binds. The poor bishop on h8 has no prospects whatsoever, e.g. 24...♗d7 25.♖fb1 (preparing to open the queenside) 25...♖fc8 26.♕d1 ♕a6 27.♗xc5 ♖xc5 28.♗g4!±.

15.♘b6 ♘d7

Black is cramped so he must seek exchanges. The thematic break 15...f5 is inefficient here since the black pieces are passive: 16.exf5 ♗xf5 17.♗e3±, V.Milov-Rincon Bascon, Dos Hermanas 2006, leaves Black with numerous weaknesses.

16.♘ca4 ♘xb6 17.♘xb6 ♘f6 18.♕c2 ♘d7 19.♘xc8 ♕xc8 20.♖b1

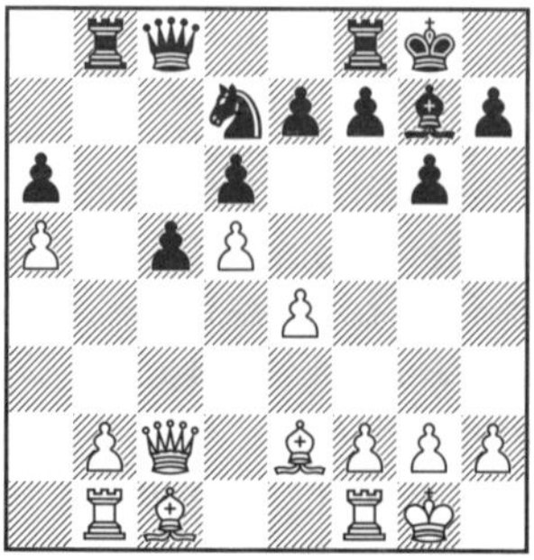

White is going to open the queenside by b2-b4. Then his bishop pair should take over the command due to the vulnerability of the a6-pawn. Black's queen will also be uncomfortable under the X-rays of the white rooks at b1 and c1.

B2. 11...♕b4?! 12.♗e2 ♘e8 13.0–0

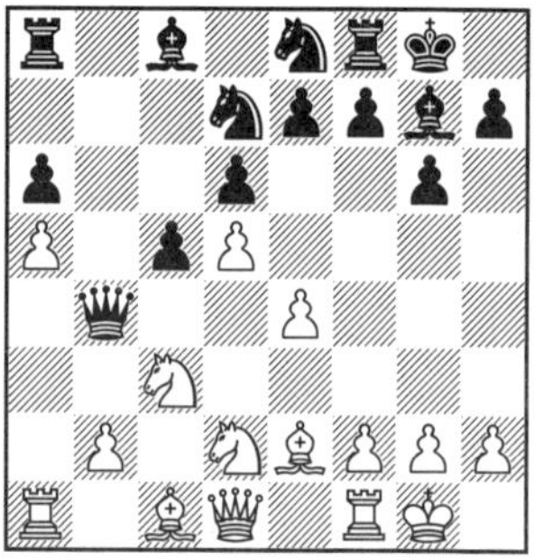

I'm not too sure what Black actually aimed with his eleventh move. If he was planning to grab a pawn by 13...♗xc3 14.bxc3 ♕xc3 15.♖a3 ♕g7, as in Porat-Papp, Budapest 2004, he should be an incorrigible optimist. White's compensation is beyond doubt because his pieces are much more active and that will be so for many moves ahead. The game continued 16.♘c4 ♘c7 17.♗b2 f6 18.f4 ♖b8, when White went for the right idea to push e4-e5, but shaped it wrongly by playing 19.♕d2?! (a superficial move) 19...♖b4 20.e5?! fxe5 21.fxe5 ♖xf1+ 22.♗xf1, when 22...dxe5! 23.d6 ♘b5 would have been about equal. Instead, he had 19.♖b3!, when 19...♘b5 would be already bad due to 20.e5! fxe5 21.fxe5 ♖xf1+ 22.♗xf1 dxe5 23.♘xe5 ♘xe5 24.♕e1±. On the other hand, 19...♖xb3 20.♕xb3 ♘b5 21.♘b6 is also grim. In this line Black is obviously lacking his strongest piece which got struck far away from the main battle.

Kiselev-Zhuravlev, Kazan 1995, saw another clumsy try to justify the sortie of the black queen: 11...♖b8 14.♖a3 ♘c7 15.♖b3 ♕d4 16.♖xb8 ♘xb8 17.♕b3 ♘d7 18.♖d1±.

These examples can explain why Black most often plays:

13...♘c7 14.♘c4 ♕b7

Now it is evident that Black transposed to line B3 losing a clear tempo on the way.

15.♘a4 ♘b5 16.♘ab6 ♘xb6 17.♘xb6 ♖a7 18.♖b1⩲

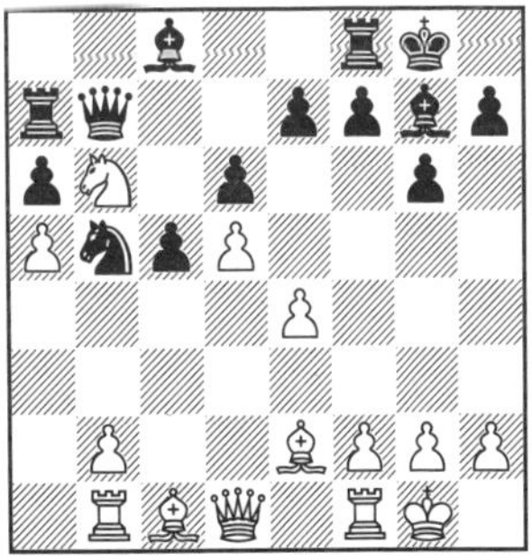

White has accomplished his main positional aim – he neutralized Black's queenside play, fixed the weak pawn at a6, and now he is ready to open up the b-file with b2-b4. Look through the model game **6 V.Milov-Abrahamyan**, Minneapolis 2005.

B3. 11...♕b7

Perhaps this is the most sensible retreat. Black retains pressure on b2, supports the weak a6-pawn and leaves c7 free for the knight manoeuvre ...♘f6-e8-c7-b5.

12.♘c4

12.♗e2 is not precise since the bishop might find a better stand on d3.

12...♘e8

Or 12...♖b8 13.♗d3.

13.♗d3

13.♗g5, which is good against 11...♕a7, fails here to 13...♘e5 and b2 is hanging.

In the positional Benko White commonly develops his light-squared bishop to e2. That allows him to keep better control of d5 and d6 in case Black pushes e6. However, 12...♘e8 indicates that Black will redeploy the knight to b5 and d4, when the bishop would be under attack on e2. Counterplay with ...f5 is also less efficient against ♗d3.

13...♘c7 14.0–0 ♘b5 15.♘a4 ♖b8

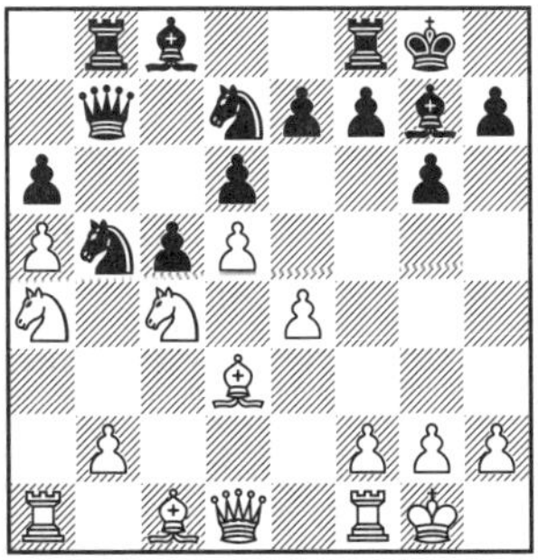

A critical position.

White's plan is to plug the b-file by ♘ab6, then open the queenside by b2-b4. At the same time, he should take care of Black's counterplay with ...f7-f5. Both aims are best served by:

16.♖b1!

Rogozenco-Heinemann, Hamburg 1998 saw 16.♘ab6 ♘xb6 17.♘xb6 ♗d7?! 18.♖b1 e6 19.♗f4 with an edge, but Black could have played 17...f5! with excellent prospects to annihilate White's centre. I was unable to find anything better than 18.♖b1 fxe4 19.♗xe4 ♗f5 20.♗xf5 ♖xf5 21.♖e1 ♘a7! 22.♕c2 ♘c8 23.b4 ♘xb6 24.bxc5 ♗d4 25.♗e3 ♗xc5 26.♗xc5 ♖c8 27.♕e2 ♖xc5 28.♖xb6 ♕xd5 29.♕xe7 ♖f7 30.♕e3 ♖xa5 31.♕c3 ♖f8 32.♖xd6, with a draw.

The text messes the enemy's plans since he now has to define the position of his knights.

16...♘e5

16...♘d4 17.♘ab6 ♘xb6 18.♘xb6 f5 is not as good as in the previous example. White is clearly better after 19.b4 ♕c7 20.bxc5 ♕xc5 21.♗d2±.

17.♘xe5 ♗xe5 18.♘b6±

White has the better chances thanks to the possibility for b2-b4. It is interesting to note that the game Markos-Tibensky, Slovakia 2001 reached a similar situation, only Black had an extro tempo since Markos firstly had played ♗e2. Nevertheless White quickly established a total dominance:

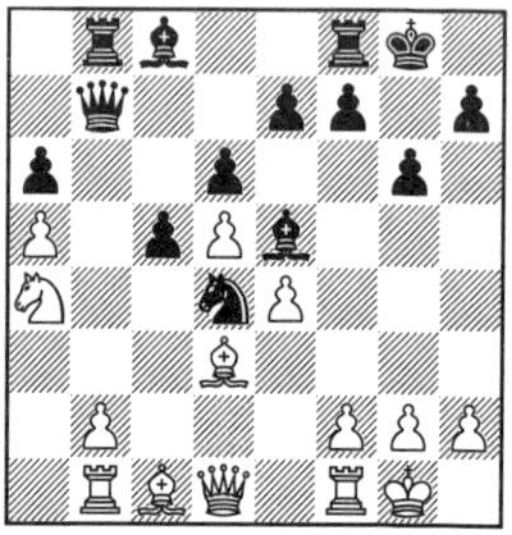

19.♗h6 ♖d8 20.♘b6 ♗d7 21.b4 cxb4 22.♖xb4 ♘b5 23.♕b3 ♗e8 24.♗c1 ♕a7, when 25.♗e3! would have been most convincing.

18...♕c7 19.♗d2 f5

This position occurred in Lapiccirella-Podini, Bratto 2000. The simple 20.♘xc8 ♕xc8 21.exf5 gxf5 22.b4± would have underlined White's advantage.

B4. 11...♕a7

This variation is similar to the previous line B3. Black leaves the b-file open for a rook, but I think that the drawbacks of this move prevail:

1. The queen is more passive on a7. It is not hitting b2 and that allows White to counter ...♘f6-e8 by ♗g5! which was impossible in line B3.

2. In some variations (especially with ...f7-f5) after ♘b6xc8 Black cannot recapture by queen which forces the rook to leave its active stand on b8 for ...♖b8xc8.

Despite the fact that once Topalov chose that very retreat (after a different move order though), I do not think that it deserves recommendation.

12.♘c4

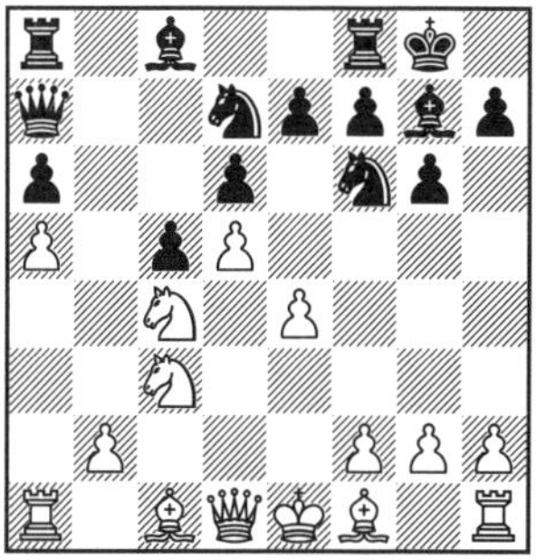

12...♖b8

Black has to be careful with the move order. 12...♘e8 13.♗g5! f6 14.♗e3 ♘c7 allowed White to develop his bishop to d3 and obtain a big advantage in Gheorghiu-Lumsdon, Brocco 1991, following 15.♗d3 ♖b8 16.0-0 ♘b5 17.♘a4 ♘e5 18.♘xe5 fxe5 19.b4+–.

13.♗e2

13.♗d3 is not good already: 12...♘e8 14.♗g5 ♘e5.

13...♘e8 14.♗g5 f6

14...♖xb2 loses the exchange to 15.♖c1±.

15.♗e3 ♘c7 16.0–0 ♘b5 17.♘a4

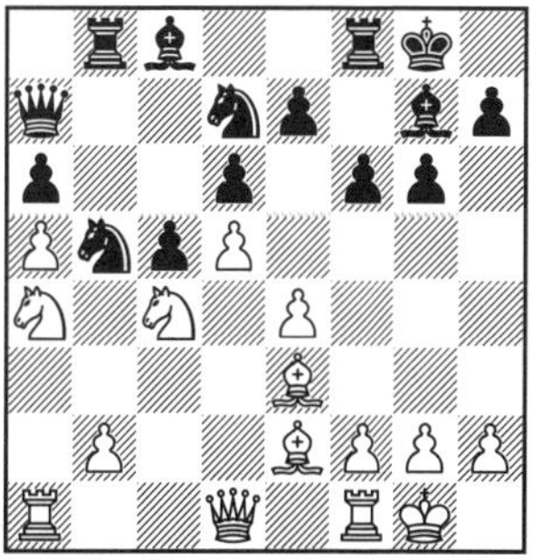

Black's strategy is a failure. He was struggling after 17...f5 18.exf5 gxf5 19.♗g5 ♘e5 20.♘ab6, C.Flear-Lumsdon, Brocco 1991, but 17...♘d4 18.♗xd4 cxd4 19.♘cb6± would have been a positional disaster due to the poor bishop on g7 and White's pawn majority on the left wing.

B5. 11...♕d8

In a number of games where Black had retreated the queen to c7, he later discovered that the c7-square was vital for the king's knight and he had to lose a tempo on ...♕d8. Therefore, it seems natural to play ...♕d8 at once. Sometimes Black even takes early on b6 and quickly returns to d8 before White threatened the queen. The pluses of the queen being on d8 are:

1. It defends the c7-pawn so ♗g5, which was awkward in line B4, is no longer a threat.
2. The queen is closer to the kingside so counterplay with ...f5 becomes less risky.
3. From d8 the queen supports the ...e7-e6 break.

On the negative side, I see:

1. The queen does not protect the a6-pawn.
2. The queen hinders the connection of Black's rooks. That could become an important factor in case the f-file opens up after ...f5.

As a whole, I do not see any reason for White to renounce his trivial plan, linked with the occupation of the b6-square:

12.♘c4 ♖b8

Black does not gain benefits by delaying this move: 12...♘e8 13. ♗e2 ♘c7 14.0-0 ♘b5 15.♘a4 ♘d4 16.♗d3

Black's knight has finally reached its destination, but it is mostly a decoration and after b4 it will be unstable. The white bishop now is directly attacking the a6-pawn. Practice has seen here:

a) 16...♖b8 17.♗g5 ♘e5 18.♘xe5 ♗xe5 19.♘b6 ♕c7 20.♖c1 (20.f4 ♗g7 21.f5↑ is another typical plan.) 20...♕a7 21.b4±, Erdos-Biro, Savaria 2002;

b) 16...♘e5 17.♘xe5 ♗xe5 18.♘b6 ♖b8 19.♗h6 ♖e8 20.f4 ♗h8 21.f5. The game Bareev-Bartel, Warsaw 1999 did not last long: 21...e6 22.dxe6 fxe6 23.fxg6 ♕h4 24.gxh7+ ♔xh7 25.♗f4 e5 26.♗g3 ♕g5 27.♘xc8 ♖bxc8 28.♗xa6 ♖c7 29.♗c4 ♗f6 30.♖xf6 1-0.

13.♗e2

13.♗d3 ♘e8 14.0-0 ♘c7 15.♘a4 ♘e5 is about equal.

13...♘e8 14.0–0 ♘c7 15.♘a4 ♘b5 16.♘ab6 ♘xb6 17.♘xb6 ♗d7

17...♘d4 leaves the a6-pawn very weak after 18.♗c4. This is something Black should be constantly concerned with while keeping the queen on d8.

18.♖b1

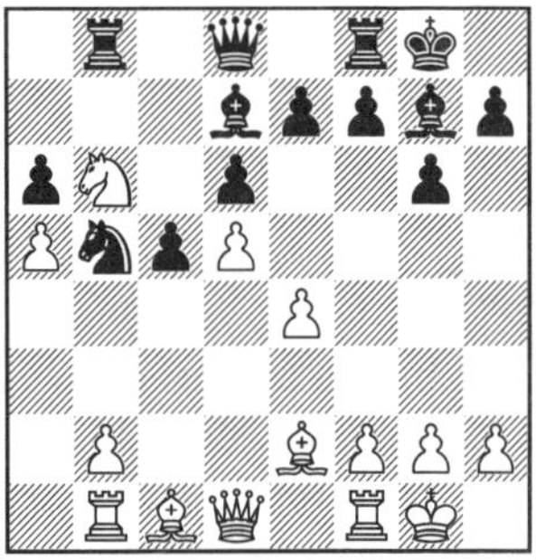

The critical position for the 11...♕d8 line. In practice Black has tried:

B5a. 18...♘c7

Preparing ...♗b5 while defending the a6-pawn.

19.♗d2

19.b4 is premature because the black knight unexpectedly returns: 19...♘b5, threatening to leap to c3.

After 19.♗e3 ♗b5 20.b4 cxb4 21.♖xb4 ♗c3 Whites lose his main trump, the a5-pawn, although 22.♖b3 ♗xe2 23.♕xe2 ♗xa5 24.♕b2 gives him sufficient compensation.

19...♗b5 20.b4±

White has accomplished his strategic aim. Black has nothing left, but to seek late counterplay in the centre:

20...e6 21.bxc5 dxc5 22.♗f4 exd5 23.exd5

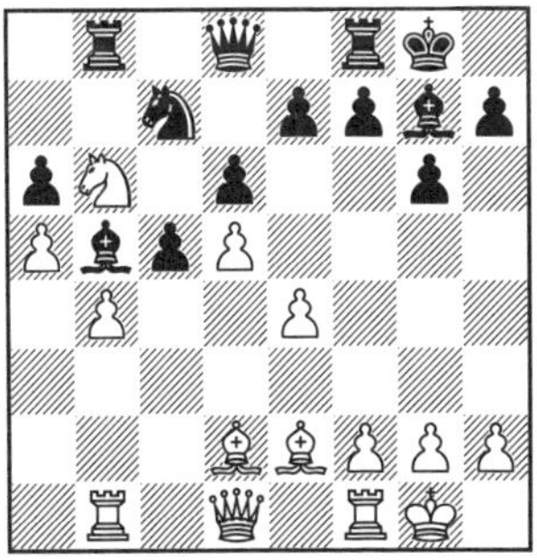

23...♖xb6

Here, in the game Mertanen-Vetemaa, Tampere 2000, White could have stabilised his advantage by the simple 24.axb6 ♘xd5 25.♗c7 ♘xc7 26.♕xd8 ♖xd8 27.bxc7±.

B5b. 18...f5 19.f3

It is good to keep Black's d7-bishop restricted. At an opportunity, we could eat it by our knight and exploit the newly arisen weaknesses on the light-squares along the h3-c8 diagonal. 19.♗d3 fxe4 20.♗xe4 is less convincing, e.g. 20...e5.

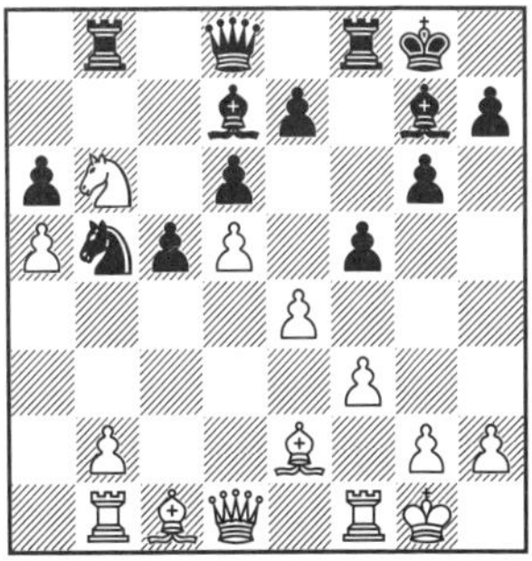

19...f4

19...♗d4+ 20.♔h1 fxe4 21.fxe4 ♖xf1+ 22.♕xf1± stresses the vulnerability of the a6-pawn.

20.♗c4 ♗d4+ 21.♔h1 ♘c7 22.b4±

Perhaps Black would have been happier here stayed his f-pawn on f7.

B5c. 18...♖xb6!? 19.axb6 ♕xb6

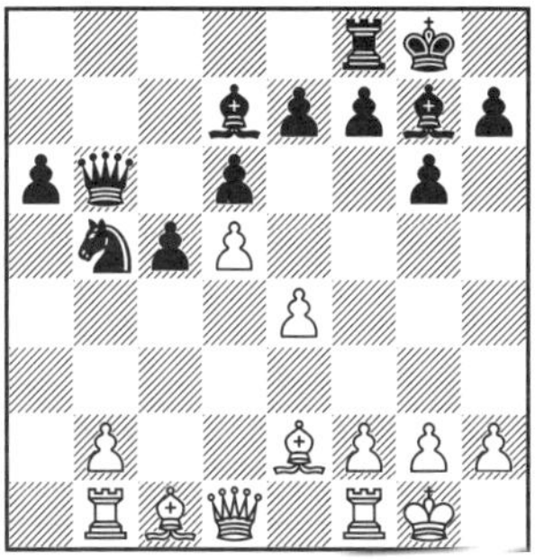

This typical exchange sacrifice always faces White with practical problems. He commonly meets it with a couple of mundane "consolidating" moves, only to discover later that Black's pressure is growing stronger and stronger. Instead, White must play very concretely and urgently find a target.

20.♗g5! h6 21.♗d2±.

See **game 5 Porfiriadis-Ermenkov**, Athens 1993. It is a good illustration of Black's resources.

Part 1

Complete Games

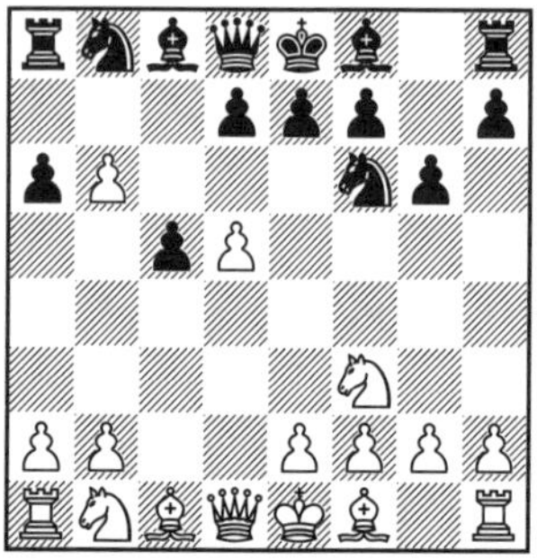

1.d4 ♘f6 2.c4 c5 3.d5 b5 4.♘f3 g6 5.cxb5 a6 6.b6

---

1. Gleizerov–Draganic
Biel 21.07.2008

1.d4 ♘f6 2.c4 c5 3.d5 b5 4.cxb5 a6 5.b6 g6 6.♘c3 d6 7.♘f3 ♗g7 8.♘d2

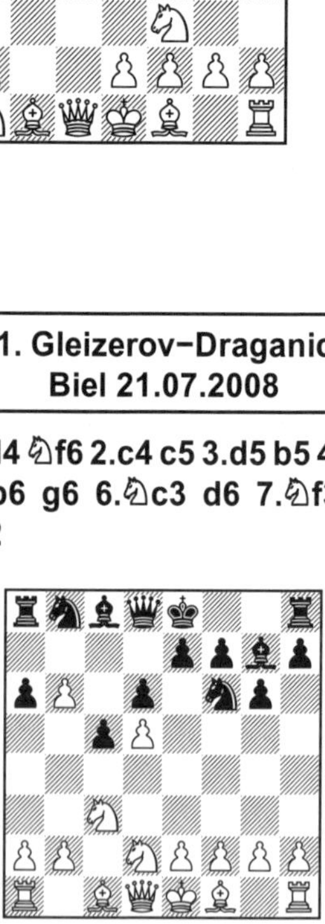

Common sense suggests that such a move cannot be the best. In my opinion, this manoeuvre should be executed only if Black had already taken on b6 by queen. Then we'll be assured that ♘c4 is with tempo. I suppose that Gleizerov wanted to prevent any pinning ideas as 8.e4 ♗g4. This position is extremely seldom seen in practice so it is not topical, but I consider it in the "Step by Step" chapter. My recommendation is 9.♕a4+ ♘fd7 10.♘d2 0-0 11.b7 ♖a7 12.♕c2 with a more harmonious setup. The problem with Gleizerov's move order is that it is not flexible. White discards too early plans connected with a kingside pawn storm without castling, or with e4-e5. He cannot even develop by ♗f4, ♕d2, which is the main reaction against ♘b8-d7xb6. In short, White's "anticipating" manoeuvre is justified only against setups with ...♕xb6 ... which is exactly what Black does in the current game!

It seems that many players do not understand the nuances in the move order. Perhaps some of them are even unaware of some interesting plans for Black, for instance, ♘f6-d7xb6.

8...♘bd7

So far so good. I would think, however, of 8...♘fd7!? having in mind to lead out the queen's knight via a6: 9.e4 0-0 10.♗e2 ♘xb6 11.0-0 a5 12.a4 ♘a6 13.♖e1 ♘b4 14.♘c4 f5 with ample counterplay.

9.a4 ♕xb6?!

Meeting halfway White's plans. What was 8...♘bd7 for?! The logical follow up of Black's previous move would have been 9...a5 10.e4 0-0 11.♗b5 ♘xb6 12.0-0 when 12...e6 13.dxe6 ♗xe6 would ensure active piece play.

In general, both sides often underestimate Black's counterattacking chances in the centre. Instead, we see a lot of inconcrete, mundane play.

10.e4 0–0 11.♗e2

11.a5! transposes to our main line from the "Step by Step" chapter. The text is a little passive.

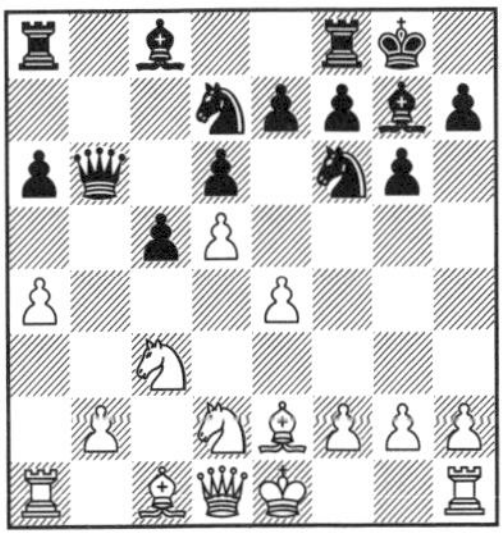

11...a5

White obtains now full control over the queenside light squares, but his central pawns are a little shaky and ...f5 is always an option to reckon with. Many other continuations also deserve attention. Note, for instance, the mean 11...♕c7 when only 12.a5! maintains the grip, while 12.0-0?! ♗b7! 13.a5 faced 13...e6 14.♘c4 ♘xe4! 15.♘xe4 exd5 16.♗f4 ♘e5 17.♗xe5 dxe5 18.♘b6 ♖ad8 with fantastic play for Black in Iotov-Giri, Enschede 2008.

12.♘c4 ♕d8 13.0–0 ♘b6

In the game Berkes-Fogarasi, Hungary 2003, Black decided to trade his bishop: 13...♗a6 14.♕c2 ♘e8 15.♗d2 (15.♗g5!) 15...♗xc4 16.♗xc4 ♘c7 17.♖ad1 ♘b6 18.b3 and here he correctly attacked the centre by 18...f5. Still, White should be better following 19.f4 ♔h8 20.♖fe1 or 20.♘b5.

14.♘a3 ♘e8

Practical experience shows that passive play in this structure commonly costs Black the point. He should seek activity in the centre so 14...e6 looks interesting. However, White retains his space advantage after 15.♗f4 exd5 16.exd5 ♖e8 17.♘ab5 ♗f8 18.♗f3, although he cannot mate Black's king as it happened in the game. The text is actually not bad, but only if Black links it with ...f5.

15.♗f4

White completely ignores the threat of ...f5 and puts the bishop under the hit of the f8-rook. 15.♗g5 is not any better since Black can shift it back by 15...f6. Perhaps the best option is 15.♖e1, in order to meet 15...f5 by 16.exf5 ♖xf5 17.♘ab5 or 15...♘c7 by 16.♗g5.

15...♘c7?

And this is already a positional mistake. Black has no play whatsoever on the queenside. 15...f5 was mandatory. White should answer 16.f3 ♘f6 and prevent the positional threat of 17...♘h5 18.♗g5 f4 by 17.exf5!.

16.♖c1 ♗a6 17.♗xa6 ♘xa6 18.b3

While Black was manoeuvring without any positional clue, White achieved the main goal of the opening – the queenside is paralysed. The next stage is to bolster up the centre.

18...♘d7 19.♘c4 ♘b4 20.♕d2 ♘b6 21.♘b5 ♘xc4 22.bxc4± ♕d7 23.♖fe1 f6 24.♗g3 g5

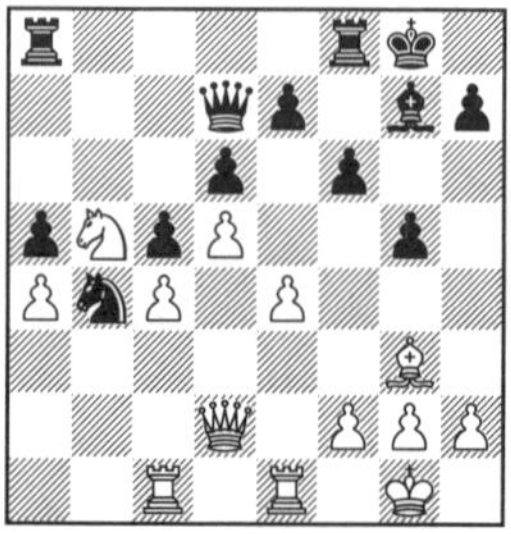

25.f4

The mobility of White's rooks make the difference in this type of positions. Both of them can be lifted onto the h-file while Black is cramped and he is lacking manoeuvring space. The rest is agony.

25...gxf4 26.♗xf4 ♖ac8 27.♖c3 ♔h8 28.♖h3 ♕g4 29.♖g3 ♕h4 30.♖f1 ♖g8 31.♖ff3 f5 32.exf5 ♕f6 33.♗g5 ♕f8 34.♖h3 ♗f6

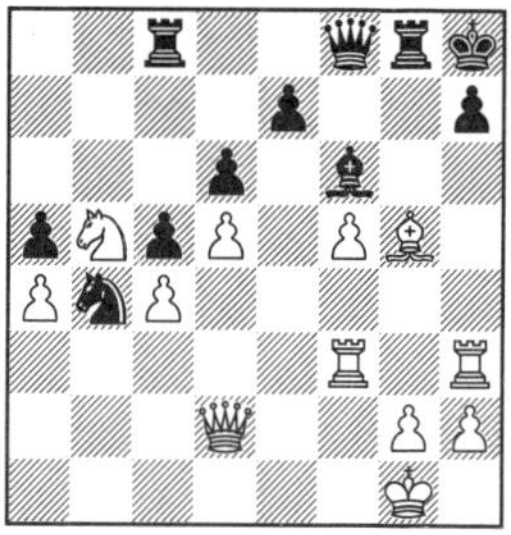

35.♖xh7+!

Black's pieces are so cramped that some tactical device sooner or later should decide the game.

35...♔xh7 36.♖h3+ ♔g7 37.♗h6+ ♔f7 38.♗xf8 ♖cxf8 39.♘c7 ♖h8 40.♖xh8 ♖xh8 41.♕e2 ♗d4+ 42.♔h1 ♗e5 43.g3 ♖h6 44.♔g2 ♔f6 45.h3 ♔xf5 46.♕g4+ ♔f6 47.♕e6+ ♔g7 48.♕xe7+ ♔g8 49.♘e6 ♖g6 50.g4 ♘d3 51.♕f8+ ♔h7 52.♕f5 ♘e1+ 1–0

---

2. Shaked–Shirov
Tilburg 1997

1.d4 ♘f6 2.c4 c5 3.d5 b5 4.cxb5 a6 5.b6 d6 6.♘c3 g6 7.♘f3 ♗g7

8.e4 0–0 9.♗e2 ♘bd7 10.a4 a5 11.0–0 ♘xb6 12.♗f4 ♘e8 13.♕d2 ♗g4 14.♖fe1 ♘c7 15.h3

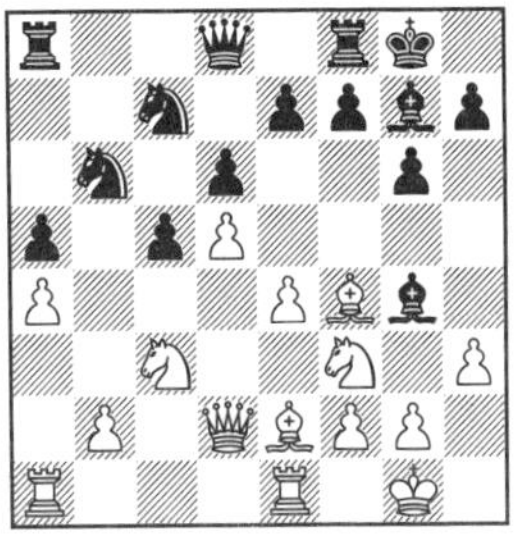

I recommend to develop the bishop to b5, but Shaked had not this option since he had chosen 9.♗e2 instead of 9.a4. Anyway, the game is a good example of play where Black trades his bishop for White's knight. Note that Black's pawn is already on a5 which offers White the b5-square. With a pawn on a6, things are more complex. In that case I suggest to preserve the king's knight by shifting it to d2, e.g. 9.a4 ♕xb6 10.♘d2!

15...♗xf3 16.♗xf3 ♘c4 17.♕c2 ♘a6 18.♘b5 ♘e5 19.♗e2 ♘b4 20.♕d2± ♕d7 21.♗g3 ♕b7 22.♖ad1 ♔h8

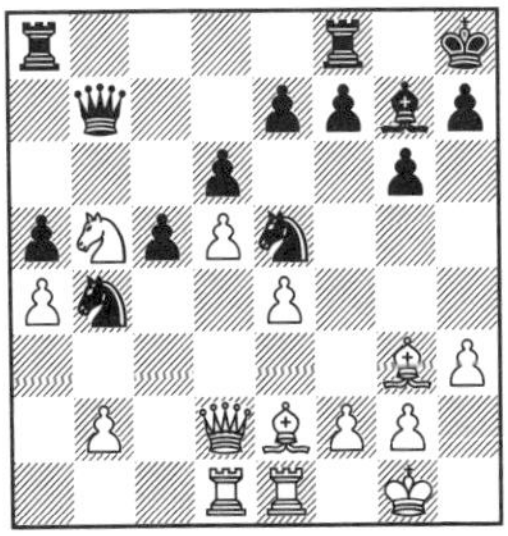

Evidently, White has won the opening battle. Black has finished all his useful moves and adopted a waiting strategy. This is a very bad sign. Besides, his last move is a mistake since now White has 23.f4 ♘d7 24.e5! and the hit on d6 would force Black to defend that pawn with 24...♕b6, depriving his knight of that square. Relatively better was 22...♘d7 23.f4 ♘b6 24.b3, transposing to the game.

23.f4 ♘d7 24.♗c4

In general, this is a good, consistent move, entirely in the spirit of the system. Still, it would be even better to catch the opportunity by 24.e5!, with a total domination. Shaked prefers to follow the well tested path with f4-f5. It is hard to blame him as this plan also assures him of the edge.

24...♘b6 25.b3 ♖ad8 26.♗h4 ♖d7 27.f5 ♕b8 28.♖f1 ♕d8 29.♖f2 ♗f6 30.♕h6

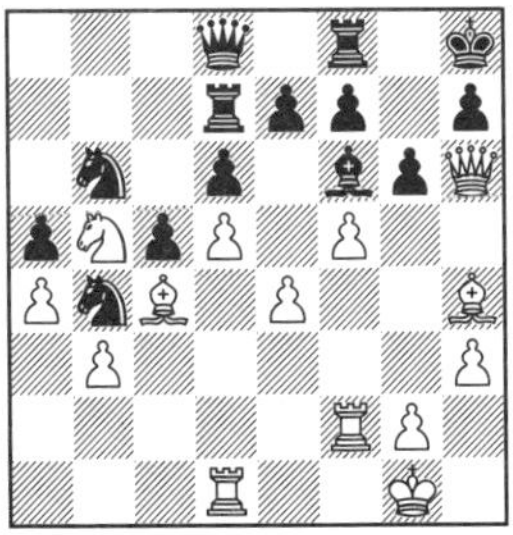

30...♖g8?!

Black seeks counterplay down the g-file, but his rook will be isolated on g6. It was better to keep harassing the queen by 30...♗g7 31.♕e3 ♗f6. The fine point is that 32.♗g5 ♗xg5 33.♕xg5 f6 would offer

Black fair chances to survive. You'll meet a similar position in game **8 Portisch-Malakhatko**, Istanbul 2000, which White won in an exemplary style by lifting both rooks to the h-file via h3. In the current game, however, White's pawn is on h3, so this method would be inapplicable.

This is one more reason to refrain from h3 in the opening!

Of course, White is able to retain an advantage, with 32.♗xf6+ exf6 33.fxg6 fxg6 34.♖df1 ♕e7 35.♕g3 ♔g7 36.h4±.

31.fxg6 ♖xg6 32.♗xf6+ exf6 33.♕f4

White has excelled in the middlegame. He has an obvious advantage, but now he has to devise a new setup to earn the full point. Most natural seems to put a rook on f5 in order to restrain any activity from Black's queen, for instance: 33.♕h4 ♘xc4 34.bxc4 ♔g7 35.♖f5 ♕e7 36.♕f4 ♖d8 37.h4±. The next moves of Shaked suggest that he expected the game to be won "by itself", but Shirov does not comply.

33...♘xc4 34.bxc4 ♕e7 35.♖dd2 ♔g7 36.♖f3 ♕e5 37.♕xe5

The endgame is definitely in White's favour, but I'd prefer to keep the queens and aim for the setup I mentioned on move 33: 37.♕e3!? ♖e7 38.♖df2 or 37...♕g5 38.♕e1. Black could capture a pawn, but 37...♕a1+ 38.♖f1 ♕xa4 39.♖df2± would be extremely dangerous for him.

37...fxe5 38.♖df2 ♘a6 39.♖b2 ♖b7 40.♔f2 h5 41.♖bb3 ♘b4 42.♖f5 ♖h6 43.♔g3 h4+ 44.♔g4 ♘c2

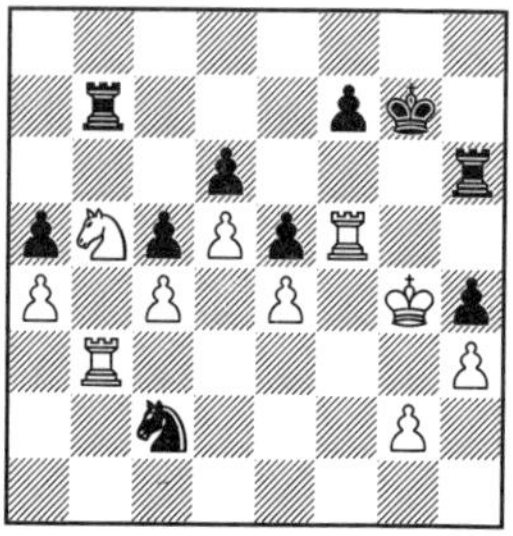

A critical position. White wins a pawn with 45.♖h5 ♖g6+ 46.♖g5 ♖d7 47.♔xh4±. Instead, he suddenly gets entangled into a mating net.

45.♖f2? ♘e1!

There is no way back for the knight, but so it is for White's king. 43.♖e3 loses to 43...♖g6+ 44.♔xh4 ♘xg2+, so the only move is:

46.g3 ♖b8 47.♖xf7+?!

Shaked has panicked. 47.gxh4 ♖g6+ 48.♔h5 ♖h8 is a mate, but 47.♖f5 f6 48.♖f2! would have offered White enough chances to save the day: 48...♖g8 (48...♖g6+ 49.♔f5 ♖xg3 50.♖xg3+ hxg3 51.♖f1↑) 49.♘xd6 ♔f8+ 50.♔f5 ♔e7 51.♘c8+ ♖xc8=. Now his game is difficult although it is still far from lost.

47...♔xf7 48.♘xd6+ ♖xd6 49.♖xb8 ♖g6+ 50.♔xh4 ♘f3+ 51.♔h5 ♖g5+ 52.♔h6 ♖xg3 53.♖b7+ ♔f6 54.♖b6+ ♔e7 55.♖b7+ ♔d8 56.♖b8+ ♔/c7 57.♖b5 ♖xh3+ 58.♔g6 ♘d2 59.♖xc5+ ♔d7 60.♖xa5 ♖g3+ 61.♔f6 ♖f3+ 62.♔g6 ♘xc4 63.♖a7+ ♔d6 64.a5 ♔c5 65.♖c7+ ♔d4 66.a6 ♘d6 67.♖c6

♖g3+? (67...♘xe4–+) **68.♔h6 ♘f7+ 69.♔h5 ♖g5+ 70.♔h4 ♖g8 71.♖f6 ♘g5 72.a7 ♘xe4 73.♖a6 ♖a8 74.d6 ♘c5 75.♖a5 e4 76.♔g3 e3 77.d7 ♘xd7 78.♖a4+ ♔d5 79.♔f3??** (79.♖a3=) **79...♘b6 80.♖a6 ♘c4 81.♔e2 ♔d4 82.♖a1 ♘b6 83.♖a6 ♘d5 84.♖a4+ ♔c3 85.♖a5 ♔c4 86.♖a4+ ♔b5 87.♖a1 ♔b6 88.♔d3 ♖xa7 89.♖b1+ ♔c5 90.♖c1+ ♔d6 91.♖d1 ♔e5 0–1**

3. Kaidanov–Petit
Torcy, 1991

1.d4 ♘f6 2.c4 c5 3.d5 b5 4.cxb5 a6 5.b6 ♕xb6 6.♘c3 g6 7.♘f3 d6 8.♘d2 ♗g7 9.e4 0–0 10.♗e2 ♕d8 11.0–0 ♘bd7 12.a4 a5

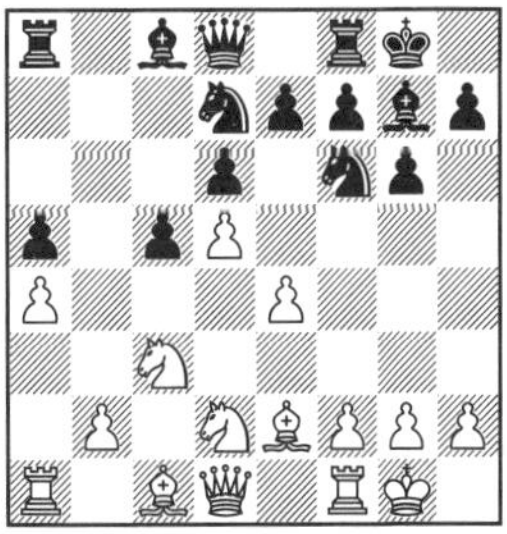

We have reached the topical pawn structure, but the placement of White's bishop at e2 (instead of b5) and the knight on d2 require different treatment. The plan with e4-e5 is no longer possible so Kaidanov adopts a light-squared strategy. It is very efficient against passive play.

13.♘c4 ♗a6

Black must undermine White's centre or he will be overrun by the e- and f-pawns as it happened in the game. He should decide whether to attack it by ...e6 or ...f5. For instance, he could try 13...♘b6 14.♘a3 e6, but then 15.♗f4 would pinpoint the weakness on d6. More interesting is 14...♘e8 15.♗f4 f5!? with unclear play. The possibility of such activity makes me prefer the setup I recommend in the "Step by Step" chapter. It allows White to conduct the game. Petit, however, clearly does not understand that he cannot survive with a passive stand.

14.♘a3 ♗xe2 15.♕xe2 ♘b8 16.♗g5 ♘a6 17.♔h1

17.♘c4! is more precise since 17...♘d7 would lose the d6-pawn. Perhaps Kaidanov was not paying much attention to the move order since he knew that this structure was clearly better for White in general.

17...♘b4 18.♖ad1

White firstly bolsters his centre before proceeding with pawn moves.

18...♖a7

After 18...♘d7 19.f4 ♘b6 White could follow the well known examples with 20.f5 ♖b8 21.♖f3.

19.f4 ♖d7 20.♘c4 ♖e8

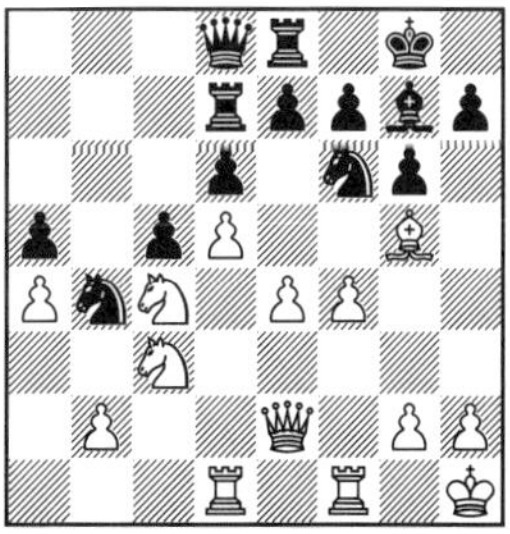

21.♗h4

Of course, Black will not run away, but still 21.e5! was good enough, without any further preparation: 21...dxe5 22.fxe5 ♘fxd5 23.♘d6+–. Black is so cramped, that the common plan with f4-f5 should also be sufficient.

21...h5 22.e5 dxe5 23.fxe5 ♘fxd5 24.e6 fxe6 25.♕xe6+ ♔h7 26.♘e4 ♕c8 27.♘g5+ ♔h6 28.♘f7+ ♔h7 29.♘ce5 ♗xe5 30.♘xe5 ♖d6 31.♖f7+ ♔h6 32.♘f3 1–0

4. Milov–Abrahamyan
Minneapolis 2005

1.d4 ♘f6 2.c4 c5 3.d5 b5 4.♘f3 g6 5.cxb5 a6 6.b6 d6 7.♘c3 ♘bd7 8.e4 ♗g7 9.a4 ♕xb6 10.a5 ♕b4

This move is a sheer provocation. It challenges White to play 11.♖a4 which would divert him from the best plan linked with ♘d2 and ♘a4. I also employed it back in 1994 against Ricardi, but nowadays it looks only as a waste of a tempo. Milov shows how White should react:

11.♘d2 0–0 12.♗e2 ♘e8 13.0–0

13...♘c7

Evidently 13...♗xc3 14.bxc3 ♕xc3 15.♖a3 ♕g7 16.♘c4 ♘c7 17.♗b2 f6 18.f4 is repulsive for Black.

14.♘c4 ♕b7

Unfortunately, the placement of the queen at b4 becomes a nuisance to Black's plans since 14...♘b5?? would lose to 15.♘a2. The recapitulation of Black's queen's sortie is: 1 tempo lost.

15.♘a4 ♘b5 16.♘ab6 ♘xb6 17.♘xb6 ♖a7 18.♖b1!

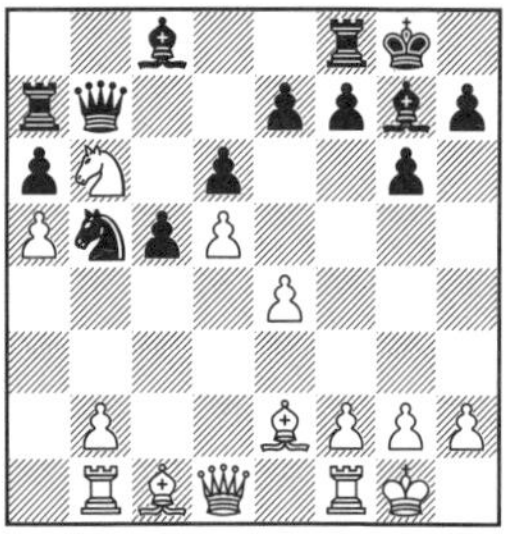

Milov's play is disarmingly simple, but very efficient. He is aiming for a setup like ♗c4, ♕d3, b2-b4. Black should not be staying idle and watching. Perhaps he should try to shift the focus to the kingside by 18...f5. Notice that White was unable to prevent that break anyway. For instance, 18.♗c4, intending to meet 18...f5 by 19.exf5 ♗xf5 20.♖e1 ♘d4 21.♗g5, does not cause any harm to Black in view of 21...♘c2 22.♖xe7 ♕xe7 23.♗xe7 ♖xe7 24.♖c1 ♖e1+ 25.♕xe1 ♘xe1 26.♖xe1 ♗xb2 27.♗xa6 ♗c3=. Returning to 18...f5, White's only reasonable answer would be 19.f3 to keep the c8-bishop restrained. (19.exf5 ♗xf5 20.♗d3 e6! is about equal following 21.dxe6 ♗xe6 22.♗xb5 axb5 23.♕xd6 ♗f5 24.♖a1 ♖f6 25.♕d8+ ♖f8 26.♕d6.) Now Black would hardly have time to organise a kingside pawn storm with 19...f4 20.♗d2 g5 because White strikes first: 21.b4 ♗d7 22.bxc5 ♗d4+ 23.♔h1 ♗xc5 24.♘xd7 ♕xd7 25.♕a4± and Black is tied up and down. 20...♗d7 would not be too helpful either: 21.b4 cxb4 22.♘xd7 ♕xd7 23.♖xb4 ♘c3 24.♕e1±.

18...♗d7 19.♗g5

Milov completely ignores ...f5, but probably he should have discouraged it by 19.♗d3!? when 19... f5 would be outright bad due to 20.♘xd7 ♕xd7 21.exf5 and White must recapture by pawn. Abrahamyan, however, wants to defend without weakening his castling position.

19...♖e8?! 20.♕d2

This move loses a tempo. 20.♗c4! was better. Then 20...♘d4 21.b4 ♗b5 22.bxc5 dxc5 23.♕d3 would be grim for Black while 20...f5 would not make sense after 19...♖e8.

20...♘d4 21.♗c4 ♗b5 22.♕d3 ♗xc4 23.♕xc4 ♘b5?!

23...e6 was called for: 24.b4 exd5 25.exd5 cxb4 26.♕xb4 ♕b8 27.h3 ♘b5 28.♖bc1 ♖c7 29.♖c6± ♗c3 30.♕a4 ♗d4 31.♖fc1 ♖xc6 32.dxc6 ♗xb6 33.axb6 ♕xb6 34.c7

24.♕d3 ♕b8

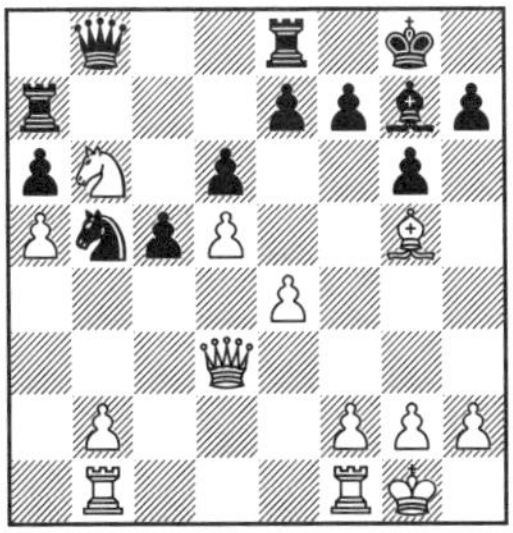

25.f4

All the previous play of White was directed to achieving b2-b4. Now 25.b4 would have been a good move which would ensure an advantage. The point is that Black's second rook cannot contest the c-file so White's heavy piece would be much more active. Quite surprisingly however, Milov turns to the kingside. This is probably a very good practical decision. Black's pieces are too discoordinated and fail to arrive at time to rescue their king. Other games also suggest that the plan with f4-f5 remains topical in the current pawn structure.

25...♖c7 26.f5!

This move achieves several goals: most importantly, it restricts Black's counterplay with ...e6 or even ...f5. It also threatens to open the f-file when the c7-rook will be unable to connect with the other one. Besides the f-file, White has other resources, too. He can attack with h4-h5 or build up a heavy pieces battery on the h-file, leaving the h2-pawn on place.

26...♘d4 27.♖bc1 ♗e5 28.♗f4

It is always good to trade Black's dark-squared bishop.

28...♗xf4 29.♖xf4 ♖f8 30.fxg6 fxg6 31.♖xf8+ ♕xf8 32.♖f1 ♕b8 33.h4! ♘b5 34.h5 ♕e8

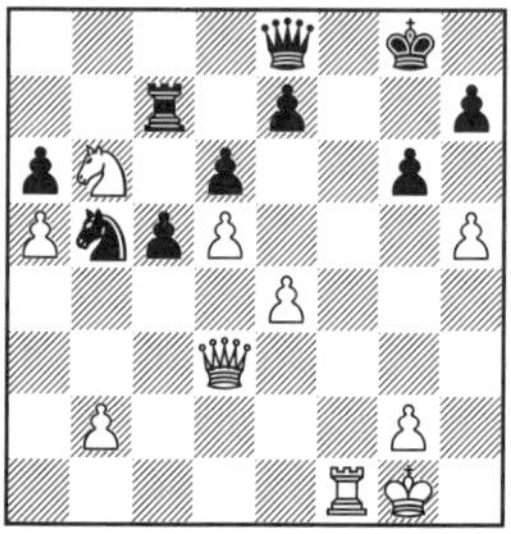

35.e5!

A typical blow of mercy in this structure. We meet it at the final stage of many Benko games. Black's position crumbles down.

35...dxe5 36.♕g3 ♘d6 37.♕xe5 gxh5 38.♖f3 h4 39.♕g5+ ♔h8 40.♕h6 ♘f7 41.♕h5 ♔g8 42.♕xh4 ♖b7 43.♕g4+ ♔h8 44.♕h5 e5 45.d6 e4 46.♖f1 1–0

---

5. Porfiriadis–Ermenkov
Athens 1993

1.d4 ♘f6 2.c4 c5 3.d5 b5 4.cxb5 a6 5.b6 d6 6.♘c3 ♘bd7 7.e4 ♘xb6 8.a4 ♖b8 9.♘f3 ♘fd7?!

Black chooses an ambitious set-up which is, however, risky, to say the least. It is not too wise to deprive the kingside of its main defender before White castled.

10.♗e2 g6 11.0–0

The most straightforward reply is 11.h4!?. Going back is out of question: 11...♘f6 12.e5, but 11...♗g7 12.a5 ♘a8 13.h5 also looks dubious.

11...♗g7 12.♘d2 0–0 13.a5 ♘a8 14.♘c4 ♘c7 15.♘a4 ♘b5 16.♘ab6 ♘xb6 (16...♘d4) **17.♘xb6 ♗d7 18.♖b1**

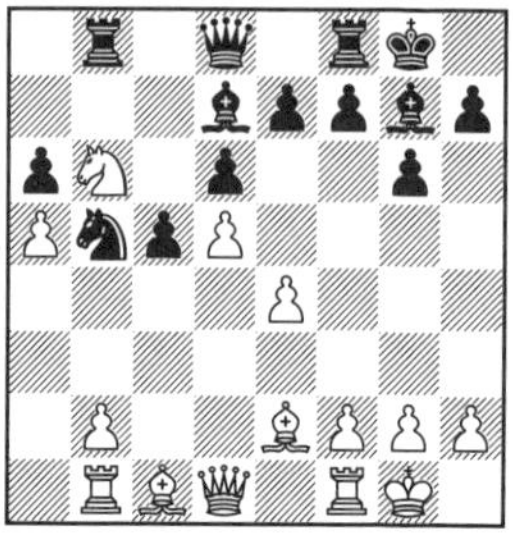

18...♖xb6!? 19.axb6 ♕xb6

White should never underestimate such sacrifices. In fact, strategically Black has the better prospects. His pressure on the queenside will be gradually increasing and White will hardly be able to save his b-pawn in the long run. His other potential weakness is the e4-pawn, and indirectly, the d5-pawn.

Instead of trying to restrain Black's queenside play, White must focus on his kingside attack. There is one very important fine point though! Black still has no weaknesses there. That would render White's attack inefficient. It is vital to create a lever which to use later. Perhaps best would be 20.♗g5! Then 20...h6 21.♗d2± would weaken g6 which could be essential in the light of future f4, and e5-e6, or h4-h5 and f2-f4-f5.

Black can ignore the threat on e7 by 20...♖b8, but the hit on e7 will remain a source of concern: 21.♗c4 a5 22.♕d3 when both thematic continuations of Black fail to 23.♗xe7:

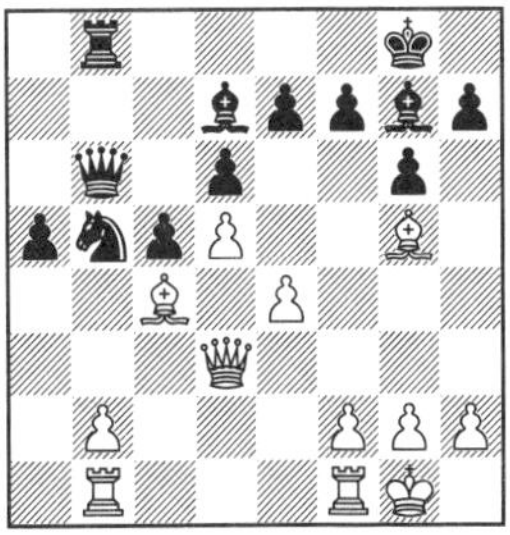

22...♘d4 23.♗xe7 f6 24.♕g3 or 22...a4 23.♗xe7 f6 24.b4!

Porfiriadis makes only one inconcrete move and his position suddenly becomes dubious.

20.♗e3?! ♖b8 21.♗c4 a5

According to the engines, White is fine, but in terms of practical chances, Black's game is easier. Here Porfiriadis realised that he lacks a plan, and decided to repair his mistake on move 20, but tactics do not work in his favour anymore. I must admit that White's choice was not wide at all. For instance, 22.h4 ♘d4 23.h5 a4 24.hxg6 hxg6 25.♗g5 ♕b4 and Black takes over the initiative since 26.♕d3 ♘b3 27.♗xb3? (27.♗xe7 ♘d2 28.♗xd6 ♖b6) would lose to 27...♗b5.

22.♗g5 ♘d4

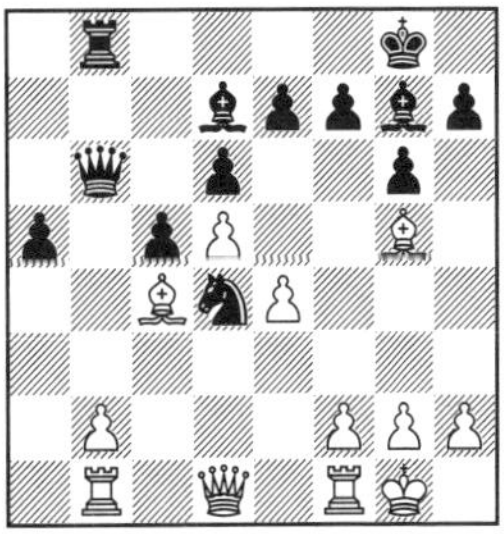

23.♖e1?!

White keeps on making mediocre moves instead of devising a plan. His only reasonable setup is linked with f2-f4, so he needs his rook on f1. Best was 23.♕d3 when Black should already take care of the hanging e7-pawn by 23...♔f8. Then 24.f4 h6 25.♗h4 a4 would be unclear, with mutual chances. Now Black is in command.

23...a4 24.f4 ♕b4 25.♕d3 ♔f8!

The five-time Bulgarian champion is conducting very well this game so far. Ermenkov could have forced play by 25...♘b5 26.♕c2 ♗d4+ 27.♔h1 f6, but he is completely confident with his position and prefers to keep all the options open. His bishop might prove more useful on g7 to protect the king.

26.f5 ♗e5?

Ermenkov overdoses the slow-playing and let his opponent slip away. The most consistent continuation of his play would have been 26...♘b3! 27.♖f1 ♘a5 with total domination: 28.fxg6 hxg6 29.♕f3 ♗e8 30.♗e2 ♘c4∓. Now the game is level again.

27.♗d2 ♕b6 28.fxg6 hxg6 29.♖f1 ♔g7 30.♗c3 ♗b5 31.♗xb5 ♕xb5 32.♕xb5 ♖xb5 33.♔f2 ♘b3

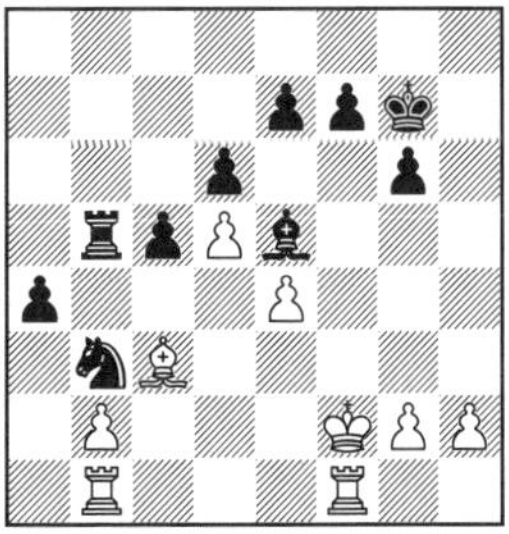

34.♗xe5+?!

This exchange leaves the b2-pawn very weak. White should have played 34.♔e3 c4=. Perhaps he was afraid of the distant passed pawn which would appear after 34...♗xc3 35.bxc3 a3, but in fact that pawn would be more of a weakness than an asset, e.g. 36.♖f2 c4 37.♖a2 ♖a5 38.h4.

34...dxe5 35.♖fd1 c4 36.d6?

This loses on the spot.

36...exd6 37.♖xd6 ♘c5 38.♔e3 ♖b3+ 39.♔d2 ♘xe4+ 0–1

---

6. Portisch–Malakhatko
Istanbul ol. 04.11.2000

1.d4 ♘f6 2.c4 c5 3.d5 b5 4.♘f3 g6 5.cxb5 a6 6.b6 ♕xb6 7.♘c3 d6 8.e4 ♘bd7 9.♗e2 ♗g7 10.♘d2 ♕c7 11.0–0 0–0 12.a4 ♖b8

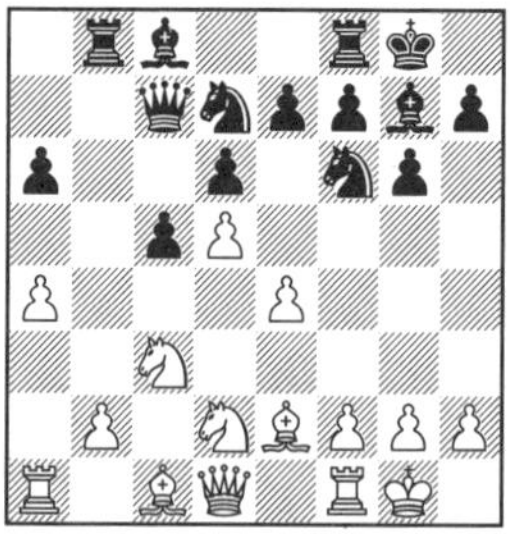

13.♘c4

I recommend 13.a5 aiming to hinder the manoeuvre ...♘d7-b6-a8(c8). It may seem paradoxical, but Black does not mind sticking his knight in the corner, as long as White cannot block the b-file with ♘a4-b6. At a8 the knight is not getting in the way of the c8-bishop and the other knight.

13...♘b6 14.♘a3 ♘fd7 15.♗d2

A fine positional move. From d2 the bishop controls b4, but most importantly, it will not be hanging after ...f7-f5 as it would be in the case of 15.♗f4?! f5!. 15.♗g5 ♖e8 16.♕d2 also looks consistent, but then 16...♘a8!? would enable serious counterplay down the b-file. For instance, ...♖b4 would be quite awkward for White.

The alternative, 15.a5 ♘a8 16.♘c4, is not especially efficient due to 16...♘e5.

15...♗b7

Malakhatko seems at a loss in this structure. I do not see any consistency in his play so far. Black cannot stay passively in these positions. If he lacks clear threats on the b-file, he must seek to undermine White's centre. In general, Black gets most action with ...f5. It does weaken e6, but at least Black can breathe, for instance: 15...f5 16.a5 ♘a8 17.exf5 ♖xf5 18.♘c4 ♘e5

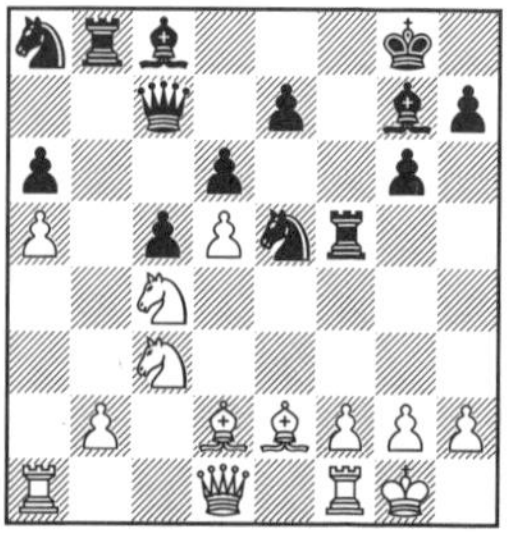

Black's pieces are active and they

generate good counterplay, e.g. 19.♘e3 ♖f4 20.♘c2 ♖f8 21.f4 ♘f7 22.♘a4 ♘h6∞.

Malakhatko apparently opts for ...e6, but White can ignore this breakthrough.

16.♖e1

Portisch does his best to discourage ...f5.

16...♖be8 17.a5 ♘c8 18.♘c4 ♘a7 19.♕c1 ♖b8 20.♗h6 ♗xh6 21.♕xh6 ♘b5

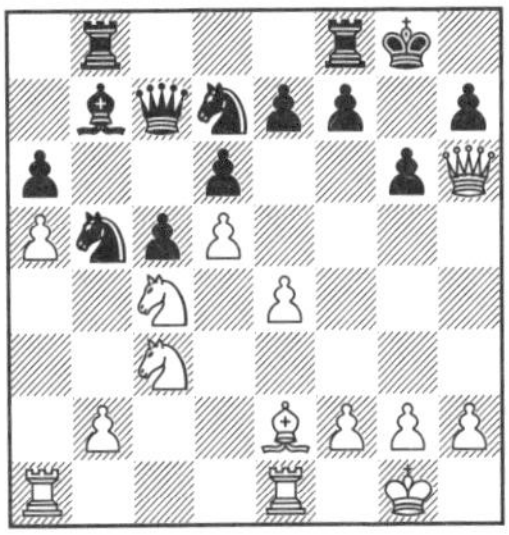

22.f4

In contrast to his opponent, Portisch perfectly knows what he wants to achieve. His plan is to push f5 and pile two heavy pieces on the h-file. So f4 is a logical, "human" move. Rybka, however, suggests an improved version of the same plan: 22.♕h4. The fine point is to anticipate ...♘f6 when White would have to retreat from h6 anyway because of the double attack ...♘g4 against ♖e3. Then 22...♖fe8 23.f4 ♘f6 23.♗d3 would deprive Black of any counterplay, and even 24.♘xb5 axb5 25.♘b6 c4 26.♗f3 would be clearly better for him since 26...♕c5+ can be met by 27.♕f2.

The immediate 22...♘f6 would miss 23.♘xb5 axb5 24.♘b6 ♗a6 (24...c4 25.b3) when the rook lift 25.♖a3 ♖fe8 26.♖h3 c4 27.g4 should be decisive.

22...e6 23.♕g5 ♘d4 24.♗d3 f6 25.♕h4 e5

Black admits the failure of his opening strategy and braces himself for a gloom defence. Amazingly, Rybka lightheartedly evaluates the position as nearly equal! In fact, Black is tied up and down. During the next stage of the game White is manoeuvring without committing himself with pawn breakthroughs.

26.f5 ♖f7 27.♖e3 g5 28.♕h6 ♔h8 29.♔h1 ♖g8 30.♕h5 ♖fg7 31.♕g4 ♗c8 32.♖h3 ♘b8 33.♖h6 ♕e7 34.♘b6 ♖f8 35.♘e2 ♗b7 36.♘g3 ♖gg8 37.♘f1 ♘d7 38.♘c4 ♖g7 39.♘fe3 ♖b8 40.♕d1 ♗c8 41.♖a3 ♗b7 42.♗f1 ♖f8 43.♘g4 ♖ff7 44.♖ah3 ♔g8

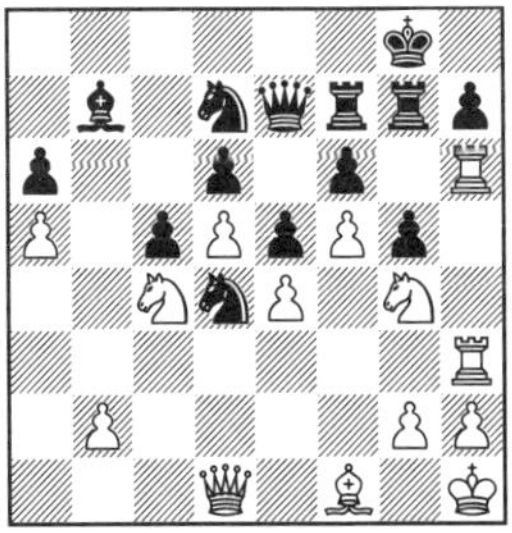

45.♕a4!

It is possible that White can win by opening the kingside with h4 and later g2-g4-g5. However, that would offer Black some counter-chances. Portisch prefers to minimise the risk and prepares to launch an offensive on the opposite wing.

45...♖f8 46.♖3h5 ♖ff7 47.♘b6 ♘f8 48.♖h3 ♕d8 49.♖c3 ♔h8 50.b4!

Typically for the pawn structure with a5 vs. a6, White's most efficient plan proves to be the b4-break. Of course, its impact here is greately enhanced by the domination of White's pieces all over the board.

50...cxb4 51.♕xb4 ♖g8 52.♖hh3 ♖gg7 53.♖h6 ♖g8 54.♖c1 ♖gg7 55.♖d1 ♖g8 56.♗c4 ♔g7 57.♕a3 ♕c7 58.♖c1 ♘d7

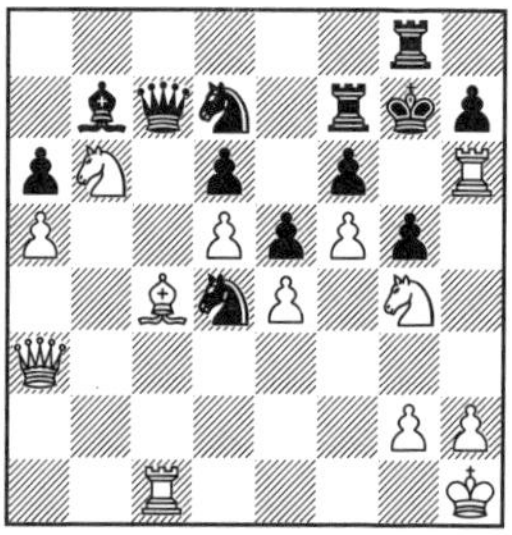

59.♖xh7+ 1–0

Part 2

Main Ideas

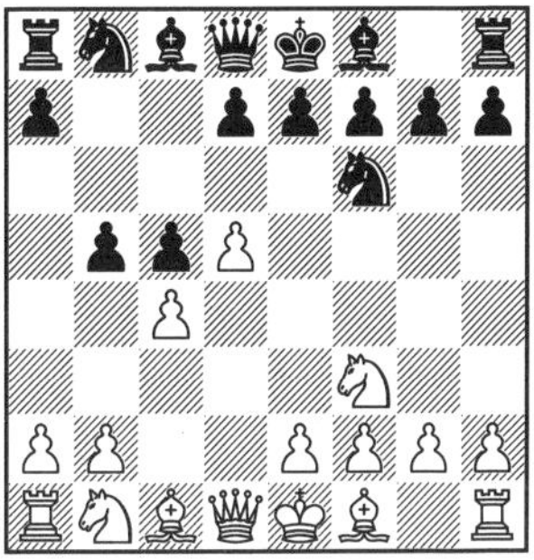

1.d4 ♘f6 2.c4 c5 3.d5 b5 4.♘f3!

4.♘f3 is the most popular way to decline the Benko. In fact, White retains a back door to real gambit lines after 4...g6 5.cxb5 a6 6.e3, but I advocate 6.b6, transposing to Part 1. In the "Step by Step" chapter I also discuss the variation 4.♕c2 which could be a solid alternative to our main repertoire.

After 4.♘f3, Black can continue in the Benko style with 4...g6 or 4... d6. We answer then 5.cxb5 a6 6.b6 reaching the main line from Part 1.

The only reason to choose the move order with 4.♘f3 is to avoid the somewhat dry positions that arise after 4.cxb5 a6 5.b6 e6.

Even if you like that line, it would be refreshing to play 4.♘f3 occasionally, since the positions we'll examine in the current chapter are often quite different from anything we have dealt with so far. Although the choice belongs to Black, there is a serious chance he will deviate from the main lines since authors like Moskalenko, Knaak and Pinski promise him good play after 4...♗b7 or 4...b4. Another consideration is that Black players may initially be willing to sacrifice a pawn for the initiative, but they often feel relieved to change tracks when offered an opportunity for that.

Even the most die-hard fans of the Benko might renounce on 4... g6 by reasons of principle as they would feel obliged to exploit the tricky move order and mess our plans by:

A. 4...bxc4

B. 4...♗b7

C. 4...b4

Still, most games feature:

D. 4...g6

E. 4...d6

I feel that White has more chances for gaining an edge in the first 3 lines than after 4...g6/d6.

A. 4...bxc4 5.♘c3 d6 6.e4

This pawn structure looks the same as in Part 1. The only difference is that the pawn is at a7 instead of a6. This should be in Black's favour since he can develop a piece on that square. For instance, if White captures on c4 by his bishop, then ...♗a6 would seriously contest the all-important c4-square. Control of that square is critical for our strategy of restraint. However, things are not that simple. First, White can recapture on c4 by knight with the manoeuvre ♘f3-d2xc4. Second, and more important, White saved tempi compared to the lines with cxb5 and b5-b6. That allows him to favorably change the pawn structure by an early e4-e5. The critical position arises after 6...g6 7.e5!? dxe5 8.♘xe5 ♗g7 9.♗xc4 0-0 10.0-0 ♗a6 11.♖e1 ♗xc4 12.♘xc4 ♘bd7

White has serious spatial advantage and he can preserve it by 13.♕f3!? ♖e8 14.♗g5 h6 15.♗xf6! ♘xf6 16.♖ad1±.

Black can prevent e4-e5, but then he will no longer have the resource ...♗a6:

6...♘bd7 7.♗xc4 g6 8.0-0 ♗g7 9.h3! 0-0 10.♖e1 ♖b8 11.♕c2

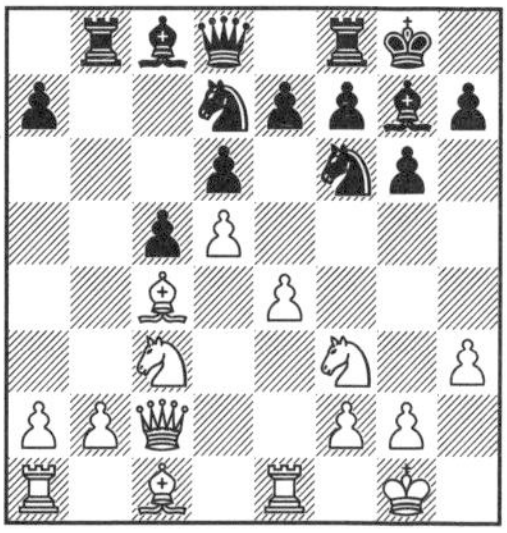

This is the main position of the line with 4...bxc4. White's plan is very straightforward. He is going to play ♗f4, ♖ad1.

Then he can prepare e5 or first organise a light-squared blockade on the queenside with b3, a4.

Should Black's f6-knight leave the kingside, White could thrust the h-pawn to h5.

For his part, Black should try to exchange pieces in order to reduce the importance of Whites space advantage.

11...♘h5, intending ...♘e5 does not work well due to the simple 12.♗e2! ♕b6 13.♘a4! ♕c7 14.♖b1 and Black's plan has failed completely.

11...♘b6 12.♗f1 ♗b7 13.♗f4 ♕c8 14.♖ad1± is also grim for Black:

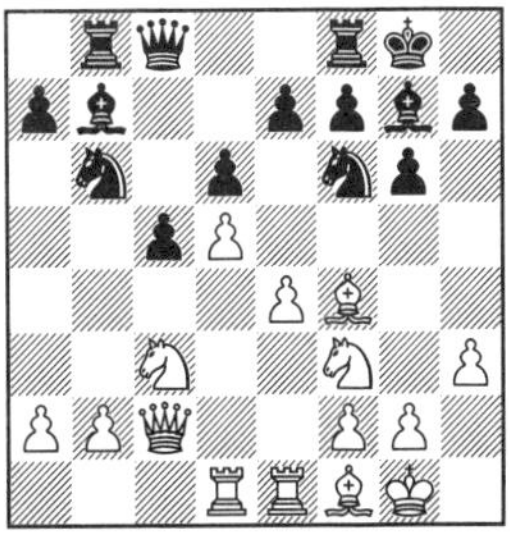

He can stay passively, but then White will be gaining space on the queenside by a4, b3. 14...♗a6 15.♗xa6 ♕xa6 does solve one problem, but it misses 16.e5 ♘e8 17.b3 with a clear edge.

These examples suggest that Black should aim for active play on the queenside:

11...♘e8 12.♗f4 ♕a5 13.♗d2 ♕b6 14.b3 ♗a6 15.♖ab1 ♘c7 16.a4 ♘e5 17.♘xe5 ♗xe5

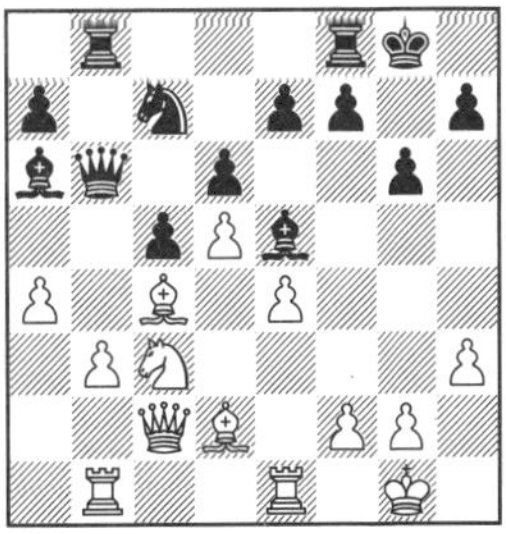

This is a model position for the Benko Declined and it deserves a detailed explanation so I devoted special attention to it in the commentaries to **game 9 O.Pavlov-Obolenskikh**, Tomsk 2008. Its main characteristic is that Black has not a trace of counterplay. White, for his part, should carefully prepare an active plan like pushing a5 and b4, or start an attack on the opposite wing with h4-h5. I prefer his chances here.

B. 4...♗b7

By attacking the centre, Black prevents any ideas with cxb5. The drawback of this line is that the b7-bishop might turn out rather useless.

Note that in this line dynamic factors prevail over structural considerations!

The activity of pieces and good coordination are paramount. We should not be afraid to part with a pawn or allow a crippled pawn chain in exchange for the initiative.

5.♕c2!

The most challenging continuation. My game against Tregubov, Ohrid 2001 convinced me that 5.a4 ♕a5+! 6.♗d2 b4 is equal. The text is linked with a promising pawn sacrifice:

5...bxc4

In this line White's centre crumbles down, but he gets in return a big lead in development and better coordination. Of course Black can still try to keep the centre closed by playing ...g6, d6 and aiming for a quick castling, but then the bishop would be misplaced on b7. Therefore, he should be consistent and, after undermining the base of the d5-pawn, strike at d5 by ...e6. At first sight:

5...♘a6 6.a3 bxc4 7.e4 e6 looks more precise as it appears that Black has gained a tempo to develop his knight. In fact, on a6 the knight stands worse than on b8! White exploits that by simply taking on e6:

8.dxe6! fxe6 9.e5 ♗xf3 10.gxf3 ♘d5 11.♗xc4 ♘ac7 12.h4

The source **game 10 Pankratov-Wang Mong Lin**, email ICCF, 1997, went on 12...♕b8 13.♘c3±.

Knaak suggests as an improvement: 12...d6, but 13.♘c3!? gives White a clear edge, e.g. 13...dxe5 14.♗d2 ♕d7 (14...♗e7 15.♖g1 ♗f6 16.0-0-0) 15.0-0-0 0-0-0 16.♘e4 ♕f7 17.♗e2±.

5...bxc4 6.e4 e6 7.♗xc4 exd5 8.exd5

This position is critical and it requires a crucial decision from Black. He cannot ignore the d5-pawn since if it survived, it would be restricting all his play. The problem is how should he take it.

8...♗xd5

After 8...♕e7+ 9.♗e3 ♘xd5 10.♗xd5 ♗xd5 11.♘c3 ♗e6 White will easily regain the sacrificed material, e.g. 12.♖d1 ♘c6 13.0-0 ♕d8 14.♘e4 ♗e7 15.♗xc5, with pressure.

9.♗xd5 ♘xd5 10.0-0 ♗e7 11.♖e1

White has great compensation for the pawn due to his pressure on the e7-bishop, for instance, 11...0-0 12.♕e4 is a hidden double attack through the X-ray to a8.

11...♘b4 12.♕e2 0-0

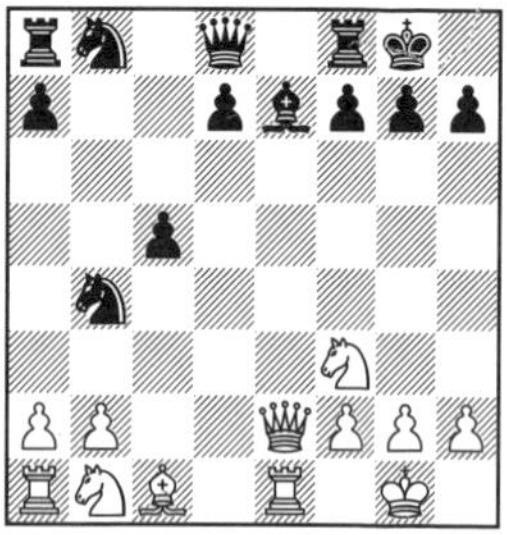

Black would be struggling even after a simple developing move like 13.♘c3, planning to leap onto d5. The game E.Toth-A.Popovics, Budapest 2007, saw instead:

13.♕xe7 ♕xe7 14.♖xe7 ♘c2 15.♗f4 ♘xa1 16.♘a3 ♘c6 17.♖e1 ♖fe8 18.♖xa1±.

C. 4...b4 5.a3

Unlike the previous line, here you should tune yourself up to long positional play. Remember that while pushing e4-e5 remains our main objective, we must first undermine the enemy pawn chain on the queenside. If Black then trades his b4-pawn for our at a3, we will get a nice square for our knight on c3 and some pressure against the stranded a7-pawn. However, that should not be enough to win the game. We will need a second weakness and it could be created by executing the thematic e4-e5.

Conversely, should Black allow a3xb4 cxb4, we might be able to win the game only on the left wing. The reason is simple – in that case Black would have two vulnerable pawns, b4 and a7. Moreover, the absence of the c5-pawn would enable the breakthrough c4-c5 and offer White the important square d4. Playing through game **9 Kir.Georgiev-Milanovic**, Bar 2008, should give you a good notion of Black's structural problems.

Now let us examine the two main pawn structures in more detail:

1. 5...♘a6

5...bxa3?! is a worse version of the text as it practically gives White an extra tempo. We can use it to push an early e4-e5, for instance: 6.♖xa3 g6 7.♘c3 ♗g7 8.e4 d6 9.e5! with a clear edge.

6.axb4 ♘xb4 7.♘c3 d6 8.e4

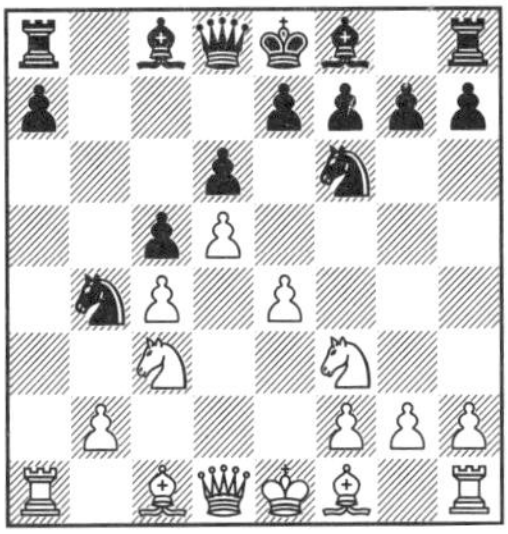

8...g6

8...e5 would have been clearly inferior after 9.dxe6.

9.♗e2 ♗g7 10.0-0 0-0 11.♗f4

White's game is a bit easier since his space advantage is very stable. I had to struggle as Black in **game 8 I.Sokolov-Kir.Georgiev**, Sarajevo 1998.

2. 5...g6

5...a5 has no advantages over 5...g6, followed by ...a5 later. On the contrary, it offers White the interesting option of a pawn sac after 6.♘bd2 g6 7.e4 d6 8.axb4 cxb4 9.c5!? which I analyse in the "Step by Step"chapter.

Practical experience has shown that tactical solutions do not favour White so we must think strategically.

Sooner or later we'll have to exchange on b4 obtaining the following structure:

Our task will be to blockade the pawn at a5 and bind the opponent with its defence. Then we'll have enough options to increase our edge by breaking through with c4-c5 or e4-e5.

9 Kir.Georgiev-Milanovic
Bar 2008

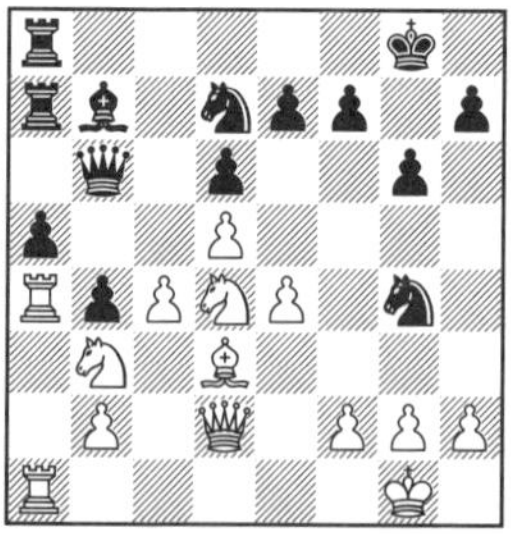

The black pieces are very passive. Especially the rooks and the bishop have no prospects at all.

But suppose Black achieved the following setup:

Black's dream setup

The doomed a-pawn from the previous example has transformed here into a monster, which is constantly threatening to leap forward. This became possible because Black had managed to manoeuvre his king's knight to c5 via d7, while the other one defends the b4-pawn from a6. Such a setup leaves the d7-square free for the bishop.

Our main task is to avoid the second scenario so we should very carefully choose the moment to exchange on b4. If we do it too early, the f6-knight will rush to the vacated c5-square.

We must wait for Black to put on d7 the queen's knight and only then capture on b4.

The delay of a3xb4 is exploitable only by b4xa3, but then Black will practically abandon any hope for active play.

6.♘bd2!? ♗g7 7.e4 0-0 8.♗d3 d6 9.0-0

Do not waste a tempo on h3. Black would have little chances to organise counterplay without his light-squared bishop. I discuss this subject on multiple occasions throughout the book.

9...♘bd7

9...♘fd7 is rather useless here as the knight cannot go to c5. We could start a kingside attack with 10.h4 ♘a6 11.h5.

9...bxa3 is a principled response to our tricky move order with a delayed exchange on b4. However, Black thus concedes to play a passive albeit solid position. White should redirect the d2-knight via b1 to c3 and take on e6 if Black attempts to close the centre: 10.♖xa3 ♘a6 11.♘b1!? ♘b4 12.h3

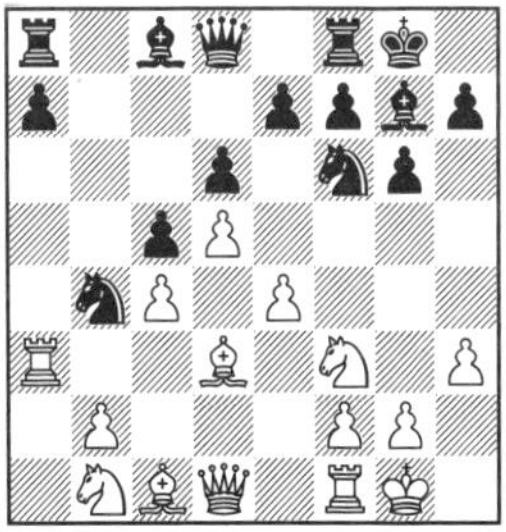

12...e5 (12...♘d7 13.♘c3 ♕c7 allows White to pursue his main positional aim with 14.♖e1 a6 15.♗f4.) 13.dxe6 ♗xe6 14.♘c3. White has the better pawn structure and possibilities for further expansion.

10.axb4!

Now we can alter the pawn structure favorably. This exchange fixes two targets – the pawns on b4 and a7, and makes possible the breakthrough c4-c5 in future.

10...cxb4 11.♘b3 a5

12.h3!

An important prophylactic move which prepares 12.♗e3.

White should be avoiding to trade his bishop for its counterpart on g7 as it deprives Black's queen of the vital squares c5 and b6.

12...♗b7 13.♖a4

White has achieved its goal and easily obtained a huge advantage in Petkov-Jianu, Galatzi 2007: 13... e6 14.♗e3 exd5 15.cxd5 ♖e8 16.♘fd2 ♘h5 17.♘c4 ♕f6 18.♕d2±.

Part 2

Step by Step

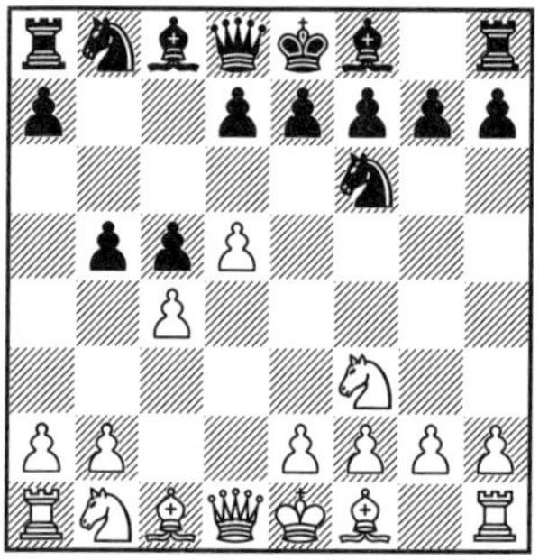

1.d4 ♘f6 2.c4 c5 3.d5 b5 4.♘f3!

White has several other decent ways to decline the gambit, as 4.♗g5, 4.♘bd2 or 4.a4, but they all look a little artificial to me. Perhaps biggest attention of the sidelines deserves:

4.♕c2

The queen is not placed greatly on that square, but it does support e2-e4. Then the mundane 4...g6 5.e4 d6 6.cxb5 ♗g7 7.♘c3 a6 8.♘f3 0-0 would offer White a nice version of the Benko Gambit Accepted. He can follow up with 9.a4 or 9.♗e2 enjoying an extra pawn with good development. In my opinion, the main drawback of 4.♕c2 is that White makes a move which is not strictly necessary and allows Black to complete his development by:

4...bxc4 5.e4 e6

After 6...g6 7.♘f3 ♗g7, the position looks very similar to line A, but the placement of the queen on c2 deprives White of the breakthrough e4-e5. Thus he must switch to calm play with 8.0-0 0-0 9.♘c3 ♗a6 and contest the light squares by 10.♘b5!? ♗xb5 (10...♕d7 11.a4 ♗b7 12.♖e1 ♘a6 13.♗f4 ♘b4 14.♕d2 a6 15.♘c3. White has a clear plan for central play.) 11.♗xb5 ♕b6 12.♗e2 ♘bd7. White's bishop pair restricts the enemy and allows different good paths: 13.♗d2 ♘g4 14.♖ab1 ♘ge5 15.♘e1± or 13.♘d2 13...♕c7 14.♖b1 a5 15.♗b5±, Moskalenko-Mihailovs, Barbera 2009.

6.♗xc4

To 6.♘c3!? exd5 7.e5, Black can sacrifice a piece by 7...♗b7 8.exf6 ♕xf6∞ or 7...♘g4 8.♘xd5 ♘xe5 9.♕e4 d6 10.f4 f5 11.♕e3 ♗e6 12.♘c3 ♘bc6 13.fxe5 d5∞.

6...exd5 7.exd5 d6 8.♘c3 ♗e7 9.h3 0-0

Now White can develop his knight to f3 or e2 (intending to prevent possible ...♗f5 by ♘g3). In both cases he maintains some small edge which, however, seems insufficient to me because Black's only weakness on d6 is easy to protect. The arising positions are too dry and cannot be a solid ground for a lifelong repertoire for White. I'm afraid that a few games at highest level would be enough to show a firm, safe stand for Black.

a) 10.♘f3 ♘bd7 11.0-0 ♘b6 12.b3 ♘xc4 13.bxc4 ♖b8 14.♗f4 ♖b4 15.♘d2 g6 16.a3 ♗f5 17.♘ce4 ♖b8 18.♖fe1 ♘xe4 19.♘xe4 ♗xe4 20.♕xe4 ♗f6 21.♖ab1 ♕d7 22.♕d3 ♖fe8 23.♖xb8 ♖xb8 24.♕g3 ♖b6 25.♗h6, Kempinski-Urban, Hamburg 1999. It is unclear how White could improve further his position after 25...♕d8 26.f4 a5, organising counterplay on the queenside.

b) 9.♘ge2 (Moskalenko's choice) 9...0-0 10.0-0 ♘bd7 11.♘g3 ♘b6 12.b3 ♖b8 13.♖e1 ♘xc4 14.bxc4 ♘g4 15.♗f4 ♗f6 16.h3, Sedlak-Vuckovic, Mataruska Banja 2007.

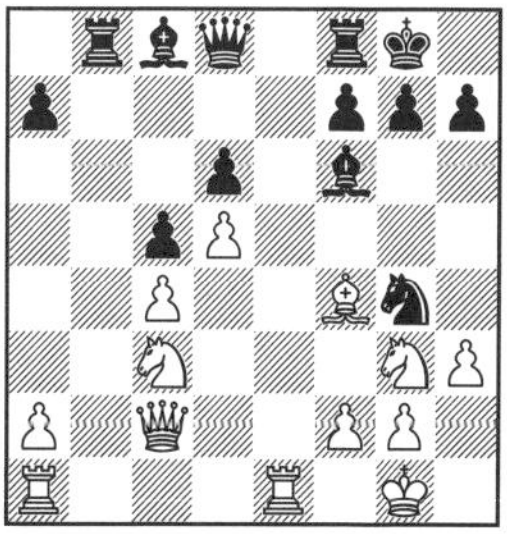

Here the simple 16...♗e5 17.♕c1 ♗xf4 18.♕xf4 ♘e5 would have been about equal since 19.♖xe5 dxe5 20.♕xe5 ♖b6 21.♘ce4 f6 22.♕f4 ♖b4 23.♖c1 ♕b6 could become dangerous for White.

It is worth mentioning that the other Black's replies to 4.♕c2 lead to more lively play with fair chances for White to gain the initiative:

4...♘a6. Play can continue with 5.a3 (5.♘c3!? is sharp and unclear) 5...bxc4 6.e4

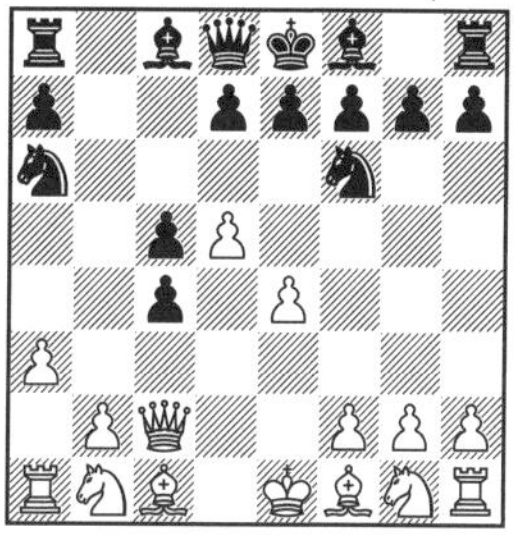

7...e6

6...♘c7 7.♗xc4 leads to the same position, but White might also contemplate 7.♘f3 having in mind to meet 7...e6 by 8.d6.

7.♗xc4 ♘c7 8.♘c3

There is no need for 8.dxe6 fxe6 9.e5 ♗b7 10.♘f3 ♗xf3 11.gxf3 d5 12.exf6 dxc4 13.fxg7 ♗xg7 14.♕xc4 ♗d4 with a rather unclear game.

8...exd5 9.exd5 d6 (9...♗b7 10.♕d3) 10.♘ge2 ♗e7 11.b4 0-0 12.0-0

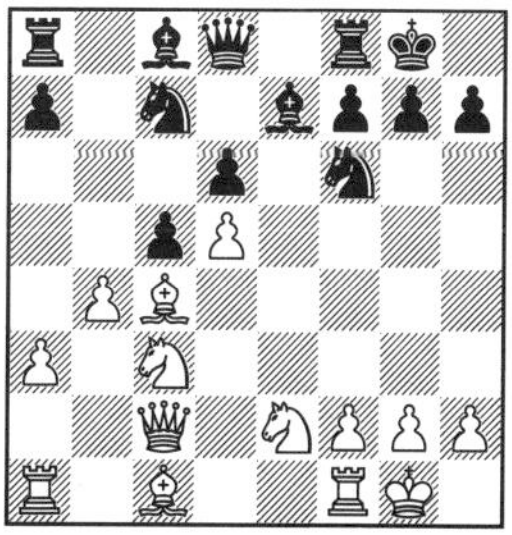

This position was tested in two games. White's space advantage assures him of an edge:

a) 12...♖b8 13.bxc5 dxc5, Malakhatko-S.Kasparov, Pavlograd 2000, when White should have exchanged the blockading dark-squared bishop by 14.♗f4 ♗d6 15.♕d2 ♖e8 16.♘g3 ♗xf4 17.♕xf4±.

b) 12...♘d7 This was played in the recent game Mamedyarov-Tregubov, Ajaccio 2008. Tregubov is one of the most devoted Benko protagonists, but I fail to grasp his idea. Perhaps he intended to recapture by knight after 13.bxc5, but 13...♘xc5 14.♗e3 would have left White with an overwhelming spatial advantage when the c7-knight would be a sorry sight. So Tregubov took by pawn 13...dxc5 and went on to lose following 14.♗f4 ♘b6 15.♗a2 ♘e8 16.♖fe1 ♘d6 17.♘g3 ♗b7 18.a4 ♗a6 19.♖ad1 ♖e8 20.♘ce4 ♘xe4 21.♘xe4 c4 22.d6 ♗f8 23.♗b1 f5 24.♘c5 ♖xe1+ 25.♖xe1 ♗xd6 26.♕xf5 etc.

Summarising: 4.♕c2 will remain a solid weapon in White's repertoire against the Benko Gambit.

Now let us return to 4.♘f3, when Black commonly chooses between:

A. 4...bxc4
B. 4...♗b7
C. 4...b4
D. 4...g6

Minor alternatives are:

4...d6 5.cxb5 a6 6.b6 reaches positions from Part 1, and

4...e6 transposes to the Blumenfeld Gambit – see Part 6.

A. 4...bxc4 5.♘c3 d6

Black cannot attack d5 by 5... e6?! 6.e4 exd5 due to 7.e5 (by the way, 7.exd5 is also clearly better for White) 7...d4 8.exf6 d5 9.♘xd4! cxd4 10.♕xd4 ♗b4 11.♗xc4± with a crushing attack in Lasinskas-Rachela, Stare Mesto 2004. Of course, Black can avoid the route by closing the centre with 6...d6 7.♗xc4 e5 8.0-0 ♗e7, but his position is very passive. Then 9.♗b5+! is perhaps simplest. The fine point is that 9...♘fd7 stumbles into 10.♘xe5. 9...♘bd7 10.♘xe5 dxe5 11.d6 ♗f8 12.f4+– is not much different, so the only move is 9...♗d7 10.♗e2 0-0 11.♘d2± with a better version of variations which I discuss later.

5...g6 6.e4 ♗g7 7.♗xc4 0-0 8.0-0 is not of independent significance.

6.e4

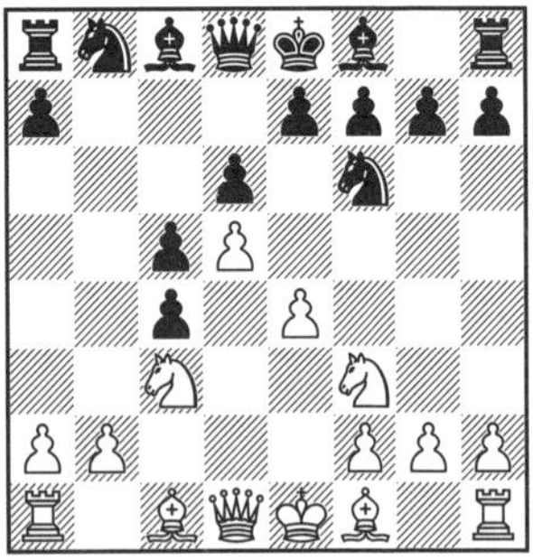

6...♘bd7

6...♗g4 does not fulfill its aim to trade the f3-knight due to 7.♕a4+ ♘bd7 (7...♗d7 8.♕c2) 8.♘d2.

In the majority of games Black opts for 6...g6. White can answer with the typical manoeuvre 7.♘d2 ♗g7 8.♘xc4 0-0 9.♗e2 ♘bd7 10.0-0

♗a6 11.♗d2 ♖b8 12.b3±, Dao Thien Hai-Gal, Bekescsaba 1996, but I think that:

7.e5 dxe5 8.♘xe5

should be more unpleasant to Black as he would have to defend a passive position without clear counterplay after 8...♗g7 9.♗xc4 0-0 10.0-0 ♗a6 11.♖e1 ♗xc4 12.♘xc4 ♘bd7±.

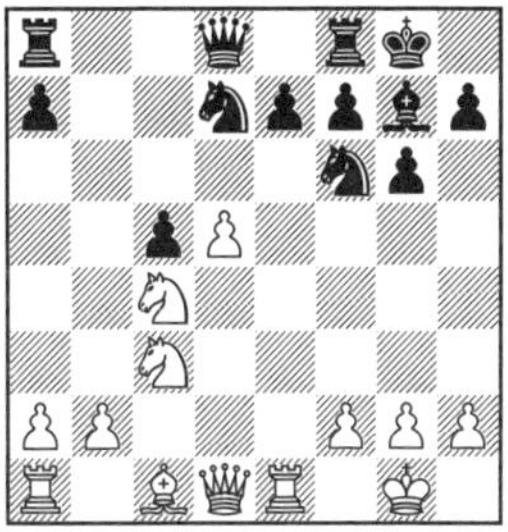

White has serious spatial advantage. His only problem is the vulnerable d5-pawn. For instance, 13.♗f4 ♘b6 14.♘e5 (exchanges favour Black) would cost a pawn after 14...♘fxd5 15.♘c6 ♘xc3 hitting the queen. That's why in Hebden-K.Arkell, Isle of Man 1995 White shifted the queen: 13.♕f3!? in order to ensure the possibility of 13...♘b6 14.♘e5 when 14...♘fxd5?? would lose a piece. The game went on 13...♖e8 (protecting e7 and renewing the threat of 14...♘fxd5) 14.♗g5 h6 and here Hebden sacrificed a pawn with some compensation – 15.♗h4 ♘b6 16.♘e5 g5 17.♗g3 ♘bxd5 18.♖ad1 e6 19.h4 ♕e7 20.hxg5 hxg5 21.♘b5 a6 22.♘a3=∞. Simple and strong, however, would have been 15.♗xf6! ♘xf6 16.♖ad1± with domination in the centre.

7.♗xc4

7.♘d2 is no longer a good option due to 7...♘b6.

7...g6 8.0-0 ♗g7 9.h3

It is better to prevent 9.♖e1 ♘g4! 10.h3 ♘ge5 11.♘xe5 ♘xe5 12.♗b5+ ♘d7 13.e5 0-0 14.exd6 exd6 15.♘e4 ♘f6 16.♗g5 ♖b8 17.♕e2 ♗f5 and Black exchanges two minor pieces.

9...0-0 10.♖e1 ♖b8 11.♕c2

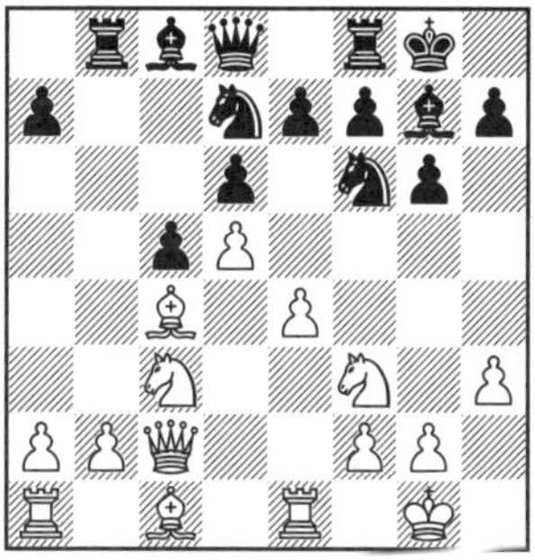

A1. 11...♘h5
A2. 11...♘e8
A3. 11...♘b6

A1. 11...♘h5

This is the only way for Black to prevent ♗f4. At the same time, he would be glad to trade some pieces by ...♘e5. However, White has a strong retort which eliminates this option and leaves Black wondering what to do further:

12.♗e2! ♕b6

Enabling ...♗a6. Exchanging the bishop would help Black equalise so White must cut across his plan by:

13.♘a4! ♕c7 14.♖b1

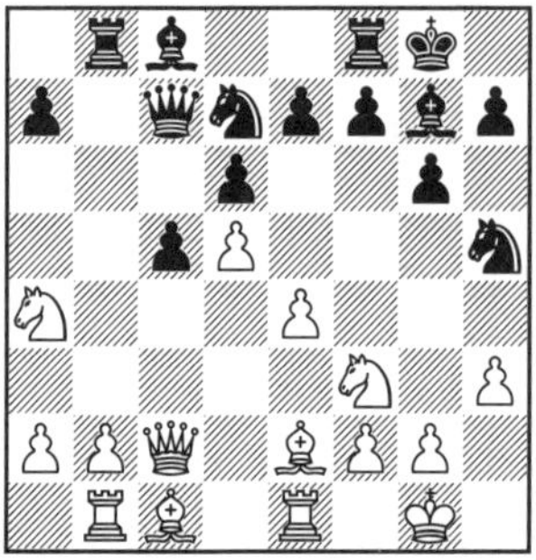

Black has not made any progress. His bishop is still stuck at c8, the knight on h5 is unemployed as well. The attempt to break in the centre with 14...e6 15.♘c3 ♘b6 should not be enough for equality as White's pieces are harmoniously attacking the opponent's weaknesses: 16.dxe6 ♗xe6 17.♘g5 ♘f6 18.♘b5 ♕e7 19.♗f4 ♖bd8 20.♖bd1±.

A2. 11...♘e8

Another typical Benko plan.

12.♗f4 ♕a5

Black has also tried 12...♘b6 13.♗f1 e6 14.dxe6 fxe6 and here Roeder-Baklan, Antwerp 1999 signed a draw, but White is clearly better after 15.♕d2±.

13.♗d2 ♕b6 14.b3 ♗a6 15.♖ab1 ♘c7 16.a4 ♘e5 17.♘xe5 ♗xe5

This is a model position for the Benko Declined and I devoted to it special attention in the commentaries to **game 9 O.Pavlov-Obolenskikh**, Tomsk 2008.

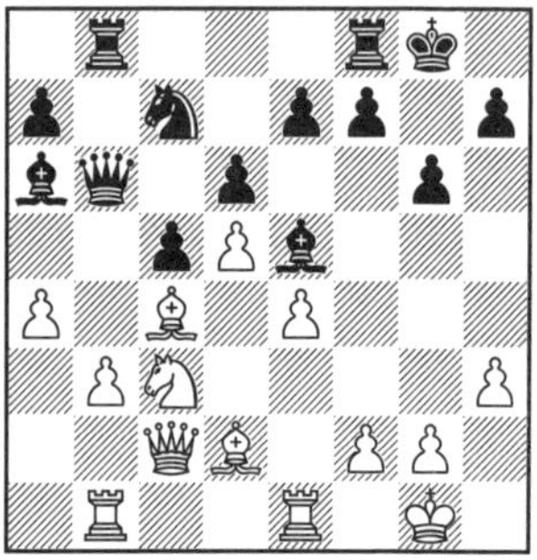

I prefer White's chances here.

A3. 11...♘b6 12.♗f1 ♗b7 13.♗f4 ♕c8 14.♖ad1±

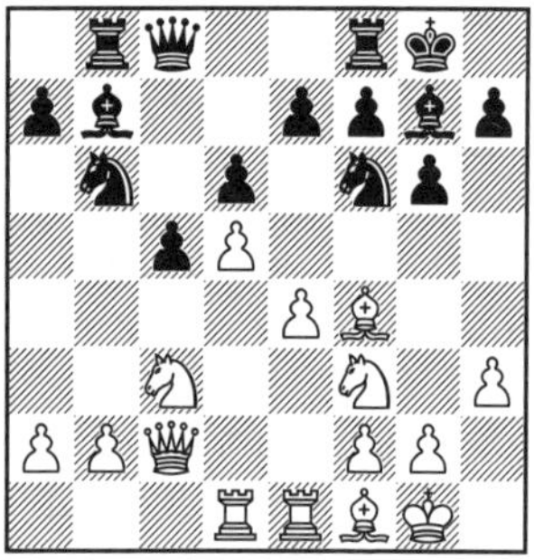

White intends to conquer the light squares on the left wing by a4, b3, restricting any counterplay.

14...♗a6 15.♗xa6 ♕xa6 16.e5 ♘e8 17.b3 ♖d8

White has a clear edge. Decent moves here are 18.a4 or 18.♕d2, maintaining the grip. Instead, the game Ding Liren-Nepomniachtchi, Sochi 2009, saw 18.♗g5. This was not necessary as Black would anyway play ...f6 or ...f5 at some moment. Still, after 18...f6 19.exf6 exf6 20.♗f4 ♕c8 21.♗g3 ♕d7, White would have been much better had he played 22.a4!±. In the game, he completely lost the track and ended up losing the d5-pawn without compensation following 22.♖e6?! ♘c8 23.♖de1 ♘c7 24.♖6e2 ♕f7 25.♕d3 (25.♘e4! ♘xd5 26.♕d2 ♖d7 27.♖d1 ♘db6 28.♘h2 with compensation) 25...h6 26.♗f4 f5 27.h4 ♖fe8 28.♗d2 ♖xe2 29.♖xe2 ♘b6 30.g3 ♘cxd5.

B. 4...♗b7

By attacking the centre, Black prevents any ideas with cxb5. The drawback of this line is that the b7-bishop might turn out rather useless at b7.

5.♕c2!

White used to play 5.a4 trying to stabilise the centre. In that case 5...bxc4 6.♘c3 e6 7.e4 would be a better for White version of the line 4.a4 where Black has more chances for equalising with ...♗a6 rather than with ...♗b7. It is well known since the game Rubinstein-Spielmann, Vienna 1922, that the tactical device 7...♘xe4 8.♘xe4 exd5 9.♘c3 d4 is countered by 10.♗xc4! dxc3 11.♗xf7+ (11.0-0!±) 11...♔xf7 12.♕b3+, with initiative.

Black experienced problems also with 5...b4 6.♘bd2 d6 7.e4 g6 8.♗d3 ♗g7 9.0-0 0-0 10.a5!, for instance, 10...♘bd7 11.h3 e6 12.a6 ♗c8 13.dxe6 fxe6 14.e5!± dxe5 15.♘g5, Shabalov-E.Hansen, Edmonton, 2008.

In this example the a5-pawn awkwardly restricts Black's queenside. Eventually, the second players improved their defence with:

5...♕a5+! 6.♗d2 b4 and in my game against Tregubov I was unable to prevent a further ...e5 with equality: 7.♕c2 d6 8.e4 ♘bd7 9.♗d3 g6 10.0-0 ♗g7 11.♗f4 0-0 12.♘bd2 ♘h5 13.♗g5 ♖ae8 14.♖ae1 e5 15.g3 ♗c8, Kir.Georgiev-Tregubov, Ohrid 2001.

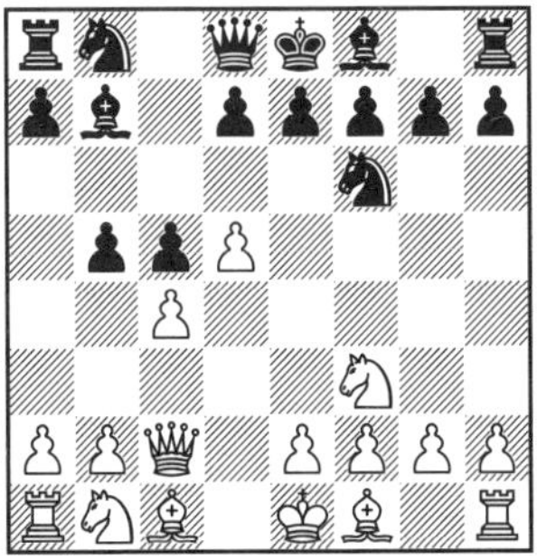

Main branches are:
B1. 5...bxc4
B2. 5...♘a6

B1. 5...bxc4 6.e4 e6 7.♗xc4 exd5 8.exd5

8...♗xd5

Black cannot ignore the d5-pawn since if it survived, it would be restricting all his play as in the game Renet-Wege, Cappelle la Grande 2008: 8...d6 9.0-0 ♗e7 10.♕b3 ♕c7 11.♖e1 0-0 12.♗g5 h6 13.♗h4 g5 14.♘xg5!±.

Another way of taking on d5 is 8...♕e7+, when 9.♗e3 is the only sensible reply. Instead, Dziuba-Balogh, Dresden 2007 saw 9.♔d1?! ♕d6 10.♖e1+ (10.♗g5 ♗xd5 11.♗xd5 as in Greenfeld-Van Haastert, Wijk aan Zee 1997 should be met by 11...♘xd5 12.♖e1+ ♗e7 13.♕d2 f6 14.♗f4 ♕xf4 15.♕xd5 ♘c6 16.♘c3 0-0-0∓) 10...♗e7 11.♗g5 ♗xd5 with Black's edge. Let us return to 9.♗e3. Then Black does win a pawn: 9...♘xd5 10.♗xd5 ♗xd5 11.♘c3 ♗e6, but White's overwhelming advantage in development should soon pay off with regaining the sacrificed material: 12.♖d1 ♘c6 13.0-0 ♕d8 14.♘e4 ♗e7 15.♗xc5 0-0 16.a3 ♖c8 17.b4 keeping pressure.

9.♗xd5 ♘xd5 10.0-0 ♗e7 11.♖e1

White has great compensation for the pawn due to his pressure on the e7-bishop. The tactical background of his idea is seen in the line 11...0-0 12.♕e4 ♘f6 13.♕xa8 ♕b6 14.♖xe7 ♘c6 15.♕xf8+, winning material. Therefore, Black should find a stable stand for his knight, and in practice he often chooses:

11...♘b4 12.♕e2 0–0

12...♘8c6 is strongly met by 13.♘c3 c4. What else?! The b4 knight is in a critical situation. 14.♕xc4, and now 14...♘c2 runs into 15.♖xe7+ ♘xe7 16.♘b5.

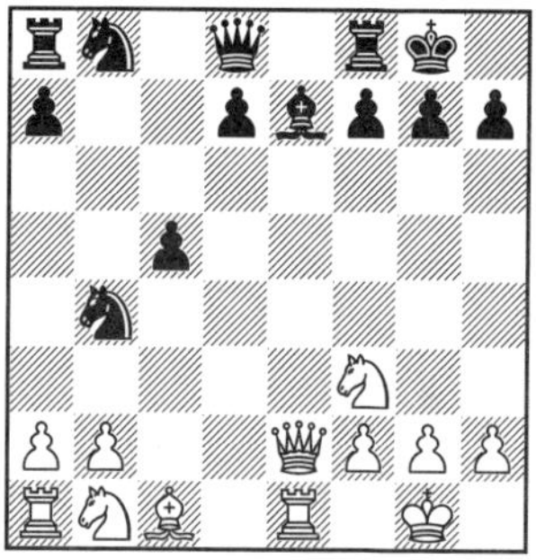

13.♕xe7

13.♘c3 might be even stronger. White would achieve total domination following 13...♖e8 14.a3 ♘4c6 15.♘d5 d6 16.♗g5 f6 17.♗f4 ♘e5 18.♗xe5 fxe5 19.♘xe5 ♗g5 20.♕c4 dxe5 21.h4± so Black should answer 13...♗f6 14.a3 ♘4c6 15.♗f4 d5 16.♕b5 ♕b6 17.♕d3 ♘e7 18.♘g5 g6 19.♘xd5 ♘xd5 20.♕xd5 ♕c6 21.♕d2±. The c5-pawn is weaker than the b2-one.

13...♕xe7 14.♖xe7 ♘c2 15.♗f4 ♘xa1 16.♘a3

White entrapped the a1-knight and the ending is somewhat better for him: 16...♘c6 17.♖e1 ♖fe8

18.♖xa1±, E.Toth-A.Popovics, Budapest 2007.

B2. 5...♘a6 6.a3!

White has achieved a perfect score of 4-0 with 6.♘c3?!, but I cannot recommend it. Black gets great compensation for the piece after 6... bxc4 7.e4 ♘b4 8.♕d1 e6 9.♗g5 (Or 9.a3 9...♘bxd5 10.exd5 exd5∓ and Black's pawn cluster in the centre is extremely annoying) 9...exd5 10.e5 ♗e7 11.exf6 ♗xf6 12.♗xf6 ♕xf6∓.

It is only a slight consolation that White can make a draw with 9.♗xc4 ♘xe4 10.♘xe4 exd5 11.♗g5 f6 12.♘e5 fxg5 (12...♕e7 13.♕h5+ ♔d8 14.♘f7+ ♔c7 15.♗f4+ ♔b6 16.♘fd6∞) 13.♕h5+ g6 14.♘xg6 hxg6 15.♕xg6+ ♔e7 16.♕f6+=.

6...bxc4

Lately Black has been trying to refrain from this move with 6... e6, but this is inconsistent because without capturing on c4, Black cannot destroy the enemy pawn centre:

7.e4 and now:

a) 7...exd5 8.cxd5 ♕e7 9.♘c3! (The game Giri-Chatalbashev, Vienna 2008 saw 9.♘bd2 c4 10.♗e2 ♘c5, when 11.d6!? ♕xd6 12.e5 ♘d3+ 13.♗xd3 cxd3 14.♕b3 ♕e6 15.♕xe6+ fxe6 16.exf6 gxf6 would have won a piece, but hardly the game.) 9...♘xd5 10.♘xb5 ♘b6 (10...♘ac7 11.♗g5 f6 12.0-0-0→) 11.♗f4 ♕xe4+ 12.♕xe4+ ♗xe4 13.0-0-0±.

b) 7...♕a5+ 8.♘bd2 exd5 9.cxd5 g6 (White also maintains his edge after 9...c4 10.♗e2 ♘c5 11.0-0 ♕a4 12.♕b1± due to his stable pawn centre.) and here both 10.♕c3± or 10.b4!? cxb4 11.♘b3!?↑ favour White.

7.e4 e6

The move order is important here. Black must attack d5 immediately since 7...♘c7 8.♗xc4 e6 would enable 9.d6 ♗xd6 10.e5 ♗xf3 11.exf6 ♗xg2 12.♖g1 ♕xf6 13.♖xg2±.

8.dxe6!

8.♗xc4!? exd5 9.exd5 ♘c7 10.♘c3! (Or 10.0-0? ♗xd5 11.♗xd5 ♘fxd5 12.♖e1+ ♘e6∓, Sachs-Miles, London 1993.) gives White fine compensation for the pawn, as Knaak points out. His variation goes 10...♘cxd5 12.♗xd5 ♘xd5 13.0-0 ♗e7 14.♖e1

14...♖c8 15.♕f5 ♘f6 16.♗h6 ♔f8. Here 17.♗f4! maintains the pressure. Undoubtedly White will regain the pawn, but he will have to exchange some pieces along the way and his advantage might wane in the process.

Let us return to 8.dxe6! Somebody might argue that taking on e6 means a collapse of White's opening strategy. In fact, this is only a temporary concession since the e-pawn will move forward, gaining space in the centre.

Knaak writes in *Chessbase Magazine 114:* “Black has to find a few precise moves, but then he has nothing to fear.” Well, nothing except for the result, I would add. Two correspondence games are pretty convincing for me.

8...fxe6 9.e5

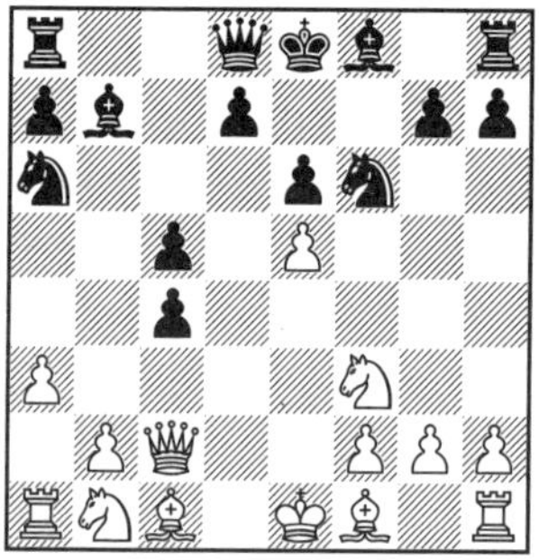

9...♗xf3

If Black does not take the chance to cripple our pawn structure, he will be simply worse after 9...♘e4 10.♗xc4 ♕a5+ 11.♘bd2 ♘xd2 12.♗xd2 ♕c7 13.0-0-0± as in Schafranietz-Gruber, Eppingen 2004.

Rybka prefers 9...♕a5+ (planning 10.♘c3 ♘b4!) 10.♘bd2 ♗xf3 11.gxf3 ♘d5 12.♗xc4↑

The white pieces are much more active. They soon will be targeted on the kingside. After castling and ♔h1, the rook will go to g1, while the b1-knight reaches d6, for instance:

12...♗e7 13.0-0 0-0 14.♕e4 ♘ac7 15.♗d3 g6 16.♘c4 ♕a4 17.♗h6 ♖f7 18.♘d6±.

10.gxf3 ♘d5 11.♗xc4 ♘ac7 12.h4

This is not White’s only attractive possibility, but it is holding good enough so far.

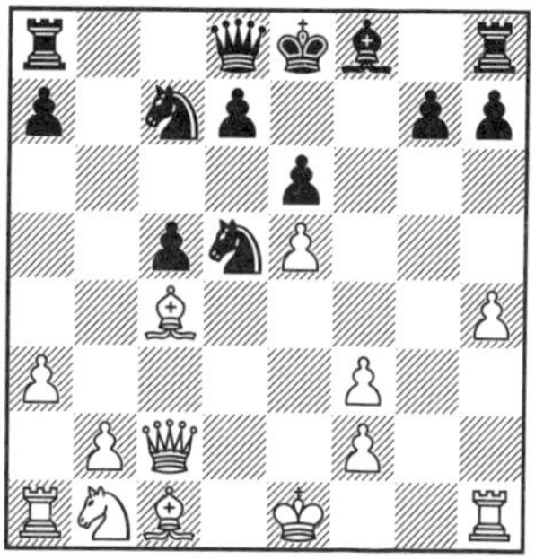

This position seems to be critical. The source **game 10 Pankratov-Wang Mong Lin**, email ICCF, 1997 went on 12...♕b8 13.♘c3 with a clear edge for White.

Knaak suggests as an improvement:

12...d6

Unfortunately, he considers only 13.♗d3 ♕d7 14.♗xh7?! 0-0-0. In my opinion, 12...d6 is positionally dubious, since Black voluntarily opens up play against our bishop pair. White does not need any extra pawns. He should be much better due to his active pieces, so any developing moves should be good. The main targets are the c5-pawn and the black king. Most natural looks 13.♘c3!? dxe5 14.♗d2 ♕d7 (14...♗e7 15.♖g1 ♗f6 16.0-0-0) 15.0-0-0 0-0-0 16.♘e4 ♕f7 17.♗e2±, but 13.♗d3 is not bad either. Only after 13...♕d7 White should choose 14.♘c3 (or 14.♗g5 dxe5 15.♘c3). 14...dxe5 (14...♘xc3 15.bxc3 dxe5 16.c4±) 15.♗g5

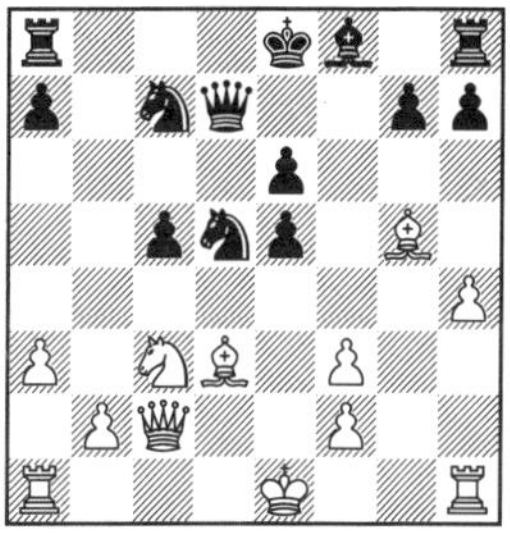

By the way, 15.♗e3 0-0-0 16. 0-0-0 ♕c6 17.♗xh7± is also in White's favour, but the text is more logical. In the diagram position Black has two sensible answers:

a) 15...♘xc3 16.bxc3 c4 17.♗xh7 ♗e7 18.♖d1 ♘d5 19.♕g6+ ♔f8 20.♗h6 ♗f6 21.♖xd5 ♕f7 22.♖d7 ♕xg6 23.♗xg6 ♖xh6 24.h5± and Black is practically a rook down.

b) 15...♗e7 16.0-0-0 c4 (16... 0-0-0 17.♘e4 ♕c6 18.♗xe7 ♘xe7 19.♘xc5) 17.♗xh7± 0-0-0 18.♘xd5 ♘xd5 19.♕xc4+ ♔b7 20.♕b3+ ♔a8 21.♗e4±.

Summarising: This alledgedly "main" line of Black against 4.♘f3 is probably one of the most pleasant for White who enjoys the bishop pair and better development.

C. 4...b4

This move came into fashion in the 80ies in response to White's attempts to use the move order with 4.♘f3 as a lead-in to cxb5. In the early games White tried to prepare e4-e5, but soon it became evident that Black can parry this positional threat by pushing ...e5 himself. A typical example is the game G.Agzamov-Plaskett, Sochi, 1984: 5.♘bd2 g6 6.b3 ♗g7 7.♗b2 0-0 8.e4 d6 9.♕c2 e5! 10.dxe6 ♗xe6 11.g3 ♘c6 and Black has easy play on the dark squares. All the attempts to improve this plan were unsuccessful. Black always managed to put in ...e5, blocking the position, for instance: 5.♘bd2 g6 6.e4 ♗g7 7.♗d3 d6 8.0-0 0-0 9.♖e1 e5 10.♘f1 a5=, Vyzmanavin-Kalegin, St Petersburg 1996.

Then the first players discovered that the early advance of the b-pawn offered a lever for opening the queenside and began playing:

5.a3

Black is unable to maintain symmetry with ...a5 so he should decide here which pawn structure on the left wing is easier to defend: with a3xb4 c5xb4 or without a pawn on b4. Both have drawbacks and give White some pull.

Note that White should better play a3 on the fifth move since later Black could take on a3 obtaining a solid position; 5.♘bd2 g6 6.e4 d6 7.a3 bxa3. White's knight is on d2 instead of its ideal place c3 and that makes the difference with line B1. The game Levitt-Hebden, Hastings 1990 went on 8.♖xa3 ♘a6 11.♖e1 (11.e5!? ♘g4 12.exd6 exd6 13.♖e1 ♘b4 14.♗b1) 11...♘b4 12.♗b1 e5=, Levitt-Hebden, Hastings 1990.

Black's main responses in the position on the previous diagram are:

C1. 5...bxa3?!
C2. 5...♘a6
C3. 5...a5
C4. 5...g6

I should also mention:

5...e6.

I found only two games in Megabase and they are not too convincing. My first thought was to sacrifice a pawn and see what happens: 6.e4 ♘xe4 7.♗d3 ♘f6 8.0-0 ♗e7 9.♖e1 0-0 10.♗f4 ♘h5 11.♗e3 ♗b7 and we have not accomplished much. The problem is that we cannot prevent the castling by 8.♗f4 due to 8...exd5 9.cxd5 ♘xd5.

Then I tried to disguise my idea with 6.♗f4, intending to meet 6...♘a6, for instance, with 7.e4! ♘xe4 8.♗d3 ♘f6 9.0-0⩱. In this line Black cannot castle since he will lose the e7-bishop.

However, I'm not sure how to proceed after 6...♗b7.

Then I checked a more straightforward way:

6.axb4 cxb4 7.♘bd2. White is about to play e4 with space advantage. Black can take the pawn and suffer after 7...exd5 8.cxd5 ♘xd5 9.♘c4 ♘b6 10.e4 ♗b7 11.♗f4 ♘c6 (11...♘xc4 12.♗xc4 ♗e7 13.0-0 0-0 14.♕d3⩱) 12.♕d2. The b4-pawn will fall soon and White will still keep the initiative.

Of course, White can also play:

6.♗g5!?, transposing to line D from Part 6 – The Blumenfeld Gambit. This is a modern variation which has been constantly evolving lately. I think that White can expect to obtain an advantage there.

C1. 5...bxa3?!

If Black was aiming for this pawn structure, he had better choose 5...♘a6, intending to meet 6.axb4 with 6...♘xb4 as in line B2. The text practically presents White with an extra tempo.

6.♖xa3 g6 7.♘c3 ♗g7 8.e4 d6

9.e5!

Of course, 9.♗d3 0-0 10.h3 ♘a6 11.0-0 ♘b4 12.♗b1 ♖e8 13.♗f4 ♘d7 14.♕e2 as in the game Kopylov-Lange, Kiel 2003, is also pleasant for White, but the text is more straightforward and gives White a clear advantage. Notice that Black cannot prevent this breakthrough by 7...d6 8.e4 ♘bd7 due to 9.♕a4 ♕c7 10.♘b5 ♕b8 11.♕a5 ♘b6 12.♘xa7. Going to d7 with the other knight – 8...♘fd7, is also dubious since we can immediately launch an attack by 9.h4 when 9...h5 will seriously weaken the kingside.

9...♘g4

Or 9...dxe5 10.♘xe5 0-0 11.♗e2 ♘e8 12.♗f4±.

10.exd6 exd6 11.♕e2+!

The point is that the endgame would be difficult so Black loses the right to castle.

11...♔f8 12.h3 ♘e5 13.♘xe5 ♗xe5 14.♗h6+ ♔g8 15.♕d2±.

C2. 5...♘a6 6.axb4

6.g3 is too slow. This development is effective only if Black plays ...e6. Instead, 6...g6 7.♗g2 d6 8.b3 ♗g7 9.♗b2 0-0 10.0-0, Davies-Votava, Rishon Le Ziyyon 1993, 10... bxa3! 11.♖xa3 ♘b4 12.♘c3 ♗d7 13.♖e1 ♘e4 14.♕c1 ♘xc3 15.♗xc3 ♗xc3 16.♕xc3 a5= simplifies Black's game.

6...♘xb4

This recapture may not be best, but it is at least consistent.

6...cxb4 casts doubts on Black's previous move. Nonetheless, it is not too clear how White should exploit it. For instance, 7.♗e3 does not gain control over c5 due to 7... e6 8.♘bd2 ♗b7∞. The same happens after 7.♘bd2 ♘c5 8.♘b3 e6. In both cases Black holds on thanks to ...e6 when his dark-squared bishop works well on the f8-c5 diagonal. Therefore White should prefer:

7.g3 ♘c5 8.♗g2 d6 and now we can already contest the dark squares in the centre more successfully: 9.♘bd2 g6 10.♘b3 ♘fd7 11.♘fd4±. The hole on c6 and the backward a-pawn will be a source of constant concern for Black.

7.♘c3 d6 8.e4

8...g6

Black allows 9.e5, but we'll see that this breakthrough is not too dangerous in the current position due to tactical reasons. 8...e5 would have been clearly inferior owing to 9.dxe6.

9.♗e2

Commonly White should not miss an opportunity to push 9.e5.

However, Black holds on after 9...♘g4 10.exd6 ♗f5! when 11.♕a4+ ♗d7 12.♘b5 exd6 is unclear. So we should analyse 10.e6!? fxe6 11.♘g5. The common 11...♗g7 12.♗e2 exd5 13.♘xd5 h6 14.♘xb4 hxg5 15.♗xg4± gives White some initiative, but the outwardly risky 11...♗h6! 12.♗e2 ♗xg5 13.♗xg5 ♘e5 14.0-0 ♘f7 15.♗e3 0-0∞ covers all the approaches to the black king.

9...♗g7 10.0–0 0–0 11.♗f4

White's game is a bit easier since his pieces are harmoniously developed and his space advantage is very stable. See **game 8 I.Sokolov-Kir.Georgiev**, Sarajevo 1998.

C3. 5...a5

This move is logical, but it delays development and White can try to punish that by tactical means. As a whole, this move order has no advantages over 5...g6, followed by ...a5 later (line B4). On the contrary, it offers White extra options.

6.♘bd2 g6 7.e4 d6 8.axb4 cxb4

9.c5!?

9.♗d3 ♗g7 10.0-0 0-0 11.♘b3 ♘bd7 transposes to line B4 which is also pleasant for White.

9...dxc5 10.♗b5+ ♗d7

Hertneck suggests 10...♘fd7 11.e5 ♕b6, but 12.♕a4 ♗a6 13.♕xa5 ♗xb5 14.♕xa8 ♗a6 is insufficient for equality. White has many good options, e.g. 15.e6 fxe6 16.dxe6 ♕xe6+ 17.♕e4 ♕f5 18.♔d1 ♗g7 19.♖e1±.

11.♗c4 ♗g7

White has full compensation due to his pawn majority in the centre. He can try to convert his edge by making an advanced passer on d6 and combining central play with a kingside attack. Black's last move concedes even more space, but at least avoids making more targets. Seirawan-D.Gurevich, Estes Park, 1986, saw instead 11...e6 12.0-0 exd5? 13.exd5 ♗h6 14.♖e1+ ♔f8 15.♘e5 ♔g7 16.♘xf7! and the game did not last long. Relatively better is 12...♗g7, but 13.dxe6 ♗xe6 14.e5 ♘fd7 15.♗xe6 fxe6 16.♕b3 ♖a6 17.♘e4 0-0 18.♘fg5 ♕e7 19.f4 leaves Black in binds.

12.e5 ♘g4 13.♕e2 0–0 14.h3 ♘h6 15.♘e4 ♘f5 16.0–0

Of course White should not hurry to regain the pawn in exchange for the initiative after 16.♘xc5?! ♕c7 17.♘xd7 ♘xd7 18.♗f4 ♘b6.

16...♕b6 17.♗f4 a4 18.♖fd1 ♘a6 19.d6±

White is steadily increasing his edge, Gostisa-D.Ilic, Kladovo 1990.

C4. 5...g6

6.♘bd2!?

The main battle in the next moves will be about control over c5 and c6. Practice has proved that tactical solutions do not favour White:

6.axb4 cxb4 7.e4 (7.♕d4 a5 8.c5 d6 9.cxd6 exd6 10.♗g5 ♗g7 11.♘bd2 0-0 and White is way behind in development) 7...♘xe4 8.♕d4 ♘f6 9.♖xa7 ♖xa7 10.♕xa7 ♘a6 11.♗e3 d6 12.♗e2 ♗g7 13.0-0 ♕d7=, V.Popov-Tregubov, St Petersburg 2004. Black can chase to trade the enemy queen from b7.

I would like to draw your attention to the fianchetto setup:

6.axb4 cxb4 7.♗e3 a5 8.g3 ♗g7 9.♗g2 0-0 10.0-0 d6 11.♘bd2 ♗d7 12.h3 a4 13.♘d4 ♕c8 14.♔h2 ♕a6 15.f4 ♖c8 16.♗g1 ♗e8 17.e4, Razuvaev-Loncar, Maribor 1996:

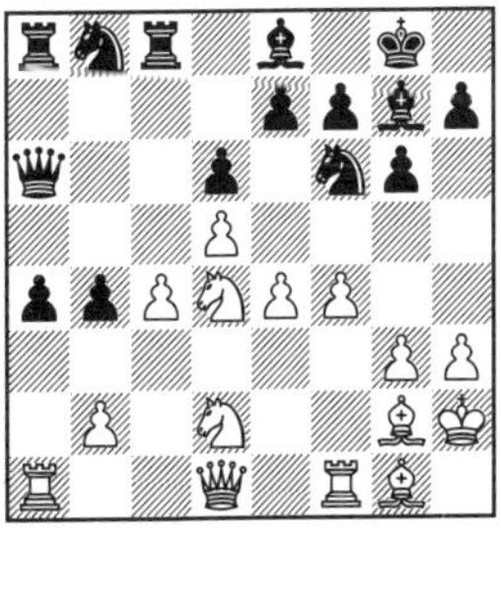

White's initiative in the centre should be more dangerous than Black's advanced a-pawn. However, this example only reinforces my conviction that White cannot make progress without e2-e4 so why not put it in early in the opening. It is also questionable should White spend a tempo on g3. It seems that natural development serves White's plans better.

The main drawback of 6.axb4 is that Black gets the opportunity to occupy c5 by directing both his knights toward that square – ♘f6-d7! and ♘b8-a6. My idea is to wait for the b8-knight to go to d7 and only then exchange on b4. The delay of a3xb4 is exploitable only by b4xa3, but then Black will practically abandon any hope for active play. I'll discuss this structure in line B4a.

6...♗g7 7.e4 0–0

This looks more safe than 7...d6 8.axb4 cxb4 which enables the pawn sac from line B3: 9.c5 dxc5 10.♗b5+ ♗d7 11.♗c4. However, I suggest to refrain from it since Black saved a tempo on ...a5 and this gives him decent chances to defend after 11...e6. Instead, 11...♗g4 12.♕c2 ♗xf3 13.♘xf3 0-0 14.0-0 ♘bd7 15.♖d1 ♘b6 16.♗b5 a5 17.♗e3 was slightly better for White in Komarov-Belotti, Belfort 1991.

8.♗d3 d6 9.0–0

Do not waste a tempo on h3. Black would have little chances to organise counterplay without his light-squared bishop.

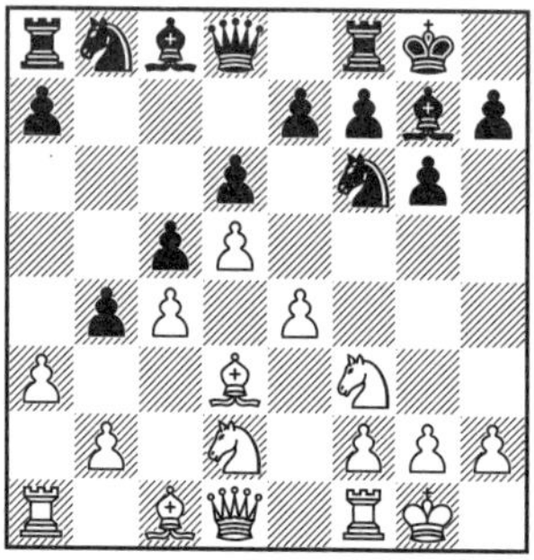

It has been easy so far, but now Black is faced with a crucial decision. He must define the pawn structure.

C4a. 9...bxa3
C4b. 9...♘bd7

9...♘fd7 is rather useles here as the knight cannot go to c5. We could launch a kingside attack with 10.h4 ♘a6 11.h5 bxa3 12.♖xa3 ♘b4 13.hxg6 fxg6 (13...hxg6 14.♗e2 ♘f6 15.♘g5) 14.♗e2 ♘f6 15.♘g5↑.

C4a. 9...bxa3

Black voluntarily cripples his queenside pawn chain. This is however justified by the awkward position of the knight which can no longer land on c3 in one move. Although this statement is literally correct, we can still redirect the d2-knight via b1 to c3 and that is perhaps White's best plan!

10.♖xa3 ♘a6

The game Duppe-S.Vajda, Gyula 2000 went on 10...e5. This move blocks the centre, bringing about a KID pawn structure. I often observe that Benko devotees do not feel comfortable when their g7-bishop is clogged by their own pawn at e5. In the above-mentioned game, after 11.♘b3 Black let the white knight to a5 and was clearly worse: 11...a6?! 12.♘a5 ♘h5 13.♖e1 h6 14.♗d2 ♘f4 15.♗f1 g5 16.g3 ♘h3+ 17.♗xh3 ♗xh3 18.♘xg5! hxg5 19.g4.

Black should have tried 11...♘a6 when 12.♘a5 would be parried by 12...♘b4. White should firstly take control of b4 by 12.♗d2 ♕b6 (12...♘b4 13.♗xb4 cxb4 14.♖a5 ♘h5 15.♖e1 ♘f4 16.♗f1 favours White who will soon push c4-c5.) 13.♕c2 (intending to double rooks on the a-file) 13...♘b4 (13...♗g4 14.♖fa1 ♘c7 15.♗a5 ♕b7 stumbles to 16.♘xe5 dxe5 17.♘xc5±) 14.♗xb4 ♕xb4 15.♖fa1 ♕b6 16.♘a5. White's initiative on the queenside is rapidly developing while Black has not even started play on the opposite wing: 16...♗d7 17.♖b3 ♕d8 18.♖b7 ♕c8 19.b4 cxb4 20.♖xb4 threatening ♘b7.

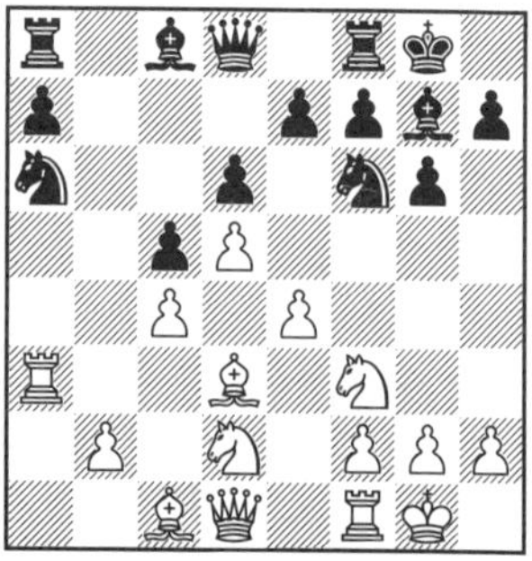

11.♘b1!?

The opening stage is over and it is time for planning the middlegame.

White has an advantage in the centre which is a stable ground for a flank attack. Obviously we have no advantage on the kingside so that the attack should be focused on the left wing. We have a better pawn structure there and the a-pawn is a target. However, it is well known that only one weakness is generally not enough for success. Where to look for a second front of attack?

That could be only the e-file and the d6-pawn. So we should be aiming for e4-e5.

White is still not fully developed for 11.e5 though. Concrete calculation shows that after 11...dxe5 12.♘xe5 Black can counterattack in the centre: 12...♘b4 13.♘df3 e6 14.dxe6 ♗xe6 15.♘g5 ♕b6 16.♘xe6 ♕xe6 17.♖e1 ♖fe8=.

Therefore, we should improve our pieces first, still bearing in mind e4-e5 as a main objective. The problem is that Black will hardly be sleeping and he will certainly anticipate our plans by playing ...e7-e5 himself, for instance: 11.♖e1 ♘b4 12.♗b1 (12.h3!) 12...e5! Black successfully petrified the centre. The game Levitt-Hebden, Hastings 1990 went on 13.♘f1 ♘h5 14.♗g5 ♕b6 15.♕c1 ♗d7 16.♘g3, when the simple 16...♘xg3 17.hxg3= would have left White without any active plan.

It is obvious that White should prepare to meet ...e5 by d5xe6. Then he will need firm control of d5 and protection of the c4-pawn. Hence the manoeuvre 11.♘b1!? – the knight goes to c3 while the bishop will remain on the f1-a6 diagonal in order to protect c4. The game might develop:

11....♘b4 12.h3 e5

The waiting game 12...♘d7 13.♘c3 ♕c7 allows White to pursue his main positional aim with 14.♖e1 a6 15.♗f4.

13.dxe6 ♗xe6

White is better following 13... fxe6 14.♘c3 ♗b7 15.♗b1.

14.♘c3 ♕b6 15.♘g5 ♗c8 16.♖e1 ♗b7 17.♗b1

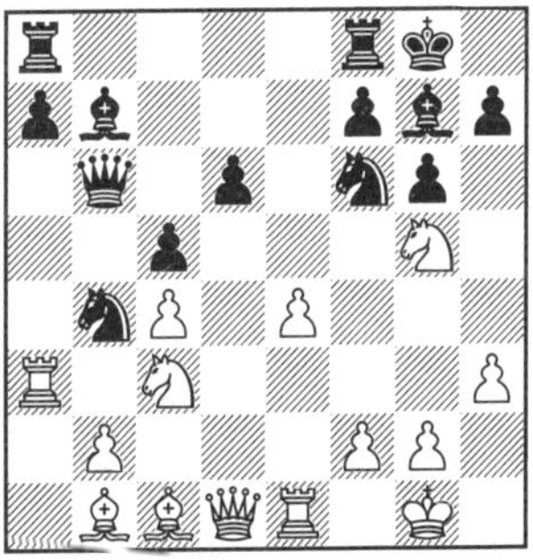

Black has activated his pieces, but his initiative is temporary. It will gradually evaporate, leaving White with the better pawn structure and possibilities for further expansion. A logical continuation would be 17...♖fe8 18.♗f4 h6 19.♘f3 ♖e6 20.♘a4 ♕c7 21.♖ae3 ♖ae8 22.♘c3±.

C4b. 9...♘bd7 10.axb4!

Now that the queen's knight took the d7-square, we can alter the pawn structure favourably. This exchange fixes two targets – the pawns on b4 and a7, and makes posssible the breakthrough c4-c5 in future.

10...cxb4 11.♘b3 a5

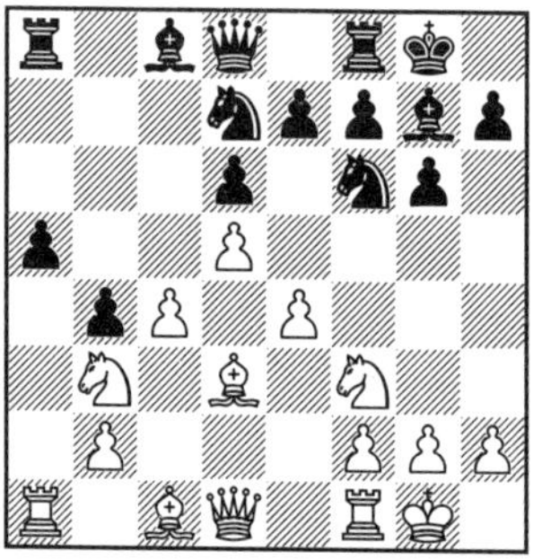

12.h3!

An important prophylactic move which prepares 12.♗e3. In **game 7 K.Georgiev-Mila novic**, Bar 2008 I developed the bishop immediately and obtained an advantage after 12...♗b7 13.♕d2 ♘g4 14.♗d4 ♗xd4 15.♘fxd4 ♕b6 16.♖a4. It is instructive to see how Black was struggling in the the midlegame with his stranded pawn at a5. However, he had 12...♘g4 13.♗d4 a4! with fair counterplay.

The text deprives Black of that resource and leaves him with a cramped position. White should avoid exchanges in such situations. Moreover, his dark-squared bishop controls the vital squares c5 and b6.

12...♗b7

Now White fixes the black pawn on a5 and his game is much easier. The problem is that Black does not seem to have a better alternative as 12...a4 loses a pawn to 13.♘bd4 ♘c5 14.♘c6 ♕c7 15.♘fd4 a3 (15...♘fxe4 16.♘b5) 16.bxa3 ♗b7 17.♘xb4 ♘fxe4 18.♘b5 ♕a5 19.♖b1±, while the other natural move 12...♕c7 will attract the attention of White's knight which will leap to b5 with a tempo: 13.♘fd4 (13.♗d2 is also slightly better for White) 13...a4 14.♘b5 ♕b7 15.♘3d4 ♘c5 16.♘c6, with a clear edge, e.g. 16...b3 17.♖e1 ♖e8 18.e5 dxe5 19.♘xe5.

13.♖a4 e6 14.♗e3 exd5 15.cxd5 ♖e8 16.♘fd2 ♘h5 17.♘c4 ♕f6 18.♕d2

White has a huge advantage, Petkov-Jianu, Galatzi 2007.

D. 4...g6 5.cxb5 a6

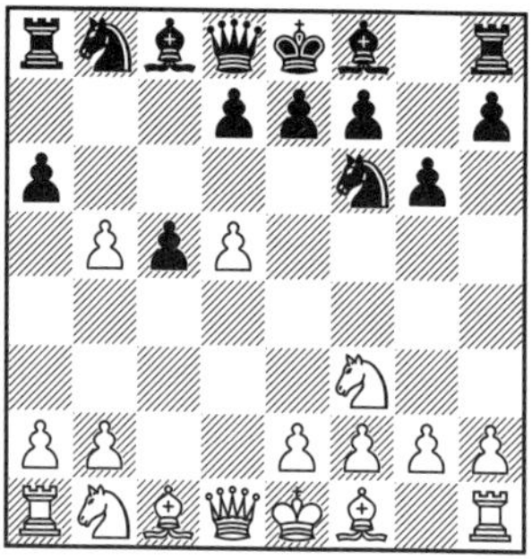

Now we play:

6.b6

Thus we reach our main line from Part 1.

Alternatives outside our repertoire are:

1. 6.♘c3 axb5 7.d6

This is hardly a good option. This variation looked promising some 20 years ago and it is still boasting with nice statistics, but White has nothing after 7...exd6! 8.e4 b4 9.♘b5 ♗a6 10.♗f4 ♕b6 11.a4 ♘c6 12.♗xd6 ♗xb5 13.♗xb5 ♗xd6 14.♕xd6 ♘xe4 15.♕d5= (15.♕d3 is rather risky) 15...♘f6 16.♕d6 ♘e4 with repetition.

2. 6.e4 ♘xe4 7.♕c2

Pinski advocates this sacrifice, but lately no one seems to be willing to part with his central pawn.7...♕a5+

7...♘d6!? 8.♕xc5 axb5 is unclear: 9.♕d4 (9.♘c3 ♗g7 10.♘xb5 0-0↑ Safarian-Allen, Canberra 1999 is a bad alternative.) 9...♖g8 10.♗f4 ♗g7 11.♕d2 ♘e4 12.♕b4 ♗b7∞.

8.♘bd2 ♘d6

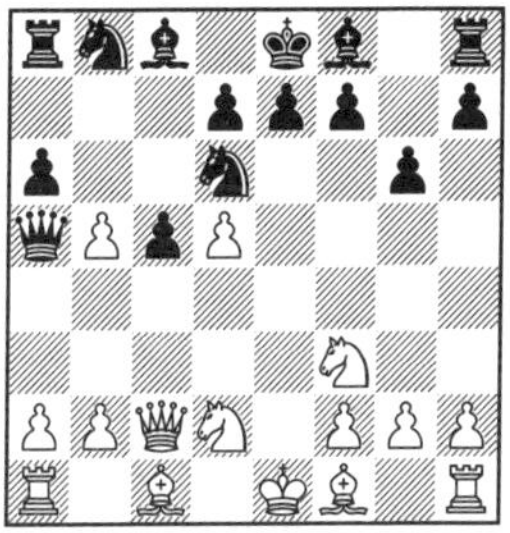

9.♕xc5

Here 9.b4!? cxb4 10.♗b2 is the only way to mess things up. At least White weakens Black's position and gets some compensation after 10...f6 (10...♖g8!? – Rybka) 11.♗d3 ♗g7 12.0-0 axb5∞.

9...♗g7 10.♗d3 axb5 11.0-0 b4 12.♕c2 when instead of 12...♕xd5?? 13.♗e4, Perez-Fuentes, Havana 1999, Black should have simply castled, retaining a better game.

3. 6.♕c2 axb5

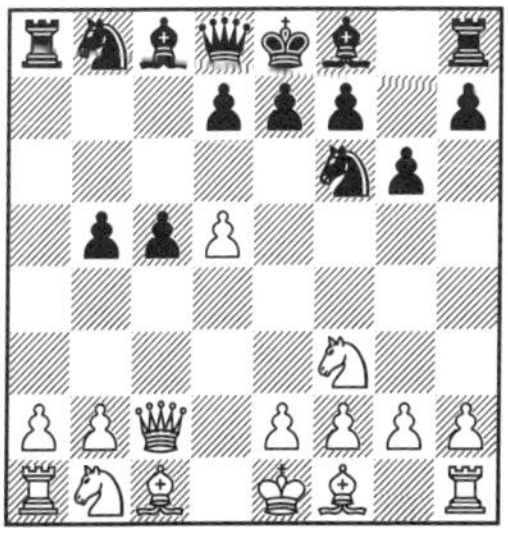

7.e4

7.♕xc5 is very risky and leads to hazy complications with good compensation for Black: 7...♘a6!? 8.♕d4 ♗g7 9.e4 ♗b7 10.♗xb5 (10.♘c3 might be better, 10...b4!? 11.♗xa6 ♗xa6 12.♕xb4 d6∞) 10...♕a5+ 11.♘c3 ♘b4 12.0-0 ♘c2 13.♕d3 ♘xa1 14.♗g5 0-0 15.♖xa1 ♗a6 16.e5 ♗xb5 17.♘xb5 ♖fb8 18.♘c3 ♘g4 19.♗xe7 ♖xb2 20.♖f1 ♘xe5∓, Vegh-Adrian, Hampstead 1998.

7...♕a5+ 8.♗d2 ♕a4 9.♕xa4 (9.♕xc5 ♕xe4+ 10.♗e3 ♘a6↑) 9...bxa4 10.♘c3 ♗g7 11.e5 (11.a3 d6 12.♗d3 ♘bd7 13.♗b5 0-0⇄) 11...♘g4 12.♗f4 f6 13.exf6 ♘xf6= 14.a3 0-0 15.0-0-0 d6 16.♖e1 ♖a7!=, Bareev-Topalov, Sarajevo 2000.

Summarising: These alternatives to 6.b6 lead to sharp play with serious Black initiative. If we wanted to play such positions, we should have better taken on a6.

E. 4...d6 5.cxb5 a6 6.b6

This line can be of independent significance only if Black does not play ...g6 now or on the next move.

I do not see any benefits for Black, on the contrary, in some lines White gets additional options. For instance, he can play e4 without ♘c3 and develop the queen's knight to d2, trying to exploit the placement of Black's queen on b6. Most probably, however, play will transpose to the main lines:

6...♕xb6

Here 6...a5 has no reason as White can answer 7.e4!

Lately 6...♘bd7 comes into fashion: 7.♘c3 and now:

a) 7...♘xb6

Black's idea is to meet 8.e4 by 8...♗g4 is another option. White might try to exploit the particular move order by 9.h3 ♗xf3 10.♕xf3 g6 11.♗e2 ♗g7 12.0-0 0-0 13.♗g5 and possibly retreat the queen to e3. However, I recommend the trivial:

8.a4, when 8...♖b8 is hardly a good idea in view of threat e4-e5: 9.a5 ♘a8 10.e4 ♘c7 (10...♘d7 11.♗c4 g6 12.♕e2±) 11.e5±.

b) 7...♖b8

This is a bit too flexible. Black is waiting for ♘d2 in order to meet it with ...♘xb6, or for a4, when ...♖xb6 would be quite good. As usual, there is no free lunch. White all these finesses, Black misses to put pressure on b2. That allows White to develop the bishop to f4 and forget about a4 in favour of some central action:

8.e4 g6 9.♗e2

9.♗d3 also looks attractive here: 9...♗g7 10.0-0 0-0 11.h3 ♖xb6 12.♕e2.

9...♗g7 10.0-0 0-0 11.♗f4!?

11.♘d2 ♘xb6 12.a4 ♘fd7 13.a5 ♘a8 14.♘c4 ♘c7 15.♘a4 ♘b5 16.♘ab6 ♘d4!, Golichenko-Baklan, Kiev 2008 is level.

11...♕xb6

Or 11...♖xb6 12.♖b1 followed by 13. ♘d2.

12.♖b1 ♘g4 13.♘d2 ♘ge5 14.♗e3 ♘f6

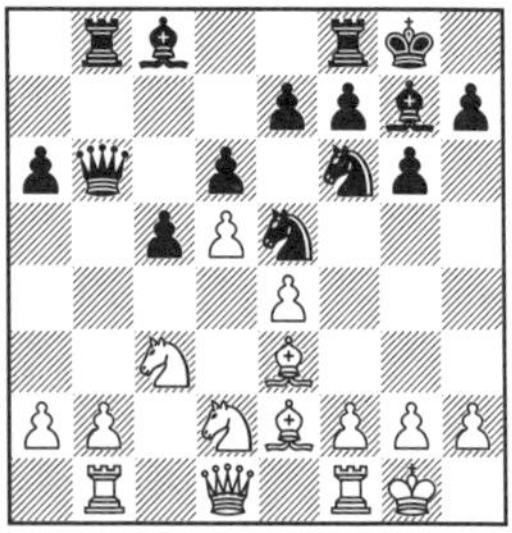

Here, in Palliser-Hebden, rapid, Halifax 21.11.2009, White missed 15.b4!±.

7.♘c3 g6 8.♘d2

Thus we have reached the main line, see Part 1. This particular position is covered on page 32.

Part 2

Complete Games

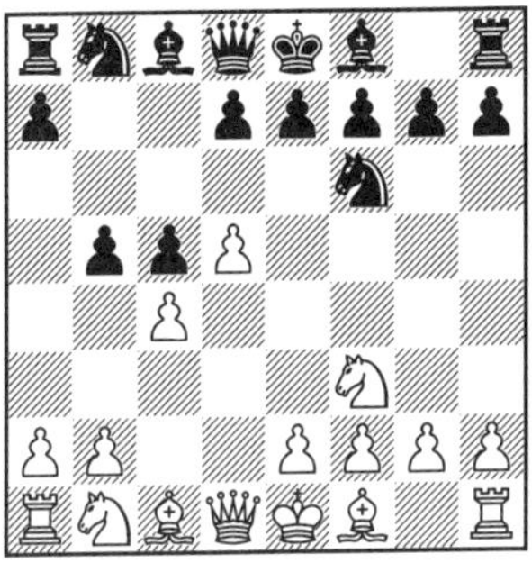

1.d4 ♘f6 2.c4 c5 3.d5 b5 4.♘f3!

7. Kiril Georgiev–Milanovic
Bar 2008

1.d4 ♘f6 2.♘f3 c5 3.d5 b5 4.c4 b4 5.a3 g6 6.♘bd2 ♗g7 7.e4 0–0 8.♗d3 d6 9.0–0 ♘bd7 10.axb4 cxb4 11.♘b3 a5

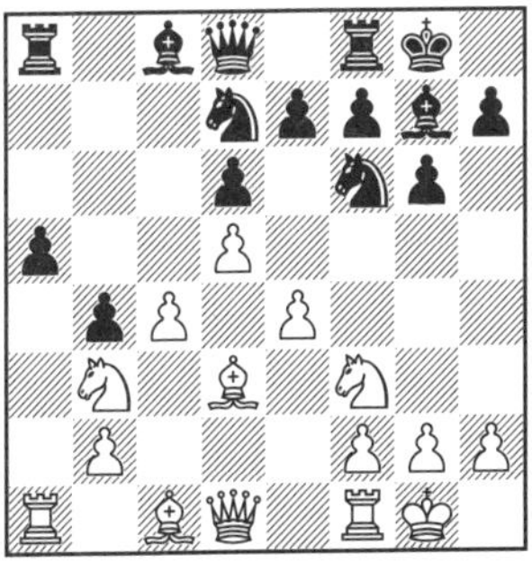

We see a typical pawn structure for the variation with 4...b4. White has two possible ways to break through the centre – c4-c5 or e4-e5. In both cases White needs to control the c5-square or the black knight would be too strong there. So far, the b3-knight is restraining its d7-counterpart, but only one move – ...a5-a4 – might change that radically. The whole Black's counterplay depends on that push. Therefore, I thought about 12.♖a4. It effectively prevents ...a4, but such a solution is too mechanical and delays development. Black can answer 12...♘g4 13.♗e2 ♘de5, clearing d7 for the bishop. Then 14.c5 dxc5 15.♘xe5 ♘xe5 16.♘xc5 ♕c7 17.♗e3 ♘d7 is only equal.

The best option is 12 h3! and Black should be struggling without sufficient space for his pieces. It is analysed in the "Step by Step" chapter.

I decided to rely on common sense and complete development:

12.♗e3

Now Black should have opted for 12...♘g4 13.♗d4 a4! After trading dark-squared bishops, Black's queen will be very comfortable on b6 or c5 and that will compensate the vulnerability of the queenside pawns:

a) 14.♗xg7 ♔xg7 15.♘bd4 ♘ge5 16.♘xe5 ♘xe5 17.♗e2 ♕b6 18.♘b5 b3 19.♕d4 ♕xd4 20.♘xd4 ♘d7 21.♘xb3 ♖b8 22.♘d4 ♖xb2 23.♖xa4 ♘c5 24.♖a7 e5. This is a forced draw although White still has some initiative after 25.dxe6 ♘xe6 26.♘xe6+ ♗xe6 27.♖e1 ♖c8 28.g3 ♗xc4 29.♗xc4 ♖xc4 30.♖e3 ♖b8 31.h4.

b) 14.♕d2 ♘de5 15.♗e2 (15.♘xe5 ♗xe5 16.h3 ♗xd4 17.♘xd4 ♘e5 18.♗e2 ♕b6 19.♔h2 20.f4 ♘d7 21.♘c2 ♘c5 22.♕xb4 ♕xb4 23.♘xb4 ♘xe4=) 15...♘xf3+ 16.♗xf3 e5 17.dxe6 ♗xe6 18.♗xg7 ♔xg7 19.♗xg4 (19.♘d4 ♘e5 20.♕xb4 ♗xc4 21.♖fc1 ♖b8 22.♕d2 ♕b6=) 19...♗xg4 20.♘d4 ♕b6 21.♘b5 ♕c5. Suddenly the a4-pawn turns into a considerable force: 22.h3 ♗e6 23.♘xd6 ♖fd8 24.♖fd1 ♔g8⩱.

12...♗b7

Milanovic prefers to enhance the threat of ...a4 by protecting the c6-square. For instance, 13.h3 a4 would be pleasant for him. The main drawback of his move is that the bishop can no longer remove a blockade of White's rook at a4, as we saw in a line on the previous page. So 13.♖a4!? would be probably best here, e.g. 13...♘b6 14.♖xa5 ♖xa5 15.♘xa5 ♘bxd5 16.exd5 ♕xa5 17.♖e1. However we both underestimated ...a4.

13.♕d2 ♘g4 14.♗d4 ♗xd4

14...a4!? should be equal.

15.♘fxd4 ♕b6 16.♖a4!

Finally I fixed the nasty pawn on a5 and everything begins to work smoothly in my favour. The bigger activity of my rooks makes the difference.

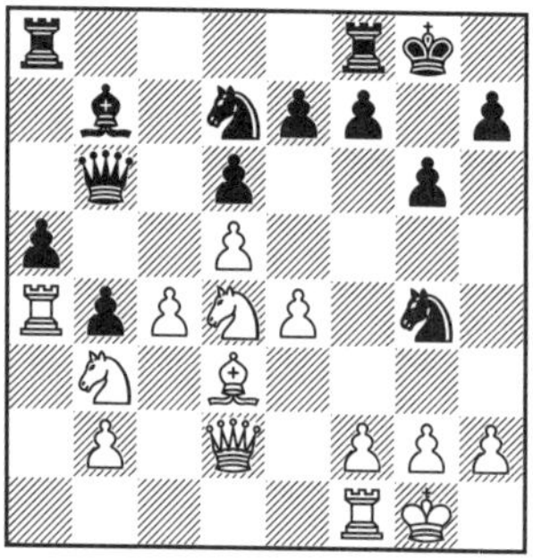

16...♖a7

Black takes a passive stand that will cost him a pawn. He could have tried to counterattack my only weakness, the c4-pawn: 16...♘ge5 17.♗e2 ♖fc8 (17...♗a6 18.♖c1 ♖ac8 19.♖ca1±) 18.♖c1 ♘f6 19.f3. Everything in White's camp is protected, but the opponent cannot claim the same – a waiting move like 19...♔h8 (or 19...♘fd7 20.f4) would lose a pawn to 20.♘xa5 ♖xa5 21.♖xb4 ♕a6 22.♖xb7.

17.♖fa1 ♖fa8 18.h3 ♘ge5 19.♗f1 ♘c5 20.♘xc5 ♕xc5 21.♘b3 ♕c7

Black has to give up the a7-g1 diagonal since the endgame following 21...♕b6 22.♕d4 would be hopeless for him.

22.♕d4

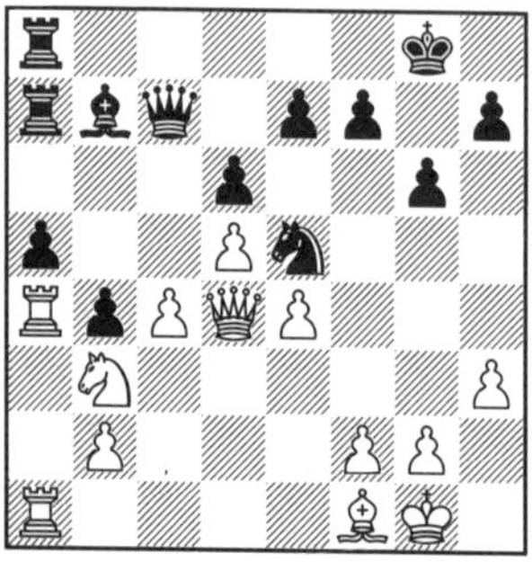

Black is already tied up and down, but it is far from easy to convert the advantage. The crisis however is imminent, since Black is unable to prevent ♖xb4 or c4-c5. For instance, 22...♗c8 23.c5 dxc5 24.♕xc5 ♕xc5 25.♘xc5 is very difficult for Black: 25...f5 26.f4 ♘d7 27.♘b3 fxe4 28.♖xa5 ♖xa5 29.♖xa5 ♖xa5 30.♘xa5 ♘b6 31.♘c6 ♔f7 32.♘xb4 ♗b7 33.♔f2+–) or 25...♗d7 26.♖4a2 g5 27.g3, threatening f2-f4.

22...♘d7 23.♖xb4 ♗xd5 24.♖xa5 ♖xa5 25.♘xa5 ♗xe4 26.♕xe4 ♕xa5 27.♖b5 ♕d8 28.b4

I transformed my advantage into a passed pawn and a bishop vs. knight in an open position and pawns on both wings. A computer might be able to hold on, but in practice Black rarely survives. My next task is to produce a passed pawn on c6 where it will be well defended by my bishop. That will free my major pieces for an attack on the king.

28...♖a7 29.g3 ♖c7 30.♗g2 ♘f6 31.♕d4 ♕c8 32.c5 dxc5 33.bxc5 h5 34.c6

The rest of the game is purely technical and it is not relevant to the opening. With my next few moves I gave away a solid part of my advantage and had to win the game once again, this time demonstrating the superiority of the bishop over a knight.

34...♘e8 35.♖b6 (36.♕b4!+–) **35...♘d6 36.♕b4 ♕d8 37.h4 ♔h7 38.♖a6 ♘e8 39.♗f3 ♘d6 40.♔h2 ♘f5 41.♗g2 ♕d4 42.♕e1 ♖a7 43.♖xa7 ♕xa7 44.♕d2 ♘d6 45.♕f4 ♕c5 46.♔g1 ♔g7 47.♕d2 e5 48.♕b2 ♘b5 49.♕a2 ♘c7 50.♕d2 ♕d4 51.♕xd4 exd4 52.♔f1 ♔f6 53.♔e2 ♔e5 54.♔d3 ♘e6 55.♔c4 ♔d6 56.♗h1 ♔e5 57.f4+ ♔d6 58.♗e4 ♔c7?** (58...f5) **59.♔d5 ♘d8 60.♔xd4 ♔d6 61.♗d5 f6 62.♔e4 ♘xc6 63.♗xc6 ♔xc6 64.f5 g5 65.g4 ♔d6 66.gxh5 1–0**

---

8. I.Sokolov–Kiril Georgiev
Sarajevo 1998

1.d4 ♘f6 2.c4 c5 3.d5 b5 4.♘f3 b4 5.a3 ♘a6 6.axb4 ♘xb4 7.♘c3 d6 8.e4 g6 9.♗e2 ♗g7 10.0–0 0–0 11.♗f4 ♗g4

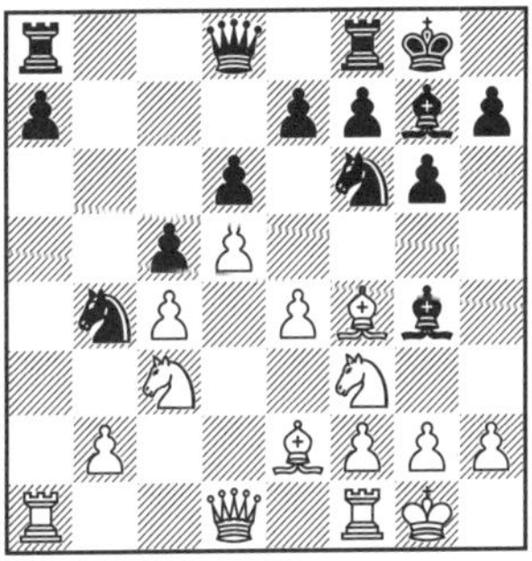

In many lines of the Benko Declined White is faced with a choice – to allow the exchange of his f3-knight or prevent it by h3. I'm inclined to think that White should not waste a tempo on this prophylaxis at an early stage of the opening. He has more important issues to deal with, such as development and control of the centre. The move h3 is often useful later, but in order to restrict the f6-knight, not the bishop.

12.h3 ♗xf3 13.♗xf3 ♘d7 14.♕d2

It is time to take stock of the opening. White has a stable pawn centre and a better pawn structure. My biggest problem is not the weak a-pawn, but the total lack of counterplay. Without the light-squared bishop, I cannot favourable open the centre with some pawn breaks as e6 or f5. Thus I should only stay passively and hope that White will not find a target. However, White does have a clear target – my king. His spatial advantage lets him easily manoeuvre pieces from one wing to the other while the h- and f-pawns can be used for ramming my castling position. Rybka light-heartedly assess my game as nearly equal, but the truth is rather different. Sokolov masterly develops his initiative.

14...♖e8

OK, this looks strange, but what else?! 14...e6 is strategically wrong no matter takes White on e6 or not. So I decided to wait and pretend that I'll push e6 some day.

15.♖a3!

As you might guessed, Sokolov's intention is not to double rooks on the a-file, but lift the a-one via the third rank and point it to my king.

15...♕b6 16.♗g4!

Plugging the g7-bishop and setting up f4 with a tempo.

16...♘e5 17.♗e2 ♖eb8

The moment of truth. I frankly admit that I have no active plan. At the same time my opponent is ready to reveal his own one.

18.h4!

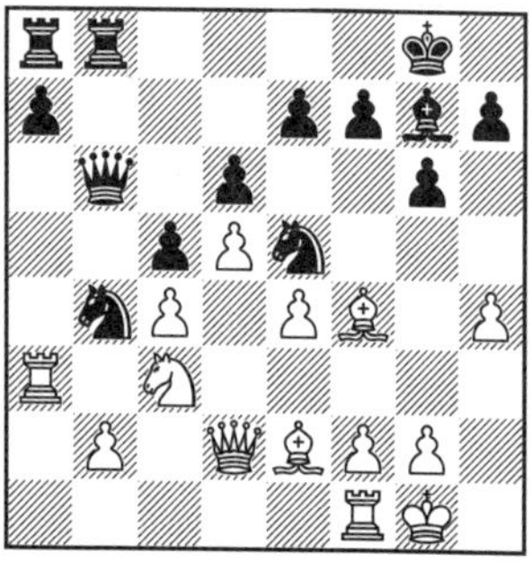

White is aiming to open the h-file, put a rook on h3 (where has my light-squared bishop disappeared!) and, possibly, the queen to h4. 18...h5 is no remedy as White can even throw in a piece sac without any calculations: 19.♗g5 ♕d8 20.f4 ♘d7 21.g4!? f6 22.gxh5 gxh5 23.♗xh5 fxg5 24.hxg5. I cannot imagine that Black could survive here.

18...♖b7 19.h5 gxh5!?

A good try. It may look like desperation, but this move does poses concrete problems to White. At least he will have to do some calculation work. In such positions the abundance of good possibilities often leads to long thinking and miscalculations.

Now a good continuation would be 20.♘d1 when neither 20...♘g6 21.♗h6 (21.♗xh5?! gives the opportunity of activating the b4-knight by 21...♘c2 22.♕xc2 ♘xf4 23.♗xf7+ ♔xf7 24.♖f3 ♗e5 25.g3 ♖g8 with counterplay) 21...♗xh6 (21...h4 22.♗xg7 ♔xg7 23.♘e3) 22.♕xh6 ♕d8 23.♕xh5 e5 nor 20...h4 21.♖h3 ♘g6 22.♗h6 ♗d4 23.♘e3 e6 are pleasant. Sokolov chooses a simple and good continuation of the attack:

20.♗xe5! ♗xe5 21.♗xh5 e6 22.♘e2 exd5 23.exd5 ♔h8?!

23...♕d8 intending 24...♕f6 was better. Now White wins a pawn and the game.

24.♖f3 ♕d8 25.♖xf7 ♖xf7 26.♗xf7 ♕f6 27.♗e6 ♗xb2 28.♖b1 ♗a1 29.♖b3 ♕g6 30.♖g3 ♕b1+ 31.♔h2 ♗e5 32.f4 ♕b2 33.♕e3 ♗g7 34.♗f5 ♖f8 35.♕e4 h6 36.♖g6 a5 37.♕e6 ♖f6 38.♕e8+ ♖f8 39.♕d7 ♖xf5 40.♕xf5 a4 41.♖xd6 1–0

---

9. O.Pavlov – Obolenskikh
Tomsk 28.06.2008

1.d4 ♘f6 2.c4 c5 3.d5 b5 4.♘f3 g6 5.♕c2 d6 6.e4 bxc4 7.♘c3 ♗g7 8.♗xc4 0–0 9.0–0 ♘bd7

Now play transposes to line A1 which I consider to be in White's favour. More testing is 9...♗a6 which I discuss in the beginning of "Step by Step" chapter.

10.h3 ♖b8 11.♖e1 ♘e8 12.♗f4 ♕a5 13.♗d2 ♕b6 14.b3 ♗a6 15.♖ab1 ♘c7 16.a4 ♘e5 17.♘xe5 ♗xe5

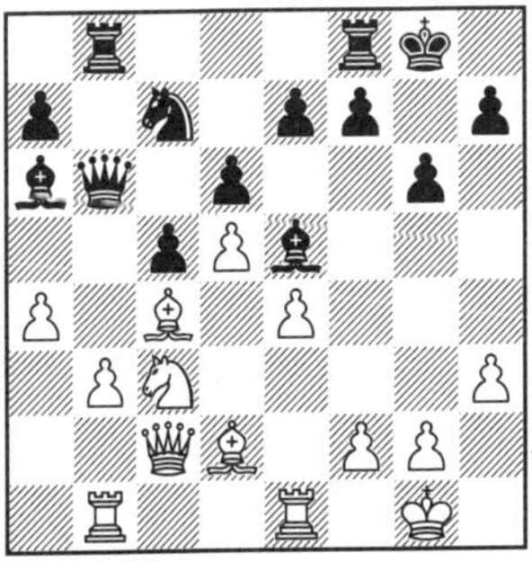

White has the better prospects here. He has successfully consolidated on the queenside where Black cannot make any progress. On the contrary, only White could attack there by b3-b4.

Black's only counterplay could be in the centre and it is linked with e7-e6. White typically opposes that by pushing f4-f5 so Pavlov's next moves are thoroughly logical. At the same time White also has other decent plans:

1. In such positions with full control of c4 and b5, White often uses his h-pawn to weaken the enemy's castling position. The immediate 18.h4, however, meets 18...♕b7 19.h5 ♕c8 20.♕d3 ♗xc4 21.bxc4 ♕d7 22.hxg6 fxg6 and White did not achieve any advantage, because the enemy's queen efficiently restricts his kingside play. That does not mean the plan with h4 is bad, only it needs to be shaped up a little, for instance, 18.♕d3 first. Black's defensive task is not trivial at all. For instance, 18...♗g7 19.h4, with initiative. 18...♖fe8 19.h4 or 18...e6 19.h4 would stress the fact that Black cannot really open the centre since White's attack will only gain in strength. The manoeuvre 18...♗c8 19.a5 ♕b7 (19...♕xa5 20.♘a4 ♖b4 21.♘b2 ♗d7 22.♕f1 ♕b6 23.♘d3±) 20.b4! cxb4 21.♘a2± leads us to:

2. The plan with b4.

After 18.♕d3 ♕b7!? White can follow up with 19.♘e2 threatening b4, e.g. 19...♗g7 20.b4!±. 19...♗xc4 20.bxc4 ♕a6 21.a5 gives White a small, but stable edge due to the gloom prospects before the knight at c7. Therefore, Black answers with 19...♕c8, when the only sensible continuation would be 20.f4 ♗g7 21.♗c3, switching to:

3. Plan with e5. This is the most common idea in the Benko structures. It requires f4 and in the game White decided to not beating about the bush but play straightforwardly:

18.f4!? ♗d4+ 19.♔h1 ♗c8

19...♗xc4 20.bxc4 ♕a6 is quite bad here as 21.♘b5 is a double attack. After ♘xb5 22.cxb5 ♕b7 23.f5 ♗e5 24.♖f1± Black is totally cramped.

19...♘e8 would be useless since after 20.♕d3 Black must return to c7: 20...♘c7 when White can choose between 21.e5 and 21.♘e2 ♗g7 22.f5 ♖fe8 23.♘g1 ♗xc4 24.bxc4 ♕a6 25.a5.

20.♘e2 ♗g7

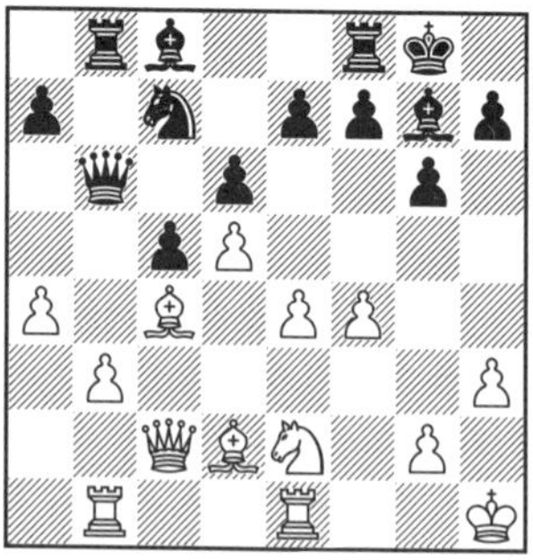

21.f5!?

White is persistently gaining space and restricting the opponent. The main idea of this move is to discourage ...e6 (and ban ...f5). Instead, 21.♗c3 ♗xc3 22.♘xc3 ♘e8 is not too impressive. White, however, would have achieved a clear advantage without any risks with plan 2:

21.a5 ♕b7 22.b4 cxb4 23.♖xb4 ♕a8 24.♖xb8 ♕xb8 25.♖b1 ♕a8 26.♗e3±, eyeing the a7-pawn. We see a striking difference in the strength of the pieces of the two armies.

21...♘e8

Black is wisely shifting the knight to the kingside. 21...♘a6 22.♗c3 ♘b4 23.♕d2 ♗d7 24.♗xg7 ♔xg7 25.♘f4→ would be too dangerous for him.

22.g4?!

White has played by the book until now, but here he makes a strange move. I do not understand why should he weaken his king without any necessity. He had at least two much better options:

22.b4 cxb4 23.♖xb4 ♕c7 24.♖xb8 ♕xb8 25.♗e3±;

22.♘g1!? ♘f6 23.♘f3 a5 24.♗c3 ♘d7 25.♗xg7 ♔xg7 26.fxg6 fxg6 27.e5±.

The latter one would have fitted best in White's schema. Now White's edge evaporates. He can hardly win with a naked king.

22...♘f6 23.♘g1 ♘d7 24.♘f3 ♘e5 25.♘xe5 ♗xe5 26.♕d3

26.♗c3 ♗xc3 27.♕xc3 f6 28.♕d3= would have sealed the position.

26...♔g7 27.♕e3 ♗a6 28.a5 ♕b7 29.♕d3 ♗xc4 30.bxc4 ♕d7 31.♖b3 ♖xb3 32.♕xb3 e6 33.♖f1 exd5 34.exd5 f6!

Eliminating all the tricks with the pawn sac on f6, e.g. 34...♖e8 35.a6 ♕d8 36.f6+ although Black still should be able to survive after 36...♗xf6 37.♕f3 g5 38.h4 ♕e7 39.hxg5 ♗d4 40.♖b1 ♕e2⇄.

35.♔g2 ♖f7 36.♕e3 gxf5!

The simplest. Now 37.♖xf5 ♕a4 38.♕e4 would be about equal, but probably in the time trouble the opponents made some mistakes.

37.♕h6+? ♔g8 (37...♔h8!) **38.♖b1 ♕c8 39.♔f3 fxg4+ 40.hxg4 ♖b7 41.♖xb7 ♕xb7 42.♕h5 ½–½**

A draw was signed here, but Rybka suggests 42...♕b3+! and White has no good continuation: 43.♗e3 ♕d1+ 44.♔e4 ♕c2+ 45.♔f3 ♔f8∓ with an extra pawn.

---

10. Pankratov–Wang Mong Lin
EM/TT/F/01 ICCF email, 1997

1.d4 ♘f6 2.c4 c5 3.d5 b5 4.♘f3 ♗b7 5.♕c2 ♘a6 6.a3 bxc4 7.c4 e6 8.dxe6 fxe6 9.e5 ♗xf3 10.gxf3 ♘d5 11.♗xc4 ♘ac7

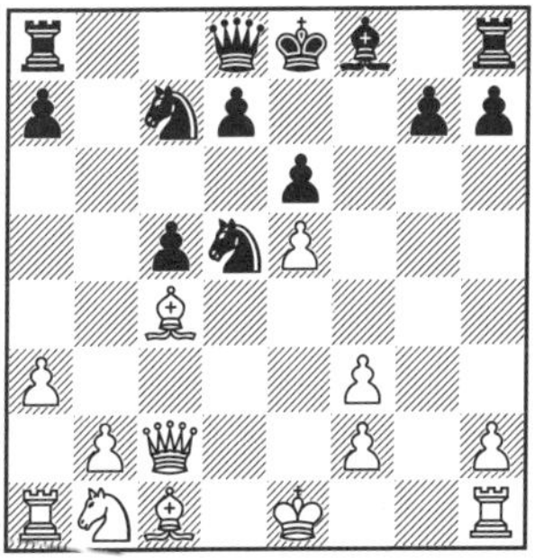

12.h4

Static factors are in Black's favour due to the doubled pawns on the f-file. However, the position is very sharp and the activity of White's pieces should prevail in the evaluation. In principle, White's plan includes quick development, so 12.♘c3 looks more consistent. This is a good move indeed, but it allows 12...♘xc3 13.bxc3 d5, when White should capture 14.exd6 to keep the centre open. Thus he will help Black's development. Although White will be exerting strong pressure after 14...♗xd6 15.♗e3 0-0 16.♖d1 ♕e7 17.♕e4, for instance, ♔h8 18.♗d3 g6 19.c4 ♖ad8 20.h4, it would be even better to make another useful move and see Black's next one.

12...♕b8

Knaak suggests 12...d6, but White is not forced to take it. Instead, he can answer 13.♘c3 or 13.♗d3 ♕d7 14.♘c3. I analyse these options in the "Step by Step" chapter. The text looks more consistent as Black tries to keep play closed.

13.♘c3 ♘xc3

In another correspondence game Black decided to castle on the kingside, but he was crushed after 13...♗e7?! 14.♗d3 ♘xc3 15.bxc3 ♘d5 16.f4 0-0 17.♗xh7+ ♔h8 18.♗g6 1-0, Pankratov-A.Tsvetkov, Russia 1999/Corr 2002.

14.bxc3 ♕b7 15.♕d3

Rybka suggests 15.♔e2± ♖b8 16.♗e3, but that would allow Black to exchange the queens with 16...♕b2 17.♔d3 ♕xc2+ 18.♔xc2 ♗e7. Similar positions arise from the Taimanov variation in the Sicilian. It is not easy to break them. Naturally, Pankratov prefers to keep the queens.

15...♘d5 16.♖b1 ♘b6 17.♖g1 ♕c7 18.♕e4 ♖b8 19.♗d3 ♘d5 20.♖xb8+ ♕xb8 21.♗g5

21...♔f7

Black has not time for regrouping with 21...♘e7 22.♔d2 ♘c6 in view of the sudden mate 23.♕g6+!! hxg6 24.♗xg6#. Pawn eating does not solve the problem of developing the kingside: 22...♕b2+ 23.♗c2 ♘d5 (23...♕xa3 24.♖b1) 24.♖b1 ♕xc3+ 25.♔e2 ♔f7 26.♖b7 ♘b6 27.♖xa7, with a huge advantage.

22.♗c4 h6

Black weakens the g6-square, but he has not a good choice anyway: 22...♘xc3 23.♕f5+ ♔e8 24.♗xe6 or 22...♕b7 23.♗d2 ♗e7 24.♔e2 g6 25.h5 ♖g8 26.hxg6+.

23.♗d2 ♕b2 24.♕g6+ ♔e7 25.♗xd5 exd5 26.♖g4 ♕b8 27.♕f5 ♕b3 28.a4 ♔d8 29.h5 ♔e7

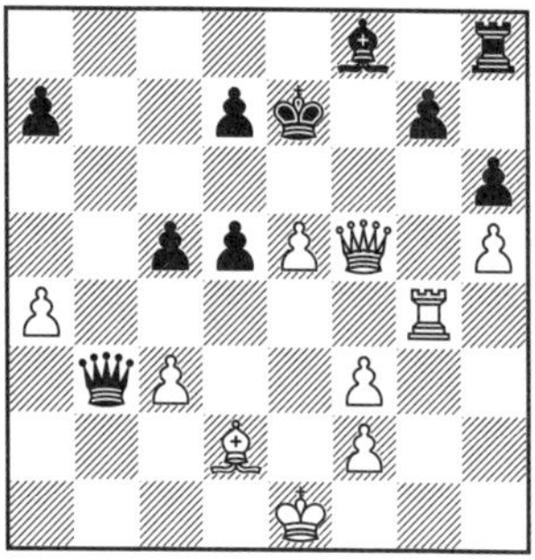

30.c4

Finally White finishes the game off. The d5-pawn cannot leave its place because of the hanging c5-pawn: 30...dxc4 31.e6.

30...♕xa4 31.cxd5 ♕a1+ 32.♔e2 ♕a6+ 33.♕d3 ♕xd3+ 34.♔xd3 ♔e8 35.d6 ♔f7 36.f4 ♔e6 37.♔e4 ♔f7 38.♔d5 1–0

It is difficult to pinpoint any serious Black's mistake in this game! Maybe he should blame the opening!

Part 3

Main Ideas

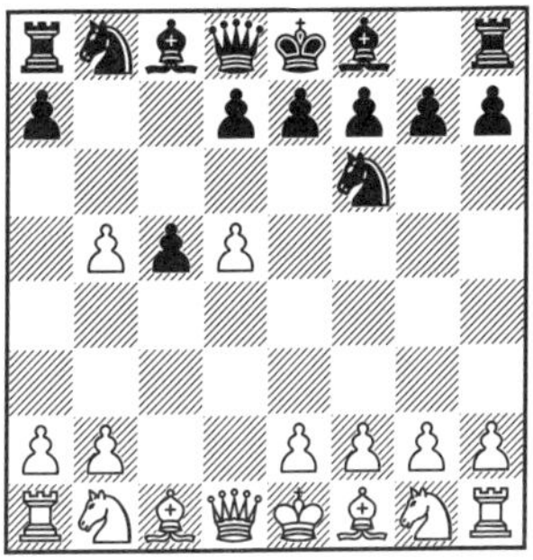

1.d4 ♘f6 2.c4 c5 3.d5 b5 4.cxb5

In this part I examine the direct approach to the b6-system. White takes on b5 immediately and meets

4...a6 with **5.b6**

My only reason to leave it as an alternative way is the possibility for:

5...e6 6.♘c3 ♘xd5!

This line is in no way a miraculous solution of Black's opening problems. The mere fact that the main line after 14.♗c3 gives White, according to Megabase, the amazing edge of 73% over a sample of 22 games (only two Black victories, one of them in a blitz game) speaks for itself. White plays practically with a draw in the pocket and the only question is would he convert his better pawn structure into a point or not. Pogonina has been the most stubborn protagonist of Black's side lately, but despite her home preparation, she is often struggling right from the opening.

Still, the arising positions are too dry and might not appeal to some players. Perhaps it would be a good idea to have both move orders in your repertoire in order to avoid being too predictable for the opponents.

Now I will briefly consider another option of Black on the sixth move – 6...♗b7. It is much sharper and brings about fresh positions with an open centre after 7.e4 exd5 8.exd5 d6

One possible plan here is to advance the pawns on the kingside and stake all on a direct attack. I offer as a main line the positional approach: to use our space advantage for organising a piece attack on the enemy king.

Firstly, we have to ensure a stable stand for out light-squared bishop:

9.a4! a5 (9...♕xb6 10.a5 ♕c7 11.♘f3 ♗e7 12.♗c4 0-0 13.0-0 ♘bd7 14.h3 ♖fe8 15.♗f4 is clear and easy to handle.) 10.♗b5+ ♘bd7 11.♘ge2!

There are two things to remember about this line:

1. To play a4;

2. Then to put the king's knight to e2 in order to ensure protection of our pawn at d5.

11...♗e7 12.0-0 0-0 13.♖e1 ♘xb6 14.♘f4 ♖c8

15.♕f3 ♘fd7 16.♗d2 ♘e5 17.♕e4

White consolidated and his space advantage is a strong argument in his favour.

See **game 11 Dreev-Kutuzovic**, Sibenik 2006.

Now let us return to:

6...♘xd5 7.♘xd5 exd5 8.♕xd5 ♘c6

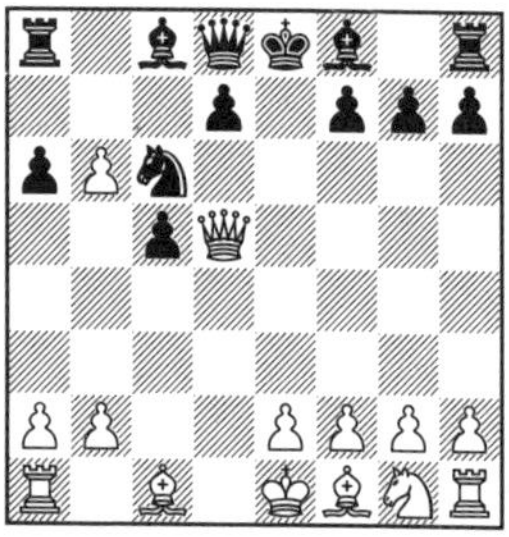

9.♘f3!

Note the move order! The threat of 10.♘e5 0-0 11.♘xc6 dxc6 12.♕xd8 hinders Black's development.

9...♖b8 10.e4

10.♗d2 is also possible, but it is unnecessary to offer the enemy a wider choice without gaining any benefits from that.

10...♗e7 11.♗c4 0-0 12.0-0 ♖xb6

Game 12 Dreev-Banikas, Panormo 2001 explains why it is not so good for Black to shift the knight from the centre by 12...♘a5. In that case White's queen goes to h5 with chances for attack.

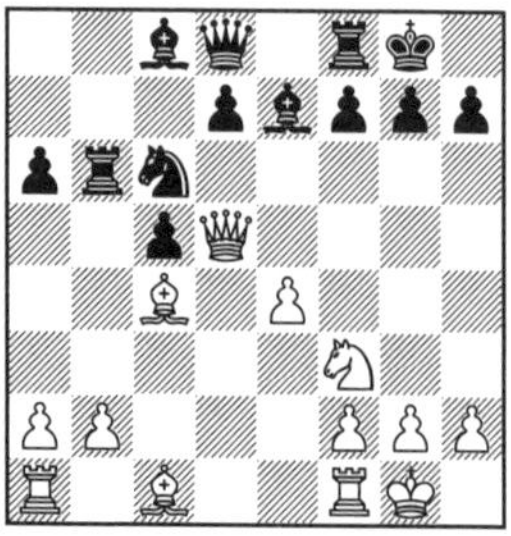

13.♗d2!

White finishes his development

and activates the rooks. The point is that in the line 13...♖xb2 14.♗c3 ♖b6 15.♖ad1 d6 16.♕h5 ♗d7 he is not obliged to regain the pawn immediately, but can double rooks first with 17.♖d2!± with strong pressure.

13...d6 14.♗c3

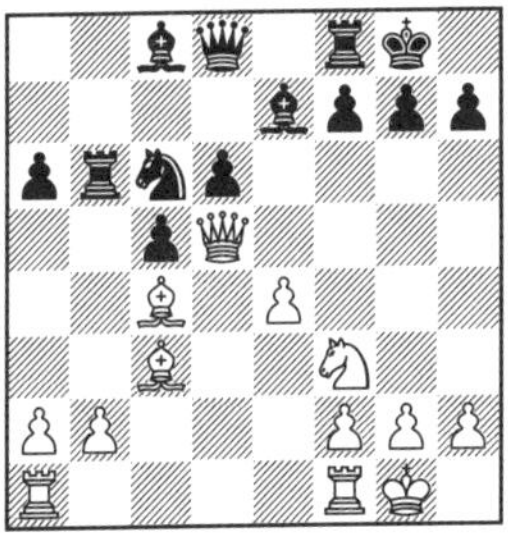

This is the starting position of the 5...e6 system nowadays.

White's minor pieces are more active and better coordinated so in the following moves Black will try to trade them all. We cannot avoid that, but even the heavy pieces endgame is slightly better for White and we can be squeezing the opponent for many moves. Let us examine the most typical positions that arise:

1. 14...♗e6 15.♕d3 ♘b4?! 16.♕e2 ♗xc4 17.♕xc4 d5 18.exd5 ♕xd5 19.♘e5±.

Model Position 1

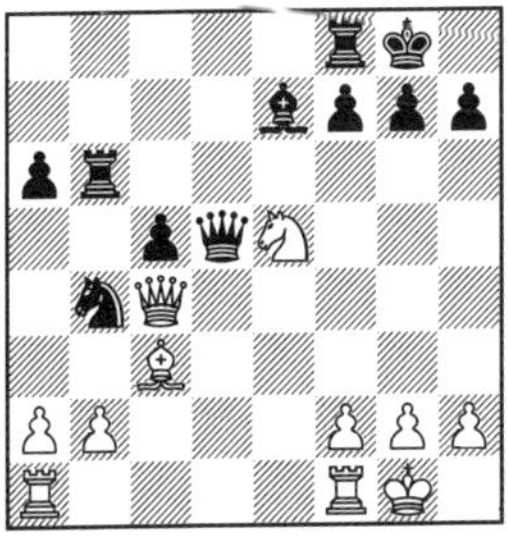

In practice Black never survives here. See **game 15 Stefanova-Pogonina**, Solin 2007. White trades queens and invades the queenside by a rook via the d-file.

2. 14...♗e6 15.♕d3 ♗xc4 16.♕xc4 ♗f6! 17.♖ad1 ♗xc3 18.bxc3 ♕f6 19.♖d3 ♖e8 20.♕a4 ♔f8 21.♖fd1 ♘e5 22.♘xe5 ♕xe5 23.♖e3 ♕f4

Model Position 2

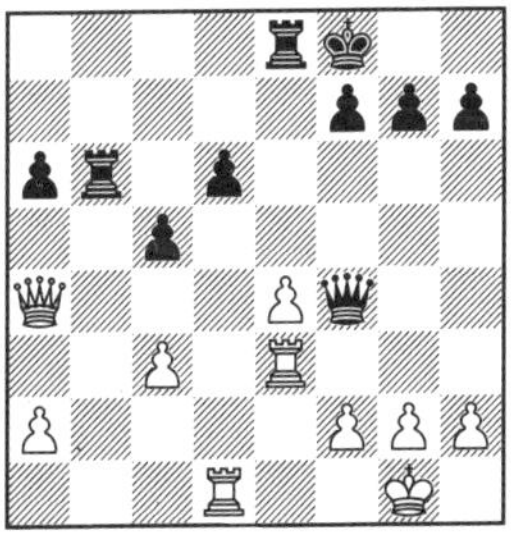

White has some practical chances, linked with the breaktrough c4-e5, aiming to take on c5 and make a passer. See **game 14 Kuljasevic-Andrews**, ICC INT 2007, where White had a dangerous initiative, but the game was eventually drawn.

14...♗f6 offers White a choice:

3. To aim for Model Position 2 with 15.♕d3!? ♗g4! (16.♗xe6 fxe6 17.♖ad1 with some edge) 16.♖ad1!

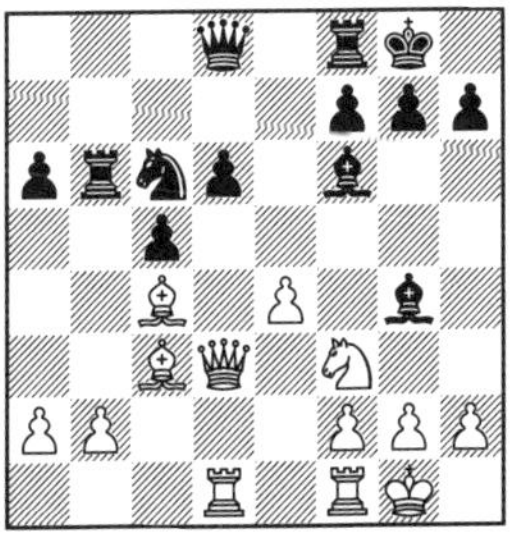

16...♗xc3 17.bxc3 ♗xf3 18.♕xf3 ♘e5 19.♕e2 ♘xc4 20.♕xc4 ♕f6.

4. To seek complications with 15.♖ad1 ♗e6 16.♕d3 ♘b4 17.♕e2

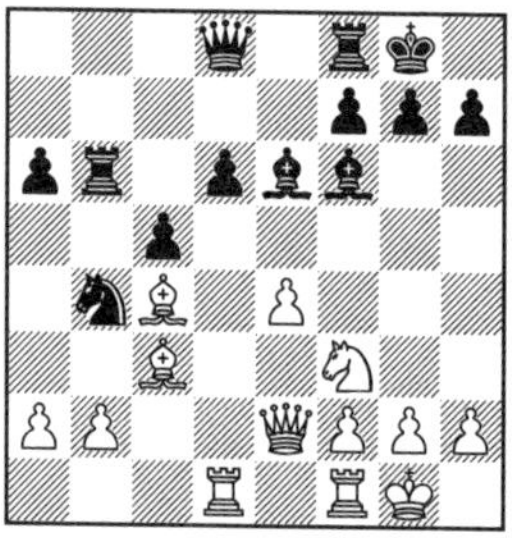

17...♘xa2! 18. ♗xa2 ♗xa2 19.♗a5

I won **game 13 Kiril Georgiev-Vaisser**, Ohrid 2001, but the exchange sacrifice should give Black sufficient counterplay.

Conclusion:

White should be ready for a long technical game with only a slight advantage. The more minor pieces, the more his space advantage is tangible. This variation could be a cold shower to aggressive players who choose the Benko Gambit to obtain sharp play.

Finally, my advice about the best placement of White's heavy pieces:

The queen's rook should go to d1. The other one might be needed on e1.

The queen should stay in the centre, at d3 or e2. It has no business on h5 despite looking "active" there.

Part 3

Step by Step

1.d4 ♘f6 2.c4 c5 3.d5 b5 4.cxb5

4...a6

4...e6 is a seldom seen attempt to lure White into the Blumenfeld Accepted: 5.dxe6 fxe6 6.♘c3 ♗b7! 7.♘f3 ♗e7. I do not recommend such an approach as it suites well Black's plan of intercepting the initiative. Instead, we should answer:

5.♘c3! ♗b7 6.e4 exd5 (6...a6 is a bad version of the Benko Accepted: 7.♘f3 axb5 8.♗xb5 ♕a5 9.♕e2 ♗e7 10.♗d2 ♕b6 11.d6+–, Golod-Danzer, Bad Wiessee 2000) 7.exd5 d6 8.a4 a6 9.a5±. White is clearly better.

5.b6 e6

The alternatives transpose to the main lines of Part 1.

5...♕xb6 6.♘c3 g6 7.♘f3 ♗g7 8.e4 d6; 5...d6 6.♘c3 g6 7.♘f3 ♗g7 8.e4 0-0.

Only 5...a5?! 6.♘c3 ♗a6 is of independent significance. This tricky line enjoyed a burst of popularity in the beginning of the 90ies and it is still occurring in tournaments. Perhaps Black counts on 7.f4 d6 8.♘f3 ♕xb6 9.e4 ♗xf1 10.♖xf1 with supposedly better game for White, but Black has counterplay there. Instead, White should aim for a much better endgame by checking from a4 after 7.e4 ♗xf1 8.♔xf1 d6

a) 9.♕a4+!?

Introduced by the game Semkov-Berndt, Sitges 1993. White hinders the enemy's development. The point is that 9...♘bd7 will face 10.f4 ♕xb6 11.e5 when, in order not to lose a piece, Black must completely concede the centre: 11...dxe5 12.fxe5

♘g8. White's pieces are very active, e.g. 13.♘f3 e6 14.dxe6 fxe6 15.♔f2 c4+ 16.♗e3 ♗c5 17.♗xc5 ♕xc5+ 18.♔f1 ♘h6 19.♖d1 ♕e7 20.♘e4 ♘f7 21.♔f2±.

9...♘fd7 10.♘f3 ♕xb6 11.e5 ♕b4

A critical position for the variation with 9.♕a4+. White's best is:

12.♕b5! dxe5 13.♘xe5 ♕xb5+ 14.♘xb5 ♘xe5 15.♘c7+ ♔d8 16.♘xa8 ♘bd7 17.f4 ♘d3 18.♔e2, Jabbar-B.Gonzalez, Curitiba 2009, when simplest would have been 18.♗d2±.

b) 9.♘f3 ♘bd7

9...♕xb6 allows 10.e5 dxe5 11.♘xe5 g6 12.♕a4+ ♘fd7 with a clear edge for White in the endgame after 13.♘c4 ♕b4 14.a3! ♕xa4 15.♘xa4 ♗g7 16.♗f4±. Another good option is 13.♗g5 ♗g7 14.♘xd7 ♘xd7 15.♖e1 ♗f6, Akobian-Pinski, Yerevan 1999, 16.h4!±.

10.♕a4 ♕xb6 11.e5 dxe5 12.♘xe5 ♖d8

12...g6 would transpose to the previous comment, but the text is not any better:

13.♗g5

13.g3 ♕b7 14.♕c6± is simple and good, but White wants to finish off the opponent quickly.

13...♕xb2 14.♖c1 ♕b4 15.♕c6+–, Iotov-Petkov, Pleven 2005.

Summarising: White should put his queen to a4 and force the opponent to take on e5. The ensuing endgames are clearly in his favour.

6.♘c3

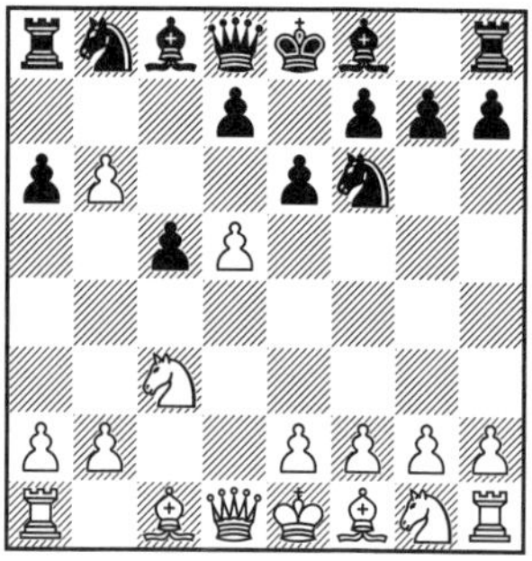

A. 6...♗b7

B. 6...♘xd5! (6...exd5)

A. 6...♗b7 7.e4 exd5 8.exd5 d6

In this line Black hopes to win the d5-pawn. His play is simple and straightforward. He focuses three minor pieces on d5 and tries to place a fourth decisive hit with his queen – either from a8 or f7. Black's problem is that if his plan fails, his bishop at b7 will be rather useless. The open e-file also works in White's favour, causing headache to the bishop at e7. Finally, even if Black does win that pawn, most likely he will lose in return its d6-one (if something worse does not happen to his king).

It looks that White has a wide choice, but in fact he must play very precisely.

It looks natural to develop the bishop to c4 from where it will be defending the d5-pawn. However, that would mean to fall into Black's strategic trap and assume a defensive stand. Then the enemy's opening choice would be justified. Practice has seen many games where White was gradually losing ground in such a scenario.

A more aggressive version of this idea is to play 9.g4!? and defend the d5-pawn from g2 while using the g-pawn to oust the f6-knight from its perfect attacking/defending position.

General principles are against such an approach. In open positions it is better to play with pieces and activate them maximally. Obviously a bishop on g2 does not look great. At the same time, it covers the white king, replacing the pawn which had went forward. In practice Black fails to tame the white pawn avalanche and often gets crushed:

9...♗e7 (but not 9...♘bd7? in view of 10.g5 and the knight must retreat to g8) 10.♗g2 0-0 11.g5

This looks more consistent than the slower 11.h3 although in Cheparinov-Simonet, Andorra 2001 White won nicely.

11...♘fd7 12.h4

In the game Tella-Salmensuu, Helsinki 2002, White pushed the other pawn, but after 12.f4 ♘xb6 13.♘ge2 a5 14.0-0 ♘a6 15.h4 f5 Black defended successfully. White should aim for an attack with the h-pawn. In that case his rook is better off at h1:

12...♘xb6 13.♘ge2 a5 14.♘g3 ♗a6 15.f4 ♕e8 (Or 15...♖e8 16.♔f2 ♘8d7 17.♘f5 ♗f8 18.h5 with unclear position where White still has the initiative.) 16.♔f2 f5 17.♖e1 ♖a7 18.b3 ♕f7 19.♗b2 ♖c8 20.h5 ♗b7 21.♕c2 ♖f8 22.♘b5 ♖a8 23.g6 ♕e8 24.♕c3 ♖f6 25.♘xf5 ♘c8 1-0, Esen-Rouchouse, Kemer 2007. I do not advocate this plan because it contradicts the spirit of the book. It involves considerable strategic risk and double-edged positions.

Instead, White has a clear plan to dominate in the centre.

9.a4!

Aiming to ensure the b5-square for the bishop.

A1. 9...♕xb6
A2. 9...a5

A1. 9...♕xb6

This is too passive so it is no wonder that Black seldom lets the a-pawn to a5:

10.a5 ♕c7

White must define here his further plan.

Knaak has a favourite setup which he likes to play against many different openings. He expands on the kingside, pushing back the f6-knight and trying to run Black over with a pawn avalanche. It assumes development of the king's knight on e2 in order to keep an open lane to the f-pawn:

11.♗c4 ♗e7 12.♘ge2 0-0 13.0-0 ♘bd7 14.f4. I know only of the game Knaak-Mainka, Germany 1991, which did not last long: 14...♕d8 (This is quite consistent. Black manoeuvres his knight to c7.) 15.♕d3 ♘e8 16.g4 ♘c7 17.♗d2 ♖e8 18.g5 ♗f8 19.h4 ♖b8 20.♘g3 ♗c8 21.b3 g6 22.♘ce4 f5 23.gxf6 ♘xf6 24.♘g5 ♗g7 25.♖ae1↑ h6? 26.♕xg6 hxg5 27.fxg5 ♘g4 1-0.

It is not easy to come up with a good plan for Black, because he is cramped and basically he should be waiting and looking for counterchances. A possible continuation is also 14...♖fe8 15.h3 g6 16.g4 ♗f8 17.♘g3 ♖e7 18.g5 ♘e8 19.f5 ♘e5 20.b3 ♗c8 21.f6 ♖d7 22.♗f4±.

However, once again I choose as main line the most clear positional plan:

11.♘f3 ♗e7 12.♗c4 0–0 13.0–0 ♘bd7 14.h3 ♖fe8 15.♗f4

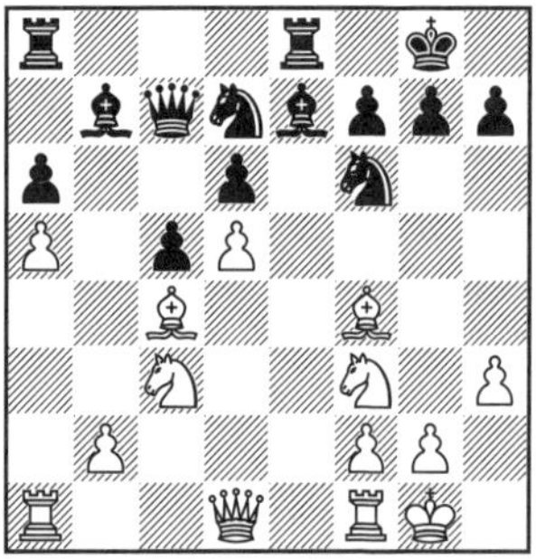

White is slightly better here due to the weak black pawn at a6. He can hardly achieve anything substantial though without b2-b4. This breakthrough would allow him to put pressure on Black's most awkward piece, the bishop at b7. In Vyzmanavin-Luco, Cap d'Agde 1994 Black chose a dubious redeployment of his minor pieces and lost control of the important square b6: 15...♘f8?! 16.♖e1 ♘g6 17.♗h2 ♖ad8 18.♕d3 ♕c8 19.♘a4±.

Instead, 15...♗f8 would have been better. I suppose that White should not change rooks then, but build pressure on the queenside with 16.♕d3 h6 17.♖fb1!? ♖e7 18.♗d2 ♘e5 19.♘xe5 ♖xe5 20.♗f4 ♖ee8 21.b4 cxb4 22.♖xb4 ♖ac8 23.♗d2±.

A2. 9...a5 10.♗b5+ ♘bd7 11.♘ge2

Again, we should prefer development to tactical stabs with 11.♗g5 ♗e7 12.♗xf6 ♗xf6 13.♕g4. Black is OK after 13...h5 14.♕f5 g6 15.♗xd7+ ♔e7 16.♕f4∞.

11.g4 is possible, but it is rather risky.

11...♗e7 12.0–0 0–0 13.♖e1 ♘xb6 14.♘f4 ♖c8

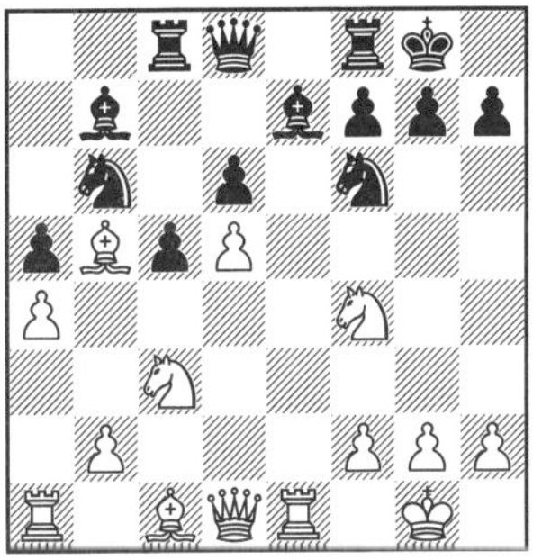

15.♕f3

The game Barsov-S.Polgar, Wijk aan Zee 1997, saw 15.b3. This move is unnecessary as White anyway cannot impose control over c4. It also wastes a tempo and leaves the c3-knight hanging. The game went 15...♘e8 (15...♘fd7 does not protect d6. White can use that by 16.♖a2 ♗f6 17.♘e4 ♗e5 18.♘d3, when 18...♘xd5 19.♘xe5 ♘xe5 20.f4 ♘g6 21.f5 ♘e5 22.f6 would give him a terrible attack.) 16.♖a2 ♗f6 17.♘e4 ♗e5 18.♖ae2 ♘f6=. Instead, 6.♕f3 ♗f6 17.♗d2 ♗e5 18.♗c6 would have been more enterprising.

15...♘fd7 16.♗d2 ♘e5 17.♕e4

White has consolidated and his space advantage is a strong argument in his favour. See the brilliant **game 11 Dreev-Kutuzovic**, Sibenik 2006.

B. 6...♘xd5 7.♘xd5 exd5 8.♕xd5 ♘c6 9.♘f3

This move is more precise than 9.e4 because it practically forces Black to answer 9...♖b8 instead of developing with ...♗e7.

9...♖b8

The point is that 9...♗e7 allows White to cripple severely Black's pawn chain on the queenside: 10.♘e5 0-0 11.♘xc6 dxc6 12.♕xd8 ♗xd8 (12...♖xd8 is even worse: 13.♗f4 ♗f6 14.♖d1 ♖d4 15.e3± Karpov-L.Christiansen, Wijk aan Zee 1993) 13.b7 ♗xb7 14.♗e3 c4 15.0-0-0.

9...♗b7 has nearly disappeared from tournaments due to: 10.♘e5 ♕e7 11.♗f4.

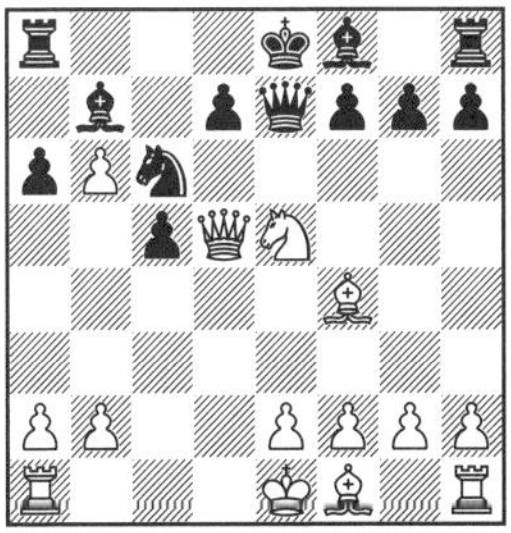

Now 11...g5 12.♘xc6 ♗xc6 13.♕xg5! (13.♕e5 gxf4 14.♕xh8 ♖b8 gives Black some counterplay) 13...♕xg5 14.♗xg5 ♖b8 15.h4! ♗g7

(or 15...♖xb6 16.♖h3 ♗d5 17.♖d3 ♗c4 18.♖d2 ♗g7 19.e3±) 16.♖h3± was rather convincing in Zueger-Manor, Bern 1990.

11...♘d8 is more unclear, but I think that 12.♕d1 gives White a clear edge. (The alternative is 12.♕d2 g5 13.♗g3 f5 14.f4 ♗g7 15.0-0-0 d5 16.e3 0-0 17.♗e2 ♘e6 18.♔b1±) The idea of this move is to prevent counterplay with 12...g5 13.♗g3 f5 14.e3 f4 in view of 15.♕h5+) Therefore Black has to concede to a worse position after 12...♘e6 13.♗g3 ♘d4 14.e3 ♘f5 15.♘c4 ♘xg3 16.hxg3±, Malek-Kersten, Marburg 2006.

10.e4

In his earlier games Dreev preferred 10.♗d2, but the text limits Black's options which is a sufficient argument in its favour. In my game against Vaisser, 2001, the bishop's move led to a simple transposition after 10...♗e7 11.♗c3 0-0 12.e4 ♖xb6 13.♗c4 d6 14.0-0 ♗f6 15.♖ad1.

10...♗e7 11.♗c4 0-0 12.0-0

White cannot gain benefits by delaying castling: 12.♗d2 ♖xb6 13.♗c3 d6 (13...♘b4!? 14.♕d2 ♗b7 15.0-0-0 is very sharp and unclear.) 14.♕d3 ♗f6 15.♖d1

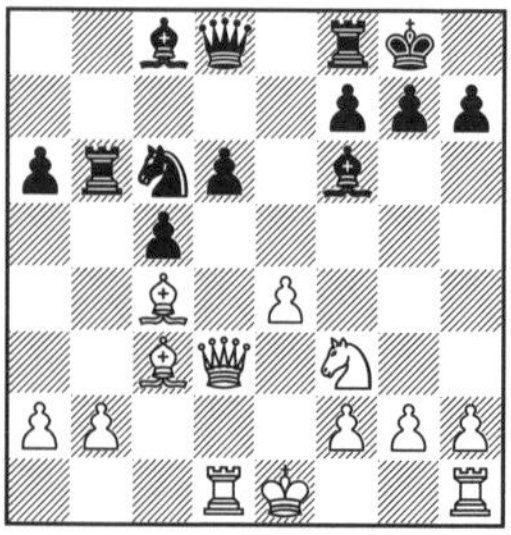

It looks like White's pressure on d6 hinders Black's plan, but after 15...♗xc3+ 16.bxc3 ♗g4 17.♕xd6 ♕xd6 18.♖xd6 ♖b1+ 19.♖d1 ♖b2 Black's compensation is enough for holding the draw.

12...♖xb6

The older continuation is 12...♘a5 13.♗d3 ♖xb6. It is not a good idea to shift the knight from the centre. Look at the model **game 12 Dreev-Banikas**, Panormo 2001 with detailed commentaries by Dreev.

12...♘d4?! 13.♘xd4 ♗b7 14.♕b3 cxd4 15.♗xd4 ♗xe4 16.f3 favours White.

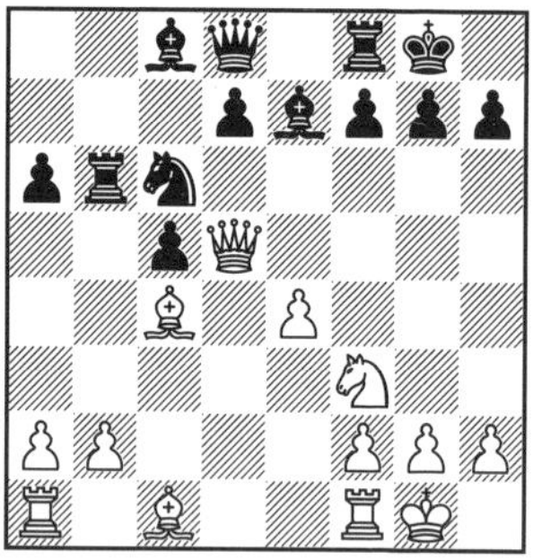

13.♗d2! d6

Practice has seen Black struggling after accepting the greek gift: 13...♖xb2 14.♗c3 ♖b6 15.♖ad1 d6 16.♕h5 ♗d7 (16...♗f6 17.e5 g6 18.♕h6 ♗g7 19.♕e3±, Thorfinnsson-Zueger, Ohrid 2001) 17.♖d2! (17.♖xd6 ♘d4 18.♖xb6 ♕xb6 19.♖d1 ♗a4 was only equal in V.Gaprindashvili-Zarkua, Agana 2007) 17...♗e8 18.♖fd1 ♔h8 19.♖xd6±, for instance, 19...f6 20.♖xd8 ♗xh5 21.♖xf8+ ♗xf8 22.h3

♗xf3 23.gxf3 ♘d4 24.♔g2 ♗d6 25.a4±.

14.♗c3

14.♕h5 ♗f6 15.0-0 ♗e6 16.♗xe6 fxe6 17.e5 dxe5 (17...♘xe5 18.♘xe5 ♗xe5 19.♗a5 ♕b8 20.♗xb6 ♕xb6 is a bit risky for Black.) 18.♖fe1 occurred in a few games and Sasikiran even beat Tregubov in 2006, but I have no idea what White had planned to do against the most natural centralising reply:

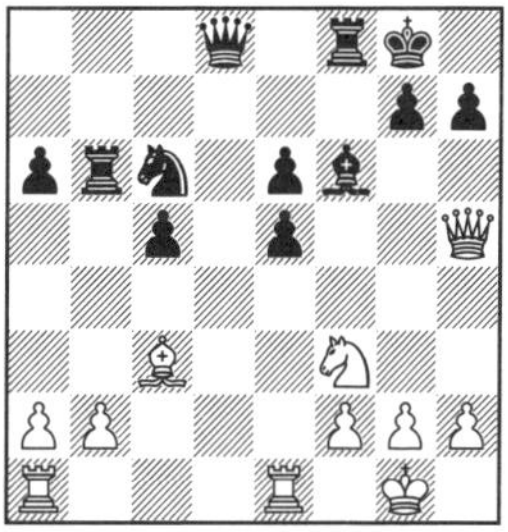

18...♕d5, for instance, 19.♖ad1 ♘d4 20.♘g5 ♗xg5 21.♕xg5 ♖f5∓ or 19.♘g5 ♗xg5 20.♕xg5 ♖f5 21.♕e3 ♘d4∓.

18...♕e8 should be equal after 19.♕g4 ♘d4 20.♖e4 ♘xf3+ 21.gxf3 ♖d6 22.♖ae1 ♕c6=.

After 14.♗c3, Black's main options are:

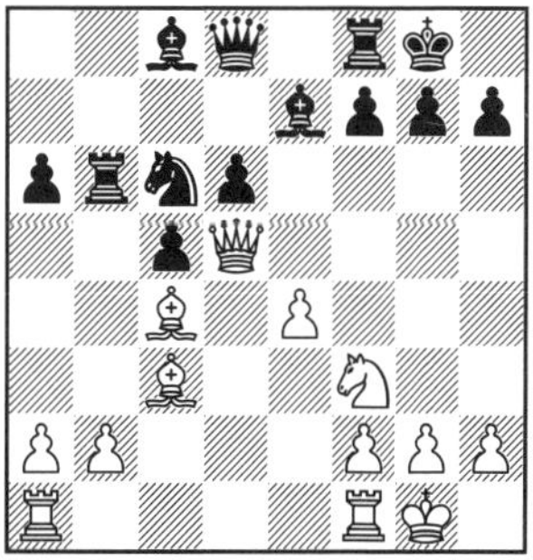

B1. 14...♗e6
B2. 14...♗f6

B1. 14...♗e6

This move is not bad, provided that Black links it with the idea from line B2 – to exchange all the minor pieces.

15.♕d3 ♗xc4

In many games Black tried to get rid of the backward d6-pawn, but that only weakened the c5-one: 15...♘b4?! 16.♕e2 ♗xc4 (the typical blunder 16...d5? 17.exd5 ♘xd5 18.♗a5 often occurs even in tournament games!) 17.♕xc4 d5 18.exd5 ♕xd5 19.♘e5. Computers may assess this position as nearly equal, but in practice Black never survives. See the model **game 15 Stefanova-Pogonina**, Solin 2007.

15...♗f6?! is best met with 16.♗xe6 fxe6 17.♖ad1± as mentioned in line B2.

16.♕xc4 ♗f6! 17.♖ad1 ♗xc3 18.bxc3 ♕f6

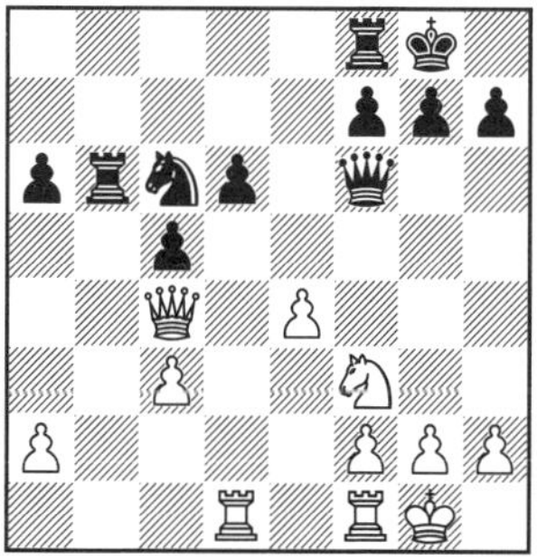

This position differs from line B2 only by the the presence of the knights. However, Black can always trade them by ...♘e5, thus reaching a drawish heavy pieces endgame after 19.♖d3 (19.♖d2 ♘a5 20.♕d3 ♕e6∓) 19...♖e8 20.♕a4 ♔f8 21.♖fd1 ♘e5.

White's game is still somewhat easier due to his space advantage, ensured by the e4-pawn. See the interesting **game 14 Kuljasevic-Andrews**, ICC INT 2007, where White had a dangerous initiative, but the game was eventually drawn.

B2. 14...♗f6

This rare move seems best although things are not that simple as you will see from my victory over Vaisser in the "Complete Games" chapter.

In the later game Krush-Golubenko, Moscow 2008, White tried to improve by **15.♕d3!?**, anticipating 15...♗e6 which could be answered by 16.♗xe6 fxe6 17.♖ad1 with some advantage, e.g. 17...♘b4 18.♕e2 ♕e7 (18...♘xa2 19.♗a5 ♖xb2 20.♕xb2) 19.♗xf6 gxf6 20.b3± ♘c6 21.♖d3 e5 22.♘h4 ♘d4 23.♕h5. However Black can swiftly eliminate all the minor pieces with 15...♗g4!

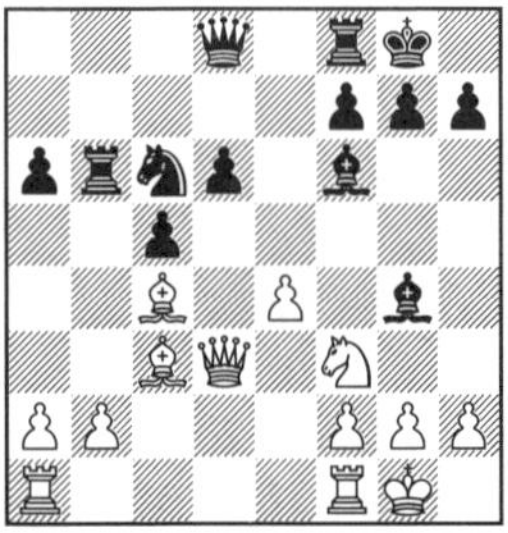

After 16.♖ad1! ♗xc3 17.bxc3 ♗xf3 18.♕xf3 ♘e5 19.♕e2 ♘xc4 20.♕xc4 ♕f6 play would be very similar to Kuljasevic-Andrews. The position is deceptively simple, but Black experiences some practical problems. He does not have any threats while White can accomplish e4-e5 or push a4-a5 thus underlining the weakness of the a6-pawn. No wonder that in the game Black avoided that position, but with a strong bishop vs a knight White had a serious edge after 16.h3 ♗h5 17.♖ad1 ♗xc3 18.bxc3 ♗xf3 19.♕xf3 ♖b2 20.♕g3 ♘e5 21.♗d5 ♕f6 22.f4 ♘g6 23.e5 dxe5 24.fxe5 ♕e7 25.♖f5±. Of course, Black should have taken on f3, aiming for the previous variation with h3 instead of ♖d1.

15.♖ad1 ♗e6 16.♕d3 ♘b4 17.♕e2

The latest game in this line was Iotov-Szamoskozi, Albena 2009, which saw 17.♗xb4 ♗xc4 18.♕xc4 ♖xb4 19.♕xa6 ♖xb2 20.♖xd6= (20.e5 ♖b6 21.♕a7 ♗e7 22.a4=) 20...♖xa2 with an inevitable draw.

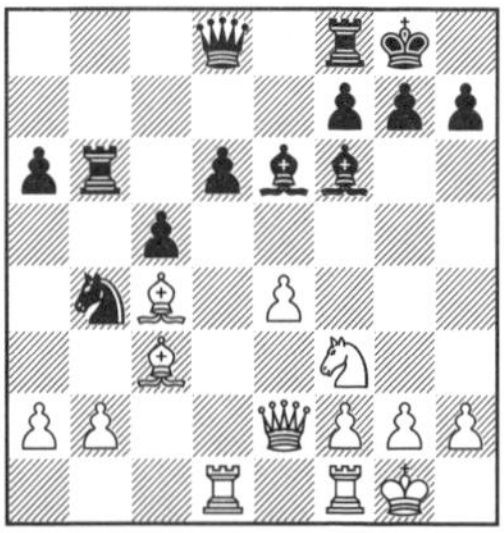

17...♘xa2!

This move should give Black sufficient counterplay. See **game 13 K.Georgiev-Vaisser**, Ohrid 2001.

Part 3

Complete Games

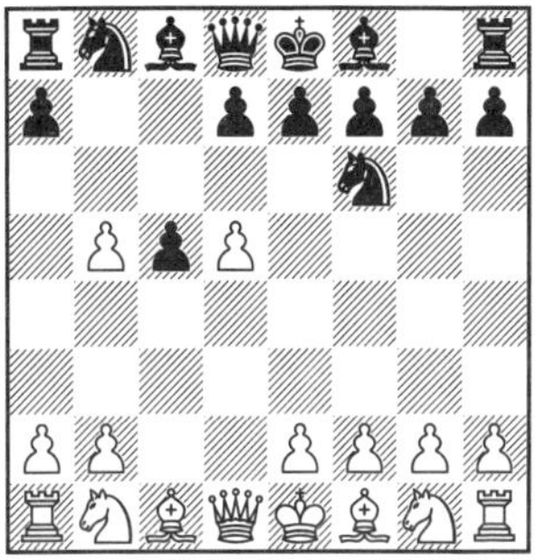

1.d4 ♘f6 2.c4 c5 3.d5 b5 4.cxb5

---

11. Dreev–Kutuzovic
Sibenik 26.09.2006

1.d4 ♘f6 2.c4 c5 3.d5 b5 4.cxb5 a6 5.b6 e6 6.♘c3 ♗b7 7.e4 exd5 8.exd5 d6 9.a4 a5 10.♗b5+ ♘bd7 11.♘ge2 ♗e7 12.0–0 0–0 13.♖e1 ♘xb6 14.♘f4 ♖c8 15.♕f3 ♘fd7 16.♗d2 ♘e5 17.♕e4

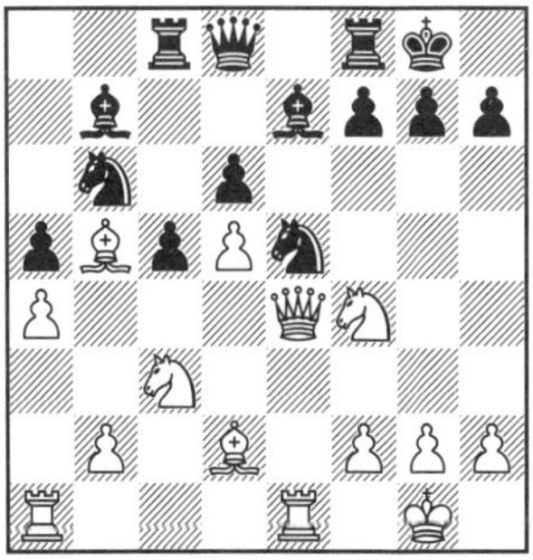

During the last moves White has been preoccupied with completing development while protecting the d5-pawn. Now we can take stock of the opening stage. White has achieved a big spatial advantage.

His main plan is to use his active pieces to strike at the kingside.

When things come to concrete play, he can ignore the pawn at d5 in order to ensure additional forces for a decisive attack on the lonely black king.

Black has three "local" weaknesses – the a5-pawn, the d6-pawn, the hanging bishop at e7, and one "global" worry – the only defender of his castling position is the knight at e5. This piece looks rock solid in the centre, but in fact White needs only 2-3 moves to oust it by f4. That could happen if Black stays passively, for instance:

17...h6 18.♘h5 ♖c7 19.♕e2 (19.f4 ♘g4) 19...♘g6 20.f4 ♕a8 (20...♘xd5 21.♘xd5 ♗xd5 22.♗xa5) 21.f5 ♘e5 22.f6 with destruction.

Apparently Black should try

to continue with his assault on the d5-pawn. One possible way is to give access to his queen to a8 by 17...♖c7. Then White must hurry in order to keep the initiative: 18.♗d3! ♘xd3 (18...g6 loses the a5-pawn to 19.♘b5 ♖d7 20.♗xa5±) 19.♕xd3. White parted with an important bishop, but without his centralised knight Black's defence looks difficult. White's cavalry should prevail, for example: 19...♗f6 20.♘e4 ♗e5 21.♗xa5 ♖e7 22.♘g5 g6 23.♕h3 h5 24.♘xh5, or 19...♕a8 20.♕g3 g6 (20...♘xd5 21.♘h5) 21.♘h5 ♘xd5 22.♘xd5 ♗xd5 23.♖xe7! ♖xe7 24.♘f6+ ♔g7 25.♗c3+–. Even the best defence 19...♗g5 20.♘e4 ♗xf4 21.♗xf4 ♗xd5 22.♘xd6 ♖d7 23.♕g3 clearly favours White.

With his next move Black pursues several goals: he removes the bishop from its vulnerable stand at e7, indirectly hits once more d5 by threatening to capture on f4, and he brings a defender to his kingside.

17...♗g5 18.♖ad1

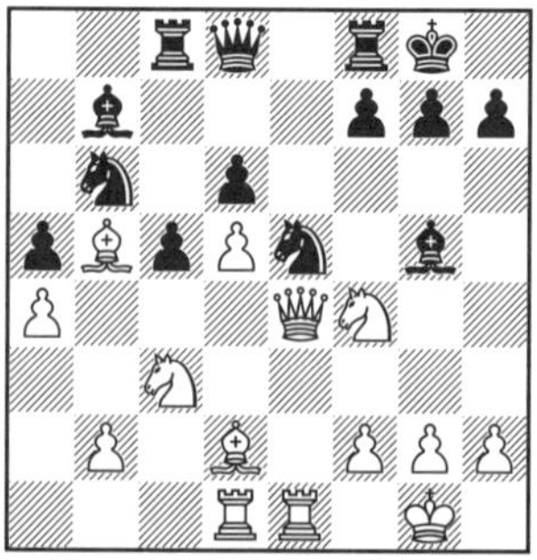

This is a critical position since Black must define his setup on the kingside. Instead, he can hardly persist with his campaign against the d5-pawn with 18...♖c7 19.♕c2 ♕a8 as he risks to be run over after 20.♘h5 ♗xd2 (20...♗e7 21.f4 ♘g4 22.♗d3 g6 23.h3±) 21.♕xd2. White's threats would force Black's queen to return: 21...♕d8, but that would not save him due to the thematic: 22.f4! ♘g4 23.h3! ♘h6 (23...♘f6 24.♘xf6+ ♕xf6 25.♘e4 ♕g6 26.f5 ♕xf5 27.♕xa5±) 24.♘e4 ♘f5 25.♕d3 ♔h8 26.♘ef6 ♗c8 27.g4 gxf6 28.gxf5 with a big edge.

Rybka prefers 18...h6 19.♕e2 ♖c7

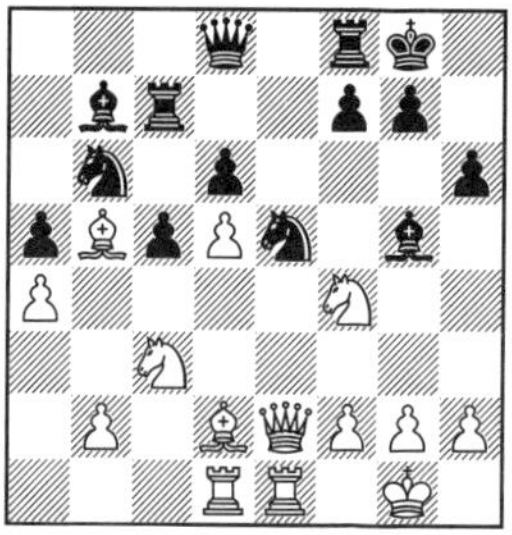

Now White wins a tempo by:

20.h4! facing Black with an unpleasant choice:

a) 20...♗xh4 21.♘e4 ♖e7 22.♗xa5 ♗c8 23.♕d2 ♗f5 24.♘xc5±;

b) 20...♗xf4 21.♗xf4 ♖e7 22.♕h5 ♘g6 23.♗g3 ♖xe1+ 24.♖xe1 ♘e7 25.♘e4 ♘ec8 26.♗c6±;

c) 20...♗e7 21.♘e4 ♕a8 22.♘h5 ♗xd5 (22...f5 23.f4 ♘g4 24.♘xd6 ♗xd6 25.♕e6+ ♔h7 26.♕xd6 ♘xd5 27.♗d7±) 23.♗c3 ♗xe4 (23...f5 is bad in view of 24.♗xe5 dxe5 25.♘c3 ♗e4 26.f3 ♗xh4 27.fxe4 ♗xe1 28.♕xe1 f4 29.♖d6±) 24.♕xe4 ♕xe4 (24...f6 25.♕e2±) 25.♖xe4 when a5 is hanging, e.g. 25...♖a8 26.♘xg7! ♔xg7 27.♖xe5+–.

Black decides to anticipate the attack by moving the other pawn, but eventually it turned out that the long dark-squared diagonal was seriously weakened:

18...g6 19.♕c2± ♗e7 20.♘e4 ♖a8

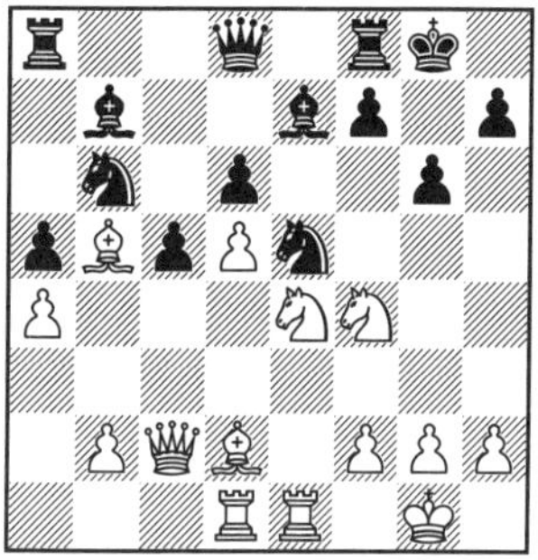

Black admits the complete failure of his opening strategy. Now the game moves on to the stage of conversion of White's big positional advantage. Dreev executes it brilliantly. His next aim is to destroy Black's only stronghold at e5.

21.♗c3± ♘bd7 22.♕d2 ♗c8 23.♖e2 ♖a7 24.♖de1 ♕b6 25.♘d3 ♘xd3 26.♕xd3 ♘e5 27.♕g3 f5 28.♘xd6! ♗xd6

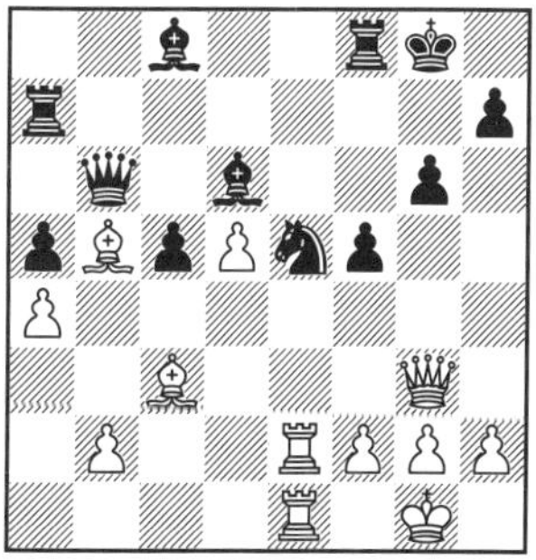

29.♖xe5!

29.♗xe5 was safe and sound, but apparently Dreev was playing for the galleries. He wants to crown his strategy with total domination on the dark squares.

29...f4 30.♕g5 f3 31.♖e8 ♖af7 32.♖xf8+ ♖xf8 33.♖e7 ♖f5 34.♕h6 1–0

---

12. Dreev–Banikas
EU–Cup 17th Panormo 2001
Comments by Dreev from Chess Stars book "My 100 Best Games"

1.d4 ♘f6 2.c4 c5 3.d5 b5 4.cxb5 a6 5.b6

I play that line regularly against the Volga Gambit – White does not accept the pawn sacrifice and that leads to quite different positions in comparison to the line 5.bxa6. Some two years before this game, I had written a special article on that subject, which was published in the German magazine *Schach*. I had shared with my readers my understanding of that variation in details in this article. Naturally, chess theory develops permanently; fashion changes and evaluations of positions sometimes even contradict each other. Still, it seems to me that most of the contents of my article remain upto-date even now. Frankly speaking, I had no idea whether my opponent had studied my theoretical work before our game or not...

One of the basic plans for Black against the 5.b6 system is – d7-d6, g7-g6, ♗f8-g7 and depending on circumstances – capturing on b6 with the queen, or with the knight. It is interesting, but still somewhat slow for Black to play: 5...a5 6.♘c3 ♗a6 –

with the idea to develop quickly the light squared bishop and to trade it for its white counterpart, preventing White's castling in the process. Still, tournament practice has confirmed that after White's energetic reply 7.f4!, followed by ♘f3 and e2-e4 – the position is in his favour.

My opponent chose the sharpest line, in which Black opens up the centre immediately:

5...e6 6.♘c3 ♘xd5 7.♘xd5 exd5 8.♕xd5 ♘c6

GM H.Banikas had not played the Volga Gambit in any game before our tournament; nevertheless I had expected that variation as an eventual possibility. The point was that in the previous round, in the game Portisch – Banikas, that position had already appeared on the board. The eminent Hungarian veteran chose an unfavourable line for White – 9.♗g5 ♕xb6 10.♕e4+ ♗e7 11.♗xe7 ♘xe7 12.♕c2 (In case of 12.♕xa8, ♗lack can at least force a draw with: 12...♕xb2 13.♖d1 ♕c3+ 14.♖d2 ♕c1+.) 12...♖b8 (It also seemed good for Black to continue with the simple move 12...d5!?, with an advantage for him.) 13.b3 – and after: 13...c4 14.♘f3 cxb3 15.axb3 ♕xb3 16.♕xb3 ♖xb3, Black remained with an extra pawn.

I decided to follow my own recommendation from the article, so I played:

9.♘f3

This is the best for White and now Black is practically forced to reply with:

9...♖b8 10.e4

White's other possibility to fight for the opening advantage is the move 10.♗d2 and one of its ideas is to place the bishop quickly on the c3-square, from where it protects the b2-pawn and it is aimed at Black's kingside. I have tested the move 10.♗d2 in several games and quite successfully at that. Therefore, I recommended it in my article and I made a conclusion there that although the move 10.e4 (Naturally, I analyzed thoroughly that move too in my article...) was also possible, Black, as a rule after it, could manage to solve his opening problems. During the game, it came to my mind that my opponent should have been familiar with this publication and he might have been specially prepared for our game, so I decided to play 10.e4, moreover that during the period after the appearance of the article I had succeeded in finding some additional possibilities for White in this variation. I still consider the move 10.♗d2 up to the point in this line, though...

10...♗e7 11.♗c4 0–0 12.0–0

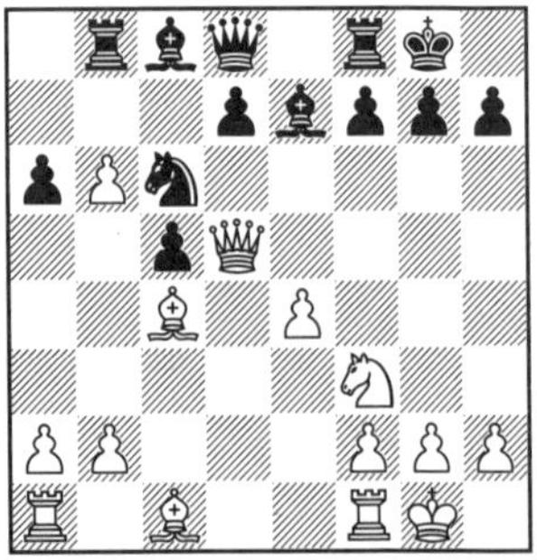

12...♘a5

Black avoids the main variation and he continues with a seldom played line. The idea behind 12...♘a5 is quite obvious he wishes to repel White's bishop away from the a2-g8 diagonal. The drawback of that move is evident too – Black's knight is decentralized.

13.♗d3 ♖xb6 14.♕h5 ♗b7

In the game Lautier-Koch, France 1999, Black played an interesting move – 14...d5 and after: 15.exd5 g6 16.♕h6 ♕xd5 17.♖e1 ♖e6 18.♖xe6 ♗xe6 19.♘g5 ♗xg5 20.♗xg5 ♕d4 21.♗d2 ♕xd3 22.♗xa5 ♗xa2 23.♖e1 ♕d6 24.h4 f6 25.♗c3 ♗f7 26.♖e4, the opponents agreed to a draw.

15.♗d2 ♖d6

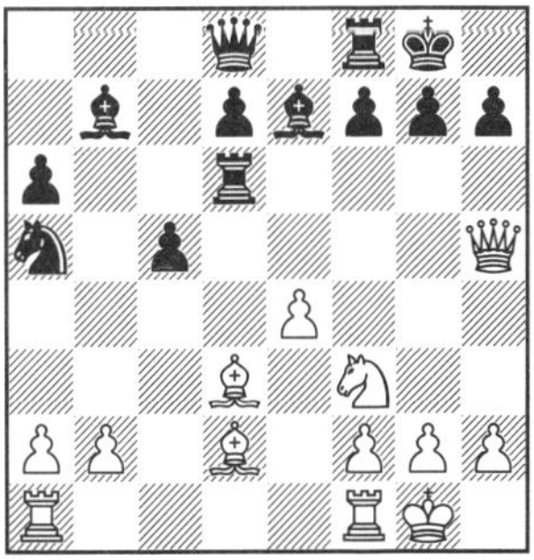

Black has tested in practice 15...♖e6. Following 16.♖fe1, White's position is preferable.

16.♖ad1

This is a novelty. In the game Arakelian-Sumaneev, Briansk 1995, White went back with his bishop 16.♗c2. I did not like to lose a tempo for the retreat of the bishop and I played a useful move protecting it indirectly.

16...♘c6 17.♗f4

The most natural try here is 17.♗c3, but I did not like Black's possible reply 17...♘d4.

17...♖g6!

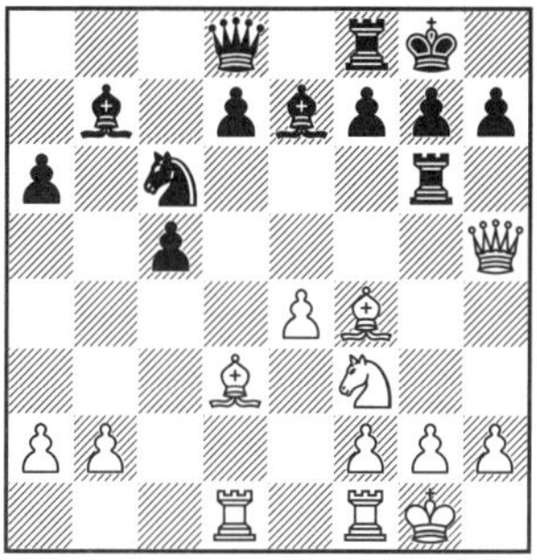

18.♗c4

That is an imprecision and it became the reason that my opponent could have equalised the position, as we are going to see later.

Naturally, the pawn-advance 18.e5 would have been too optimistic. Black has two good possibilities after that: 18...♘d4 19.♘e1 h6 20.♗e3 ♖b6, or 18...♖xg2+ 19.♔xg2 g6, followed by ♘c6-d4.

Meanwhile, I should have played the move 18.♖fe1, protecting my pawn and preserving the threat e4-e5. During the game I thought that the consequences of 18...♘d4 might be quite unclear, but later in my home analyses, I understood that after 19.♘xd4 cxd4 20.a3, White's position should be better.

18...d6

Now, it seems that White's pieces are perfectly placed and his advantage should be overwhelming. In fact, things are far from simple. For example, White cannot play 19.e5?, due to 19...♘d4. I was considering the move 19.♖fe1, but Black could counter that with 19...♗c8!. After White's only move 20.h3, Black redeploys his bishop – 20...♗e6 and his position is quite acceptable. Here, I thought for a long time before playing:

19.h3

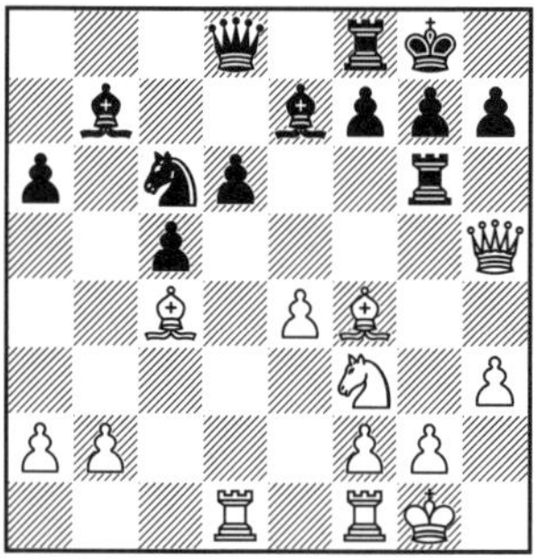

This move is motivated not so much by the need to ensure a leeway for the king, but to prevent Black's maneuver ♗b7-c8-e6. Now, 19...♗c8 is of course bad, for example, because of 20.e5.

It looks like the position will soon be clearly in favour of White, particularly if Black does not play actively enough. My positional advantage seemed to be guaranteed and it was supposed to increase, since Black's bishop could hardly be redeployed. My opponent found here a wonderful possibility to avoid the positional bind:

19...♕a8!

White now obviously needs his rook on e1, but unfortunately I had to lose a tempo for the move h2-h3. Here, after 20.♖fe1, Black organizes some counterplay after the knight-manoeuvre – 20...♘b4.

I did not have too much time left on the clock at that moment. My opening advantage seemed to be dissipating and I understood that I would fail to consolidate my position. Therefore I decided to act in a completely different fashion:

20.♗g5 ♕d8

The game is rather unclear after 20...♗xg5 21.♘xg5 ♖h6 22.♗xf7+ ♔h8 23.♕e2 ♘d4.

21.♗e3 ♕a8 22.♗g5 ♕d8 23.♗d2 ♗f6

Here the move 23...♕a8 would have been senseless, because of 24.♗d5. In order for Black's battery to begin functioning, he should remove his knight somewhere, but White has taken the b4-square under control.

24.♗d5 ♕a8 25.♗c3 ♘e7 26.♗xf6 ♖xf6

Black could have played here more calmly – 26...♘xd5 27.exd5 ♖h6! (This is better for Black than: 27...♖xf6 28.♖fe1.) 28.♕g5 ♖g6 and that might lead to a possible repetition of moves.

Now, the fight becomes fierce again and its development is favourable for me...

27.♘g5 h6 28.♗xf7+ ♖8xf7

29.♘xf7 ♖xf7 30.♖xd6 ♗xe4 31.♖fd1 ♖f8

I had too little time left to be able to apprehend all thc fine points of that tricky position, but I had the feeling that White's prospects should be preferable.

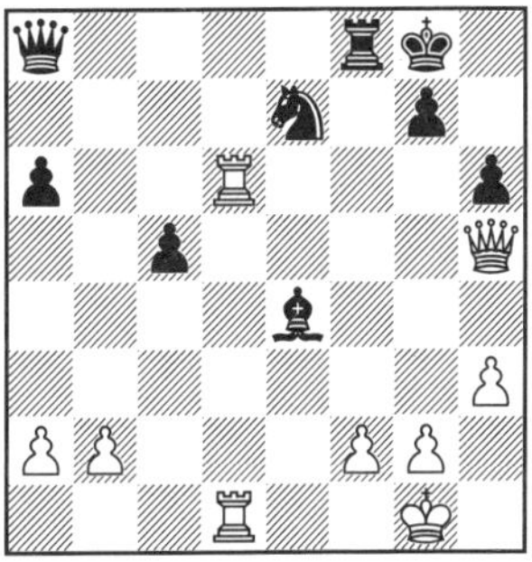

32.♖d7!?

I considered the other possibility too – 32.♕e2!?, but I made up my mind to follow with the penetration of the rook.

32...♘f5 33.♕g6 ♕c6?

Black has certain problems now. For example in case of 33...♔h8, White can continue with 34.♕b6!?. Possibly, Black had to try 33... ♕e8!?. The exchange of queens becomes quite probable in many variations and that would lead to an endgame. Instead, H.Banikas tried to exchange queens outright and thus he in fact was making me a present. I was in a severe time-trouble at that moment, so ...unfortunately I did not accept it...:

34.♕xc6?

Naturally, I saw the move – 34.♖1d6, but I never connected it with the pawn-advance g2-g4 (attacking Black's knight...) in the line: 34...♕a4 35.g4!+– ♕b4 (or 35...♕c2 36.gxf5 ♕c1+ 37.♖d1) 36.♖d2!. In case of 34... ♕b5, White can follow with the simple: 35.♕e6+ ♔h8 36.♖d8+–.

So, as you have already seen – the move 34.♖1d6 was winning quite easily.

34...♗xc6 35.♖c7 ♖f6 36.f3

I was reluctant to continue with 36. ♖c1, because of: 36...♘d4 37.♖xc5 ♖g6, although it might have been quite reasonable to play like that and to follow later with 38.g4.

36...♔h7

That is an unnecessary loss of time. Black could have equalised with 36... ♘d4! and if 37.b4 (It is better for White to play 37.♔f2.) then Black would have the resource 37...♖d6! and it would be White who would have to worry about how to make a draw...

37.♖c1 ♘d4?!

That is already a serious imprecision and the reason was that Black was also short of time. It would have been much better for him to follow with 37... ♗d5 and after: 38.b3 ♘d4 39.♔h2, the position would have been equal. Now, White can collect three pawns for his knight after: 39.♖1xc5 ♘e6 40.♖xg7+ ♔xg7 41.♖xd5 ♘f4 42.♖d7+ ♔f8, but that would not change the correct evaluation of the position...

38.♖xc5 ♗b5 39.♖e7 ♖g6

Black had better play here 39...♖d6.

40.♔f2 ♖d6

White's rooks now are a bit misplaced, they are badly coordinated and they come under attack by Black's pieces. Therefore, my plan was to consolidate my position by exchanging a couple of rooks.

41.♖e4!

Now, Black cannot play 41...♘e6 42.♖c2 ♗d3, because of 43.♖d2.

41...♗d7 42.h4 ♘e6 43.♖c2 ♔g6 44.♔e3 ♔f6 45.♖d2

So, I managed finally to accomplish what I wanted – the rooks would soon be exchanged. Black's position without rooks would be extremely unpleasant and maybe even lost.

45...♖xd2 46.♔xd2 a5

My next plan included the following: I wanted to improve maximally the placement of my kingside pawns and then to create a passed pawn on the queenside. It is tremendously difficult for Black to resist that plan successfully on both sides of the board.

47.b3 ♗c6 48.♖c4 ♗d7 49.♔e3 ♔e5 50.h5 ♔d5 51.g4 a4

Now, my task becomes much easier. Black's pawn-advance a6-a5 was more or less reasonable, but his last move just speeds up his demise. The rest is quite simple.

52.♖c3 axb3 53.♖d3+ ♔c6 54.♖xb3 ♔d6 55.♖b4 ♗c6 56.a3 ♘g5 57.♖f4 ♘e6 58.♖f5 ♗e8 59.♖a5 ♗c6 60.♖a7 ♘c7 61.♔f4 ♘d5+ 62.♔g3 ♘c7 63.f4 ♗d7 64.♖b7 ♘d5 65.a4 ♘f6 66.a5 ♔c6 67.a6 ♘e4+ 68.♔h4 ♘c5 69.♖b8 ♘xa6 70.♖g8 ♘c5 71.♖xg7 ♘e6 72.♖f7 ♔d6 73.♔g3 ♗e8 74.♖h7 ♗b5 75.♖xh6 ♔e7 76.f5 ♘g5 77.♖g6 ♘e4+ 78.♔f4 ♘f6 79.h6 1–0

13. Kir.Georgiev–Vaisser
EU–ch playoff 15', Ohrid 2001

1.d4 ♘f6 2.c4 c5 3.d5 b5 4.cxb5 a6 5.b6 e6 6.♘c3 ♘xd5 7.♘xd5 exd5 8.♕xd5 ♘c6 9.♘f3 ♖b8 ♗e7 11.♗c3 0–0 12.e4 ♖xb6 13.♗c4 d6 14.0–0 ♗f6 15.♖ad1 ♗e6 16.♕d3 ♘b4 17.♕e2 ♘xa2!

17...♗xc4 18.♕xc4 ♕e7 is passive and leaves White on top after 19.♖d2±!

18.♗xa2 ♗xa2 19.♗a5 ♖xb2 20.♕xb2

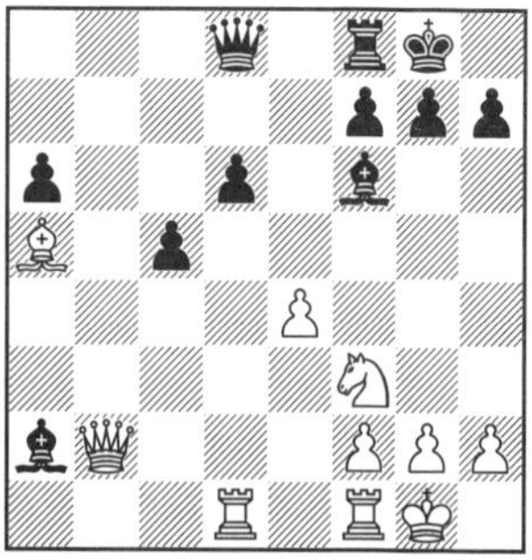

20...♗xb2

White wins the exchange, but the enemy bishops, working in unison with the passed c-pawn, are very strong. The less pieces on board, the better for me. In the game I managed to trade queens and a pair of rooks which gave me some advantage. My task would have been more difficult after 20...♕xa5. Of course, White is not risking to lose, but he will probably have to return the exchange in order to stop the c-pawn. Then the game would be a draw. Here is my analysis:

a) 21.e5 dxe5 22.♖a1 e4=.

b) 21.♕d2 ♗c3!

Again, Black has less problems with more pieces on the board. 21...♕xd2 22.♖xd2 ♗c4 23.♖c1 ♗b5 24.♖xd6 ♗e7 25.♖d5 gives White some pull, for instance 25...♗c6 26.♖dd1 ♗xe4 27.♖d7 ♖e8 28.♖e1 and Black still has to struggle for the draw.

22.♕xd6 ♗b3 (22...♗c4 23.♖b1) 23.♖c1 c4

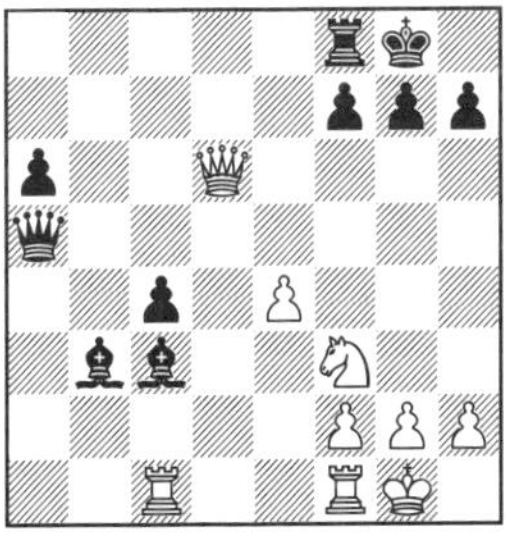

I do not see how to improve White's position here. 24.♘d4 looks most attractive, but Black manages to put in motion his a-pawn just in time: 24...♗xd4 25.♕xd4 ♕d8 26.♕c5 a5=. Sooner or later White will have to take on c4.

c) 21.♕c2

This line is similar to b). 21...c4 22.♖xd6 ♗b3 23.♕c1 c3 24.♕e3 ♖c8. It is difficult for White to create threats. All the variations seem to lead to a dead draw: 25.♘d4 ♗xd4 26.♖xd4 c2 27.♖c1 ♕b5 28.♕c3 ♖b8 29.g3 a5 30.♖xc2= or 25.♖c1 ♗e7 26.♖d3 ♗b4= 27.♘d4 ♗c4 28.♖dxc3 ♗xc3 29.♖xc3 ♕d8.

21.♗xd8 ♖xd8 22.♖d2 ♖b8 23.♖xd6 h6 24.♖fd1

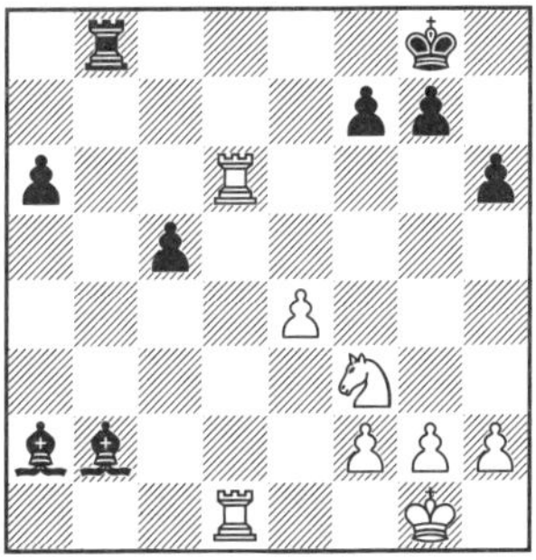

24...♗c4

Suddenly it turns out that Black's passed pawns are not as mobile as they look. He cannot avoid the trade of his rook which is a big achievement for me. It is well known that the batery ♖+♗ works much better vs ♖♖, than a single bishop vs a single rook, because the two different pieces complement each other.

In the diagram position 24...c4 cannot force a draw because instead of falling into the trap by 25.♖xa6? 25...♗b3 26.♖e1 c3 27.♘d4 c2 28.♘xb3 ♖xb3 29.♖c6 c1♕ 30.♖exc1 ♗xc1 31.♖xc1 h5!= with a position from any endgame primer, White would follow up his main plan of swapping the rooks: 25.♖d8+ ♖xd8 26.♖xd8+ ♔h7 27.♖c8 c3 28.♘d4

♗b1 29.♘e2 c2 30.♖c5 and Black is in impasse. Then 30...a5 31.♖xa5 c1♕+ 32.♘xc1 ♗xc1 33.♖a1 regains the piece and the resulting position with symmetrical pawns is a win. I'm not too sure about the same ending with an additional a-pawn for Black. It would arise after 29...♗xe4 30.♘xc3. I suppose that White has very good winning chances though.

Vaisser's decision to stay passively is wrong. He gets a much worse version of the variations I have discussed. Note however, that the game was a playoff for the European championship and time control was only 15 minutes.

25.♖d8+ ♖xd8 26.♖xd8+ ♔h7 27.♖c8 ♗a3 28.♘e5 ♗e6 29.♖a8

Now the a-pawn perishes and the light-squared bishop is passive on e6 so the game is over.

29...c4 30.♖xa6 ♗b2 31.♘f3 c3 32.♖c6 ♗a2 33.♘d4 ♗b1 34.f3 ♗a3 35.♖xc3 ♗b2 36.♖c4 ♗d3 37.♖a4 1–0

---

14. Kuljasevic–Andrews
USA tt ICC INT 2007

1.d4 ♘f6 2.c4 c5 3.d5 b5 4.cxb5 a6 5.b6 e6 6.♘c3 ♘xd5 7.♘xd5 exd5 8.♕xd5 ♘c6 9.♘f3 ♖b8 10.e4 ♗e7 11.♗d2 0–0 12.♗c4 ♖xb6 13.♗c3 d6 14.0–0 ♗e6

14...♗f6 is slightly more precise as Black achieves to trade all the minor pieces faster. In the game Black still had to work for that.

15.♕d3 ♗xc4 16.♕xc4 ♗f6 17.♖ad1 ♗xc3 18.bxc3 ♕f6 19.♖d3 ♖e8 20.♕a4 ♔f8 21.♖fd1 ♘e5 22.♘xe5 ♕xe5 23.♖e3 ♕f4

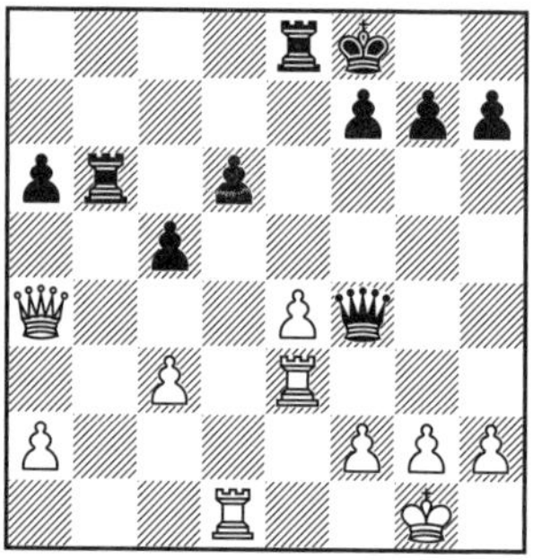

White has some practical chances, because his rooks are better coordinated and one of them can be lifted to the kingside. Also, the a6-pawn is a bit more vulnerable than the a2-one. One important resource of White might be the breakthrough e4-e5, aiming to take on c5 and make a passer. The next few moves aim to prepare it. Interestingly, Rybka assesses this position as dead equal, but humans would undoubtedly take White here.

24.g3 ♕g4 25.♔g2 g6 26.♖d5 ♕e6 27.♕a5 ♖eb8 28.c4 f6

White has made some progress. Black's castling position is weakened and the f6-pawn is a target. Now best would have been 29.h4 in order to provoke ...h5. The queen at a5 is binding the black rooks.

29.♕c3 ♖b2 30.♕d3 ♔e7

(see next diagram)

31.♕a3

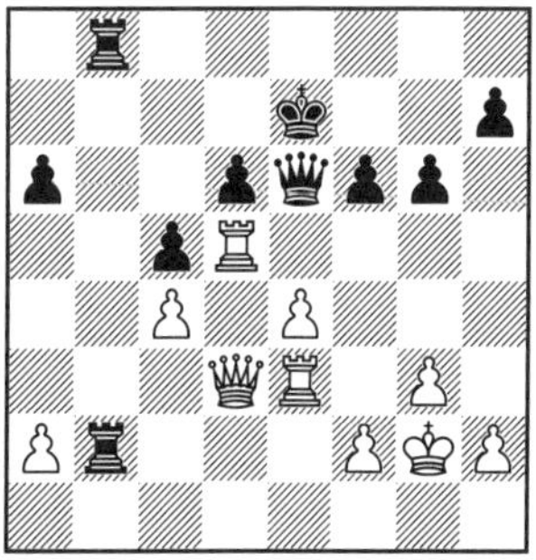

Kuljasevic is too hesitant. He should have staked everything on the attack. For instance, 31.♖f3 ♖xa2? 32.♕e3± would give him a tremendous pull, e.g. 32...♔f7 33.♕h6 ♖h8 34.h4 ♖b2 35.h5. Instead, he gives the opponent time to retreat the king back to g7.

31...♖8b6 32.♕a5 ♔f7 33.h3 ♔g7 34.g4!

White is planning g4-g5.

34...♔f7 35.♖f3 ♕xe4 36.♕c3 ♕e7 37.g5 f5 38.h4

38.♕h8 ♕xg5+ 39.♖g3 ♕h6 40.♖xf5+ gxf5 41.♕g8+ ♔f6 42.♕h8+ ♔e6 43.♕e8+ is only a draw.

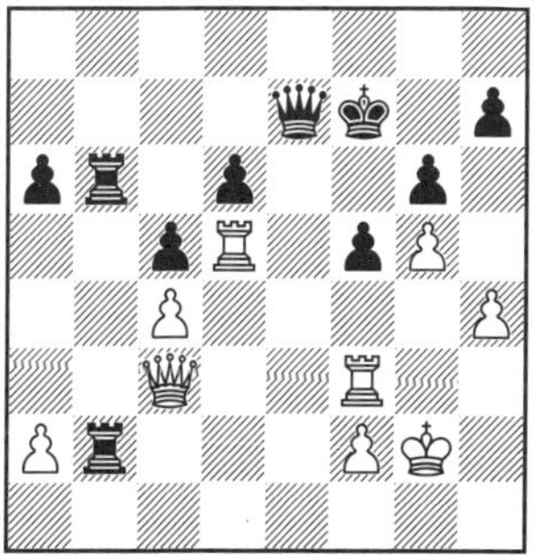

38...♕e4!

The best defence is to stay active. 38...♔g8 39.♖e3 ♕f8 (39...♕d8 40.♕e1) 40.h5 keeps an initiative, for example, 40...♕d8 41.hxg6 hxg6 42.♖h3 ♕xg5+ 43.♖g3 ♕e7 44.♕f3 ♕e4 45.♖xg6+ ♔h7 46.♕xe4 fxe4 47.♖g4 ♔h6 48.♔g3 ♖b1 49.♖xe4 ♖g1+ 50.♔f3 ♖g6 51.♖d2±. After the text Black should be able to organise some perpetual check.

39.♕f6+ ♔g8 40.♖dd3 ♕g4+ 41.♖g3 ♕e4+ 42.♖df3 ♖b8 43.h5 ♕e5?

Finally Black errs. He had to find the idea 43...f4! 44.hxg6 (44.♖h3 gxh5 45.♕xd6 ♖xf2+=) 44...♖xf2+! 45.♔xf2 ♕c2+ 46.♔g1 ♖b1+ 47.♖f1 ♖xf1+ 48.♔xf1 ♕xc4+ 49.♔g1 fxg3 50.♕d8+=. Now his position collapses:

44.hxg6 ♖xf2+ 45.♖xf2 ♕e4+ 46.♔h3 ♕h1+ 47.♖h2 ♕f1+ 48.♔h4 ♕f4+ 49.♔h5 ♖b7 50.♖e2 1–0

---

15. Stefanova – Pogonina
Solin 13.12.2007

1.d4 ♘f6 2.c4 c5 3.d5 b5 4.cxb5 a6 5.b6 e6 6.♘c3 exd5 7.♘xd5 ♘xd5 8.♕xd5 ♘c6 9.♘f3 ♖b8 10.e4 ♗e7 11.♗c4 0–0 12.0–0 ♖xb6 13.♗d2 d6 14.♗c3 ♗e6 15.♕d3 ♘b4 16.♕e2 ♗xc4 17.♕xc4 d5 18.exd5 ♕xd5 19.♘e5

Black has gotten rid of the backward pawn, but that only made the rest of her queenside even more vulnerable. Still, her play is reasonable enough as the rook at b6 becomes operational along the 6th rank and as a whole, Black's pieces obtain some activity.

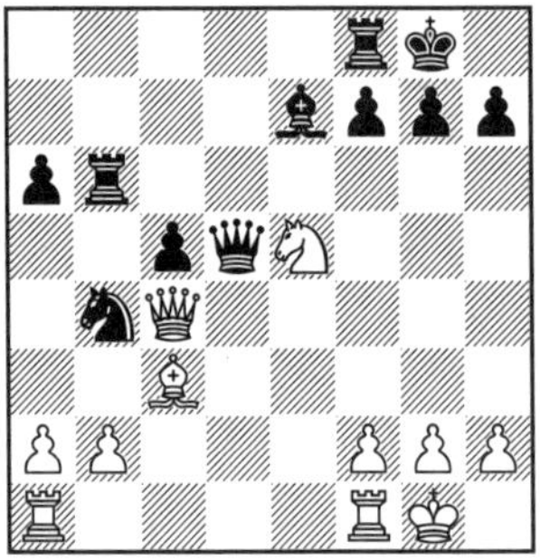

White will aim to trade queens and a pair of rooks to reduce the enemy's counterplay. Note however, that White needs one rook to attack more effectively the weak black pawns. White can also exchange any of the minor pieces, but she would prefer to keep them both since the black knight has not a stable stand.

As a whole, the game will be often decided by the fate of Black's knight. If it finds an active position, chances would be about equal.

In earlier games in this line Black tried to incorporate the knight onto d4, but that did not work well as the white rook invaded Black's camp along the d-file. Here are some examples:

19...♖e6 20.♖fd1 ♕xc4 21.♘xc4 22.♖xd8+ ♗xd8 23.a3 ♘c6 24.♔f1 ♗e7 25.♖e1, Iskusnyh-Pogonina, Moscow 2006:

Here most consistent would have been 25.♖d1±. The knight cannot reach d4 as that square is controlled by the bishop at c3.

In the game Iotov-Ntiloudi, Kalamaria 2008, Black decided to trade the defender of d4 by 21...♗f6 22.♗xf6 ♖xf6, but the weakness of the c5-pawn did not allow the b4-knight to shift over to d4: 23.♘e3! ♖b8 24.♖d2 ♖fb6 25.b3 a5 26.♖c1 ♘a6 27.♘c4 ♖b5 28.♖d6±.

Finally, 19...♖d6 20.a3 ♘c2 also failed to 21.♕xd5 ♖xd5 22.♘c6! ♗g5 23.♖ad1 ♖xd1 24.♖xd1 ♖c8 25.♖d6± and the black knight missed again its goal, Lomineishvili-Pogonina, Kemer 2007.

Apparently Pogonina learned a lesson and in the current game she heads with the knight to d3.

19...♖d6 20.a3 ♘d3 21.♖ad1 ♕xc4 22.♘xc4 ♖d7

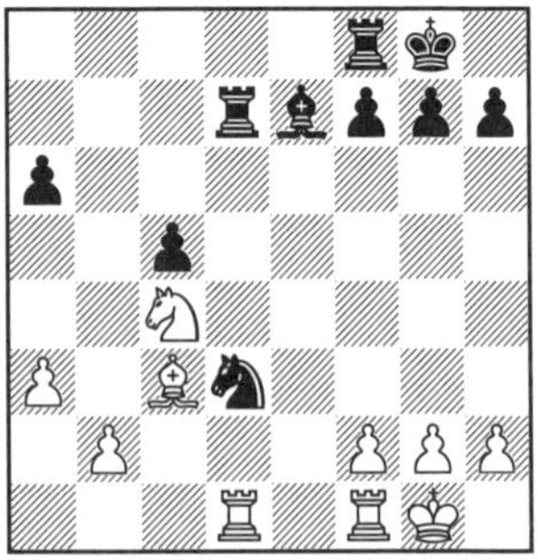

In the previous examples Black had difficulties due to the raving white rook that ruled over the board from the d-file. Now the situation is rather different. Black guarded both rooks and the d3-knight seems to effectively bar the d-file. Still White's game is preferable due to her better pawn structure.

23.♖fe1

23.♖d2 ♗f6 24.♗xf6 gxf6 25.♔f1 ♖d4 26.♖e3 ♖fd8 27.b3 is also slightly better for White, but Stefanova prefers to have at least one rook free for action.

23...♖fd8 24.♘b6 ♖b7 25.♖e3 ♔f8 26.♘c4 ♖bd7 27.g3 ♗f6 28.♔f1 ♗xc3 29.bxc3

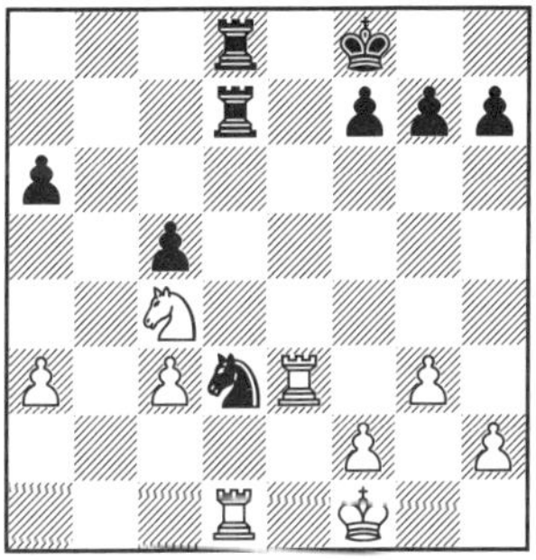

A very instructive position. It perfectly illustrates White's advantage in this opening line. The activity of the rooks and the unstable state of the d3-knight make the difference here. White is threatening with ♖b1 so Pogonina correctly seeks exchanges.

29...♘e5 30.♖xd7 ♘xd7 31.♖d3

Black's worst nightmare has become true. White gained control over the d-file and now she is going to hit the weak queenside pawns. There is still a lot of fight ahead though.

31...♔e7 32.♖d6 ♘b8?

After this awful move Pogonina should be lost. She had to activate her pieces with 32...♘f6 33.♖xa6 ♘e4 34.a4 ♖d1+ 35.♔g2 ♖a1 and while the distant passer should give White some edge, the outcome would have been unclear. Now White calmly finishes off her opponent.

33.♖b6 ♔d7 34.♖b7+ ♔e6 35.f4 g6 36.♔e2 ♘d7 37.♖a7 ♘b8 38.♘e5 f6 39.♘d3 c4 40.♘b2 ♖d5 41.♖xh7 ♘d7 42.♘xc4 ♖c5 43.♔d3 ♖d5+ 44.♔c2 ♖c5 45.♘d2 ♖a5 46.♘b3 ♖d5 47.♘d4+ ♔d6 48.h4 ♖a5 49.♘b3 ♖d5 50.♖g7 ♔e6 51.♘d4+ 1–0

The Budapest Gambit

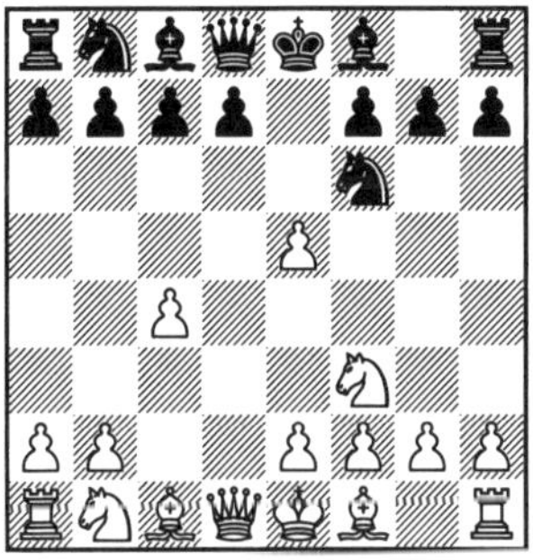

Part 4

Main Ideas

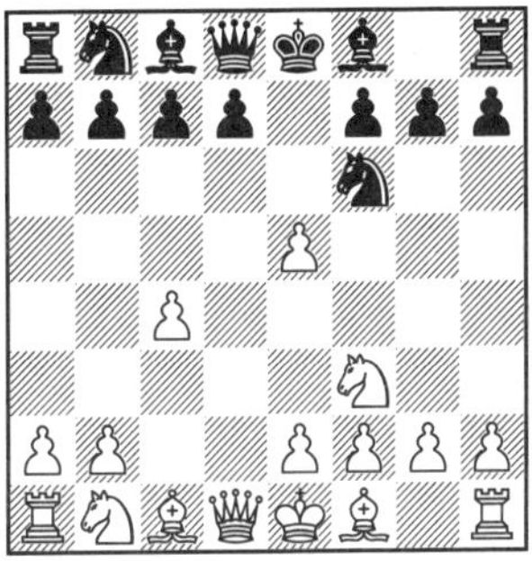

1.d4 ♘f6 2.c4 e5 3.dxe5

This gambit was born at the end of the 19th century in Budapest, in the game Adler-Maroczy, 1896. Although it was occasionally employed by famous players as Alekhine, Euwe, Reti, Vidmar, Tarrasch, Tartakower, Bogoljubow, the gambit has never made it to the big stage. Lately only Mamedyarov and Short of the top grandmasters seem to fire it as a surprise weapon, mostly in rapid games. Is it refuted or should we speak about a whim of fashion?

I think there are two main reasons for that state:

1. The pawn structure that arises from the Budapest Gambit, is basically in White's favour. It is much more flexible for the first player, who has a number of good strategic plans. He can play on the queenside and prepare c4-c5 (by b4, if needed), or he can thrust f4-f5, even f6, with a dreadful kingside attack. He can also be just maintaining a grip on the centre by lining up his pawns on e4 and f4, watching his time for a possible break with c5 or e5.

Black's pawn formation, on the contrary, is very solid, without weaknesses, but entirely defensive. It does not provide a positional foundation for any active plan. Thus the second player is restricted to piece play only. If he fails to take the opponent by surprise in the opening and allows his pieces to be repelled from the kingside, he must brace himself for a long defence.

2. Due to Black's rigid pawn structure, this opening is very meagre on strategic ideas. Essentially, Black faces time and again one and the same setup, with the only difference being the position of the dark-squared bishop (at c5 or e7). Such an approach to the game is unacceptable at higher level. Even if the gambit were totally sane and sound (and it is not!), using it regularly would reduce the creative potential of the player. Chess is too rich to downgrade it to only one schema. Young players often underestimate such factors while building their opening repertoire. They seek quick results and clear, "easy", plans, but that severely limits their positional understanding. As a result, they badly "float" in unfamiliar structures. Even endgame play is affected, since many endings inherit some strategic concepts from the opening. A narrow range of pawn formations in your opening repertoire leads to a deficit of weapons later in the game.

General principles are good, but when facing a rare opening, we often prove unprepared for concrete play. This is understandable, since it is inefficient to spend a lot of time preparing for a line which might occur in a game or two per year. Black players count on that and use the surprise weapon in rapid games when we'll lack time for calculation. That explains the decent results of Black in some branches of the Budapest Gambit.

I'm going to arm you with a solid repertoire, which should keep you on the safe side while being logical and clear. I will not be arguing which is the best variation against the Budapest Gambit. I think that any major system against it should be good enough for a small edge, but the learning overhead for some sharp variations is rather big.

Basic Plans and Pawn Structures

After 1.d4 ♘f6 2.c4 e5 3.dxe5 Black chooses between 3...♘e4?! and 3...♘g4. They lead to completely different play so we can speak of independent openings: 3...♘e4?! is commonly defined as Fajarowicz Gambit while 3...♘g4 is actually the "true" Budapest Gambit.

The Fajarowicz's idea is to check from b4, aiming to hinder White's normal development. In this system Black focuses on play in the centre. He adopts a sharp gambit style and many variations feature an early clash that often leads to miniatures.

The Budapest Gambit is deceptively slower at first, but it demands crucial decisions from White around move 12.

The Fajarowicz Gambit

3...♘e4?! 4.a3!

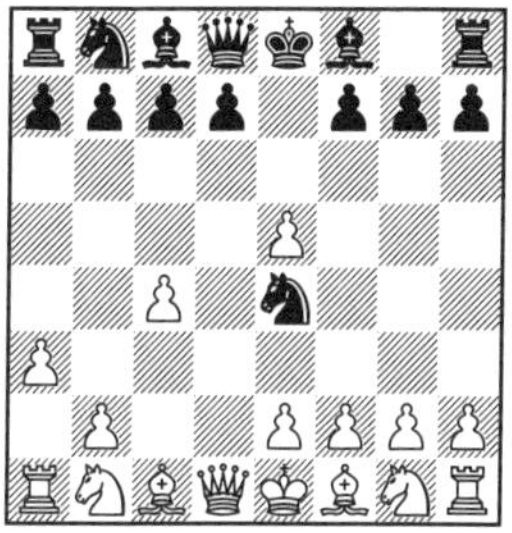

This simple prophylactic move cuts across Black's main idea to check from b4 and it casts a strong doubt on the whole system. Practice has seen Black trying many answers, with discouraging results though.

You should remember that White's plan is to win tempi with ♕c2 and aim for quick development. He can often return the extra pawn, but obtain an overwhelming advantage in the centre:

1. 4...d6 5.♕c2! ♗f5 (5...d5 6.♘c3!) **6.♘c3!**

The *gist* of the plan with 4.a3. White is winning after 6...♘g3 7.e4 ♘xh1 8.exf5. The same idea can be met in another version: 4...♘c6 5.♘f3 d6 6.♕c2! ♗f5 7.♘c3.

2. 4...♕h4

In this line Black regains the pawn, but dramatically falls behind in development.

5.g3 ♕h5 6.♗g2

6...♕xe5 7.♕c2 ♘f6 8.♘f3 ♕h5 9.♘c3 ♗e7 10.h3

White is much better, Van Wely-Alburt, New York 1994.

3. 4...b6 5.♘f3 ♗b7

Lately Black acknowledged that f5 is a bad square for the bishop and began to fianchetto it. However, he could hardly hope to regain the pawn, nor could he contest the centre. White is much better after:

6.♘bd2 ♘c5 7.b4 ♘e6 8.♗b2 d6 9.exd6 ♗xd6 10.e3 0-0±.

Black plays 3...♘g4

4.♘f3

White's plan is not to defend the e5-pawn, but focus on quick harmonious development.

4...♗c5 5.e3 ♘c6 6.♘c3 0-0 7.♗e2 ♘gxe5 8.♘xe5 ♘xe5 9.0-0 ♖e8 10.b3! a5 11.♗b2 ♖a6

Critical position

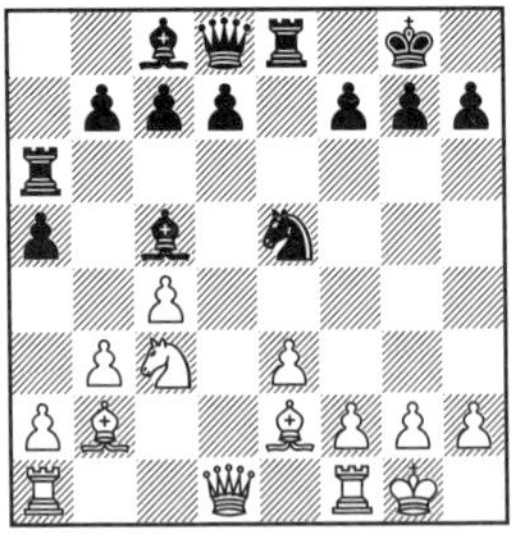

You'll be facing this position in the majority of your games. The manoeuvre ...♖a8-a6-h6, introduced by Drimer, is the main incentive for Black players to choose the Budapest Gambit nowadays. They hope to catch us unprepared and win a miniature with an impetuous attack on the h-file.

Our first task should be to neutralise the lying in ambush c5-bishop before the a6-rook reached h6. That should not be done at any cost though. For instance, 12.♘a4 or 12.♘e4 would achieve this goal, but our knight will be misplaced.

I recommend:

12.♕d5!

with the following branches:

1. 12...♗a7 13.c5! ♖h6

We also attack 13...♖ae6 or 13...♖g6 by 14.f4!

14.f4!

Moskalenko considers in his book only 14.♘e4?

14...♘c6

14...♕h4 is bad owing to 15.fxe5 ♕xh2+ 16.♔f2 ♖xe5 17.♖h1!

15.♘b5

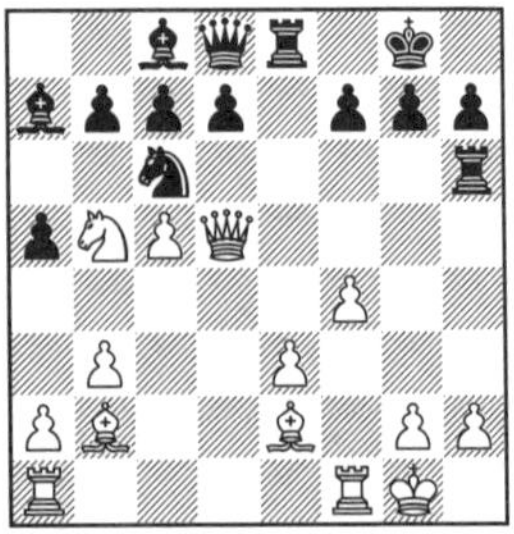

White has a huge advantage. The allegedly most dangerous black pieces, the Drimer rook on h6 and the dark-squared bishop, are isolated and unable to return in defence. The e3-pawn is a greek gift. If Black takes it, he will be crushed along the e-file: 15...♕h4 16.h3 ♖xe3:

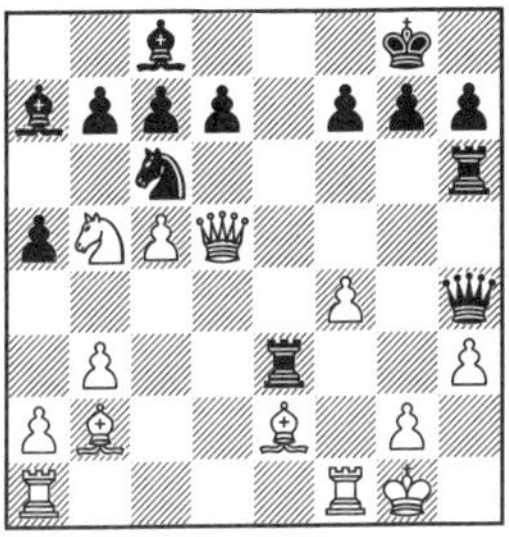

This position occurred in Lalic-Mukic, Yugoslavia 1988 when 17.♗g4, preventing the sacrifice on h3, would have fixed White's advantage.

Our stem **game 17 Flear-Taddei**, Chalons en Champagne 02.05.2009, featured:

15...♕e7 16.♘xa7 ♕xe3+ 17.♖f2 ♘xa7 18.♗c4±.

See the rest of it in the "Complete Games" chapter.

2. 12...♗f8 13.♘e4 ♖ae6

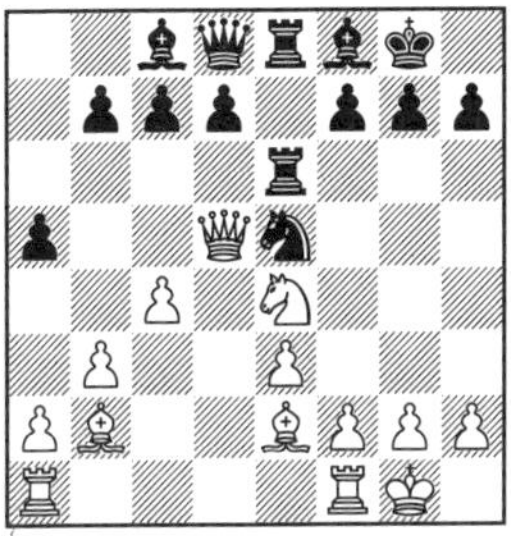

Both Black's bishop are passive. The pawn structure is in White's favour and Black has no dynamic factors to compensate for that. White maintains pressure in the centre by 14.c5 c6 15.♕d4 or 14.♘g3 b6 15.♖ad1 d6 16.♖fe1 ♗d7 17.♕d2 ♖h6, Bischoff-Hort, Dortmund 1989, when 18.h3 deserves attention – 18...♕g5 19.a3 ♖h4 20.♕c2 ♗c6 21.b4.

Points to remember:

- Castle before developing the dark-squared bishop;
- Fianchetto the queen's bishop on the main diagonal;
- Shut in the enemy bishop by 12.♕d5! ♗a7 13.c5!;
- Repel the active knight at e5 by f2-f4;
- Exploit the misplacement of the h6-rook.

Middlegame Plans

In the Budapest Gambit White's basic strategic plan is to occupy the centre with f4 and e4:

Game 16. Polugaevsky–Nunn
Biel 1986

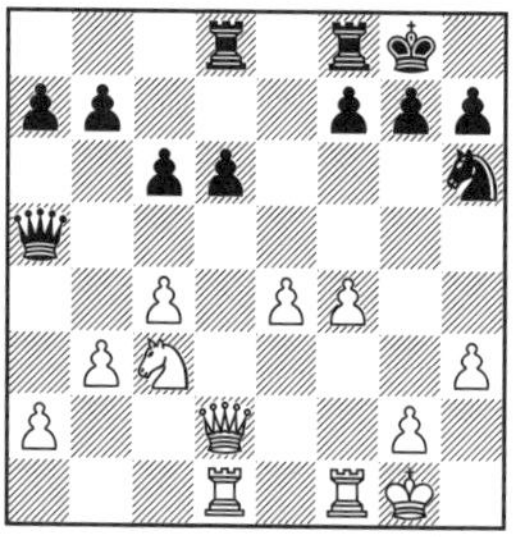

Position after 20.e4

White's grip on the centre would allow him to prepare in future an attack on either wing, e.g. with b3-b4 or g2-g4. Nunn did not want to stay passive and countered with 20...f5, but the opened e-file will be in White's favour. See the "Complete Games" chapter.

Zueger–Abdelnabbi
Dubai 1986

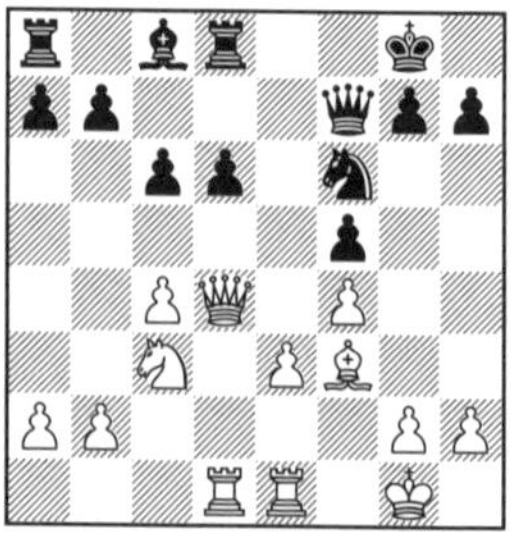

Position after 19...♕f7

White could have increased his advantage by the thematic move 20.e4!. White's pressure on d6 is not enough for winning. He should open the centre in order to extend the scope of his actions.

Sideif Sade–Lodhi
Teheran 1991

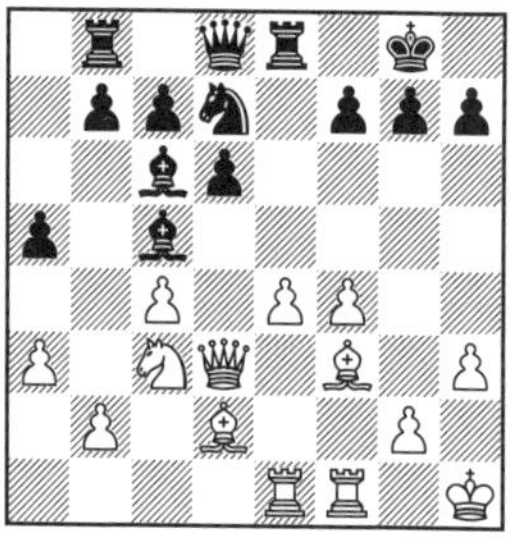

Position after 18.♖ae1

This is a typical position for the setup with ...d6. Black renounced the rook lifting via a6 and adopted a passive stand, avoiding to weaken the pawn at d6.

The natural plan here is connected with b2-b4. The game saw further 18...♘f8 19.♗g4 ♕f6 20.♗e3 ♗xe3 21.♖xe3 ♖a8 22.b4±.

Notice the setup of White's kingside pawns. They should be on h3 and g2. Shift them slightly, on g3 and h2, and Black would have had a satisfactory game thanks to the weakened light squares h3 and g4. In that case Black's bishop would be rather active on the c8-h3 diagonal.

Tactical Motives

The plan with the Drimer rook weakens Black's last rank and provides preconditions for sacrificing the e-pawn, aiming to open the e-file. We already saw such development in the games Flear-Taddei and Lalic-Mukic. Here are two more examples from tournament practice:

Gulko–Kochyev
Lvov zt 1978

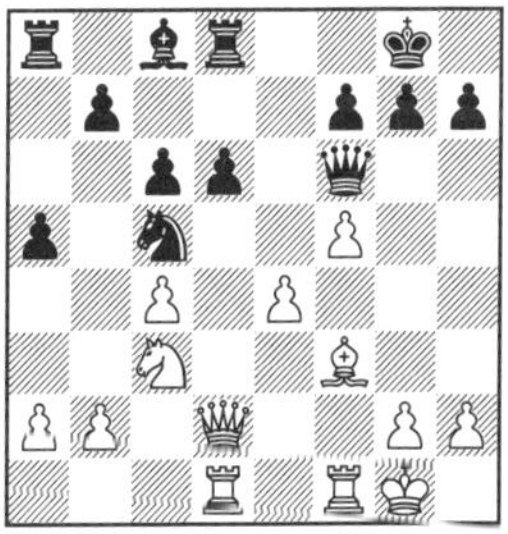

Position after 19...♖d8

20.e5!! (opening up the centre) 20...♕xe5 21.♖fe1 ♕f6 22.♕xd6 ♕xd6 23.♖xd6 ♗d7 24.♖e5 with a decisive advantage.

Semkov–Gutierrez Martinez
Sitges 1993

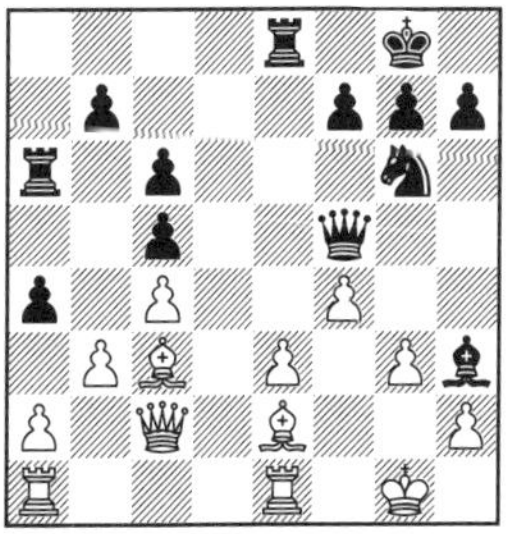

Position after 20...♕f5

21.e4 ♖xe4 22.♗d3 ♖xe1+ 23.♖xe1 ♕d7

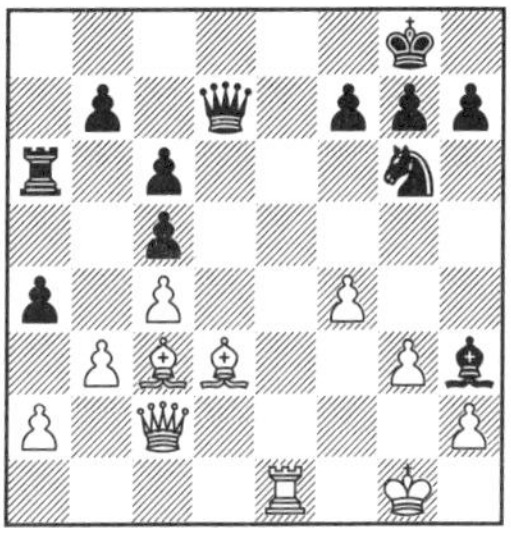

Now White fires another typical shot for the Budapest Gambit:

24.f5! axb3 25.axb3 ♘f8 26.f6! gxf6 27.♗xf6 ♘g6 28.♕d2 ♕g4 29.♕h6 ♘f8 30.♗xh7+ 1-0

Finally, an example of the other thematic break of White:

Spassky–Klaman
Leningrad 1957

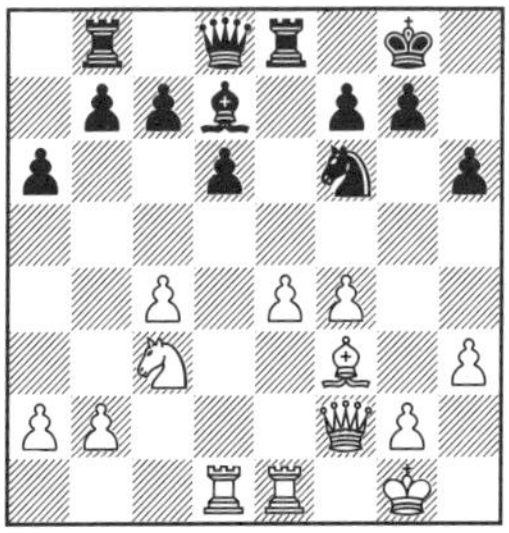

Position after 18...h6

19.c5 dxc5 20.♕xc5 b6 21.♕f2 ♕c8 22.e5, with a huge advantage.

The thrust c4-c5 can be also executed as a pawn sacrifice, in order to ensure the opening of the centre.

Part 4

Step by Step

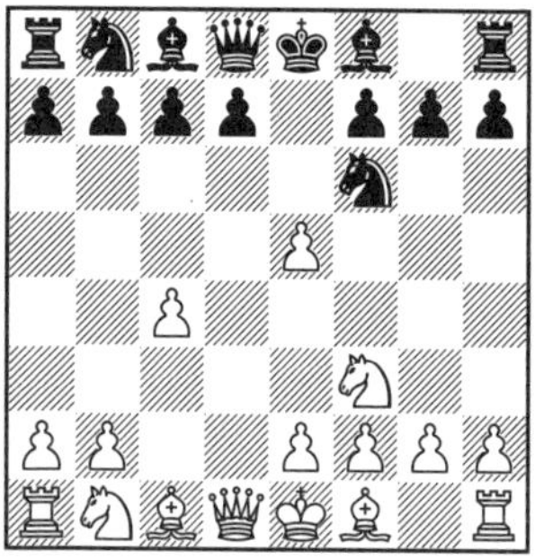

1.d4 ♘f6 2.c4 e5 3.dxe5

A. 3...♘e4?! (Fajarowicz Gambit)
B. 3...♘g4

A. 3...♘e4?! 4.a3!

4.♘d2 also gives White a stable advantage, but the text hinders Black's development and practically retains the extra pawn.

A1. 4...d6
A2. 4...♘c6
A3. 4...♕h4
A4. 4...b6

4...♗c5 does not work here since 5.e3 a5 loses a piece to 6.♕d5 ♕h4 7.g3 c6 8.♕d3.

A1. 4...d6 5.♕c2!

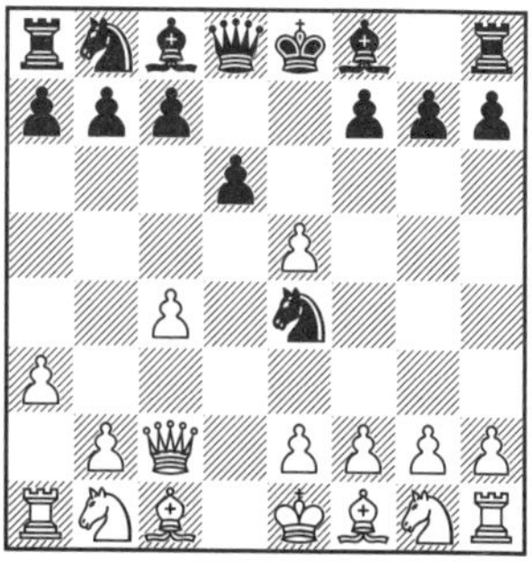

This is the main idea of 4.a3. White wins tempi, attacking the advanced knight. The tactical reason behind the queen's move is that 5...♗f5 is bad due to 6.♘c3! and Black is lost no matter how he takes the rook at h1, , e.g. 6...♘g3 7.e4 ♘xh1 8.exf5 dxe5 9.♗e3 ♘c6 10.♖d1 ♕f6 11.♘d5 ♕d6 12.c5+– CapNemo-Der Rentner, playchess. com 2006.

5...♘c5 is too passive. White can simply take on d6 and play on with an extra pawn, but Rybka suggests to stay active with 6.♘f3! dxe5 7.♘c3 ♘c6 8.♗e3 ♘e6 9.♖d1 ♕f6 10.g3, when Black cannot complete development: 10...♘cd4 11.♗xd4 exd4 12.♘e4 ♕g6 13.♘xd4 ♘xd4 14.♖xd4±. So Black follows up with:

5...d5 6.♘c3! ♘xc3 7.♕xc3

White has traded the active knight and remains a pawn up.

7...d4

7...dxc4 8.♘f3 ♗e7 9.♗f4 0-0 10.♖d1 is grim for Black.

8.♕g3

Any other retreat is also good: 8.♕b3 c5 9.e3 ♘c6 10.♘f3 or 8.♕d3 c5 9.♘f3 ♘c6 10.e3 ♗g4 11.♗e2±.

8...♗e6 9.e4 ♘c6 10.♗d2 d3

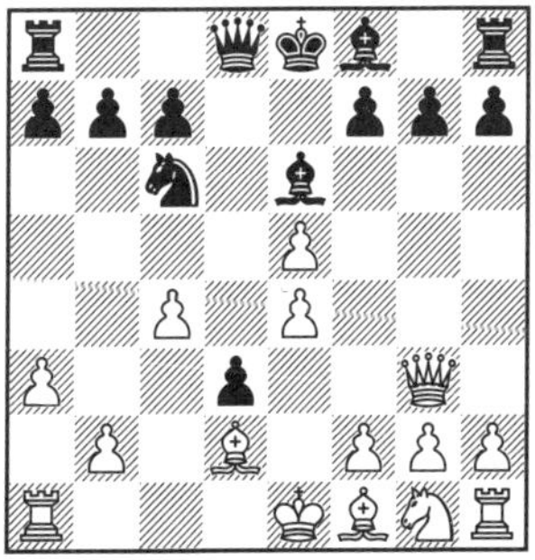

This position occurred in S.Atalik-Fette, Groningen 1999.

Here, instead of 11.♗xd3 ♘xe5 12.♗c2 ♘xc4 13.♗c3 ♗d6±, White should have stayed active with 11.0-0-0!±.

A2. 4...♘c6 5.♘f3 d6

5...a5 does not make much sense as White obtains a huge advantage with simple moves: 6.♕d5 ♘c5 7.♘c3 ♗e7 8.♗f4 d6 9.exd6 cxd6 10.e3 ♗e6 11.♕d1± or 6.♕c2 d5 7.e3 ♗e6 8.♘bd2 ♘c5 9.cxd5 ♗xd5 10.♗b5 ♗e7 11.b3±, Grabarczyk-Vospernik, Pula 1998.

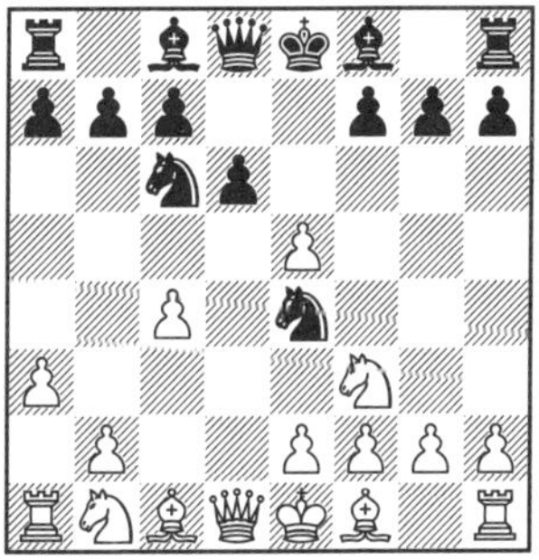

6.♕c2

Of course, 6.exd6 ♗xd6 7.♘bd2 ♗f5 8.♘xe4 ♗xe4 9.e3! ♕f6 10.♗d3 is also better for White, but it is easier to remember that we always meet ...d6 by ♕c2.

6...d5

6...♗f5 typically fails to 7.♘c3: 7...♘g3 8.e4 ♘xh1 9.exf5 dxe5 10.♗e3 ♘d4 11.♕e4 ♘xf3+ 12.gxf3+–, Vl.Georgiev-Olgag, Izmir 2006, or 7...♘xf2 8.♕xf5 ♘xh1 9.e6± fxe6 10.♕xe6+ ♕e7 11.♕d5 h6

12.g3 g5 13.♗g2 ♘xg3 14.hxg3 ♗g7 15.♗h3, Reshevsky-Bisguier, New York 1955.

7.e3 ♗g4

7...♗e6 8.♗e2 g5 9.cxd5 ♗xd5 10.0-0 reminds me to a better version for White of the Hennig-Schara Gambit. Black is behind in development so he cannot find time for attack: 10...g4 11.♘fd2 ♘g5 (Or 11...♘xd2 12.♗xd2 ♘xe5 13.♗c3 ♕f6 14.♖d1 ♕e6 15.♗xe5 ♕xe5 16.♘c3 ♗d6 17.♗b5+ c6 18.♖xd5+–) 12.♖d1 ♘xe5 13.♘f1 ♘gf3+ 14.♔h1 c6 15.e4 ♗d6 16.exd5 ♕h4 17.♗f4 ♕xf2 18.♗e3 ♕h4 19.dxc6 ♘xh2 20.g3 ♕h3 21.♘xh2 1-0, Knaak-Pachow, Germany 2007.

8.cxd5 ♕xd5 9.♗c4 ♕a5+ 10.♘bd2

10.b4 works, too: 10...♗xb4+ 11.axb4 ♕xa1 12.♕xe4 ♗h5 13.e6 ♗g6 14.exf7+ ♔f8 15.♕f4 ♕xb1 16.0-0 ♕e4 17.b5+– Bisguier-Ljubojevic, Malaga 1971.

10...♗xf3 11.gxf3 ♘xd2 12.♗xd2 ♕xe5 13.♗c3+– ♕e7 14.0–0–0 ♘e5 15.♗d5 c6 16.♗xe5 cxd5 17.♖xd5

Here Black resigned, Havik-Hamer, Gibraltar 2008.

A3. 4...♕h4

In this line Black regains the pawn, but dramatically falls behind in development.

5.g3 ♕h5 6.♗g2

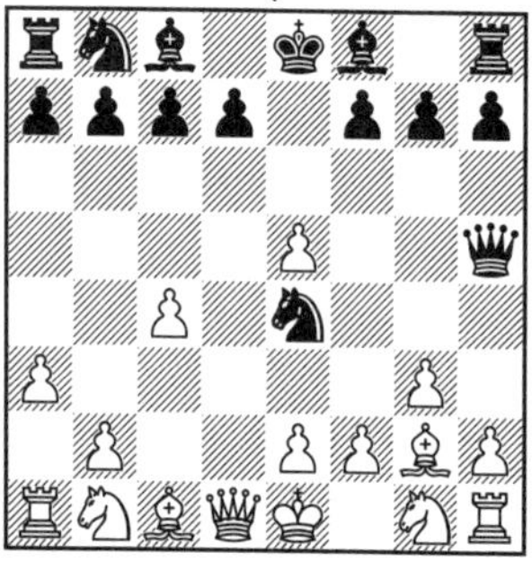

6...♕xe5

The attempt to recapture on e5 without giving more tempi finished badly in Gyimesi-Kahn, Budapest 1995: 6...♘c5 7.♘c3 ♘c6 8.f4 d6 9.♘b5 ♘e6 10.♗f3 ♕g6 11.e4 f5 12.♗h5 1-0.

7.♕c2

Gaining an extra tempo by hitting the e4-knight. 7.♘f3 ♕c5 (7...♕h5 8.0-0 d6 9.♘d4 ♘f6 10.♘c3± G. Flear-Bellon Lopez, Bern 1991) 8.♘d4 ♘f6 9.♘c3± is also in White's favour, of course.

7...♘f6 8.♘f3

Or 8.♘c3 d6 9.♘f3, Thorfinnsson-D.Olafsson, Reykjavik 2001.

8...♕h5 9.♘c3 ♗e7 10.h3

White is much better, Van Wely-Alburt, New York 1994.

A4. 4...b6 5.♘f3 ♗b7 6.♘bd2

Black is trying to finish development somehow, hoping to regain the pawn in future.

6...♘c5

Alternatively:

a) 6...♕e7 7.♕c2 ♘xd2 8.♗xd2 ♘c6 9.♗c3 0-0-0 10.0-0-0± and White is a clear pawn up, Hillarp Persson-Romero Holmes, Benidorm 2003.

b) 6...a5 7.♕c2

7.♘xe4 ♗xe4 8.♕d4 ♗b7 9.♕g4?! ♕e7 10.♗g5 ♕e6 11.♕xe6+ dxe6 12.h4 ♘d7 13.♗f4 h6 14.h5⩲ Eliet-Herbrechtsmeier, France 2001.

7...♘c5 8.b3 ♘c6 9.♗b2 ♗e7 10.e3 f6 11.♗e2 fxe5 12.♘xe5 0-0 13.♘d3 ♗h4 14.0-0± ♕e7 15.♘xc5 bxc5 16.♗f3 ♖ab8 17.♗e4+–, Alber-Roeschlau, Moerlenbach 2004.

7.b4

7.e3 a5

Or 7...♘c6 8.b4 ♘e6 9.♗b2 a5 10.b5 ♘e7 11.♗d3 g5 12.♘e4 ♗xe4 13.♗xe4 ♖b8 14.h4 1-0 Postny-Herges, Andorra 2005.

8.b3 ♘c6 9.♗b2 ♗e7 10.♗e2 0-0 11.0-0⩲ gives White a stable edge, but it is still better to gain space on the queenside.

7...♘e6 8.♗b2 d6 9.exd6 ♗xd6 10.e3 0–0

Black is undeveloped, so any attempt to display activity should be punished: 10...a5 11.c5 bxc5 12.bxc5 ♗xc5 13.♗c4 0-0 14.♕b3 ♗c8 (14...♗xf3 15.gxf3!+–) 15.♘e4↑.

11.♕c2 a5 12.♗d3 h6 13.b5

The positional solution 13.c5 bxc5 14.b5± is also appealing.

13...♘c5 14.♗h7+ ♔h8 15.♕c3 f6 16.♕c2 ♘bd7 17.0–0±

B. 3...♘g4 4.♘f3

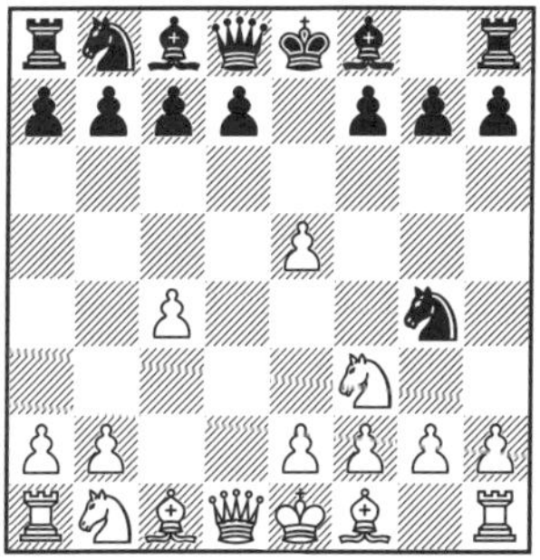

B1. 4...♘c6
B2. 4...♗c5

B1. 4...♘c6 5.♗g5

5.♗f4 is a very good option, but it transposes to the well known Rubinstein line 4.♗f4 ♘c6 5.♘f3 which has accumulated a lot of theory. Mostly in White's favour, to be sure. The text achieves one of the main positional aims of White in the Budapest – to eliminate Black's dark-squared bishop. Thus White will be assured of a small, but lasting edge.

5...♗e7

5...♗b4+?! 6.♘c3 f6 7.exf6 ♘xf6 8.e3± hardly deserves attention.

6.♗xe7 ♕xe7 7.♘c3

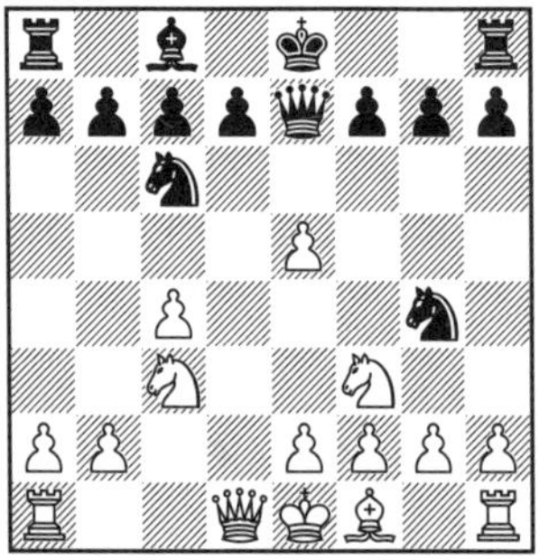

7...0–0

Black does not gain benefits from capturing on e5 before castling. In many variations the g7-pawn is hanging and White takes over the initiative:

a) 7...♘gxe5 8.♘d5 (8.♘xe5 ♘xe5 9.e3 "only" transposes to the main line) 8...♕d8 (8...♘xf3+?! 9.gxf3 ♕d8 10.♖g1 and Black has not an acceptable way to defend the g7-pawn, e.g. 10.g6 11.♕d2±, Andrews-Thompson, Jackson 1988) 9.♘xe5 ♘xe5 10.♕d4! Now Black is forced to weaken the kingside by 10...f6 when White can choose between the sharper 11.f4 ♘c6 12.♕e4+ ♘e7 13.0-0-0 c6 14.♘c3 0-0 15.e3 d6 16.♗e2→, or the solid 11.e3 d6 12.♗e2 0-0 13.♖d1 c6 14.♘c3 ♘f7 15.0-0⩲.

b) 7...♘cxe5 8.♘d5 (8.♘xe5⩲ or 8.♕d4!? are good alternatives) 8...♕c5 (Or 8...♕d6 9.♕d4 c6 10.h3±; 8...♕d8 9.h3 ♘xf3+ 10.exf3 ♘f6 11.♕e2+±) 9.e3 ♘xf3+ 10.♕xf3 d6 11.♕e4+ ♗e6, Farago-Mestrovic, Bibinje 2006, 12.b4! ♕c6 13.♗e2±.

c) 7...♕c5 8.e3 ♘gxe5 9.♘xe5 ♕xe5 (9...♘xe5 10.♘d5±) 10.♗e2 0-0 11.♕d2 ♕c5 12.0-0±. Due to the weakness of c7, Black now has to prevent ♘d5 by 12...♘e7, but 13.♖ac1 will start an offensive on the queenside by b4 or ♘d5.

8.♘d5 ♕d8 9.e3 ♘gxe5 10.♘xe5 ♘xe5 11.♗e2 d6 12.0–0

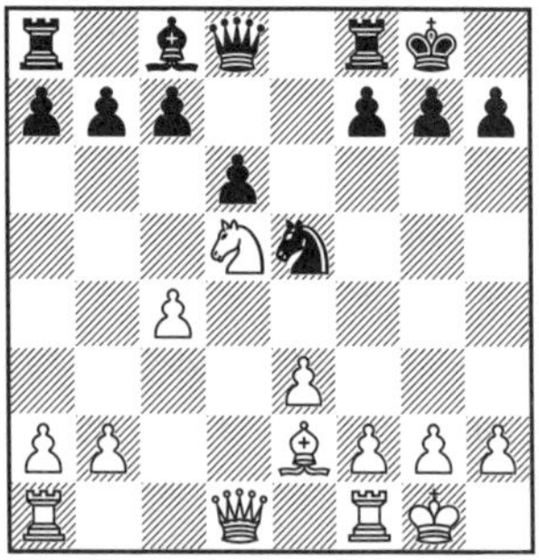

I was intrigued to read Moskalenko's note about this position, in his comments on the game Polugaevsky-Nunn, Biel 1986: "What was Polugaevsky expecting in this balanced position? He was probably waiting for his opponent's mistakes – and they duly came." Well, he answers himself the question. It is normal for humans to err in cramped positions without counterplay. The only thing I disagree with is the assessment "balanced position". In my opinion (and of many other grandmasters I know), White has a lasting pressure, due to his obvious spatial advantage and flexible broad centre.

White's game is extremely easy. He has two promising plans:

1. To thrust c4-c5, possibly after some preparation with b2-b4;

2. To expand on the kingside by f2-f4-f5. Should Black stop it by f7-f5, then e3-e4 would favourably open play.

White has scored 5:1 according to Megabase. The only victory of Black was Zueger-Abdelnabbi, Dubai 1986, which went:

13...c6 (there was a transposition in the opening, which accounts for the particular numbering of moves) 14.♘c3 ♕e7 15.♕d4 f5 16.f4 ♘d7 17.♖fe1 ♘f6 18.♖ad1 ♖d8 19.♗f3 ♕f7

White has played very well so far and now he could have increased his advantage by the thematic move 20.e4! Instead, he mixed up plans by 20.c5, allowing Black to close the centre with 20...d5 and hold on.

The model **game 16 Polugaevsky-Nunn**, Biel 1986 featured 12...c6 13.♘c3 ♗e6 14.b3±, see "Complete Games".

12...♗e6 probably should be met by 13.b3, intending to follow Polugaevsky's example and after 13...c6, retreat to c3. In Rechlis-Kaposztas, West Berlin 1987, White answered 13.♖c1 c6 14.♘f4 ♕e7 15.♕d4 which was also good enough for an edge.

Moskalenko suggests:

12...♘d7

He wants to follow up with ...♘d7-c5 and ...a5, but that does not change the pawn structure which is favourable for White. We can reply simply by:

13.♕d4

Or perhaps 13.b4!? a5 14.a3±.

13...♖e8

Gulko-Kochyev, Lvov zt 1978 shows that 13...a5 does not help Black: 13.f4 ♖e8 14.♗f3 ♘c5 15.e4 c6 16.♘c3 ♘e6 17.♕d2 ♕f6 18.f5 ♘c5 19.♖ad1 ♖d8

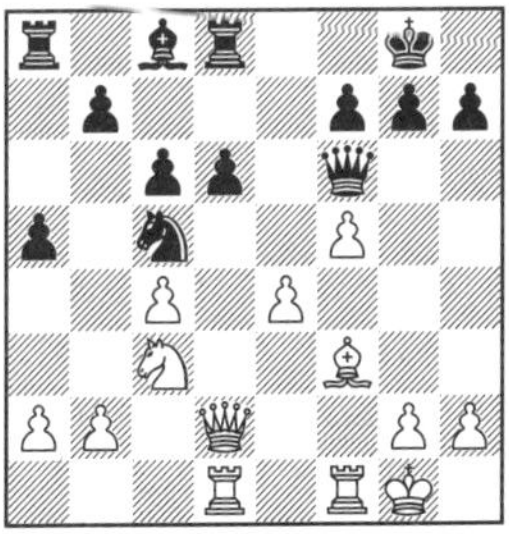

20.e5!! (opening up the e-file) 20...♕xe5 21.♖fe1 ♕f6 22.♕xd6 ♕xd6 23.♖xd6 ♗d7 24.♖e5, with a decisive advantage.

14.b4±

Of course, White could follow the plan of Spassky/Smyslov against the Budapest Gambit with 14.♗d3 ♘c5 15.♗c2 a5 16.f4 ♗e6 17.♖f3 f6 18.♖g3, with an initiative all over the board, but the text is more consistent:

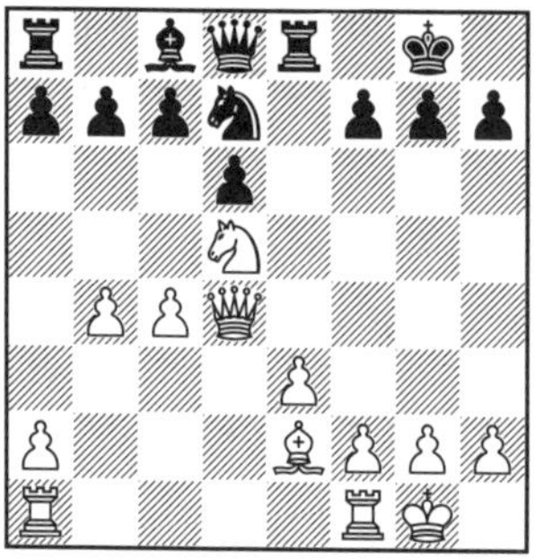

In modern chess, White would pay generously to obtain such a position in the Slav, the Queen's Gambit or the Queen's Indian and similar popular openings. I do not believe that it would appeal to the fans of the Budapest Gambit either. Black will be struggling for many moves ahead.

B2. 4...♗c5

This plan was introduced by Maroczy in 1896. By attacking f2, Black achieves to shut in the c1-bishop. White will have to fianchetto it to b2 which will distract the bishop from the critical square h6. That can seduce Black to lift his queen's rook via a6 to the kingside. The manoeuvre ...♖a8-a6-h6 is the cream of Black's strategy.

I propose to encourage this idea and take advantage of the misplaced rook. In order this plan to work, we'll need to neutralise the "Maroczy" bishop.

We start with:

5.e3 ♘c6 6.♘c3

Forget about attempts to clutch to the extra pawn with moves like ♕d5. We'll execute this attack later, only when Black put his rook to a6.

6.b3 ♘gxe5 7.♘xe5 ♘xe5 8.♗b2 is hardly good either since Black overtakes the initiative with 8...d6 9.♗e2 ♕g5 10.0-0 ♗h3 11.♗f3 0-0-0 Anastasian-Yermolinsky, 1987.

6...0–0

Capturing on e5 before White played ♗e2 is considered to be dangerous in view of the possible plan with f4, ♗d3:

6...♘gxe5 (6...♘cxe5 7.h3 ♘xf3 8.♕xf3 ♘e5 9.♕g3) 7.♘xe5 ♘xe5 8.f4 ♘c6 (8...♘g6 9.♗d3) 9.♗d3

Spassky won a nice game with this setup with a tempo down (he played firstly ♗e2, then ♔h1), but later Black discovered that White's attack was not so dreadful as it seemed. Still, if Smyslov also adopted a year later the same plan, it should be viable. The critical position arises after 9...d6! 10.0-0 0-0 11.♘e4 (11.♕h5 f5), when it is not too clear how Black should proceed further. In any case, 11...♗b6 looks dubious since White can sac a pawn to free the c4-pawn for his bishop: 12.♕h5 g6 13.♕h6 f6 14.c5 dxc5 15.♗c4+ ♔h8 16.b3 with attack. Moskalenko advocates 11...♕h4, while I suppose that 11...♕e7 may be a little more precise. Apparently White's bishop pair after 12.♘xc5 dxc5 13.a3 should ensure some edge, but the game will be strategically unbalanced.

Summarising: Spassky's plan with f4 is possible, but I'm not sure it is the best. I would opt for the more natural approach: 7.♘xe5 ♘xe5 8.♗e2, transposing to the main line.

7.♗e2 ♘gxe5

7... ♖e8 is slightly more popular move order, but I do not see a substantial difference for our plan.

8.♘xe5 ♘xe5 9.0–0

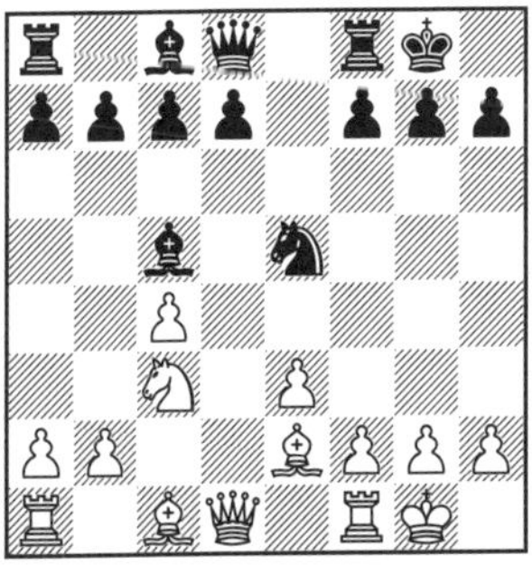

9...♖e8

I suspect that the natural developing move 9...d6 is stronger and Alekhine's intuition did not fail him when he chose it against Ibanez in 1926. However, nowadays the Budapest Gambit is played mostly by weaker players who do not care too much about the strategic laws of chess. They want to leave the 6th rank free for the rook lift ...♖a8-a6-h6. Our task should be to encourage them to fulfil this manoeuvre!

After 9...d6 we should change tactic and attack first by 10.f4 (since 10.b3 ♕h4 11.♘a4 ♗b6 12.♘xb6 axb6 is about equal) 10...♘d7

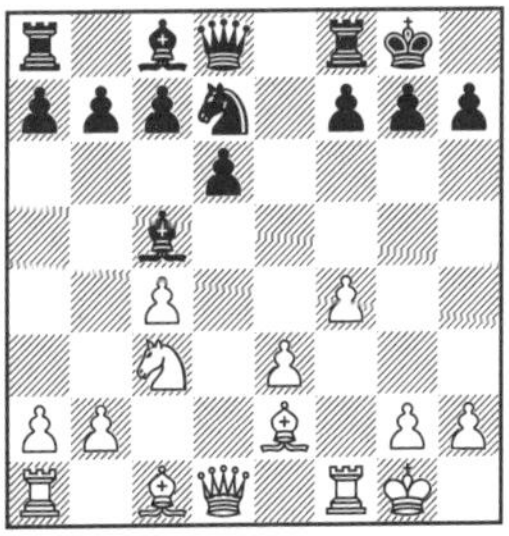

11.♗f3

Sideif Sade-Lodhi, Teheran 1991 saw 11.♔h1!? ♖e8 12.e4 ♘f6 13.♗f3 ♖b8 14.h3 ♗d7 15.♕d3 ♗c6 16.a3 a5 17.♗d2, with a spatial advantage: 17...♘d7 18.♖ae1 (18.b3 ♕f6 19.♘d5 ♗xd5 20.cxd5 ♗d4 21.♖ab1 ♘c5 22.♕c2 ♖a8 23.b4 axb4±) 18...♘f8 19.♗g4 ♕f6 20.♗c3 (20.♕c2! ♘g6 21.♘d5 ♗xd5 22.cxd5± was stronger) 20...♗xe3 21.♖xe3±.

11...♖b8 12.♕d3 ♘f6 13.♗d2 (13.♘a4 ♖e8 14.♘xc5 dxc5 15.♕xd8 ♖xd8 16.e4 ♗g4 17.♗e3 b6 18.♖ad1 ♗xf3 19.gxf3 ♘e8 20.f5±) 13...c6

14.h3 (14.♘a4±) 14...♕b6, Lautier-Rogers, Novi Sad 1990. Here the obvious 15.♘a4± would have been clearly better for White.

Summarising: after 9...d6 White occupies the centre with f4 and e4, then seeks to trade the black dark-squared bishop. The opponent has no counterplay.

10.b3 a5

10...d6 is a more natural move, but it has a major drawback – after 11.♘a4 the only active piece of Black will be exchanged at a convenient moment and he will have to struggle for two results only. It is important however to not rush with the exchange, but provoke firstly some weakening of the queenside. Moskalenko gives 11...b6 12.a3 or 12.♘xc5 bxc5, but 12.♗d2! (to drag the pawn to a5) 12...a5 13.♘xc5 is a completely different story due to 13...bxc5 14.f4 ♘d7 15.♗f3± ♖b8 16.♗xa5, while 13...dxc5 14.♗c3± is also solidly better for White.

Black's backup alternative is 11...♗f5, when, again, White should make a developing move: 12.♗b2! The fine point is that if Black tries to provide a retreat square for his bishop, for instance, 12...♕e7 13.♕d5 c6 14.♕d2± a6, we'll capture on c5 and our queen will obtain a fine post at a5. I found also the game Pachman-Goetz, Bayern 1994, which saw 11...♗b6 12.♘xb6 axb6 13.♕d4 ♘c6 14.♕c3 ♕g5 15.♗b2 f6 16.♖fd1 ♗e6 17.♗f3 ♕g6 18.♗d5 ♗f7 19.e4 ♘d8 20.f3± when the opponents signed a draw, but White's position is obviously more pleasant. He could organize a breakthrough on the queenside by a4-a5 or c4-c5.

10...a5 is certainly more aggressive as it prepares the rook lift ...♖a6, while keeping a retreat for the c5-bishop to f8, for instance, 11.♘a4 ♗f8.

11.♗b2 ♖a6

Again, 11...d6 is possible, but rather passive. White replies with 12.♘a4 when Black has the following options:

a) 12...♗a7 13.c5!

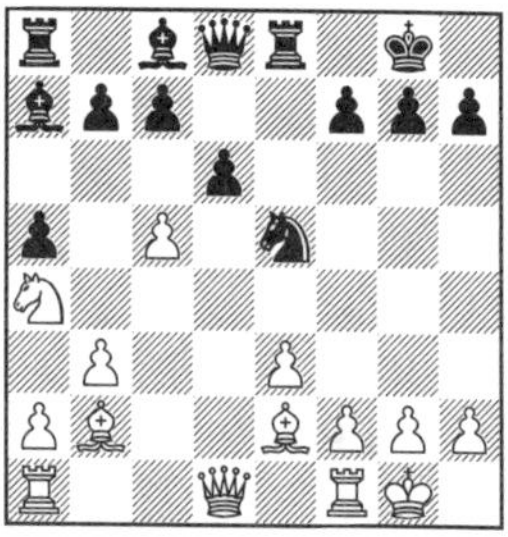

Black's strategy is a failure. He cannot close the centre by 13...d5 in view of 14.♕d4 f6 15.♖ad1 ♗e6 16.e4±. The blitz game Tkachiev-Mamedyarov, Moscow 2008 went instead: 13...♗d7 14.cxd6 ♗xa4 when Rybka points out to 15.dxc7±.

b) 12...b6 13.♘xc5 bxc5 14.f4! ♘d7 15.♗f3 ♖b8 16.♗c6!

An excellent idea. White has the bishop pair and better development. He only needs an open file to increase his pressure, e.g. 16...♖xe3 17.♕d2 ♖e8 18.♖ae1↑. That's why in Kunsztowicz-Sahlender, Germany 1989 Black went for 16...♖e7 17.♖f3 f6 when 18.♗c3± would have been the simplest solution.

c) 12...♗f5 13.♕d5! c6 14.♕d2

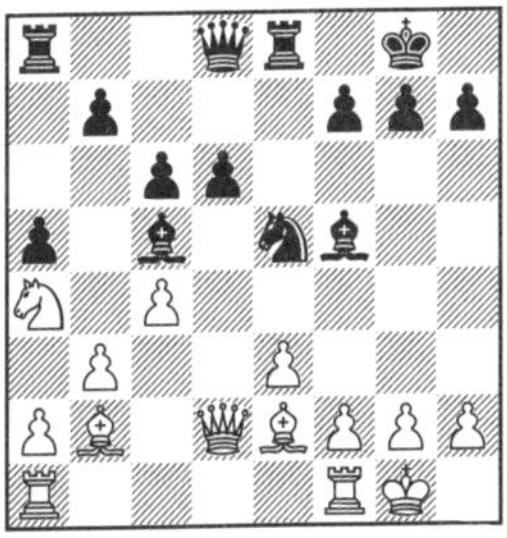

White induced weaknesses and he is now ready to take on c5, for example, after 14...♕c7 15.♘xc5 dxc5 16.♖ad1 f6 17.f3±. Perhaps Black should step back: 14...♗a7 15.♖ad1 ♕g5 (15...♕h4 16.♗d4±) 16.f4 ♕h6 17.♗d4 ♗xd4 18.♕xd4 (18.exd4!?) 18...♘g4 19.♗xg4 ♗xg4 20.♖d2 ♕g6 21.♕xd6 ♖xe3 22.♘c5 and the looming endgame is grim for Black because of the awkward situation of his bishop, e.g. 22...b5 23.h3 ♗f5 24.♕xg6 hxg6 25.g4±.

12.♕d5!

A critical position. It is important to shut in the c5-bishop, but that should be done at the expense of development. 12.♘a4 or 12.♘e4 are not impressive since White makes a second move with his knight and, on top of that, misplaces it.

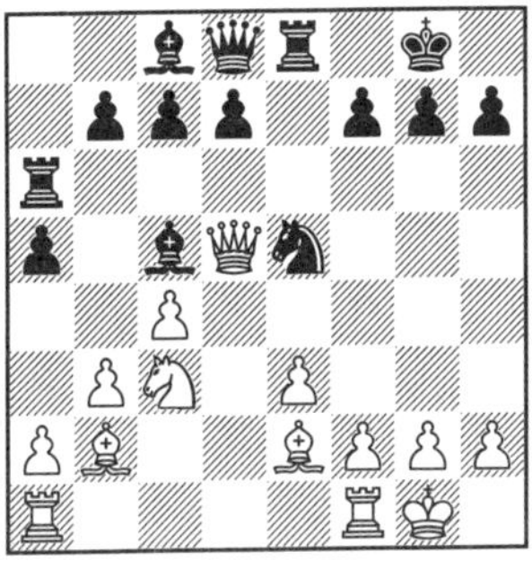

The text has been known since the 80ies, but White often shaped it wrongly. In the diagram position I will examine:

B2a. 12...♕e7
B2b. 12...♗f8
B2c. 12...♗a7

B2a. 12...♕e7 13.♘e4 ♗a7 14.♘g3 d6 15.c5 ♖c6 16.cxd6 ♖xd6 17.♕xa5

White soon won in Bagaturov-Schoetzig, Seefeld 1999: 17...♘c6 18.♕c3 ♕g5 19.♖ad1 ♖h6 20.♖d5 f5 21.♘xf5 ♖g6 22.♘g3 1-0.

B2b. 12...♗f8 13.♘e4

a) 13.♖ad1 ♖d6! 14.♕xa5 ♖a6 15.♕d5 ♖d6 leads to a repetition;

b) 13.c5 ♖h6 14.f4 ♘c6 (14...♕h4? loses to 15.fxe5 ♕xh2+ 16.♔f2 ♖xe5 17.♖h1) 15.♗c4 ♕e7 and the c5-pawn falls without due compensation.

13...♖ae6 14.c5

This is the most ambitious move, but the natural 14.♘g3 is a solid alternative. White had a tiny edge in Bischoff-Hort, Dortmund 1989 which went 14...b6 15.♖ad1 d6 16.♖fe1 ♗d7 17.♕d2 ♖h6, when 18.h3 deserves attention – 18...♕g5 19.a3 ♖h4 20.♕c2 ♗c6 21.b4. White maintains the initiative.

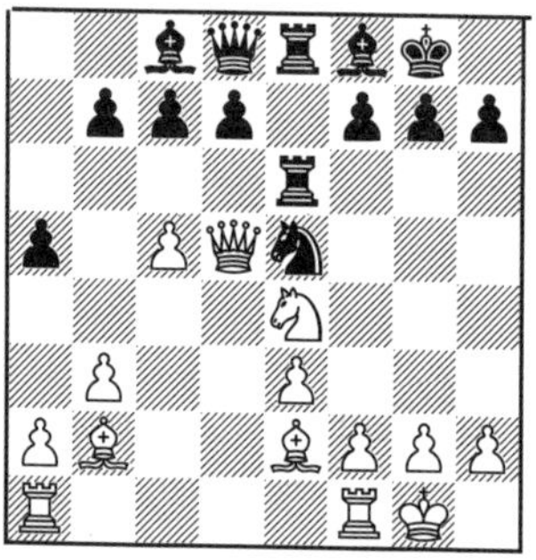

14...c6

14...d6 15.cxd6 ♘g6 loses to 16.♘g5+–, Farago-Chatalbashev, Val Thorens 1996.

15.♕d4

15.♕d2 ♕h4! gives Black just enough counterplay: 16.♘d6 ♗xd6 17.cxd6 ♖g6 18.f4 ♘g4 19.♗xg4 ♖xg4 20.♗d4 c5! 21.♗xc5 b6! 22.♗xb6 ♗b7.

15...♘c4 16.♕xc4 ♖xe4 17.♕c2

17.♗d4 d5 18.cxd6 ♗xd6 19.♗f3 ♖h4 20.g3 ♗g4 21.♗xg4 ♖xg4 22.♖ad1 is slightly better for White due to his control over the open d-file. Later he will try to put his e- and f-pawns in motion.

17...d5 18.cxd6 ♗xd6 19.♖fd1

White's pieces are well placed, his kingside pawn chain is flexible. This allows him to react adequately to Black's stabs and deflect any tactical threat. It is good for him to change one pair of rooks and advance in the centre. In many variations Black's rook can prove badly displaced on the kingside, for instance:

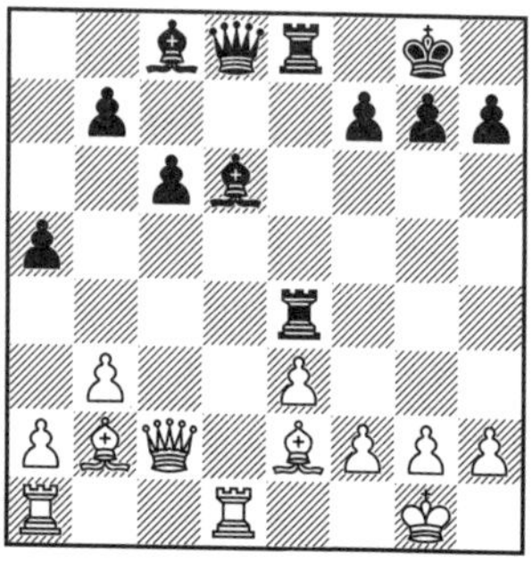

a) 19...♕c7 20.g3 (20.h3 works too, but it provides a lever for Black's attack, so it is more demanding from White) 20...h6 21.♗c3 ♗b4 22.♗d4 ♕e7 23.♗d3 ♖g4 24.f4! c5 25.♗e5 f6 26.♗b2 ♕xe3+ 27.♕f2±.

b) 19...♕e7 20.g3 (threatening 21.♗d3) 20...♖e6 21.♖d2 ♗b4 22.♖d4±.

B2c. 12...♗a7

Moskalenko decorates this retreat with an "!" sign. It is the most aggressive indeed, but probably dubious.

13.c5!

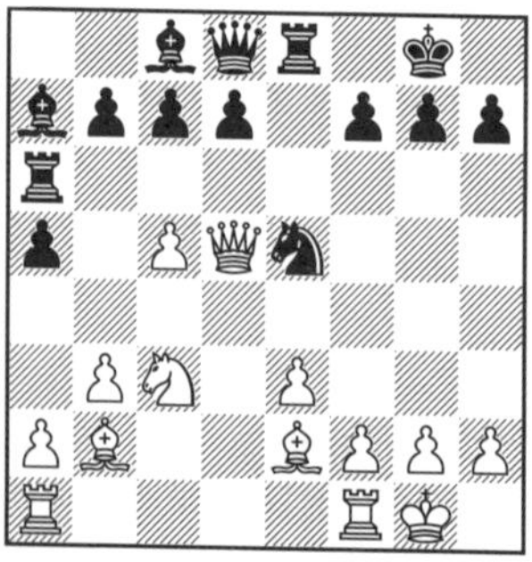

13...♖h6

Black is struggling after 13...♖ae6 14.f4! ♘c6 15.♘b5 ♖xe3 16.♗c4 ♕e7 17.♘xa7 ♘xa7 18.♗d4±.

We could attack 13...♖g6 the same way: 14.f4 ♘g4 15.f5 (Rybka suggests: 15.♗xg4 ♖xg4 16.♘b5 ♗b8 17.♕f3 d5 18.cxd6 c6 19.♘c7 ♗xc7 20.dxc7 ♕xc7 21.e4 f5 22.♖ae1±) 15...♖g5 16.♗xg4 ♖xg4 17.h3 c6 18.♕d6 ♖b4 19.♘a4 f6 20.♗d4±, with a tragicomical position for Black.

14.f4!

Moskalenko considers only 14.♘e4?

14...♘c6

14...♕h4 is bad owing to 15.fxe5 ♕xh2+ 16.♔f2 ♖xe5 17.♖h1! We know this motive from previous lines. 17...♖xd5 18.♖xh2 ♖f5+ 19.♔g1 ♖xh2 20.♔xh2 ♗xc5 21.♗f3±.

15.♘b5

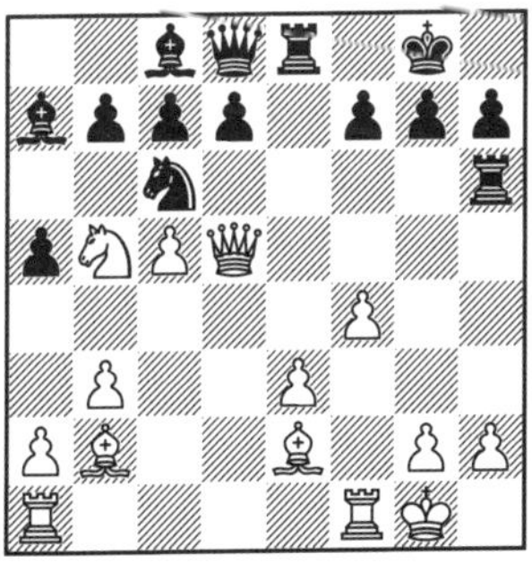

15...♕e7

Lalic-Mukic, Yugoslavia 1988 went 15...♕h4 16.h3 ♖xe3 17.♗c4? ♖e7? and White won nicely, using the clumsy "lifted"rook at h6: 18.♘xa7 ♘xa7 19.♖ae1 ♔f8 20.♕g5 ♕xg5 21.fxg5 ♖xe1 22.♗xg7+ ♔g8 23.♖xe1 ♖e6 24.♗xe6 fxe6 25.♗h6 ♔f7 26.♖f1+ ♔g6 27.g4 1-0. However, 17...♖he6! 18.♘xa7 ♖xh3! 19.gxh3 ♖g6+ 20.♕g2 ♖xg2+ 21.♔xg2 ♘xa7 22.♖ae1 ♔f8 23.♖e3 is totally messy.

The right stand for the bishop is 17.♗g4! in order to prevent sacrifices on h3. Then Black is in a predicament: 17...♗b8 18.♕d2 ♖e7 19.♖ae1±. We often observe this tactical motive – White opens up the e-file in order to underline the weakness of the last rank.

I have also analysed:

15...♗b8 16.♗c4 ♕e7 17.♖f3 d6 18.cxd6 cxd6 19.♕g5 with a dolid edge, for example, 19...♘e5 20.♖f2 ♕xg5 21.fxg5 ♘xc4 22.gxh6 ♘xb2 23.♖xb2 ♗d7 24.a4;

16.♘xa7 ♕xe3+ 17.♖f2 ♘xa7 18.♗c4±

See the finish of our stem **game 17 Flear-Taddei**, Chalons en Champagne 02.05.2009 in the "Complete Games" chapter.

Part 4

Complete Games

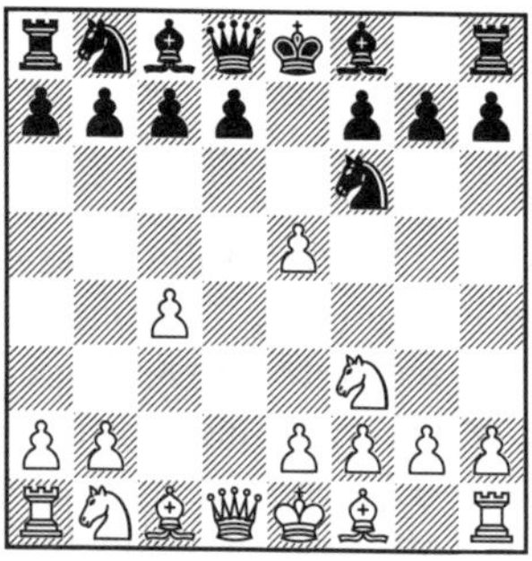

1.d4 ♘f6 2.c4 e5 3.dxe5

16. Polugaevsky–Nunn
Biel 26.07.1986

1.d4 ♘f6 2.c4 e5 3.dxe5 ♘g4 4.♘f3 ♘c6 5.♗g5 ♗e7 6.♗xe7 ♕xe7 7.♘c3 0–0 8.♘d5 ♕d8 9.e3 ♘gxe5 10.♘xe5 ♘xe5 11.♗e2 d6 12.0–0 c6 13.♘c3 ♗e6

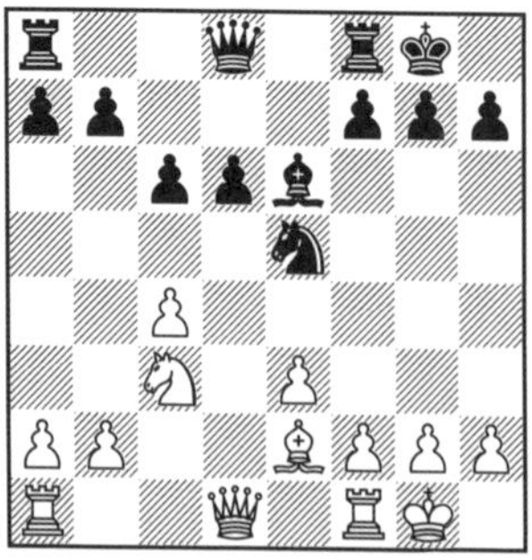

14.b3

White will be enjoying a lasting pull if he succeeds in fixing the backward pawn on d6. Thus the battle in the opening is focused on preventing ...d6-d5. Keeping that in mind, White should refrain from an early b2-b3, because the hanging knight on c3 would provide Black with some counterplay. It would have been better to defend c4 by 14.♕d4. Then 14...c5 15.♕f4 f5 16.♖ad1 is clearly better for White, as well as 14...f5 15.♖ad1 ♘f7 16.f4 when 16...♕b6 17.♕xb6 axb6 does not solve Black's problems since the b6-pawn is very weak.

14...♕a5

Generally, White would like to put in e3-e4, in order to enhance his grip on the centre. Black can prevent it by 14...f5, but that would only alter the pawn structure without really equalising. White could prepare e3-e4, maintaining his space advantage: 15.♕d4 ♕c7 16.♖ad1 ♘f7 17.f4 ♖fe8 18.e4± (or 18.♗h5 first). By the text, Nunn activates his pieces.

15.♕d2?!

The queen takes a shaky stand. Instead, 15.♕d4 keeps the pressure. The fine point is that Black cannot trade one of his minor pieces as in the game: 15...♖ad8 (15...f5? 16.♕xd6±) 16.f4± ♘g4? in view of 17.f5. So he would have to continue 16...f6 17.♖fd1 ♘d7

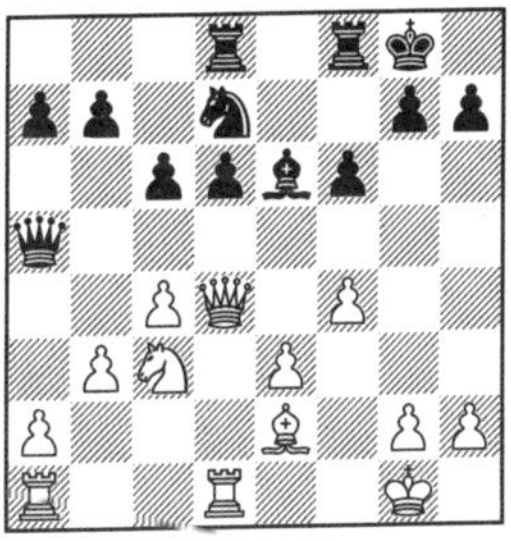

18.♖ab1 ♘b6 (18...♕b6 19.♘a4 ♕xd4 20.♖xd4±) 19.e4. White has achieved his positional goal.

15...♖ad8 16.f4 ♗g4

Nunn correctly seeks exchanges in a cramped position, but he should have traded the other piece: 16...♘g4! Then 17.f5 would be impossible due to 17...♗xf5; 17.h3 ♘f6 18.♖ad1 d5 is equal, so White should try 17.♗xg4 ♗xg4 18.h3 ♗e6 19.♖ad1 ♖fe8 (19...d5 20.cxd5 ♗xd5 21.♘xd5 ♖xd5 22.♕xa5 ♖xa5 23.♖f2±) 20.♖f2, with a level game.

17.♗d1 ♗xd1 18.♖axd1 ♘g4

18...♘d7 19.♘e4 ♕xd2 20.♖xd2±.

19.h3 ♘h6

19...♘f6 is more natural, but 20.♘d5 ♕xd2 21.♘xf6+ gxf6 22.♖xd2 ♖fe8 23.♔f2 ♔f8 24.♖fd1 ♔e7± would leave Black with a split kingside pawn formation.

20.e4

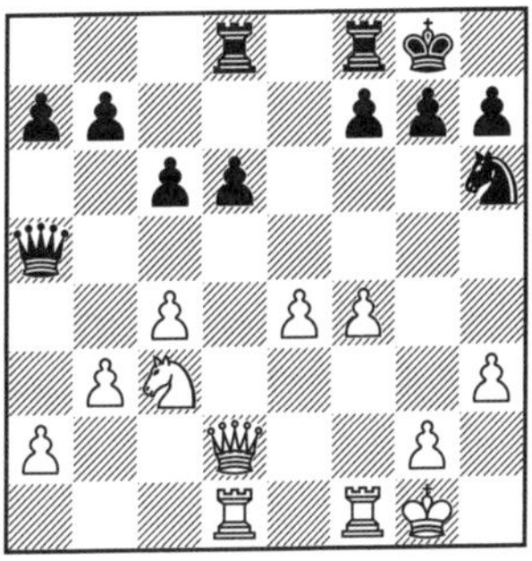

White has finally managed to occupy the centre. Of course, Black can attack it by ...f7-f5, but that would not eliminate White's edge since he will obtain a pawn majority on the kingside. At the same time, the open e-file would be in his favour.

20...f5 21.♖fe1 ♖fe8 22.♔h2 fxe4 23.♖xe4 ♖xe4 24.♘xe4 ♕h5

White maintains pressure in the ending after 24...♕xd2 25.♖xd2 ♘f7 26.♔g3± due to his more active pieces. Besides, he has a clear plan of pushing the kingside pawns.

25.♘g5 ♘f7 26.♘f3

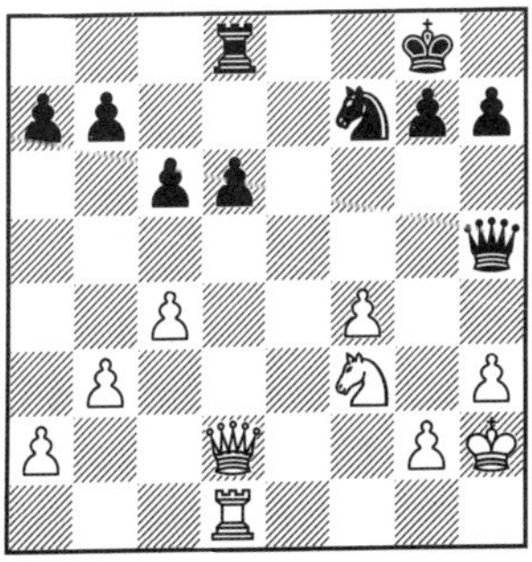

26...d5?!

Seemingly, Black achieved his goal and got rid of his weakness. In fact, his position is rapidly crumbling down. His pieces lack coordination, the last rank is weak. Perhaps he should have made a *luft* by 26...h6. That would not save him from trouble after 27.♖e1 d5 28.g4 ♕g6 29.c5, with total domination, but at least he is not losing material. 26...♕f5 27.♖e1 d5 28.♘d4 ♕d7 29.♘e6 ♖c8 30.♘c5 ♕c7 31.♕d4+– is not helpful either.

27.♕e3 ♕f5

It turns out that 27...dxc4 loses a piece after 28.♖xd8+ ♘xd8 29.♕e7.

28.cxd5 cxd5 29.g4 ♕c2+ 30.♖d2 ♕c7 31.♖xd5 ♖f8 32.♔g3

Black is totally helpless. White's pieces work in an impressive cooperation. The f3-knight covers all the access squares around the king at g3. White is winning not because of the extra pawn, but because Black has no counterplay to oppose to the kingside pawn storm.

32...♘d8 33.♕e5 ♕c8 34.♕e7 ♕c1 35.♖f5!

The same tactical motive again! The weakness of the last rank is haunting Black throughout the game.

35...♘f7 36.♕xb7 g6 37.♖f6 ♕b2 38.♕e7 ♕xa2 39.♕e6 ♕a1 40.h4 ♔g7 41.g5 a5 42.f5 gxf5 43.h5 ♕c3 44.♖xf5 ♕c7+ 45.♔h3 ♕c3 46.h6+ ♔g8 47.g6 hxg6 48.♕xg6+ ♔h8 49.♖xf7 1–0

17. G.Flear–Taddei
France 02.05.2009

1.d4 ♘f6 2.c4 e5 3.dxe5 ♘g4 4.♘f3 ♗c5 5.e3 ♘c6 6.♘c3 0–0 7.♗e2 ♘cxe5 8.♘xe5 ♘xe5 9.0–0 ♖e8 10.b3 a5 11.♗b2 ♖a6 12.♕d5!

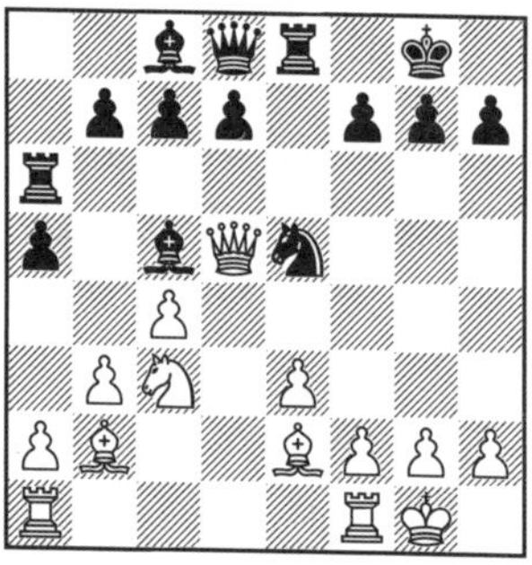

Remember this position! It is the cornerstone of our repertoire. White develops the queen, repels the c5-bishop, and starts an offensive in the centre.

12...♗a7

12...♗f8 is better, but such a move would cancel all attacking plans of Black.

13.c5 ♖h6 14.f4! ♘c6 15.♘b5 ♕e7 16.♘xa7 ♕xe3+ 17.♖f2 ♘xa7 18.♗c4

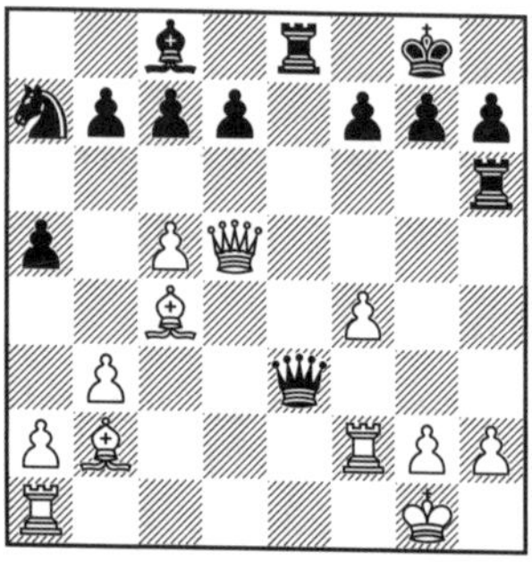

In this line, White often sacrifices the e3-pawn in order to open the e-file. Then the only way for Black to prevent the invasion of enemy rooks will be to give up the exchange. For instance: 18...♕e7 19.♖e2 ♖e6 20.♕d4 ♕f8. However, White should aim for a bigger edge by 19.f5! Naturally, Black decides to trade queens.

18...♖e7 19.♗d4 ♕e4 20.f5

A bit too quiet. Flear lets some part of his advantage slip away. He should not have given Black tempi for development. After 20.♕xe4 ♖xe4 21.♗e5 d6 22.cxd6 cxd6 23.♖d2± the raving bishops rule over the board.

20...c6

20...♕xd5 21.♗xd5 ♖e8 22.f6 g6 23.♖ff1 ♘c6 24.♖fe1 ♖f8 would have offered more chances for survival.

21.♕xe4 ♖xe4 22.♗c3

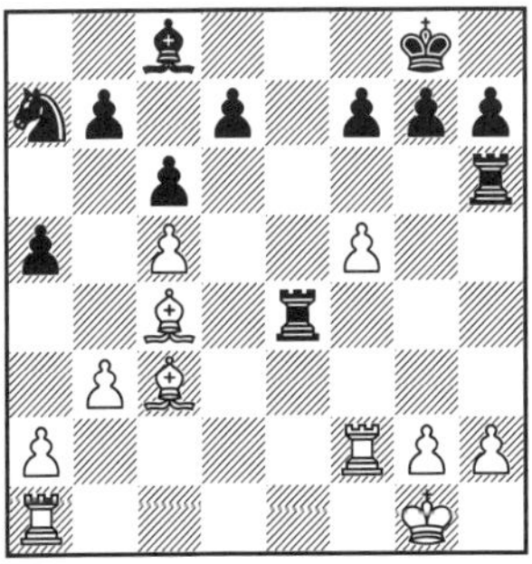

A typical situation for the Drimer rook at h6. It is cut off from the main battle and it is unclear how it could join the rest of Black's forces. When we take also into account the ridiculous knight at a7, we can confidently predict that White's win is close.

22...d5 23.♗d3 ♖e8 24.♖e1 ♖xe1+ 25.♗xe1 ♔f8 26.a4! ♗d7 27.g3!

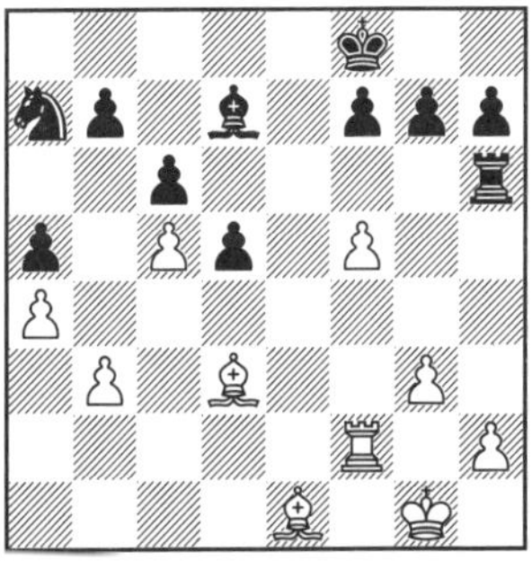

An excellent work of Flear! The Drimer rook is railed off and awaiting to be eaten by White's bishop.

27...♘c8 28.♗xa5 f6 29.♔g2 ♔f7 30.♗d2 ♖h5 31.g4 ♖g5 32.♗xg5 fxg5 33.b4 ♘e7 34.b5 ♘g8 35.b6 ♘f6 36.a5 ♗c8 37.♖a2 1–0

This is a model game for the Budapest Gambit. Black players should find a major improvement in order to resurrect the Drimer manoeuvre ...♖a8-a6-h6.

The Albin Counter Gambit

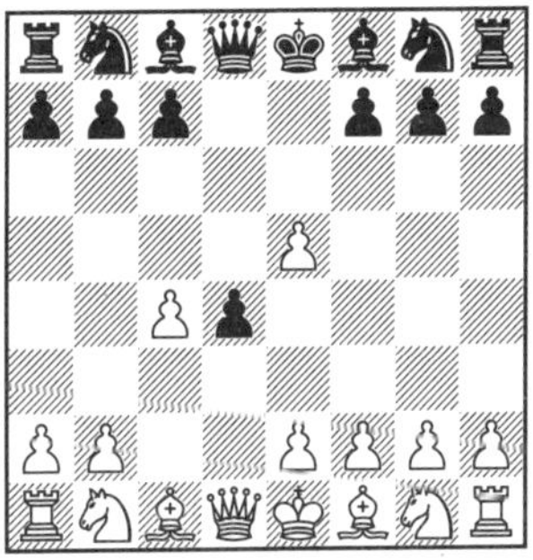

Part 5

Main Ideas

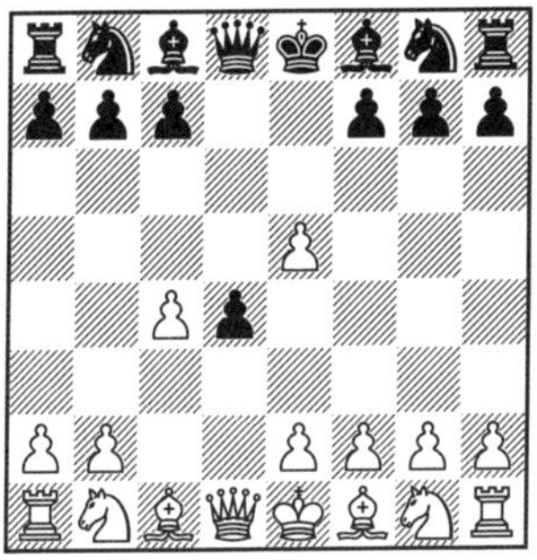

1.d4 d5 2.c4 e5 3.dxe5 d4

This gambit appeared in the last decade of the 19th century. It is obviously inspired by the Falkbeer Counter Gambit: 1.e4 e5 2.f4 d5 3.exd5 e4. However, the analogy is superficial, since in the Albin Counter Gambit White's kingside is safe, without any weaknesses. That gives him an easy game with a serious advantage.

4.♘f3 ♘c6 5.a3!

5.g3 is more popular, but I believe this is going to change quickly. The bishop's fianchetto is too slow and allows Black to get the game he wants – an easy development with castles on different sides and sharp play. "When you have opposite attacks going, the quantity of pieces is often more important than their quality," says GM Soltis. Indeed, our extra pawn would not count for much in such scenario.

The move 5.a3 assumes a more active approach to the centre. Beside covering the b4 square, White wants to expand on the queenside and develop the bishop to b2. Even in the very first game, according to Megabase, E.Lasker-Albin, New York 1893, the world champion chose this plan and discovered most of the main ideas which I recommend 120 years later: 1.d4 d5 2.c4 e5 3.dxe5 d4 4.♘f3 ♘c6 5.a3 ♗g4 6.h3 ♗xf3 7.gxf3 ♘xe5 8.f4 ♘c6 9.♗g2 ♕d7 10.b4 a6 11.♗b2 ♖d8 12.♘d2 ♘ge7 13.♘b3 ♘f5 14.♕d3

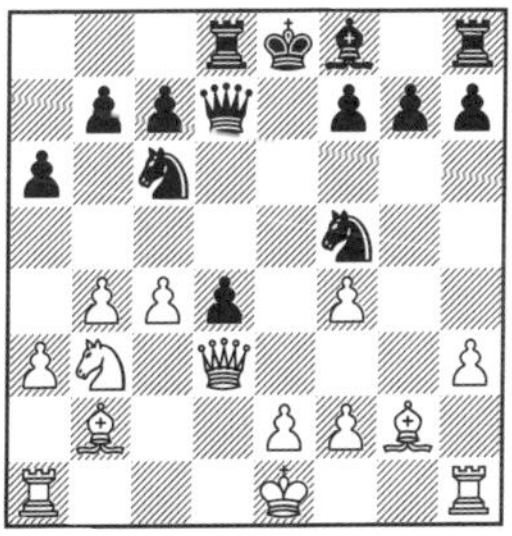

White's pieces are perfectly placed. Lasker castled long and won the game.

Black has not found convincing arguments against Lasker's plan. In the diagram position he tried nearly every possible move.

I will not discuss at length 5...♗f5 6.e3 and 5...f6 6.exf6 ♘xf6 7.e3, since Black has not even a trace of compensation in these variations.

A. 5...a5

Black prevents b4, but falls behind in development. He will have to concede the bishop pair in order to save the *gist* of his opening strategy – the d4 pawn.

6.♘bd2 ♗g4 7.h3 ♗xf3 8.♘xf3 ♗c5

9.h4!

This position was tested in 2007 in a number of blitz games between Bulgarian IMs Semkov and Panbukchian. Black cannot regain the pawn (9...♘g8-e7 10.h5!), so it is unclear what should he do at all:

9...♕d7 10.g3 ♘h6 11.♗h3+–, Semi-Panbuk, playchess.com 2007;

9...h6 10.g3 ♕e7 11.♗f4 0-0-0 12.♕a4 f6, Semi-Panbuk, playchess.com 2007, 13.exf6 ♘xf6 14.b4 axb4 15.♕a8+ ♘b8 16.♗h3++–.

B. 5...♗g4 6.b4

Now 6...♗xf3 7.exf3 ♘xe5 8.♖a2! ♗e7 9.f4± is unappealing for Black, so he should keep on developing.

6...♕d7 does not make sense since the d4-pawn looks doomed anyway. Remains:

6...♕e7 7.♘bd2 0-0-0 8.♗b2 ♘xe5 9.♘xe5 ♕xe5 10.h3 ♗h5 11.g4 ♗g6 12.♗g2 ♘f6 13.♘f3

White wins the d4-pawn with the better position, Gelfand-Radjabov, Almaty 2008.

C. 5...♗e6

In 2009, Bauer, Pert and other higher rated players preferred this move. Black postpones his plans for regaining the e5-pawn in favour of bolstering the d4-pawn.

6.♘bd2 ♘ge7 7.♘b3 ♘f5 8.♕d3

White defends the c4-pawn and threatens to win d4 with 9.g4. The game Grandelius-A.Smith, Ballerup 2009 saw further:

8...a5 9.♗f4 a4 10.♘bd2 h6 11.h4 g6 12.♘e4 ♗e7 13.♖d1 ♘xh4 14.♘xh4 ♗xh4 15.e3±.

D. 5...♘ge7 6.b4 ♘g6 7.♗b2 a5 8.b5 ♘cxe5

9.♕xd4!?

The endgame offers White a lasting advantage. Black should practically play for two results only. Such a scenario is usually the worst of all for any gambit player. Note that the topical line here is 11.♗xd4 ♘xc4 12.♕c2 ♘d6 13.♗d3 ♕g5 14.f4 ♕h4, Topalov-Morozevich, Amber-rapid 14th Monte Carlo 2005. It is also recommended by Avrukh in his repertoire book. That increases the chance your opponent will be taken by surprise. Anyway, prepared or not, Black is going to struggle for many moves ahead.

9...♕xd4 10.♗xd4 ♘xc4 11.e3 ♘d6 12.♘bd2 ♗d7 13.a4 f6

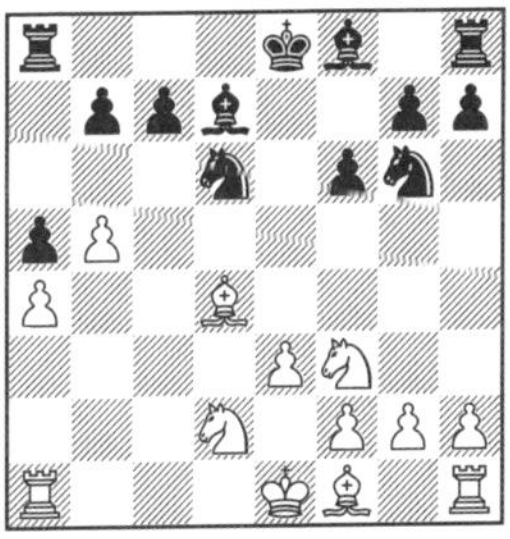

White's advantage is stable since it is due to his better pawn structure. The pawns at a4 and b5 paralise Black's queenside. The only way to break this grip would be ...c6, but then the b6-square becomes rather weak and the a5-pawn would be even more vulnerable – see the game Peralta-Perez Candelario, Ayamonte 2006 on page 163. Should Black try to defend that pawn by ...♘f5 and ♗b4, White retreats ♗c3 and exchanges on b4. The black pawn would be soon lost at b4, see **game 18. Levin-Szoen**, Pardubice 2006.

Points to remember:

- Aim for early b4, ♘d2-b3, ♗b2;
- The main target is the d4-pawn;
- Do not play g3 unless Black had changed already on f3;
- Trade queens in the line 5.a3 ♘ge7 6.b4 ♘g6 7.♗b2 a5 8.b5 ♘cxe5 9.♕xd4 and make Black struggle for the draw.

Part 5

Step by Step

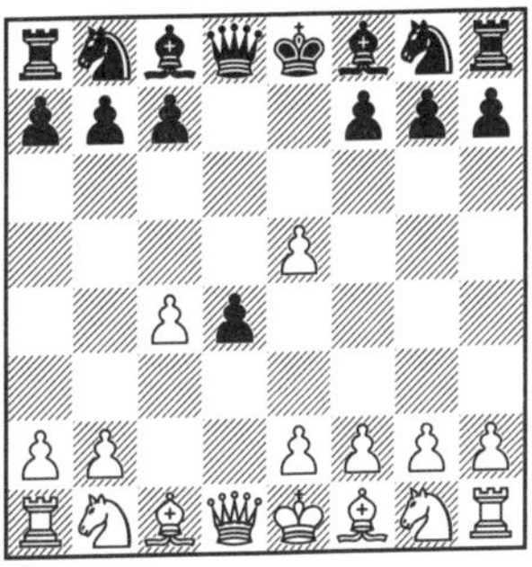

1.d4 d5 2.c4 e5 3.dxe5 d4

4.♘f3 ♘c6 5.a3

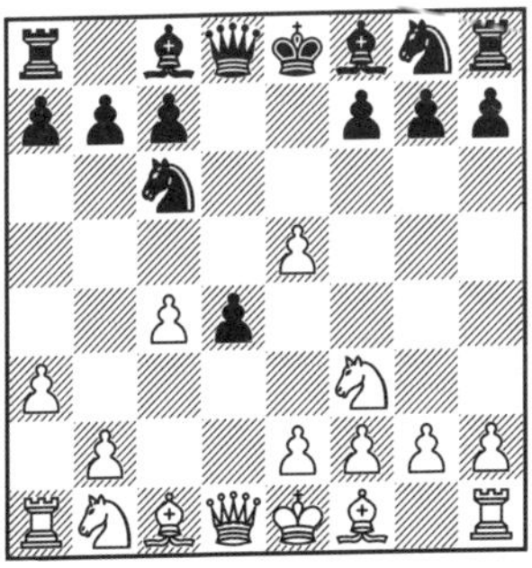

A. 5...a5
B. 5...♗g4
C. 5...♗e6
D. 5...♘ge7

Minor alternatives are:

a) 5...f6
Black has not even a trace of compensation after 6.exf6 ♘xf6 (or 6...♕xf6 7.♗g5 ♕g6 8.♘bd2 ♗g4 9.♕b3 ♖b8 10.e3±, Kolossovski-Grcic, Canberra 1999) 7.e3 ♗g4 8.♗e2 dxe3 9.♕xd8+ ♖xd8 10.♗xe3 ♗e7 11.♘c3 a6 12.0-0±, Aleksandrov-Ahmed, Abu Dhabi 2009.

b) 5...♗f5 6.e3 dxe3 (6...d3 7.♘c3 ♘ge7 8.e4 ♗g4 9.♕xd3 ♕xd3 10.♗xd3 ♗xf3 11.gxf3±, Karttunen-Jackson, Liverpool 2006) 7.♕xd8+ ♖xd8 8.♗xe3 ♘ge7 9.♘c3 ♘g6 10.♘b5 ♖d7 11.♘fd4 ♘xd4 12.♘xd4 ♗g4 13.f3, Gallego Jimenez-Ferron Garcia, Barcelona 2000. White is much better with any reasonable move: 13...♗h5 14.g4, or 14.e6!? fxe6 15.♘xe6, or even 14.0-0-0 ♘xe5 15.♗e2±.

A. 5...a5

This is Black's most logical answer. He prevents b4, thus enabling ...♗c5. At an opportunity, the a-pawn could go further, to fix the hole at b3. On the other hand, Black compromises his queenside and a future castling there becomes dubious. That overweighs all other factors.

6.♘bd2

6...♗g4

The threat of 7.♘b3 does not leave Black much of a choice.

6...♗e6 7.♘b3 ♕d7 8.e3 is grim for him.

After 6...♘ge7 7.♘b3 ♘f5 8.e3 looks the simplest (8.♗g5 ♗e7 9.♗xe7 ♕xe7 10.♘bxd4 ♘cxd4 11.♘xd4 ♕xe5 12.e3 0-0 13.♘xf5 ♗xf5± is also good, to be sure). Play might continue 8...dxe3 9.♕xd8+ ♘xd8 10.fxe3 ♗e7 11.♗d2 ♘c6 12.♘bd4 ♗d7 13.♗d3 ♘h4 14.0-0 ♘xf3+ 15.♘xf3 ♗e6 16.♗c3 ♗c5 17.♔f2, with an extra pawn and better pieces.

7.h3 ♗xf3

7...♗h5 saves the bishop pair, but deflects the bishop from the queenside, which White can exploit immediately by 8.♕a4 (8.♕b3 has similar ideas, but it gives some counterplay with 8...♖a6 9.♕b5 ♖b6 10.♕d5 a4) 8...♕d7 (8...♘ge7 9.g3 ♘c8, as in Furman-Byvshev, Vilnius 1949, gives White a big advantage: 10.♗g2 ♗e7 11.♘xd4 or 10...♘b6 11.♕b5 ♗xf3 12.♗xf3 ♕d7 13.0-0 ♗e7 14.♖d1 a4 15.b4+–) 9.♕b5 (eyeing the poor h5-bishop) 9...♗g6, Dus Chotimirsky-Marshall, Hamburg 1910, 10.♘b3+–.

8.♘xf3 ♗c5

Or 8...♘ge7 9.e3 dxe3 10.♗xe3 ♘g6 11.♕b3+–, Tripoteau-Garzon, France 2004.

Bulgarian IM Panbukchian stubbornly defends this position, at least in blitz games. The editor of this book Semkov showed perhaps the most convincing refutation of Black's strategy:

9.h4!

White anticipates the manoeuvre ...♘g8-e7-g6, which will be prevented by h4-h5. In addition, White could develop his light-squared bishop to h3. Here are two blitz examples:

9...♕d7 10.g3 ♘h6 11.♗h3+–,

Semi-Panbuk, blitz, playchess.com 2007;

9...h6 10.g3 ♕e7 11.♗f4 0-0-0 12.♕a4 f6, Semi-Panbuk, blitz, playchess.com 2007, when instead of 13.♗h3+(wich is clearly better for White, of course), White is winning with 13.exf6 ♘xf6 14.b4 axb4 15.♕a8+ ♘b8 16.♗h3++–.

B. 5...♗g4 6.b4

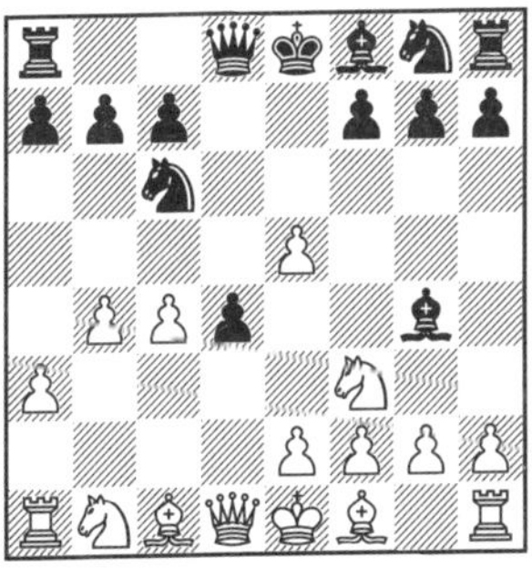

More popular is 6.♘bd2. Commonly play transposes to our main line, but in some cases White can use the particular move order to lead out the c1-bishop. The fine point is that Black is not really threatening to capture on f3 since that would help White to develop the f1-bishop:

6...♗xf3 7.exf3 ♘xe5 8.♖a2! (8.f4 ♘g6 9.g3 ♘f6 10.♗g2 ♕e7+ 11.♔f1 is enough for some advantage, but why not prevent the check from e7?!) 8...♗e7 9.f4 ♘g6 10.g3 ♘f6 11.♗g2 c6 12.♖d2±.

Another attempt to pinpoint drawbacks in 6.b4 is to insert 6...a5 7.b5 ♗xf3 8.exf3 ♘xe5 9.f4 ♘g6 (9...♘d7 10.♕xd4 ♗e7 11.♗e2 ♘c5 12.♕e3 ♘f6 13.0-0±) 10.♖a2 ♗c5, but White can take over the initiative with 11.f5 ♘6e7 12.♕g4±.

That's why in practice Black opts for:

B1. 6...♕d7
B2. 6...♕e7

Note also 6...♘ge7 7.♗b2 which is mentioned in line D. Here we draw benefits from having played 6.b4 instead of 6.♘bd2 – the d4-pawn is hanging.

B1. 6...♕d7 7.♘bd2

7...♘ge7

Black has not time for 7...0-0-0 due to the shaky state of the d4-pawn: 8.♗b2 ♕e6 (8...f6 9.exf6 ♘xf6 does not offer Black any compensation, e.g.: 10.♕a4 d3 11.e3 ♔b8 12.b5 ♗xf3 13.gxf3±, Broman-Visti, Finland 2000) 9.♕b3 ♗xf3 10.♘xf3 ♘xe5 11.♘xd4, Monin-Czebe, Zalakaros 1991, when 11... ♕xc4? loses to 12.♕h3+! ♔b8 13.e4+–.

8.h3 ♗e6 9.b5 ♘a5 10.♕a4 b6 11.♗b2

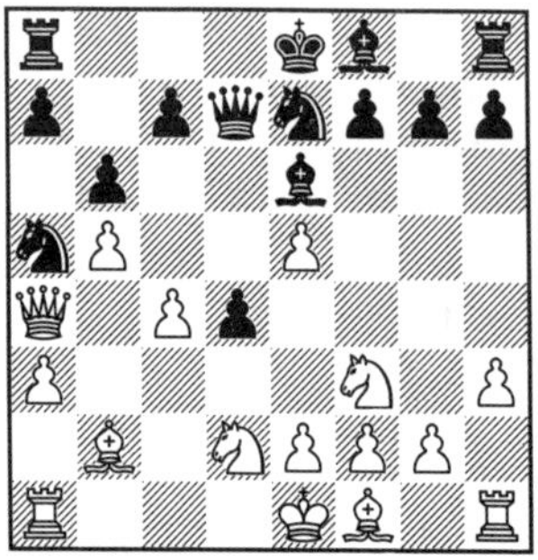

Black loses a pawn:

11...c5 12.bxc6 ♘exc6 13.♘xd4 ♗c5

Or 13...♘xd4 14.♕xd7+ ♔xd7 15.♗xd4 ♘xc4 16.♘xc4 ♗xc4 17.0-0-0 ♔e6 18.♔b2±.

14.e3±

The game Farago-Vl.Bukal Jr, Austria 2008 saw further 14...0-0 when simplest is 15.♘xe6.

B2. 6...♕e7 7.♘bd2 0–0–0 8.♗b2 ♘xe5

Mind the trap 9.♘xd4?? ♘d3#!

9.♘xe5 ♕xe5 10.h3 ♗h5 11.g4 ♗g6 12.♗g2

It is possible to start with 12.♕a4 ♔b8 13.♗g2, but I am following the blitz game Gelfand-Radjabov, Almaty 2008:

12...♘f6 13.♘f3 ♕e8

13...♕f4 is best met by 14.♕a4! (14.♗xd4 c5 15.bxc5 ♗xc5 16.e3 ♕c7 17.♕a4 ♔b8 18.0-0 h5 19.g5 ♘d7 20.♖ad1 f6 21.♖d2 ♗e4 22.♖fd1±) 14...♔b8 (14...h5 15.g5 ♘e4 16.♕xa7 c5 17.♖d1±) 15.0-0. Not only the d4-pawn will fall, but White's pieces are also more active.

14.♘xd4 h5 15.♕b3 hxg4 16.hxg4 ♖xh1+ 17.♗xh1 ♘e4 18.♕e3 ♕e5 19.f4 ♕e7 20.0–0–0

White is a healthy pawn up.

C. 5...♗e6 6.♘bd2 ♘ge7 7.♘b3 ♘f5

7...♗xc4 is inconsistent since the d4-pawn is more important than the c4-one. White was better in the game Ivanisevic-Khenkin, Subotica 2008: 8.♘bxd4 ♕d5 (or 8...♘xd4 9.♕xd4 ♕xd4 10.♘xd4 0-0-0 11.e3 ♗xf1 12.♖xf1±) 9.♕c2 ♘xd4 10.♘xd4 ♕xd4 11.e3 ♕xe5 12.♗xc4±.

8.♕d3

White defends the c4-pawn and threatens to win d4 with 9.g4. The prophylaxis 8...h5 weakens g6, so ...f6 would be dubious. White follows up with 9.h4 ♗e7 10.♗g5±.

8...a5 9.♗f4 a4 10.♘bd2 h6

10...♗e7 allows, beside 11.h4±, 11.g4!? ♘h4 12.♘xh4 ♗xh4 13.♗g2 ♗xg4 14.♖g1 ♕d7 15.♗xc6 bxc6 16.♘e4±.

11.h4 g6 12.♘e4 ♗e7 13.♖d1 ♘xh4 14.♘xh4 ♗xh4 15.e3±

We have been following the game Grandelius-A.Smith, Ballerup 2009. White has decisive domination in the centre.

D. 5...♘ge7 6.b4 ♘g6

6...♗g4 7.♗b2 ♘f5 leves Black in a worse position without any compensation for the pawn after the simple 8.♘bd2 (Avrukh gives 8.♕d3 g6 9.♕e4 ♗xf3 10.exf3±) 8...g6 9.b5 ♘a5 10.h3 ♗xf3 11.exf3± ♗g7 12.f4 f6 13.♗d3 ♕d7 14.0-0±, Rogozenco-Ardelean, Eforie Nord 2008.

7.♗b2 a5

The a5-pawn will be a constant source of concern for Black later in an endgame, but the queens are still on the board and Black should care about the activity of his pieces. In the variation 7...♘cxe5 (7...♘gxe5) 8.♘xe5 ♘xe5 9.e3 ♗e6 10.c5 ♘c6 11.exd4 ♗e7 12.♗b5 0-0 13.♗xc6 bxc6 14.0-0 ♗f6 White remains a clear pawn up, but he can hardly convert it. So it would be better to opt for a better middlegame with 10.♗xd4 ♘xc4 11.♕c2 ♘d6 12.♗d3±, as Avrukh suggests. This is a better version of the game Topalov-Morozevich, which I examine below.

8.b5 ♘cxe5

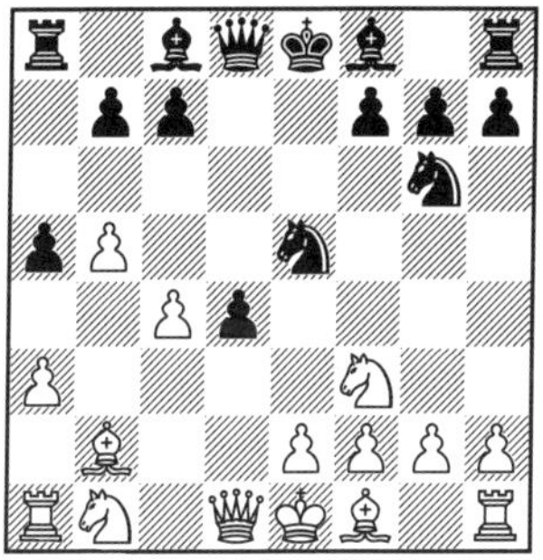

9.♕xd4!?

This move has been introduced in the game Karpov-Kasimdzhanov, Tallinn 2006. I think that the legendary positional intuition of the ex-world champion did not fail him. He leads the game into an endgame with a lasting advantage, where Black should practically play for two results only. His choice was even better from a psychological point of view, since Kasimdzhanov is an excellent tactician who loves hazy complications. Instead, he was faced with a boring defence.

“At first, I thought that Black should not have serious problems here, since the weak white pawns on the queenside should provide me with enough counterplay,” Kasimdzhanov recalls. “However, soon

I began experiencing some difficulties."

Note that Karpov's choice on move 11 is probably not the best, but still Black's task is not easy.

I have another important argument in favour of the queens trade – after the game Topalov-Morozevich, Amber-rapid 14th Monte Carlo 2005, 11.♗xd4 ♘xc4 12.♕c2 ♘d6 13.♗d3 ♕g5 14.f4 ♕h4+ has been all the rage.

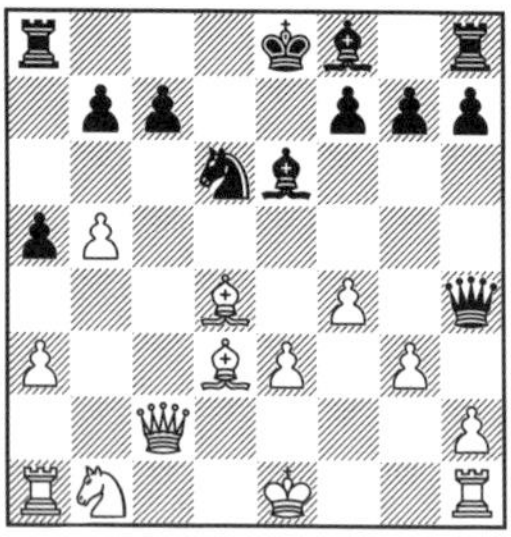

Avrukh also recommends it in his repertoire book. He considers 15...♕h3, which was suggested as an improvement, and gives the following main variation: 16.e4 ♖d8 (16...0-0-0 17.♘d2 ♕g2 18.♖g1 ♕xh2 19.b6 c6 20.♕c3→) 17.f5 ♘xe4 18.fxe6 ♕xe6 19.♗c4 ♕e7 20.♗e3 ♘xg3 21.hxg3 ♕xe3+ 22.♕e2±. You should certainly follow the development of this line, but it has one major drawback from my point of view: it is heavily dependent on a computer analysis. One can never be sure that Black has not found something along the way, perhaps even not entirely correct, but still difficult to refute over the board or in rapid chess.

With my suggestion, on the contrary, you'll be sure to get a decent position which you could play on understanding, with fair winning chances. It is very unlikely that this assessment can undergo dramatic changes.

Megabase counts 6 games in this variation so far, where White won 3 and drew the rest.

9...♕xd4 10.♗xd4 ♘xc4

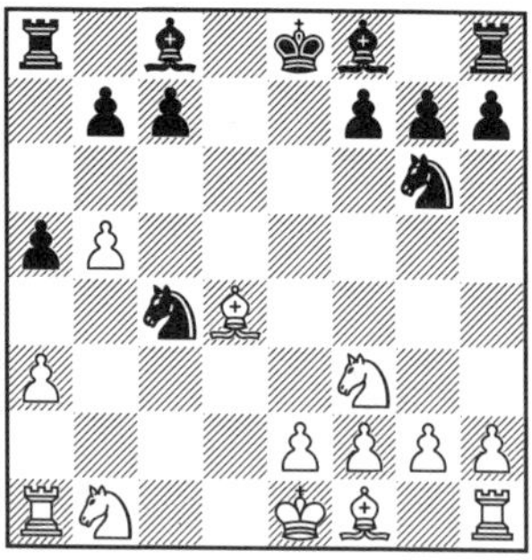

11.e3

In the source game, Karpov chose 11.♘fd2. Perhaps he wanted to remove the active knight, thus minimising Black's possibilities for counterplay. Kasimdzhanov answered 11...♘d6 (In his commentaries, he suggests as an improvement 11...♘xd2 12.♘xd2 ♗d7, but White still keeps a small plus after 13.e3 f6 14.♗e2±) 12.a4 ♘f5 13.♗c3 ♗c5 14.e3 0-0 15.♘b3 ♗b6 16.♘1d2 ♘d6 17.♘c4 ♘xc4 18.♗xc4

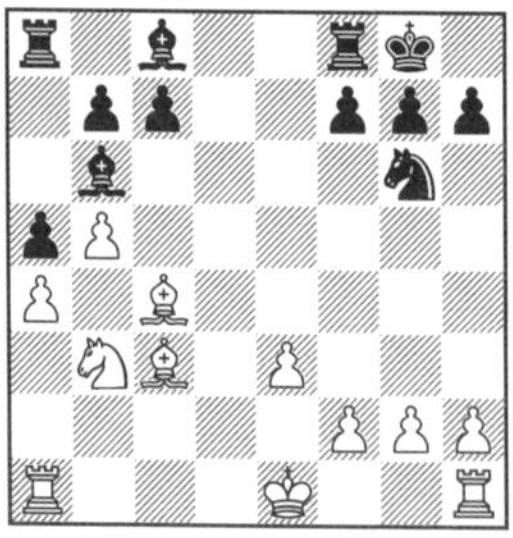

White is better due to his coordinated minor pieces and the weakness of the a5-pawn. The game went

18...♖e8 19.0-0 ♘e5 20.♗e2

Game 19 Sarkar-Nikolayev, Colonie 2008, reached the same position by different move order (following 11.e3 ♘d6 12.a4 ♘f5 13.♗c3 ♗c5 14.♘bd2 0-0 15.♘b3 ♗b6 16.♘fd2 ♘d6 17.♘c4 ♘xc4 18.♗xc4 ♖e8 19.0-0 ♘e5). White preferred 20.♗d5!? ♗e6 21.♖fd1⩲, the engines even point out to 21.♗xb7! ♖a7 22.♘d2±.

20...♗e6 21.♘xa5 ♖xa5 22.♗xe5 ♗b3, when 23.♗d1! would have won a pawn.

I think that White should not spend a tempo on a second move by an already developed piece.

11...♘d6 12.♘bd2 ♗d7 13.a4 f6

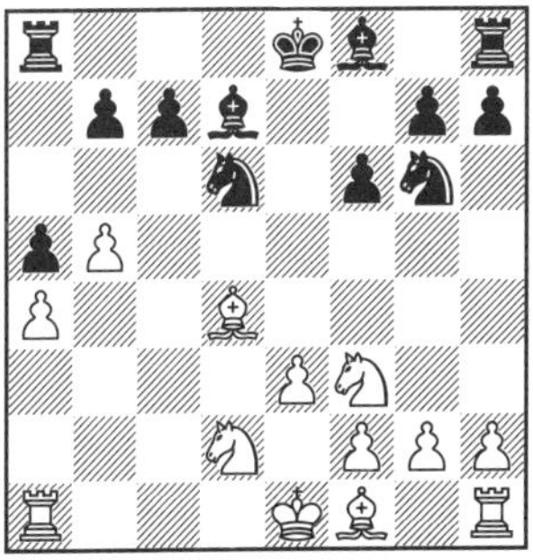

The pawn structure has crystallised. White has better control of the centre, and well coordinated pieces. He has gained an obvious spatial advantage on the queenside where he fixed two targets – on a5 and c7. Black could get rid of the latter by ...c7-c6, but then the square b6 would become very weak.

14.♗d3

Perhaps 14.♗e2 is not worse. Besides, any normal setup should give White better chances. There is no big difference whether White puts his bishop to d3 or e2. Furthermore, I suppose that the placement of White's king should not affect the evaluation either. It can go to the right wing, but staying in the centre, on e2, does not look bad. All that freedom is due to the fact that White's advantage is structural. It bears a stable character and one piece should not affect it.

Let us examine the game Peralta-Perez Candelario, Ayamonte 2006:

14.♗e2 ♘e7

Avrukh suggests as an improvement 14...♘f5 15.♗c3 ♗b4, but the simple 16.♗xb4 axb4 17.0-0 faces Black with the question how to defend the b4-pawn. For instance, 17...♘ge7 18.♖fb1 c5 19.bxc6 ♘xc6 20.♘e4± saves the pawn, but not the game.

15.0-0 ♘d5 16.♖fc1 c6 17.bxc6 ♗xc6 18.♗c5 ♘f5 19.♘b3

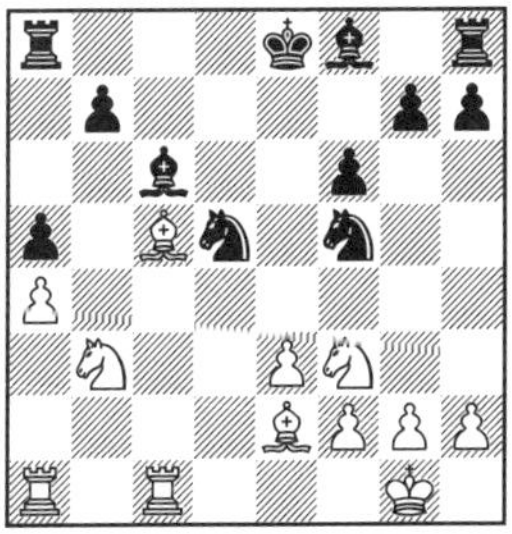

White is already so much ahead in development, that the opponent can hardly avoid material losses.

The game went on 19...♘b4 20.♗b6 ♗d7 21.♗xa5 ♘c6 22.♗b6 ♗e6 23.♘c5 ♗xc5 24.♗xc5 ♔f7 25.♖cb1 ♘a5 26.e4 ♘e7 27.♘d4 ♗d7 28.♘b5 ♘g6 29.♘d6+ ♔e6 30.♗g4+ 1-0

14...♗e7

Stojanovic-Tadic, Vrsac 2007 saw 14...♗f5 15.♗e2! when Black should think how to finish development. He opened way to his bishop with 15...♘e4? to lose after 16.g4 ♘xd2 17.gxf5 ♘b3 18.fxg6 ♘xa1 19.♗xa1+− . The engines "seriously" consider 15...♗d7?!, but, of course, this is not a solution as play transposes to Peralta-Perez Candelario with an extra tempo for White.

15.0-0

As I have mentioned, 15.♔e2 is also an option.

15...0-0 16.♖fd1 ♖fd8

16...c6 17.♗c5 cxb5 loses a piece to 18.♗xg6±.

17.♖ac1⩲

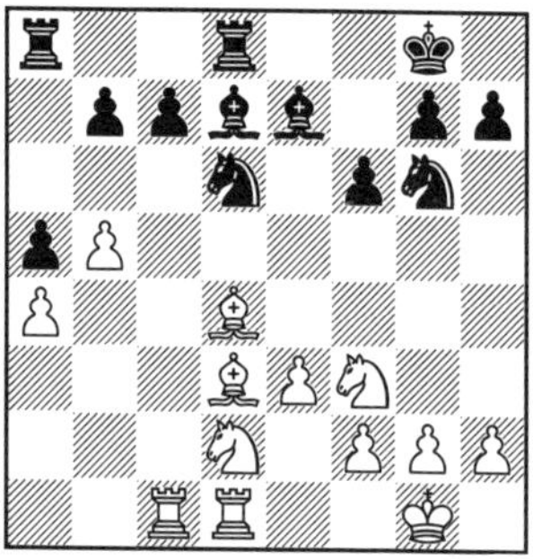

White's game is clearly more pleasant. Black cannot easily disentangle his pieces. For instance, 17...c6 leaves his minor pieces hanging: 18.♘c4 cxb5 19.♘b6! ♖ab8 20.♗xg6 (20.♘xd7 ♖xd7 21.axb5⩲) 20...hxg6 21.♖c7 bxa4 22.♖xd7 ♖xd7 23.♘xd7 ♖d8 24.♘b6±.

Part 5

Complete Games

1.d4 d5 2.c4 e5 3.dxe5 d4

18. Levin–Szoen
Pardubice 27.07.2006

1.d4 d5 2.c4 e5 3.dxe5 d4 4.♘f3 ♘c6 5.a3 ♘ge7 6.b4 ♘g6 7.♗b2 a5 8.b5 ♘cxe5 9.♕xd4 ♕xd4 10.♗xd4 ♘xc4 11.e3 ♘d6 12.♘bd2 ♗d7 13.a4 ♘f5 14.♗c3 ♗b4

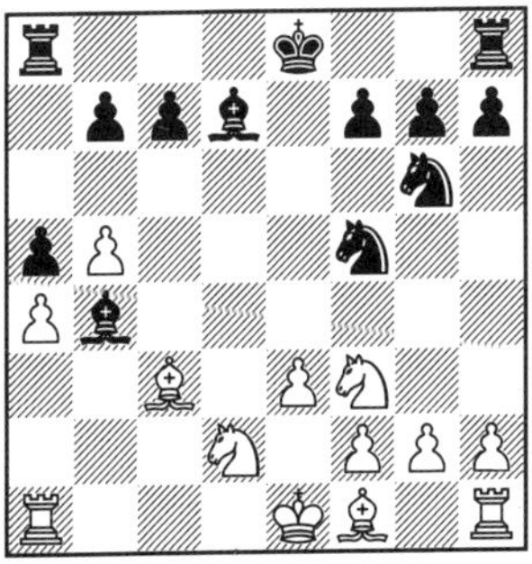

15.♗xb4

This exchange is positionally correct, but White could have delayed it for a couple of moves, for instance: 15.♖c1 f6 16.♗d3 0-0-0 17.♗xb4 axb4 18.♖c4±.

15...axb4 16.♗d3 ♔e7 17.♔e2 c5 18.bxc6 bxc6 19.♘b3 ♘d6 20.♖hc1

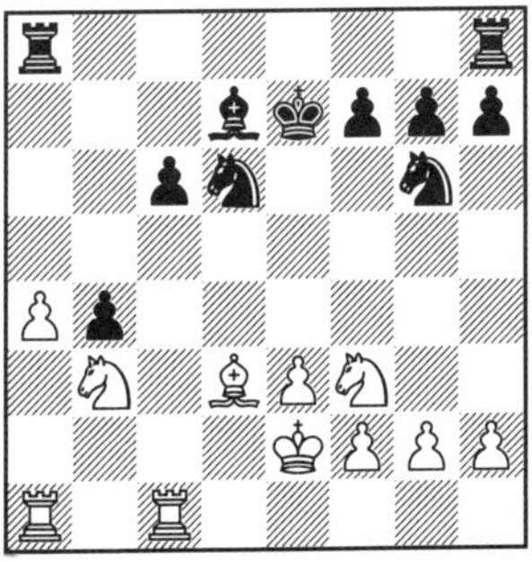

White has a large advantage since all his pieces are active.

20...♖hc8 21.♘c5 f6 22.♖ab1 ♖cb8 23.♘a6 ♖b6 24.♘xb4 ♔e8 25.♗c2 ♘e7 26.♘a2 ♖ba6 27.♘d2 ♘d5 28.♗b3

White is a clear pawn up and the rest should be a matter of technique. Perhaps the best plan was to begin with gaining space in the centre, e.g. 28.g3 ♖a5 29.e4±. Instead, White looks like being waiting for the game to get won by itself.

28...♗f5 29.♖a1 ♖b8 30.♘c3 ♘b4 31.e4 ♗d7 32.♘a2 (32.♘c4) **32...♖a5 33.f3 ♔e7 34.♘xb4 ♖xb4 35.♖a2** (35.♗d1 f5 36.exf5 ♘xf5 37.♖ab1±) **35...f5 36.exf5 ♘xf5 37.♔f2 c5 38.♖e1+ ♔d8 39.♗e6?** (39.♖e5 ♘d4 40.♗g8±) **39...♘d4?**

Perhaps the opponent were in time trouble. 39...♗xe6 40.♖xe6 ♖axa4 41.♖xa4 ♖xa4 42.♖e5 ♖a2= was dead equal.

40.♗xd7 ♔xd7 41.♖e5 ♘c6 42.♖g5 g6 43.♖c2 c4 44.♖g4 ♘e5 45.♖d4+ ♔e6 46.f4 ♘d3+ Draw

Strange decision, as 47.♔e3 ♘e1 48.♖cxc4 ♖xc4 49.♖xc4 ♘xg2+ 50.♔f2 keeps the extra pawn.

---

19. Sarkar–Nikolayev
Colonie, 01.09.2008

1.d4 d5 2.c4 e5 3.dxe5 d4 4.a3 ♘c6 5.♘f3 ♘ge7 6.b4 ♘g6 7.♗b2 a5 8.b5 ♘cxe5 9.♕xd4 ♕xd4 10.♗xd4 ♘xc4 11.e3 ♘d6 12.a4 (12.♗d3) **12...♘f5 13.♗c3 ♗c5 14.♘bd2 0–0 15.♘b3 ♗b6 16.♘fd2 ♘d6 17.♘c4 ♘xc4 18.♗xc4 ♖e8 19.0–0 ♘e5**

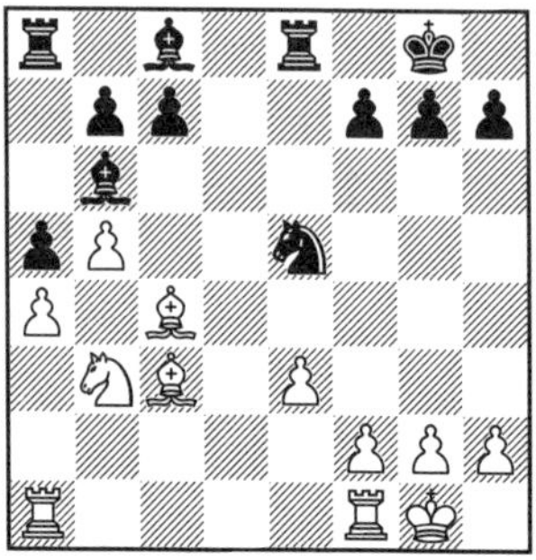

The same position arose (with transposition) in the source game for the 9.♕xd4 line, Karpov-Kasimdzhanov, 2006. The ex-world champion chose 20.♗e2 ♗e6 21.♘xa5! with an edge. Sarkar opts for the more challenging:

20.♗d5!? ♗e6 21.♖fd1

21.♗xb7! ♖ab8 22.♘d2!±

21...f6 22.♗xe5 (22.♖ac1⩲) **22...fxe5 23.♔f1 ♔f7 24.♔e2 ♗xd5 25.♖xd5 ♔e6 26.♖d2 ♖ed8 27.♖c2 ♖d5 28.♖ac1 ♖ad8 29.♔f3 ♖f8+ 30.♔e4⩲**

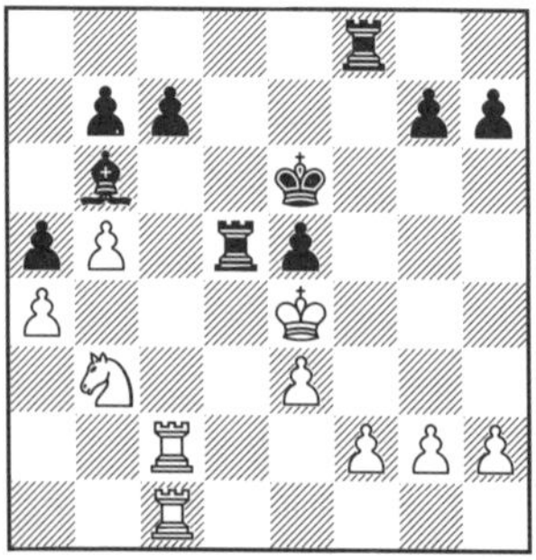

30...♖f6 31.f3 ♔d6? 32.♖c6+ bxc6 33.♖xc6+ ♔d7 34.♔xd5 ♗xe3 35.♘xa5 ♗g1 36.♖c1 ♗xh2 37.♖h1 ♗f4 38.♖xh7 ♗h6 39.♖h8 ♖f4 40.♘c6 1–0

The Blumenfeld Gambit

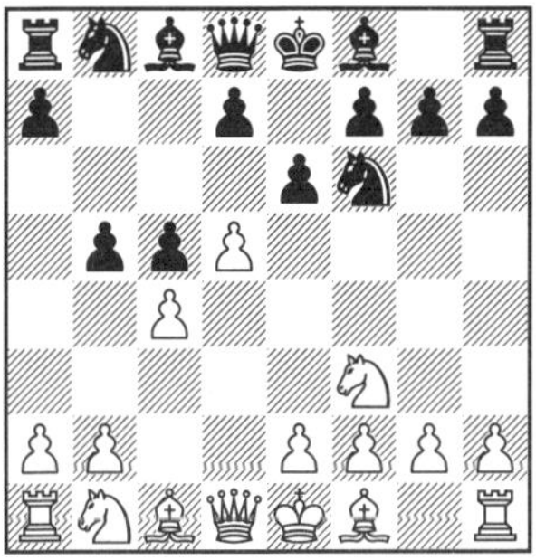

Part 6

Main Ideas

1.d4 d5 2.c4 e6 3.♘f3 c5 4.d5 b5

A Little Background

Twenty years ago the Blumenfeld Gambit was considered to be a rather dubious opening. The old books recommended 5.♗g5! and the verdict was that White had a clear advantage. The efforts of Nisipeanu, however, stirred new life into that system. In the last five years, many 2600+ grandmasters included it in their repertoire. Black began to refrain from ...h6 (on the 5th move or after 5...exd5 6.cxd5) and his results improved considerably. White discovered that it was not so easy to break the enemy's defence and turned to 5.cxb5. I saw many commentaries, claiming that accepting the Blumenfeld was "the best system" against it. That only encouraged more players to test it with Black since the ensuing positions offered them a strong initiative and fair compensation for the pawn. Look at one of my games:

Kiril Georgiev–Nisipeanu
EU–Cup Fuegen 2006

1.d4 ♘f6 2.♘f3 e6 3.c4 c5 4.d5 b5 5.dxe6 fxe6 6.cxb5 d5 7.g3 a6 8.bxa6 ♗d6 9.♗g2 0-0 10.0-0 ♘c6 11.b3 ♗xa6 12.♗b2 ♕e8 13.♘bd2 ♖d8 14.♖e1 ♘g4 15.h3

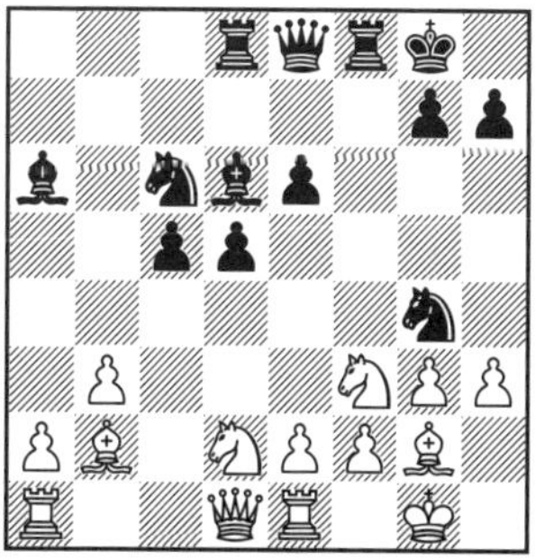

15...♘xf2!? 16.♔xf2 ♘d4

"One of the most complicated positions that I have reached in my entire chess career", writes Nisipeanu.

17.g4 h5 18.g5 ♕f7 19.e3?

In the opening, I chose the most challenging line. Then in the diagram position I picked up the gauntlet and provoked the piece sacrifice. My intuition did not let me down as I felt that White should be able to defend successfully. However, my last move loses the game! Instead, 19.♔g1! would have left Black without compensation. Nisipeanu finished the attack in grand style:

19...♘xf3 20.♘xf3 ♗h2 21.♗f1 ♕c7 22.♗xa6 ♕g3+ 23.♔e2 ♕g2+ 24.♔d3 c4+ 25.♔c3 ♖xf3 26.♕d4 ♖f2 27.♕b6 ♗e5+ 28.♔b4 ♖b8 29.♗b7 ♗xb2 30.♕xe6+ ♔h8 31.♔c5 ♗xa1 32.♗xd5 ♕xg5 33.♖xa1 c3 34.h4 ♕xh4 35.e4 c2 36.♖c1 ♕g5 37.♕h3 ♕xc1 0-1

The moral of this game is that accepting the gambit involves a considerable risk and is impractical. A single mistake can cost a whole point. Now I'm inclined to think that White has better ways to combat the Blumenfeld:

5.♗g5!

Basic Plans and Pawn Structures

The idea of the bishop move is to enable e2-e4. White is ready to part with the bishop pair, but bolster the pawn wedge at d5 and finish development quickly. The cornerstone of White's strategy is the d5-pawn. It should be kept there at any cost.

Do not even think about trading it for e6, unless you win by force.

Black has tried many continuations in answer to 5.♗g5. I'm going to consider them separately as they bring about different pawn structures:

A. 5...h6 6.♗xf6 ♕xf6 7.♘c3!

This variation is rather dubious for Black. The fine point is that he is unable to exploit the placement of White's knight on b5 after:

7...b4 8.♘b5 ♔d8, because ...a6 would never work, due to ♕a4, threatening a check from a5. The b2-pawn is irrelevant and can be sacked without calculations. Black could be crushed right in the opening.

B. 5...♕a5+ 6.♘bd2

In the "Step by Step" chapter I also consider 6.♕d2. It is undoubtedly slightly better for White, but our general strategy against the Blumenfeld is to checkmate the opponent. Therefore, playing an endgame does not comply with our plans.

6...bxc4

6...♘e4 is dubious owing to 7.b4 ♕xb4 8.♖b1±.

7.♗xf6 gxf6 8.e4

White has a pleasant game. He should castle quickly without paying too much attention what Black is doing. The bishop should go to e2, both rooks – to e1 and d1. Then Black will be so cramped, that he will be lacking good moves. For instance: 8...♖g8 9.g3 ♖g4 10.♗e2! 10...♖xe4 11.0-0 ♖g4 12.♘xc4 ♕c7 13.♖e1 ♗b7 14.♗f1 ♘a6 15.♘e3±.

C. 5...exd5 6.cxd5 d6

This is Black's most reliable answer. He opts for a Modern Benoni structure without wasting tempi on ...h6 or ...♕a5+. His only problem is that he has not time for fianchettoing the dark-squared bishop. That makes his position passive.

White's plan should be to gain control of the c4-square and prepare e4-e5 or a kingside attack. He should also aim to exchange his light-squared bishop.

White's dream position would look like this one:

Game 22. Goldin–Leuba
Bern 1991

Position after 12.♗b5

White will exchange one (only!) knight and the light-squared bishop, and prepare e5. See the whole game in the "Complete Games" chapter.

Another model position is:

Nemet–Shamkovich
Amsterdam 1979

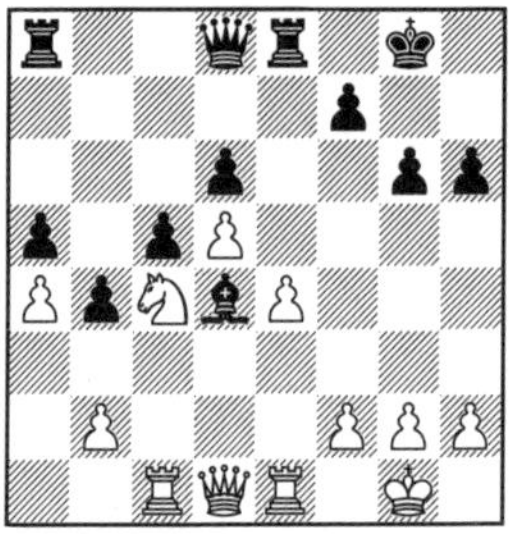

Position after 21...♗d4

It would have been nice to keep our dark-squared bishop and bind Black with the defence of the d6-pawn, but the diagram position is also in White's favour. The knight attacks two pawns and controls the important square e5. Any exchange of a heavy piece would enhance White's advantage. So he should put his queen to an active place like f3, play g3, ♔g2, h4, double the rooks on the e-file and try to open some file by e4-e5 or f4-f5. Any endgame is in his favour. Avoid playing b3, because Black will get c3 for his bishop and it will be impossible to keep both our rooks on the e-file.

Game 21 Rusev–Lilov
Plovdiv 2008

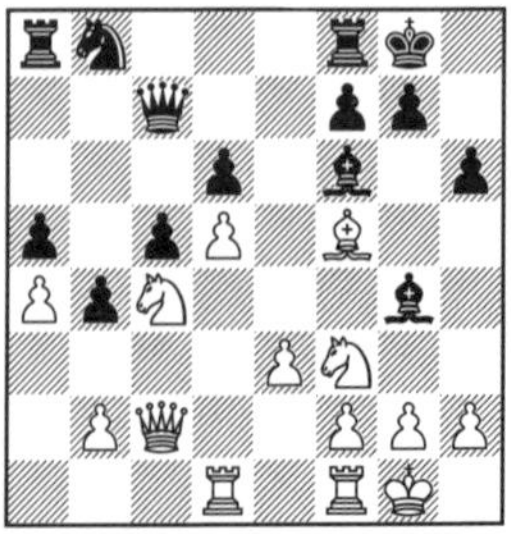

Position after 16.♗f5!

Remember this thematic move. If Black takes on f5, sooner or later he will have to defend the position from the previous example. On the other hand, 16...♗xf3 opens the g-file, which gives White additional attacking resources, as it happened in the game.

Now, armed with knowledge of the three model positions, we can move on to concrete variations.

White can aspire for a small, but lasting advantage in several lines:

1. 7.e4 a6 8.a4 ♗e7!

8...b4 would reach the structure from the first model position.

9.♗xf6 ♗xf6 10.axb5 ♗xb2 11.♖a2 ♗f6 12.♗d3 0-0 13.0-0

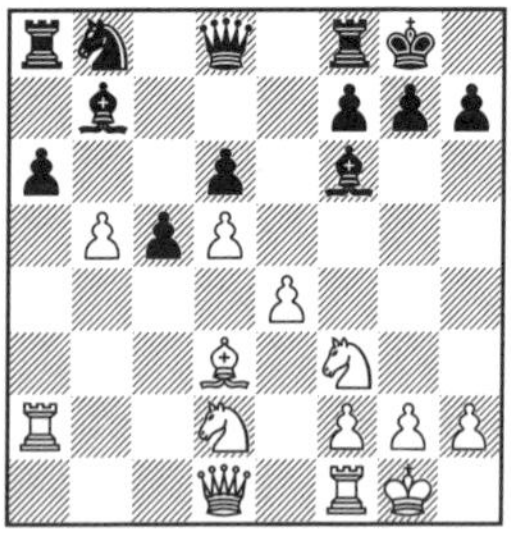

White has lasting pressure here in view of the awkward black light-squared bishop. However, Black might be able to hold it, although he was not successful in Van Wely-Feygin, Netherlands 2009: 13...♗b7 14.♘bd2 axb5 15.♖xa8 ♗xa8 16.♗xb5 ♘d7 17.♕a4 ♘b6 18.♕a5 ♕c7 19.♘c4 ♖b8 20.♖b1 ♗d8 21.♘xb6 ♕xb6 22.♕xb6 ♖xb6? (22...♗xb6 23.♗c6

♗xc6 24.dxc6 ♖a8 25.♔f1 ♖a6±) 23.♘d2 ♗c7 24.♗c6 ♖a6 25.♗xa8 ♖xa8 26.♖b7 ♗d8 27.f4+–.

2. 7.e3 a6 8.a4 b4

With this move order, White gets hold of c4, but the weakness of d5 hinders his natural development.

9.♘bd2 ♗e7 10.♘c4 a5 11.♕c2 0-0 12.♗d3

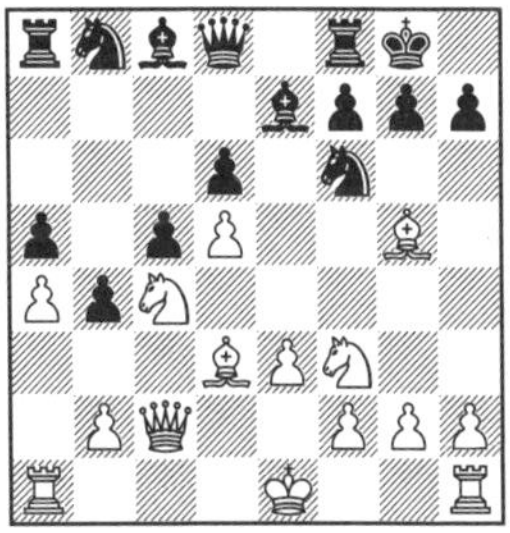

This position seems critical for the 7.e3 line. White should seek to exchange his light-squared bishop from f5, as shown by **game 21 Rusev-Lilov** and **game 20 Delchev-Ovetchkin,** Plovdiv 2008. You will find detailed explanations of the best move order in the "Step by Step" chapter.

3. 7.a4 b4 9.♗b5+ ♗d7 10.♕d3

Now the only way for Black to avoid the course of **game 22 Goldin-Leuba** is

10...♗xb5!? 11.axb5!? 0-0 12.♘bd2 ♘bd7 13.0-0 ♘b6±

Now the threat ...♘xd5 accounts for our next move: 14.♗f4 ♕d7 15.♖fe1 ♖fc8 16.b3 ♘h5 17.♗e3 ♗f6 18.♖a6. White has lasting pressure. The point is that the rook at a6 is extremely awkward for Black.

D. 5...b4

Top players like Navara and Nisipeanu opted for 5...b4 in major competitions lately so pay attention to it.

6.a3!

White should aim for a quick clash in the centre. The exchange of the a-pawn for that at c5 will enable the break c4-c5 in some lines. It also ensures control of d4 which is an excellent place for the f3-knight.

6...a5

Introduced in the game Gelfand-Nisipeanu, Kallithea 2008. This is supposed to improve on the previous game Ivanchuk-Nisipeanu, Khanty-Mansiysk 2007 which went 6...h6 7.♗h4 a5 8.axb4 cxb4 9.♘d4!? when 9...♗c5 could be attacked by 10.♘b3.

7.axb4 cxb4 8.e4!

This should be a novelty.

8...h6 9.♗xf6 ♕xf6 10.e5!

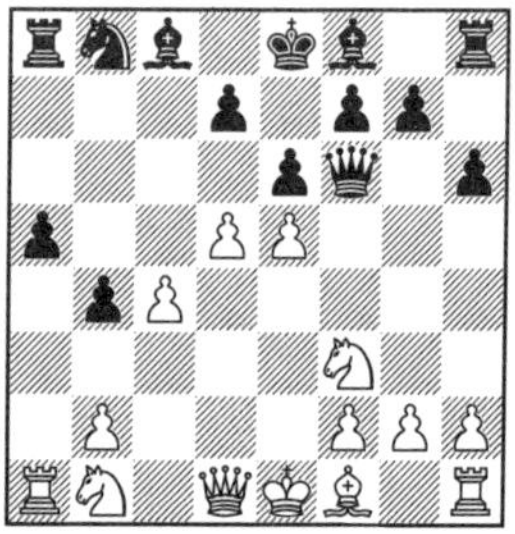

White takes over the initiative: 10...♕g6 11.♗d3! ♕xg2 12.♖g1 ♕h3 13.♘bd2, with terrific compensation for the pawn.

Typical Tactical Motives

The biggest problem of White in all the branches of the Blumenfeld is that the g5-bishop is hanging. That often allows the tactical hit ...♘xd5 (or ...♘xe4).

Position after 9.a4

Here 9... ♘xd5 equalises. White avoids that threat by retreating the bishop to f4 or by taking on f6.

White also has a thematic motive, which appears in various settings –the breakthrough e4-e5. It is often linked with a positional pawn sacrifice. Its idea is to free the e4-square for the knight and transform the d5-pawn into a passer. Black's c5-pawn also becomes vulnerable:

Williams–Rudd
Torquay 2009

Position after 11...♗g4

12.e5! dxe5 13.♘e4 ♕f4 14.♘fd2 h5 15.♘c4 ♕h6 16.♘xe5±.

Analysis

Position after 17...g6

18.e5! dxe5 19.♗e4 ♘d7 20.d6 ♕c8 21.♖fe1 ♖e8 22.h4, with an excellent compensation.

Neverov–Ghaem Maghami 2009

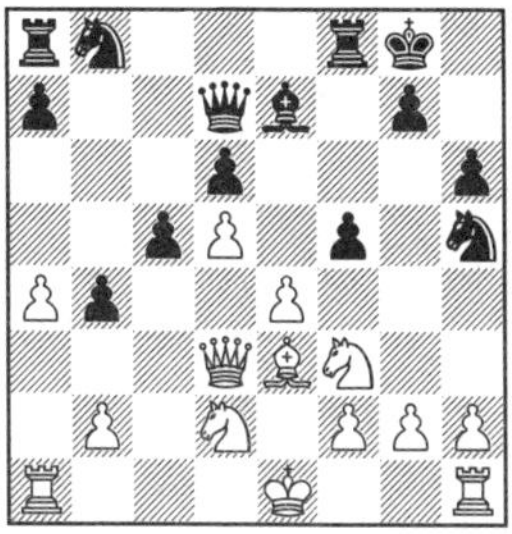

Position after 14...♕xd7

15.e5!!± f4 16.♗xc5 dxc5 17.♘e4±

Part 6

Step by Step

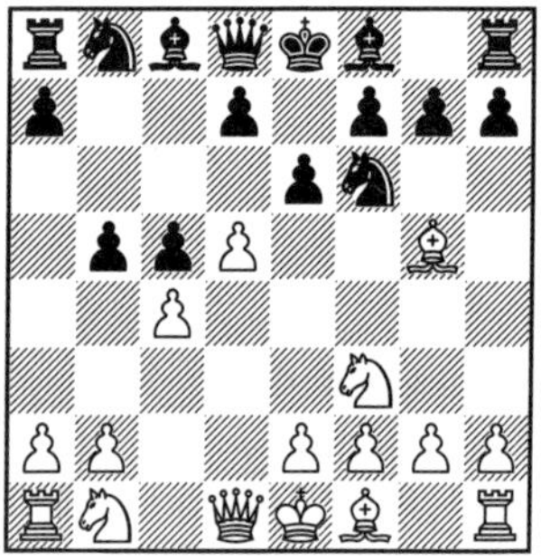

1.d4 d5 2.c4 e6 3.♘f3 c5 4.d5 b5 5.♗g5

A. 5...h6
B. 5...♕a5+
C. 5...exd5
D. 5...b4

A. 5...h6 6.♗xf6 ♕xf6 7.♘c3!

This variation is rather dubious for Black. It would make some sense if he could exploit the placement of White's knight on b5 after:

7...b4 8.♘b5 ♔d8, but ...a6 never works, due to ♕a4, threatening a check from a5. The funny game Azmaiparashvili-Miroshnichenko, Kallithea 2009, lasted only 19 moves: 9.e4 g5 (9...♕xb2 10.♖b1 ♕f6 11.♗e2, with full compensation) 10.e5 ♕g7 11.h3 ♗b7 (11...a6 12.♕a4) 12.♕a4 a5 13.0-0-0 h5 14.h4 g4 15.♘g5 exd5 16.cxd5 f6 17.♘e6+ dxe6 18.dxe6+ ♔c8 19.♘a7+ 1-0.

8...♘a6 is more stubborn, but this move renounces the threat of ...a6 and offers White a comfortable edge after 9.e4 g5 (perhaps Black should grab a pawn in order to at least have an extra material for his bad position after 9...♕xb2 10.♗d3) 10.e5 ♕f4 11.♗d3 g4 12.♕d2 ♕xd2+ 13.♘xd2 ♗g7 14.f4, Najer-Malakhov, Moscow 2003.

I will also mention Black's attempt to play in the Benko style: 7...a6 8.e4 g5 9.cxb5 ♗g7, when we could follow the receipt from the first part of our book: 10.b6!.

Summarising: Black is lagging behind in development and with a severe space deficit. His game is very unpleasant and he is understandably losing 75% in practice.

B. 5...♕a5+

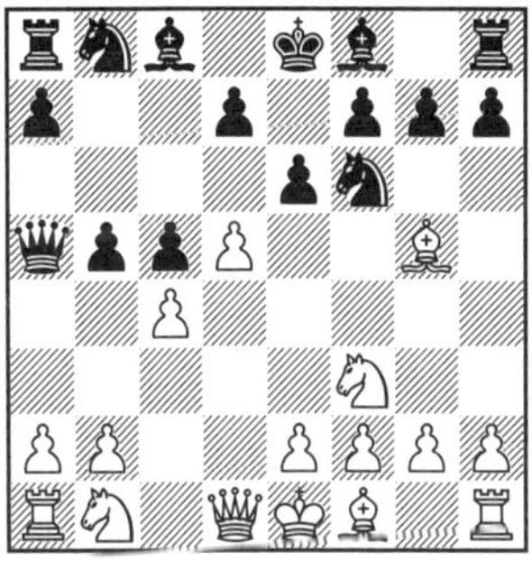

B1. 6.♕d2
B2. 6.♘bd2

I will leave the choice between these two answers to you. The trade of queens is certainly more solid and gives White a slight edge, but the second option is probably a sterner test of Black's check.

Practice has often seen 6.♘c3, but White's game is not so easy and clear as in the main lines, since Black keeps a flexible pawn formation and the bishop pair:

6...♘e4 7.♗d2 ♘xd2 8.♘xd2 (Or 8.♕xd2!? b4 9.♘e4 ♗e7 10.e3 0-0 11.♗e2 ♗b7 12.0-0) 8...b4 9.♘ce4 f5 10.♘g3 g6 with complex play.

B1. 6.♕d2 ♕xd2+ 7.♘bxd2

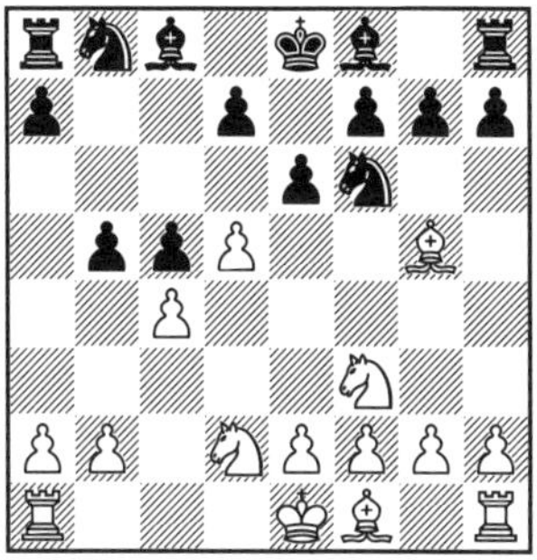

7...bxc4

Alternatively:

a) 7...exd5 8.♗xf6 gxf6 9.cxd5 ♘a6 10.e4 ♖b8 11.♗e2 ♘c7 12.0-0 ♗d6 (12...d6 13.a4 bxa4 14.♖xa4 a6 15.♘c4 ♗d7 16.♖a2±) 13.a4 a6 14.axb5 axb5, Dautov-Lobron, Bad Homburg 1998, 15.♘h4 ♗c5 16.♖a7±;

b) 7...♘a6. Intending to disturb White's development by threatening to check from c2. However, it turns out that the king is rather comfortable on d1.

8.e4

This is better than 8.♖c1 bxc4 9.e4 exd5 10.♗xf6 gxf6 11.exd5 ♖b8 12.♘xc4 ♘b4 13.d6 ♘xa2 14.♖a1 ♘b4 15.♖xa7 ♖g8, with counterplay.

8...♘b4

Or 8...bxc4 9.♗xc4 h6 (9...♘c7 10.d6±) 10.♗xf6 (10.♗h4!? may be stronger) 10...gxf6 11.0-0-0 ♖b8 12.♖he1 ♗g7. This is the game Najer-D.Gurevich, Las Vegas 2003. White is slightly better. This could be underlined by 13.♘b3± ♖b4 14.♗f1, when 14...c4 would give White the d4-square.

9.♔d1 bxc4 10.♗xc4

10...h6

Obtaining the bishop pair and keeping the e-file closed. Obsivac-Hudecek, Czechia 2006 saw 10... exd5 11.exd5 d6 12.♖e1+ ♗e7 13.♗xf6 gxf6 14.a3 ♘a6, when simplest is 15.♔c2 ♔f8 16.♖e3 ♘c7 17.♖ae1±.

11.♗xf6 gxf6 12.a3 ♘a6 13.♔c2 ♖g8 14.g3 ♘c7 15.♖ad1 ♗b7 16.♖he1 0-0-0 17.♘b3 ♘e8, Ostergaard-Ward, Hillerod 1995. White has a space advantage and a clear target – the c5-pawn.

The best continuation now is 18.♖e3±, defending the f3-knight and preparing e5 or ♖c3.

8.e4

The move order is not important. 8.♗xf6 gxf6 9.e4 should transpose to the main line.

8...♗b7

Gaining the bishop pair advantage. 8...♘a6 is not precise since after 9.♗xc4 White can decide to keep the bishop.

9.♗xf6

Now 9.♗xc4 does not work due to 9...exd5 10.♗xf6 dxc4 11.♗c3 f6.

9...gxf6 10.♗xc4 ♘a6 11.♖d1 ♖g8 12.0–0 ♘c7 13.♖fe1

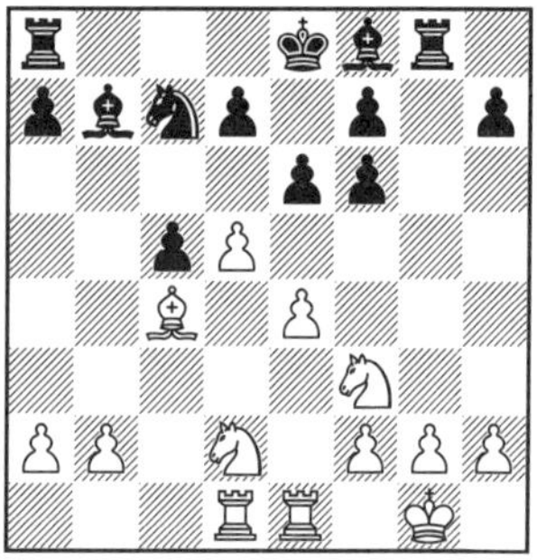

13...0–0–0

13...d6 gives White a tempo for regrouping: 14.♘b1 0-0-0 15.♘c3⩲ f5 16.exf5 exd5 (16...♗g7 17.dxe6 ♗xc3 18.exf7 ♖g7 19.♖xd6 ♖f8 20.bxc3 ♗xf3 21.g3+–) 17.♘xd5±, Vilkov-Shtepa, Kaluga 1996.

14.♘b3 f5

This breakthrough is Black's only active possibility. 14...exd5 15.exd5 ♖e8 16.g3⩲ is simply grim.

15.♘e5 fxe4 16.d6 e3

Here, in Solozhenkin-V.Ivanov, St Petersburg 1996, White should have played 17.g3±.

B2. 6.♘bd2 bxc4

a) 6...♘e4 is known to be dubious owing to 7.b4 ♕xb4 8.♖b1 ♕c3 9.♖b3 ♕a5 10.♖xb5 ♕c3 11.♖b3 (11. g3±) 11...♕a5 12.♗f4 ♗d6 13.♕c2±;

b) 6...♗e7 7.e4 ♘xe4 8.b4± is similar.

7.♗xf6 gxf6 8.e4

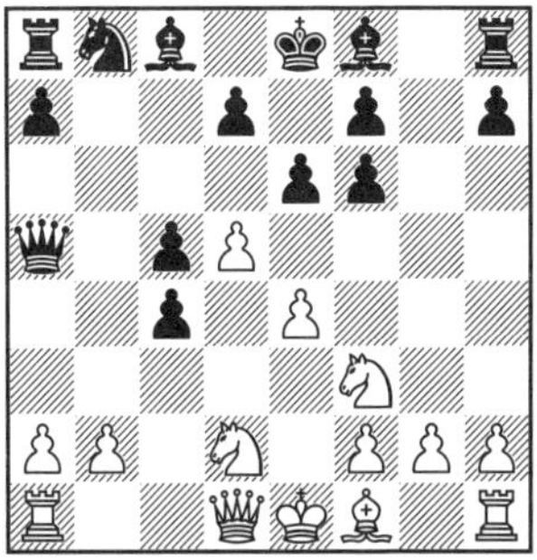

8...♖g8

Black's only compensation for the worse pawn formation is the possibility for activating the rooks on the open files. At the same time, Black should not waste tempi on grabbing a pawn with 8...c3 9.bxc3 ♕xc3 10.♗e2 ♖g8 11.0-0, as White will comfortably castle and enforce a firm grip on the centre. Black's extra pawn does not matter in such positions.

9.g3

The engines suggest 9.♖c1 in order to prevent 9...c3 However, 9.g3 c3?! 10.bxc3! ♕xc3 11.♗e2 ♘a6 12.♖c1 ♕a5 13.a3 ♘c7 14.0-0 is clearly in White's favour, for instance, 14...♗a6 15.♗xa6 ♕xa6 16.♘c4⩱.

9...♖g4

9...♗a6 10.♕c2 ♗h6 occurred in Agamaliev-Sharapov, Polanica Zdroj 2000, when instead of 11.♗xc4, 11.♗e2!± would have been very strong.

10.♗e2!

White's main aim should be to castle and repel Black's annoying rook. Then his space advantage and better coordination will tell. Play might continue:

10...♖xe4 11.0–0 ♖g4 12.♘xc4 ♕c7 13.♖e1 ♗b7 14.♗f1 ♘a6 15.♘e3± ♖g6 16.a3 0–0–0 17.♕a4 ♕b6 18.♖ad1.

C. 5...exd5 6.cxd5 d6

The most fashionable reply. Black is developing, without wasting time on h6 or checks. The resulting Modern Benoni structure is generally in White's favour, but things are complicated here in view of the hanging d5-pawn.

6...h6 is dubious because it offers White an important tempo. After 7.♗xf6 ♕xf6 8.♕c2 d6 9.e4 a6 10.a4 b4 (or 10...bxa4 11.♕xa4+ ♘d7 12.♕c6 ♖b8 13.♗xa6 ♗xa6 14.♖xa6 ♕xb2 15.0-0 ♕xb1 16.♖a7 ♕b5 17.♖xd7 ♕xc6 18.dxc6 ♖c8 19.♖a1 ♖xc6 20.♖b7 ♗e7 21.♖aa7 ♗f6 22.♖xf7 ♖b6 23.♔f1±) 11.♘bd2 Black is unable to cope with the threat e4-e5:

a) 11...g5 12.e5 dxe5 13.♘e4 ♕f4 14.♘fd2±;

b) 11...♘d7 12.♗d3 g5 (12...g6 13.0-0 ♗g7 14.♘c4 0-0 15.♖ae1 ♖e8 16.♘fd2 g5 17.e5 ♘xe5 18.♘e4±) 13.0-0 g4 14.e5 dxe5 15.♘e4 ♕d8 16.♘fd2 f5, Pert-Rudd, Liverpool 2008, when 17.d6 wins outright;

c) 11...♗g4 12.e5! dxe5

Or 12...♕e7 13.♘e4 (13.♘c4!?) 13...♕c7 (13...♗xf3 14.♘xd6+ ♔d8 15.♕f5 ♗g4 16.♘xf7+ ♔e8 17.♕xg4 ♔xf7 18.♕f5+ ♔e8 19.d6 ♕b7 20.♗e2 ♘c6 21.♗f3 ♖a7 22.0-0-0, 1-0 Williams-Rudd, Torquay 2009) 14.0-0-0±.

13.♘e4 ♕f4 14.♘fd2 h5 15.♘c4 ♕h6 16.♘xe5±.

6...♕a5+ 7.♘c3 ♘e4 8.♗d2 ♘xd2 9.♘xd2 d6 10.e4 a6 11.a4 b4 is bringing Black very disappointing results. His main problem is that he is lacking counterplay.

12.♘cb1 ♗e7 13.♗d3 0-0 14.0-0 ♗f6 15.♘c4 ♕d8 16.a5 ♖a7 17.♘bd2 g6 18.f4 ♗g7 19.♕f3 ♖e7 20.♖ae1 ♖fe8, Novikov-Mujic, Tuzla 1989. White chose here the typical break 21.e5 dxe5 22.d6 to eventually win the game, but he could have also opt for the other common plan in such positions – with f4-f5.

Blck can play ...a5 himself, but that pawn will be a target later:

12.♘c4 ♕d8 13.♘b1 a5 14.♘bd2 ♗e7 15.g3 0-0 16.♕c2 ♗f6 17.♗g2 ♖e8 18.0-0 ♗a6 19.f4 ♗d4+ 20.♔h1 ♖a7 21.♖fe1 ♖ae7 22.♘b3±, Leitao-B.Gonzalez, Sao Paulo 1997.

Following 6...d6, I'm going to propose you two good plans, leaving the choice to your taste.

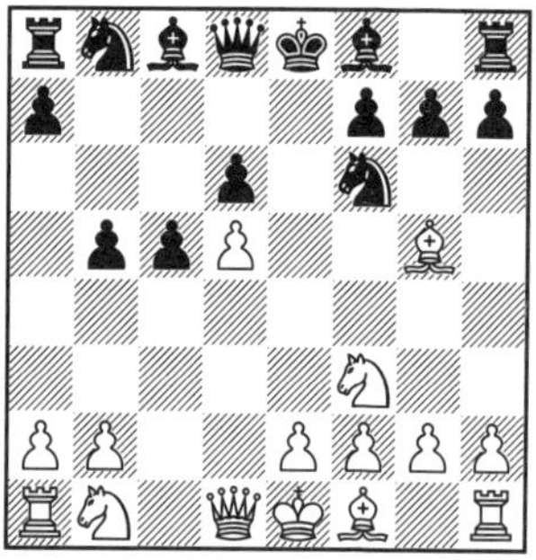

C1. 7.e3
C2. 7.a4

The first variation is very straightforward and easy to play. You need 5 minutes for preparation and there is no way that the opponent could surprise you in the opening. Perhaps that is why many strong players have adopted it lately. At the same time, Black's position is quite solid and difficult to crush.

7.a4 aims for more energetic play in the centre.

You may be surprised that I omit here 7.e4, which is by far the most popular move. In fact, the analysis of this line convinced me that White should try to improve it somehow and led me to the other two options. In the next lines I will try to explain my reasoning.

After 7.e4 a6 we reach this position:

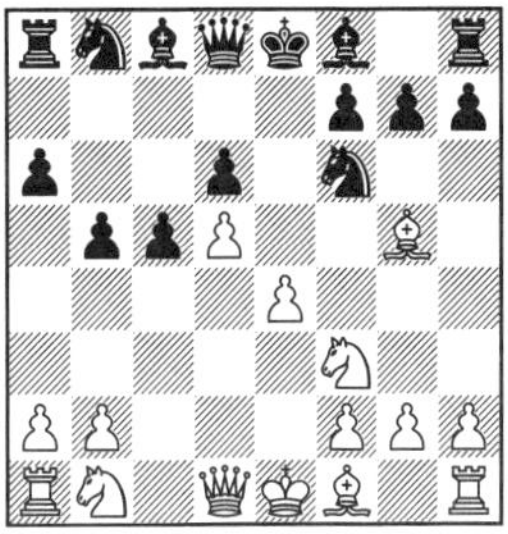

The obvious move here is:

a) 8.a4, aiming to take control over c4. However, Black has a tactical trick:

8...♗e7! when 9.axb5 is met by 9...♘xe4 10.♗xe7 ♕xe7 11.♗e2 0-0 12.0-0 ♗b7 13.♘c3 ♘f6 14.♖e1 ♕d8=, Wells-Rudd, London 2009, and 9.♘bd2 – by 9...♘xd5 10.♗xe7 ♕xe7 11.axb5 0-0=.

For many years the critical line for 8...♗e7 has been 9.♗xf6 ♗xf6 10.axb5 ♗xb2 11.♖a2 ♗f6 12.♗d3 (or 12.bxa6 ♕b6 13.♘bd2 ♗xa6 14.♕a4+ ♔e7 15.♗e2 ♗b7 16.♕c4 ♖xa2 17.♕xa2 ♘d7∓ Jobava-Ghaem Maghami, Istanbul 2004) 12...0-0 13.0-0

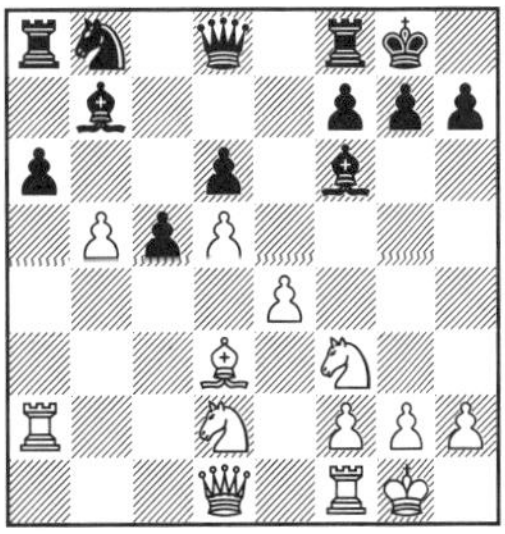

White does have lasting pressure here in view of the awkward black light-squared bishop. However, I'm afraid that this position will sooner or later be analysed till a draw. The recent game Van Wely-Feygin, Netherlands 2009 went:

13...♗b7 14.♘bd2 axb5 15.♖xa8 ♗xa8 16.♗xb5 ♘d7 17.♕a4 ♘b6 18.♕a5 ♕c7 19.♘c4 ♖b8 20.♖b1 ♗d8 21.♘xb6 ♕xb6 22.♕xb6 ♖xb6? 23.♘d2 ♗c7 24.♗c6 ♖a6 25.♗xa8 ♖xa8 26.♖b7 ♗d8 27.f4+–. I do not see, however, how White can win after 22...♗xb6 23.♗c6 ♗xc6 24.dxc6 ♖a8 25.♔f1 ♖a6 26.♔e2 ♗c7, for example, 27.♔d3 ♖xc6 28.♔c4 ♔f8 29.♔d5 ♖a6 30.♖b7 ♗d8=. Of course, this line is not too appealing for Black and statistics are rather bad for him.

Anyway, I analysed some alternatives to 8.a4:

b) 8.♕c2 ♗e7 9.♗f4 (to avoid ...♘xd5) 9...0-0, with unclear play;

c) 8.♘bd2 ♗e7 9.♗f4 0-0 10.a4

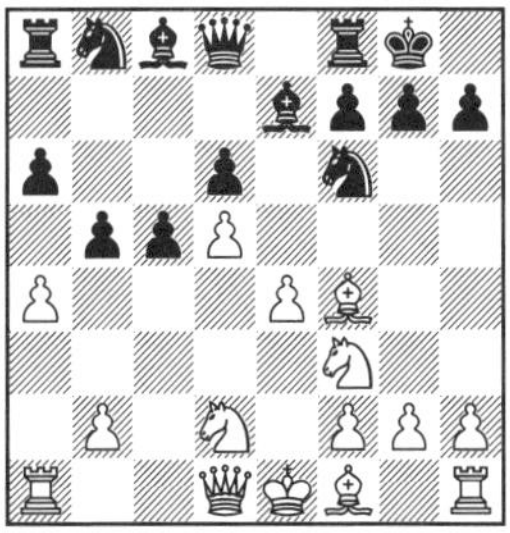

If Black now answers with 10...b4, 11.♗d3± will give us a better version of line C1. However, Black has:

10...bxa4

The game Ivanchuk-Nisipeanu, Khanty Mansiysk 2007 continued 11.♗d3 ♗d7 12.0-0 ♗b5 13.♕e2 ♘bd7 and White is slightly better, but I'm not too impressed by this approach.

11.♖xa4 ♗d7 12.♖a3 a5 13.♗e2 ♘a6 14.0-0 ♘b4 15.h3 ♖e8 16.♖e1 ♗f8 17.♗f1 a4 is hardly an improvement. Perhaps 11.♕xa4 ♗d7 (11...a5) 12.♕c2 deserves more attention.

The bottom line of my analysis is that we should somehow get in a4 b4, AND e4, preventing meanwhile the tactical trick ...♘xd5.

That leads us to the two main lines:

C1. 7.e3 a6 8.a4

8...b4

One of White's goal is fulfilled. The c4-square is in White's hands. 8...bxa4 was bad due to 9.♕xa4+ (this is more precise than 9.♗xf6 ♕xf6 10.♕xa4+ ♘d7 11.♘c3 ♖b8 12.♗xa6 ♗xa6 13.♕xa6 ♖xb2 14.0-0± Delchev-Saric, Zadar 2007, which is good also enough.) 9...♗d7 (9...♘bd7 10.♕c6 ♖a7 11.♗xf6 gxf6 12.♘c3±) 10.♗xf6 ♕xf6 11.♕b3± and the threat of ♕b7 is extremely awkward.

9.♘bd2 ♗e7 10.♘c4 a5

It is important for Black to prevent a4-a5 which would cramp Black's queenside. However, 10...0-0 is also possible since 11.a5 would be premature due to 11...♗b7.

11.♕c2

Tregubov-Ward, Reykjavik 2006 saw 11. ♗d3 ♗a6, when 12.e4 would fail to 12...♘e4. Therefore, the queen move seems more precise.

11...0–0 12.♗d3

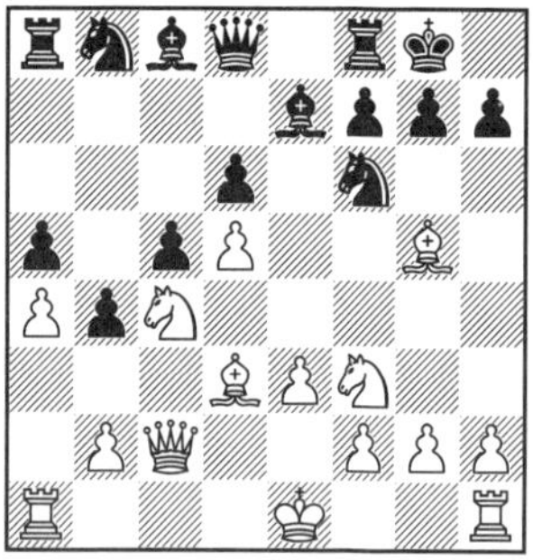

This position seems critical for the 7.e3 line. It has been tested several times by the Bulgarian grandmasters Delchev and Russev.

White's game plan is to defend d5, castle, and advance the central pawns. His space advantage suggests that the more pieces he keeps on the board, the greater his edge should be. However, the threat to the d5-pawn messes White's plan. He should part with his dark-squared bishop which considerably changes the character of the game.

12...h6

12...♘bd7 13.♖d1 h6 14.♗xf6 ♘xf6 15.0-0 ♗g4 16.b3 ♘d7 17.♗f5 is a little better for White. See **game 20 Delchev-Ovetchkin,** Plovdiv 2008.

13.♗xf6 ♗xf6 14.0–0 ♕c7 15.♗h7+

Russev played twice 15.♖ad1 against Lilov. In the first game Black answered 15...♗g4?! 16.♗f5 ♗xf3 17.gxf3 g6 and suffered, see **game 21 Rusev-Lilov**, Plovdiv 2008. A year later Lilov improved with 15...♘d7 16.b3 ♗b7 17.e4 ♖fe8=.

15...♔h8 16.♗f5

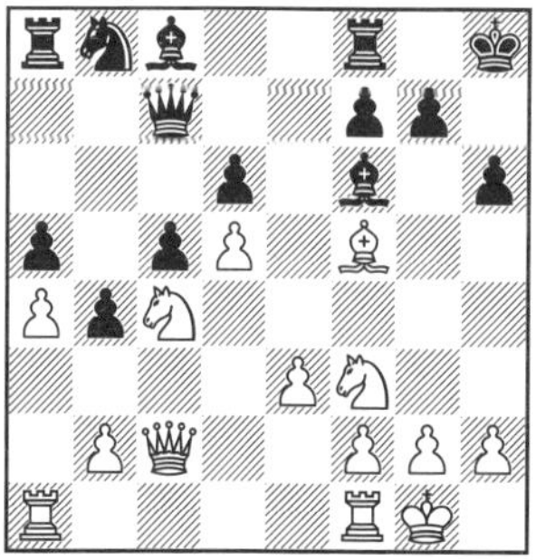

My idea is to reach a position with a knight vs. dark-squared bishop. This could happen after 16...♘d7 17.♘fd2 ♘b6 18.♗xc8±.

Should Black try to avoid it by 16...♗b7, we push 17.e4 and exploit the fact that ...♘d7 is impossible due to the fork from b6, while 17...g6 allows the interesting positional sacrifice 18.e5 dxe5 19.♗e4 ♘d7 20.d6 ♕c8 21.♖fe1 ♖e8 22.h4, with an excellent compensation.

Remains 16...♗a6 17.♘fd2 ♖d8 (enabling ...♘d7) 18.♖ab1 g6 19.♗h3 ♘d7 20.♗xd7 ♖xd7 21.♘b3 and the pressure on a5 will force Black to take on c4. In all cases White should get the above-mentioned opposition of a knight vs. bishop.

I found only one similar game in Megabase, but both opponents did not play well:

Nemet–Shamkovich
Amsterdam 1979

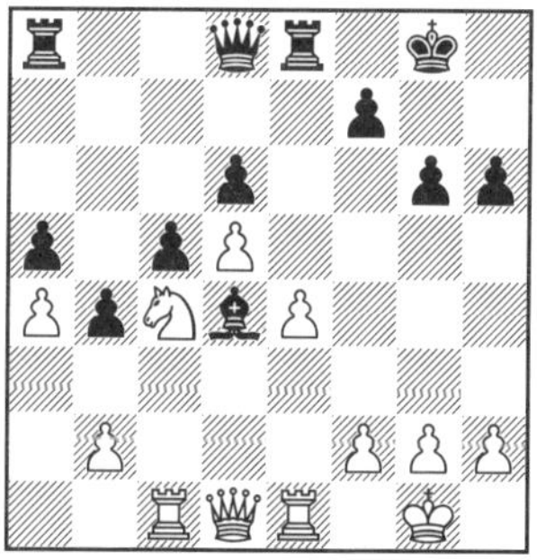

Position after 21...♗d4

22.b3?! ♖a7 23.♕c2 ♖ae7 24.♔h1 f5 25.f3 ♔g7 26.g3 fxe4 27.fxe4? (27.♖xe4!).

Let us ponder over the diagram position. The super knight at c4 attacks two enemy pawns and controls the important square e5. Any exchange of a heavy piece would increase White's advantage. So he should put his queen on an active place like f3, play g3, ♔g2, h4, double the rooks on the e-file and try to open some file by e4-e5 or f4-f5. Any endgame is in his favour.

One important thing: avoid playing b3, because Black will get c3 for his bishop and it will be impossible to keep both our rooks on the e-file.

C2. 7.a4 b4

7...h6 wastes a tempo: 8.♗xf6 ♕xf6 9.e4 b4 10.♗b5+ ♗d7 11.♕b3 ♗e7 12.♘bd2 0-0 13.0-0, with an edge.

7...bxa4 is more interesting. I propose the following setup: 8.♕xa4+ ♘bd7 9.e4 ♗e7 10.♗d2! 0-0 11.♗d3±. We'll move the bishop to c3 and the queen's knight will find a nice place on d2.

9.♗b5+

With our early breakthrough a4, we got the desired pawn structure, but Black saved the move ...a6. It is not just a tempo. The a6-square is important for Black's pieces. For instance, after 9.♗d3 0-0 10.♗f4, he can play 10...♗a6 (10...♘h5 11.♗e3 f5 12.exf5 ♗b7 13.♘bd2 ♗xd5 14.♗e4 ♗c6 15.♗xc6 ♘xc6 16.♘e4 d5 17.♘xc5 ♗xc5 18.♗xc5 ♖xf5 19.0-0 ♘f4 20.♗e3 ♕d7 21.♗xf4 ♖xf4 22.♖c1 should be better for White because the enemy pieces are unstable.) Still, White retains some edge: 11.♕e2 ♗xd3 12.♕xd3 ♘h5 13.♗e3 ♘d7 14.♘bd2 a5 15.♘c4 ♘b6 16.♘fd2±.

The text is more challenging, although not necessarily stronger.

9...♗d7 10.♕d3

White does not aim to take on b5 by queen. The queen goes to d3 in order to protect the b5-pawn in case Black exchanges the bishop himself. Otherwise White will have to defend the pawn from e2, but then d5 will be hanging, as in the game Avrukh-Volokitin, Ermioni Argolidas 2005: 10.0-0 0-0 11.♖e1 ♗xb5 12.axb5 ♘bd7 13.♘bd2 ♘b6 14.♗f4 ♕d7 (14...♖e8 15.♕c2 ♕d7! 16.♘c4 ♘xc4 17.♕xc4 ♕b7 18.♖a6) 15.♕e2 ♘h5 16.♗e3 f5 17.exf5 ♕xf5 18.♗xc5 dxc5 19.♕xe7 ♘f4 20.♕g5 ♕xg5 21.♘xg5=.

10...0–0

10...♗xb5!? now or later looks indispensable. We take 11.axb5!? and sail forth to the following position: 0-0 12.♘bd2 ♘bd7 13.0-0 (13.♘c4? ♘xe4!) 13...♘b6±

Now the threat ...♘xd5 accounts for our next move: 14.♗f4 ♕d7

15.♖fe1 ♖fc8 16.b3 ♘h5 17.♗e3 ♗f6 18.♖a6. White has lasting pressure. The point is that the rook at a6 is extremely annoying for Black. At the moment the b6-knight goes to c8 (to defend a7), we play ♖c6 and do not retreat no matter what Black is doing: 18...♖e8 19.h3 ♗c3 20.♖e2 ♖ab8 21.♘b1 ♘c8 22.♖c6 ♘e7 23.♘xc3 bxc3 24.♖c2 ♘xc6 25.bxc6±.

11.♘bd2 h6 12.♗f4 ♘h5 13.♗e3

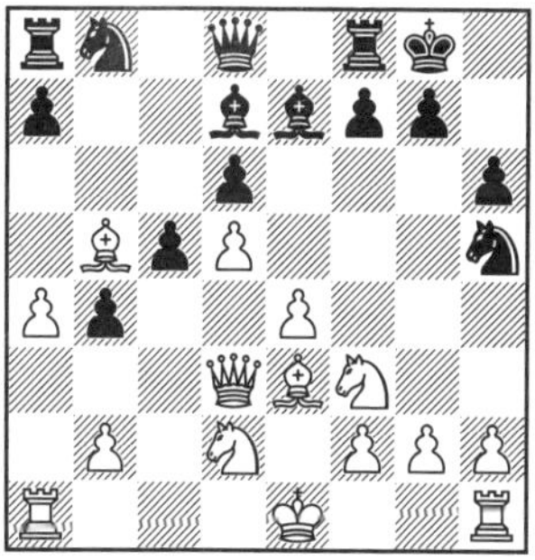

This position has been reached in Neverov-Ghaem Maghami, Dubai 2009. Black attempted to get counterplay by 13...f5 and should have been punished with 14.♗xd7 ♕xd7 15.e5!! f4 16.♗xc5 dxc5 17.♘e4±.

Of course, he had to take on b5:

13...♗xb5 14.axb5 ♘d7 15.0–0 ♘b6 16.♘c4 ♘xc4 17.♕xc4

White is clearly better. The break c4-c5 is in the air, e.g. 17...♗f6 18.e5!

D. 5...b4

This move leads to an interesting hybrid between the Blumenfeld and the Benko with 4.♘f3. It seems the most important Black's attempt to revive the gambit. Top players like Navara and Nisipeanu opted for 5...b4 in major competitions lately. I still cannot believe that it is entirely sound, but White should display energetic play in order to gain the edge.

6.a3!

White should aim for a quick clash in the centre. The exchange of the a-pawn for that at c5 will enable the break c4-c5 in some lines. It also takes control of d4 which is an excellent place for the f3-knight. One move later this idea has not the same effect: 6.e4 d6 7.a3 h6 8.♗xf6 ♕xf6 when 9.e5 is no longer possible.

6...a5

Introduced in the game Gelfand-Nisipeanu, Kallithea 2008. This is supposed to improve on the previous game Ivanchuk-Nisipeanu, Khanty-Mansiysk 2007 which went 6...h6 7.♗h4 a5 8.axb4 cxb4 9.♘d4!? when 9...♗c5 could be attacked by 10.♘b3. Stayed the bishop on g5,

Black would have had ...♗xf2+!. So Nisipeanu played 9...♗e7 10.♘b5 d6 11.c5 0-0. Here simplest would have been 12.cxd6± ♗xd6 13.dxe6 ♗e5 14.exf7+ ♔xf7 15.♘d2, with an advantage.

Here are two older examples after 6...h6 7.♗h4:

Magerramov-Nikolaev, Budapest 1990: 7...♕b6 8.♗xf6 gxf6 9.e4 ♘a6 10.♘bd2 ♗g7 11.♖b1 bxa3 12.bxa3 ♕a5 13.♕c1 0-0 14.♗d3 d6 15.0-0 ♗d7 16.♖b7±;

Lautier-Koch, Besancon 1999: 7...exd5 8.cxd5 ♗b7 9.axb4 cxb4

Here 10.♘bd2! g5 11.♗g3 ♗xd5 12.e4 would have earned White a strong initiative.

The reason behind 6...a5 is to play ...♘a6 and take on b4 by knight or even by the a5-pawn, so White has to take on b4 immediately:

7.axb4 cxb4 8.e4!

The source game saw 8.♘d4 ♗c5 9.e3 exd5 10.cxd5 0-0 11.♘b3 d6 12.♘1d2 (or 12.♘xc5 dxc5 13.♘d2 ♕xd5 14.♗xf6 gxf6 15.♗e2 ♗b7 16.♗f3 ♕d7 17.0-0 ♖d8∞) 12...♘bd7 13.♗b5 h6 14.♗h4 ♕b6, when it turned out that 15.♗c6 would stumble into 15...♗a6! 16.♗xa8 ♗xe3!. So Gelfand had to retreat 15.♗e2, losing hopes for an advantage.

I have no idea what Nisipeanu had planned on the natural move I propose. 8...d6 is outright bad in view of 9.c5!, so he must answer:

8...h6 9.♗xf6 ♕xf6 10.e5!

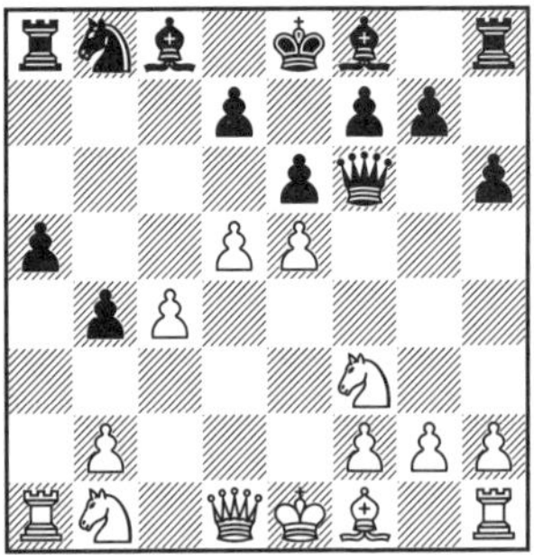

Now 10...♕d8 is too passive: 11.♗e2 ♗c5 12.0-0 0-0 13.♘bd2 ♘a6 14.♘e4±. Therefore:

10...♕g6 11.♗d3! ♕xg2 12.♖g1 ♕h3 13.♘bd2

White has terrific compensation for the pawn. For instance: 13...g5 14.♗e4 ♖a7 15.♖g3 ♕h5 16.♗c2 g4 17.♘e4 ♗e7 18.♕d4 ♖a6 19.♖xg4+–.

Have in mind that this line is totally unexplored. Watch out for new important games and keep it up-to-date.

Part 6

Complete Games

1.d4 d5 2.c4 e6 3.♘f3 c5 4.d5 b5 5.♗g5

20. Delchev–Ovetchkin
Plovdiv 02.05.2008

1.d4 ♘f6 2.♘f3 e6 3.c4 c5 4.d5 b5 5.♗g5 exd5 6.cxd5 d6 7.e3 a6 8.a4 b4 9.♘bd2 ♗e7 10.♘c4 a5 11.♗d3 0–0 12.♕c2 ♘bd7

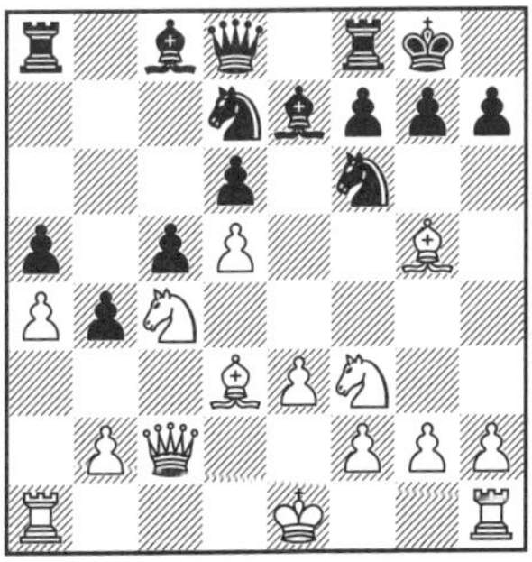

Black wants to recapture on f6 by knight, but this move allows White to keep his dark-squared bishop by 13.♗f4! 12...h6, forcing 13.♗xf6, is more precise.

13.♖d1?! h6 14.♗xf6 ♘xf6 15.0–0 ♗g4 16.b3

16.♗f5 can be met by 16...b3, so Delchev takes precautions.

16...♘d7 17.♗f5 ♗xf3 18.gxf3 ♘b6 19.♔h1 ♘xc4 20.♕xc4 ♗f6 21.♖g1

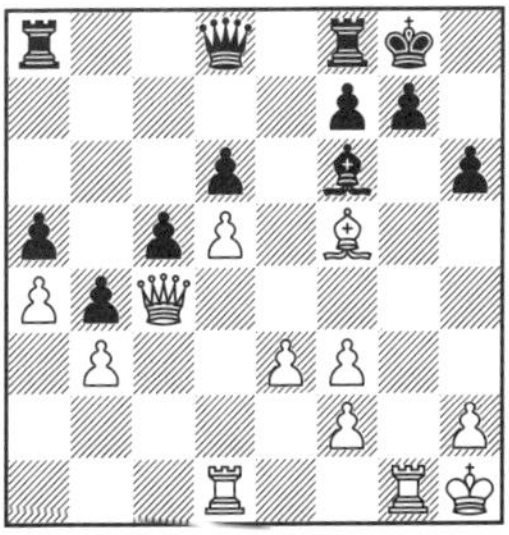

This position looks simple. However, despite the opposite coloured bishops, White retains lasting pressure, even in and endgame. Still, Black should be able to hold it.

In general, White needs one knight for his attack.

21...♖a7 22.♗d3 ♖e8 23.♖g4 ♔f8 24.♕c2 ♖e5 25.♗b5 g6 26.f4 ♖h5 27.♗e2 ♖h4 28.♖g3 ♔g7 29.♖dg1 ♔h8 30.♕e4 ♖e7 31.♕f3 ♖e8 32.♗d3 ♖g8 33.h3 ♕e8 34.♖g4 ♖xg4 35.hxg4 ♔g7 36.♔g2 ♕e7 37.♖h1 ♖h8 38.♕h3 ♔g8 39.♕f3 ♔g7 40.♔f1 ♗c3 41.♖h3 ♔g8 42.♕g2 ♗g7 43.♗c4 ♔f8 44.♔e2 ♕f6 45.♕e4 ♕e7 46.♔f3 ♕xe4+ 47.♔xe4 ♔e7 48.♗e2 ♔d7 49.♔d3 ♔c7 50.f5!

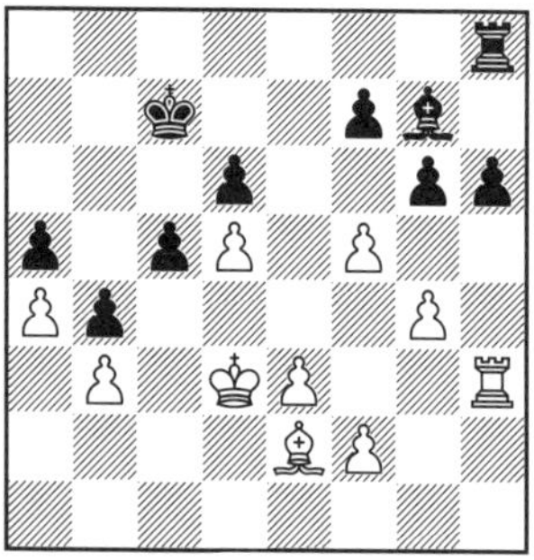

White's spatial advantage gives him some initiative. Now 50...g5? would run into 51.f6 ♗xf6 52.♖f3±.

50...gxf5 51.♖f3 ♗e5 52.♖xf5 f6 53.♖h5 ♗c3 54.♔e4 ♔d7 55.♔f5 ♔e7 56.♔f4

It turns out that 56.♔g6 ♖g8+ 57.♔xh6 ♔f7 is a draw.

56...♔f7 57.♗b5 ♗d2 58.♖h3 ♗c3 59.♖h2 ♗a1 60.♔e4 ♔g6 61.♖h5 ♖c8 62.♔d3 ♖c7 63.♖h2 ♖e7 64.e4 ♖b7 65.♗a6 ♖b8 66.♔c4 ♗d4 67.♔d3 ♗c3 68.♔e3 ♗d4+ 69.♔f3 ♔g7 Draw.

21. Rusev–Lilov
Plovdiv 14.03.2008

1.d4 e6 2.c4 ♘f6 3.♘f3 c5 4.d5 exd5 5.cxd5 b5 6.♗g5 d6 7.e3 a6 8.a4 b4 9.♘bd2 ♗e7 10.♘c4 a5 11.♕c2 0–0 12.♗xf6 h6 13.♗d3 ♗xf6 14.0–0 ♕c7

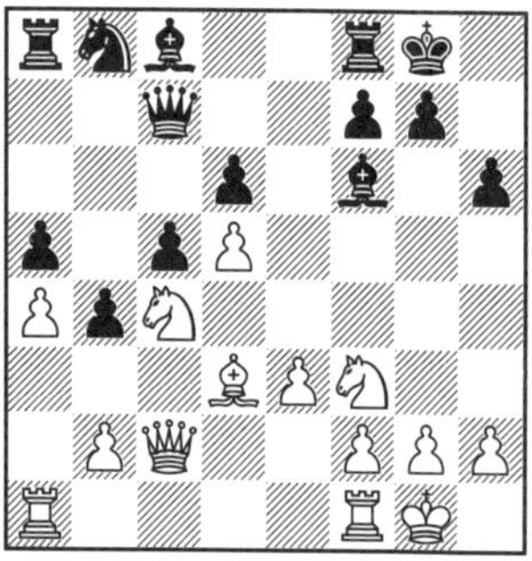

15.♖ad1?!

This move was not necessary. White should have played 15.♗h7+ ♔h8 16.♗f5, aiming to reach a ♘ vs. ♗ position.

15...♗g4

Black's bishop would stay better on a6, for instance: 15...♘d7! 16.♗f5 ♗a6 17.♗xd7 ♕xd7 18.♘fd2 ♖ae8 19.♖fe1 ♕c7 20.♖e2 ♖e7. If now Black takes on c4, White would be clearly better, because he will have a free hand on the kingside. However, he cannot advance there until the bishop is alive, since it could return on the c8-h3 diagonal.

16.♗f5! ♗xf3 17.gxf3 g6 18.♗h3 ♗g7 19.♔h1 ♘a6

White's knight makes the difference with the game Delchev-

Ovetchkin. Black's defence is difficult here.

20.b3 ♕d8 21.♖g1 ♘c7 22.♖g3 ♘e8 23.f4 ♘f6 24.♗g2 ♖a7 25.♗f3 ♔h8

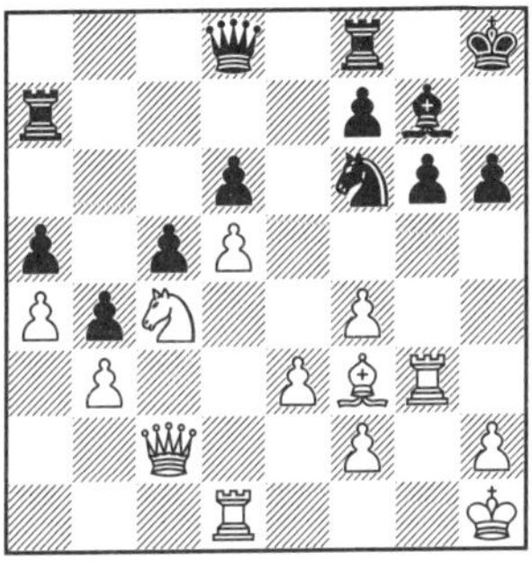

26.♖dg1

It was possible to advance in the centre by 26.e4 ♖e7 27.e5 ♘e8, but Rusev prefers to conduct an attack on the black king. I suppose he is right, because he can always return to that plan if Black finds a good way to neutralise the threat of f4-f5. Now 26...♘e8, defending the g7 bishop, looks a must, aiming to meet 27.f5 by 27...g5.

26...♘g8? 27.f5

27...g5 already loses to 28.h4.

27...♘e7 28.♗e4 ♕d7 29.f4

Black is completely helpless and can only wait to see how White will finish him off.

29...♘g8 30.♕g2 ♕d8 31.♕h3 ♘f6 32.♗f3 ♘g8 33.fxg6 f5 34.♖g5 ♕f6 35.♖h5 ♖e7 36.♗d1 ♖e4 37.♗c2?! (37.♖xf5!+–) 37...♖xc4 38.bxc4 ♕c3 39.♗xf5 ♕xc4 40.♗b1 b3 41.♕e6 ♕e2 42.♖h3 c4 43.♕xd6 c3 44.♕b6 ♕c4 45.♕c6 ♖c8 46.♕xc4 ♖xc4 47.e4 c2 48.♖xb3 c1♕ 49.♖xc1 ♖xc1+ 50.♔g2 ♖c4 51.d6 ♖xa4 52.♖b8 ♖b4 53.♖xb4 axb4 54.e5 ♗f8 55.♔f3 ♔g7 56.♔g4 b3 57.♔f5 ♗e7 58.dxe7 ♘xe7+ 59.♔e4 ♔xg6 60.f5+ ♔g5 61.h4+ ♔xh4 62.f6 ♘g6 63.e6 1–0

22. Goldin–Leuba
Bern 1991

1.d4 ♘f6 2.♘f3 e6 3.c4 c5 4.d5 exd5 5.cxd5 b5 6.♗g5 d6 7.e4 a6 8.a4 b4 9.♘bd2 ♗e7 10.♗f4 0–0 11.h3 a5 12.♗b5 ♗a6 13.♗xa6 ♖xa6 14.♕e2 ♖a7 15.0–0 ♘bd7 16.♘c4 ♘b6 17.♘fd2 ♖e8 18.♕f3

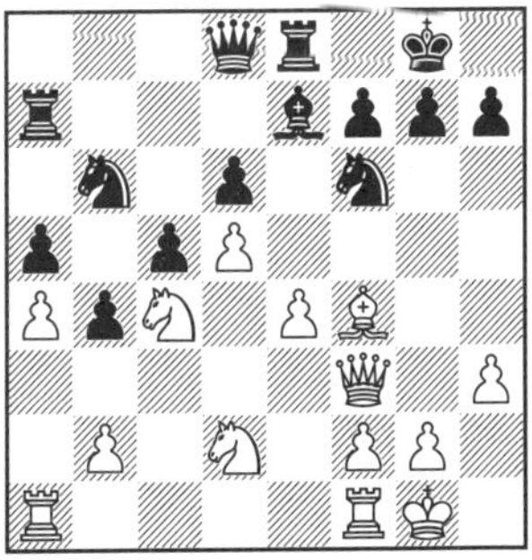

We see the perfect setup of White against the Blumenfeld. The light-squared bishops are exchanged while the dark-squared bishop is on board and eyeing the weak pawn at d6. Black has no counterplay.

18...♖a6 19.♘xb6 ♕xb6 20.♘c4 ♕b7 21.♖fe1 ♗f8 22.b3 ♘d7 23.♕g3 ♘f6 24.f3?!

A very strange move. It is true, that the ♘ vs. ♗ opposition will be in White's favour, but he had much better continuations, like 24.♕d3 ♘d7 25.e5 dxe5 26.♗xe5± or even 24.♗xd6! ♘xe4 25.♗xf8 ♘xg3 26.♖xe8 ♘e2+ 27.♖xe2 ♔xf8 28.d6+−.

24...♘h5 25.♕h2 ♘xf4 26.♕xf4

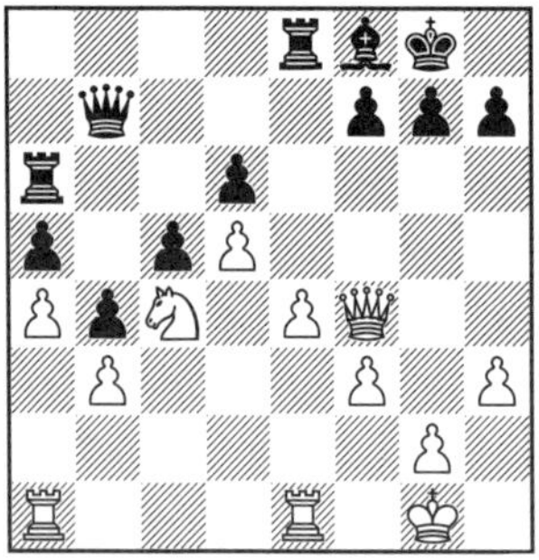

26...♕e7

Black should have tried to activate the bishop by 26...g6 27.♖ad1 ♕b8. Still, White would be better after 28.e5±.

27.♖ad1

White's next move will be e4-e5, so Black desperately attempts to discourage it:

27...g5 28.♕g4 ♗g7 29.♔h1

In strategically winning positions, it is often difficult to switch to concrete play. Here 29.e5! would have been the most straightforward way of converting the advantage: 29...dxe5 (29...♗xe5 30.f4 ♗d4+ 31.♔f1±) 30.d6±, going for a new queen.

29...♗d4 30.g3 ♖a7 31.♔g2 f6 32.h4 ♕d7?!

This loses outright. A little more stubborn was 32...♕d8 33.f4 ♖g7 34.hxg5 fxg5 35.f5±. In the game, Black loses the d6-pawn, which is decisive.

33.hxg5 ♕xg4 34.fxg4 fxg5 35.♘xd6 ♖f8 36.♖e2 ♖d7 37.♘f5 ♗e5 38.d6 c4 39.bxc4 b3 40.c5 b2 1–0

Index of Variations

The Benko Declined

The Budapest Gambit

1.d4 ♘f6 2.c4 e5 3.dxe5

The Albin Counter Gambit

1.d4 d5 2.c4 e5 3.dxe5 d4

The Blumenfeld Gambit

1.d4 d5 2.c4 e6 3.♘f3 c5 4.d5 b5